Nuts and Bolts Filmmaking

Nuts and Bolts Filmmaking

Practical Techniques for the Guerilla Filmaker

DAN RAHMEL

AMSTERDAM • BOSTON • HEIDELBERG • LONDON
NEW YORK • OXFORD • PARIS • SAN DIEGO
SAN FRANCISCO • SINGAPORE • SYDNEY • TOKYO

Focal Press is an imprint of Elsevier

Focal Press is an imprint of Elsevier
200 Wheeler Road, Burlington, MA 01803, USA
Linacre House, Jordan Hill, Oxford OX2 8DP, UK

∞ Recognizing the importance of preserving what has been written,
Elsevier prints its books on acid-free paper whenever possible.

Library of Congress Cataloging-in-Publication Data
A catalogue record for this book is available from the Library of Congress

British Library Cataloguing-in-Publication Data
A catalogue record for this book is available from the British Library

ISBN 0 2408 0546 1

For information on all Focal Press publications
visit our website at www.focalpress.com

04 05 06 07 08 10 9 8 7 6 5 4 3 2 1

Typeset by Integra Software Services Pvt. Ltd, Pondicherry, India
www.integra-india.com
Printed in the United States of America

Contents

Acknowledgements

Acknowledgements

It was a pleasure to work with the people at Focal Press on this book. The superior Focal Press staff often made the difficult seem easy. I'd like to thank Elinor Actipis for believing in the book from the start and sheparding it down the long hard road to publication. I'd also like to thank Theron Shreve, Kristin Macek, Jaya Nilamani, and all the others who had to work tirelessly in production and editing to produce this book.

It is essential that I express my gratitude to my father, Ron Rahmel, without whom creation of this book would likely have been impossible. Being an ingenious inventor and tireless experimenter, he took an active part in helping me realize projects that were initially barely formed ideas. Likewise, Marie Rahmel made contributions in time and energy that can't be understated. Thank you both.

I'd like to thank my siblings (David and Darlene) and friends (David Rahmel, Elizabeth Lee, Greg Mickey, John Taylor, Don Murphy, Frank Shindledecker, Juan Leonffu, Michelle Lecours, Ed Gildred, and Weld O'Connor) for their unconditional support. Special thanks to David and Mary Rahmel who opened their house to me when I was first getting started in Hollywood. Without their generosity, I would have never acquired the experience I needed.

Most of all, I'd like to thank the readers. By buying this book, you make it possible for all of us in the film industry to labor to produce good work. I hope the information in this book will play a part in helping you achieve all of your dreams. Thanks.

Colophon

Bembo, the typeface used for the body text of this book, has interesting historic origins as it is considered the most contemporary of all 15th century fonts. Bembo was created under the supervision of Stanley Morison (Monotype Corporation, 1929) as a modernized version of a typeface designed by Francesco Griffo da Bologna (1450–1518). Griffo worked as a type founder, cutter, and designer under the auspices of Aldus Manutius, the famed Venetian printer.

Francesco created the font for a special printing of an edition authored by Cardinal Pietro Bembo. Pietro Bembo (1460–1547) was a cardinal, friend of Lucrezia Borgia, and one-time official historian of Venice. A poet, humanist, and philologist, he was one of the first champions of Italian as a literary language.

Disclaimer

Introduction

Welcome

Guerilla filmmakers are a special breed of dreamers and idealists and geniuses and romantics. They overcome seemingly insurmountable odds almost every day. When I work on guerilla films, I see a plenty of ambition, inventiveness, and determination. Often missing, though, is proper equipment and professional technique. I wrote this book to help remedy this situation.

Most books that describe low-budget moviemaking either provide mostly inspirational anecdotes or they focus on writing scripts, handling actors, planning shooting logistics, camera selection, and so on. These books rarely address the nuts and bolts of actual production. Equipment fabrication, effective lighting, authentic art direction, set decoration, basic make-up effects, and post-production techniques are traditionally ignored. This book provides how-to information for each of these areas.

Construction details are included to replicate many expensive professional film tools for under the cost of a DVD player. The explosion in consumer and prosumer digital video cameras has supplied an opportunity for almost anyone to be a filmmaker and – with the right knowledge and equipment – to realize their vision. This book will provide quick and inexpensive remedies to the most common and difficult production challenges.

While I now work on feature films and television, my heart is still with guerilla filmmaking. As filmmakers, we make every effort to create narratives and visuals that can inspire and entertain. I assume that one or more of you reading this book will eventually be collecting golden statues at the Academy Awards or attaining your dreams of making a movie that fulfills your artistic ambition. My fondest hopes are that this book can help you on your journey.

I've set up a web site focused on filmmaking called Coherent Visual (www.cvisual.com). I would love to have your comments on any aspect of this book, particularly portions that you found difficult to understand, so that they may be improved in the future.

Thanks for purchasing this book. I believe you'll find it very useful.

Safety

Applications

I cannot stress enough the need to be careful any time you work on a construction project. Tools, adhesives, and parts can all become dangerous in the wrong circumstances. One essential asset of a guerilla filmmaker is the ability to ignore a lack of experience and barrel ahead to achieve the impossible. However, the opposite attitude should be taken when considering safety issues.

If you don't know how to use a circular saw, don't be embarrassed to ask someone that understands the tool. If a material warns of toxic fumes, ask the help desk at the hardware store what breathing gear will shield you from potential danger. Dealing with construction projects is the wrong time to boldly go where you've never gone before.

Safety gear

Proper safety gear is important for safety during most construction projects. Safety gear can be cumbersome and distracting, but preventing injury makes using this equipment essential. Further, safety gear tends to be inexpensive, readily available, and once purchased will last a lifetime. Take the time to buy and use safety gear.

The following equipment are useful for most jobs:

*   *Safety glasses* Whenever you are using power tools or any tool where flying debris can be created, use safety glasses. The glasses have thick protective lenses that will protect your eyes from projectiles and also shield them from dust and other airborne particles.

*   *Hearing protectors* Use earplugs or padded earmuffs to protect your hearing from the high-decibel whining of machinery. Padded earmuffs are much easier to use since they can be put on and removed quickly.

*   *Facemask* A basic facemask should be worn at all times when a lot of particulate matter is generated from activities such as sanding. *Do not* think that a facemask will protect you from chemical fumes or vaporized paint. Check the package to see exactly the type of protection the facemask affords.

*   *Respirator* This type of facemask is professional and contains a dual-cartridge respirator. It will protect you from paints, fumes, and toxic dusts. Although these masks are a little expensive, if you're doing a lot of work with paints, thinner, or lacquers, the investment is cheap when compared to the expense of damaging your health.

Safety guidelines

Here are some basic safety precautions that you can take with any project that can help you ensure a safe environment:

- *Find someone experienced to help you* One of the best pieces of advice that I've received is to find someone that has tools and experience with them and then work with that person. Experience only comes with time. Understanding and using tools and equipment properly can increase the safety of the environment tenfold.

- *Read the instructions* Lights, electrical gear, and even camera equipment can be dangerous if operated outside their rated specifications. Read the instructions and know the operating parameters of your equipment.

- *Read the warnings* Some of the materials you'll use (especially in prop manufacture) can be toxic or flammable during various stages of their use. Read the warning labels on any product you use and follow the specified safety precautions.

- *Work with a buddy* As long as you're not too distracted with conversation, another person can make working much safer and also much faster. Whether it's lending an extra hand for holding or cutting, a buddy can help make construction easier and safer.

- *Don't rush* Although I'm guilty of violating this guideline too, take your time and do things right. When I was constructing an apple box for this book, the day was running long and I thought instead of using a proper clamp that I would save time and simply hold the boards together with my hand. The result? I almost drove a wood screw through my hand. Rushing seldom saves much time and can often have disastrous consequences. Take your time – do it right.

- *Work in a well-ventilated area* Outdoors (depending on the time of year) is perfect for most construction projects. Fresh air dissipates paint fumes and other harmful gases.

Common Materials and Tools

Applications

I've tried to write this book so that it will be useful many years after its publication. As long as ambitious filmmakers of all ages struggle to make good films within limited budgets, I think this book has a role to play. One problem that limits any construction book's longevity is the availability of the materials and tools needed to implement the projects it contains. I myself own construction books from the 1980s that require parts that are now difficult to find.

With this problem in mind, throughout the book I've tried to stick with the most commonly available hardware parts. Most of the items are so common that I doubt they'll disappear from store shelves anytime soon. Lacking a crystal ball, however, it's impossible for me to be sure and that there won't be a better idea conceived tomorrow that would replace something as common as plumbing supplies. This chapter, then, will describe all fundamental tools and parts that you'll need to construct most of the projects. I hope that with these thorough descriptions, if any of the items become obsolete, you'll be able to find a suitable substitute or locate the part at a specialty store.

Tools

Having the proper tools for a task can save you a great deal of time. Although you can often make do with tools that aren't ideal, the right tools can help you complete a project in a shorter amount of time with far less frustration.

Below are most of the unique tools that you'll need to complete the projects in this book. Not included are common hand tools such as screwdrivers, wrenches, hammers, hacksaws, and so on. I have assumed that you either have these common implements or have access to them – otherwise you probably wouldn't have purchased this book.

PVC pipe cutter

I highly recommend that you invest the small amount of money required to buy a PVC pipe cutter (see figure 2-1). This tool can cut a length of pipe in less than 4 seconds. It makes construction with

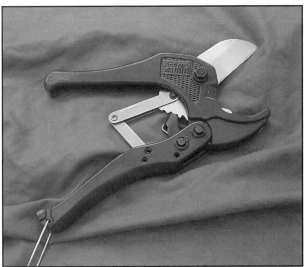

FIGURE 2.1 *PVC pipe cutter.*

PVC a joy and re-sizing PVC lengths (a common on-set job) quick and painless. Although a hacksaw is often used to cut PVC pipe, I find this tool to be much quicker, more exact, and cleaner since it doesn't create a pile of plastic dust shavings (like a saw).

A PVC pipe cutter can cuts pipes with a diameter up to $1\frac{5}{8}''$ (4.1 cm). In this book, $\frac{1}{2}''$ is the typical diameter of the pipe that you'll be using. The cutter is also handy to bring with you to the hardware store since PVC pipe generally comes in lengths of 10 ft (over 3 m). You can use the cutter (with a tape measure) to cut the shorter lengths you need right in the store, so you won't require a truck or a van to transport the long pipe.

Ratchet strap or ratchet tie-down

A ratchet strap (see figure 2-2) is an excellent tool for securing items in a car, a truck, or a garage. These straps are even commonly used to fasten a camera in place (with the aid of a hi-hat). A ratchet strap can be quickly positioned and tightened to hold your item with confidence. It's much quicker and easier to use than rope for these tasks.

When you're finished using the strap, it can be quickly released and removed. Read the instructions that come with it to learn proper use. There are many times when the user doesn't understand how to properly tighten the strap and this makes it tedious to release. Also, you can find ratchet tie-downs in a

FIGURE 2.2 *Ratchet strap or ratchet tie-down.*

variety of stores (home warehouses, hardware stores, discount retailers, etc.) so shop around. Be sure, however, to buy a high-quality strap that is explicitly labeled to handle a specific load.

Tin snips

In this book, some projects require tin snips to cut shingle flashing. As you can see in figure 2-3, there are two common types of snips. The older style shown on the left looks like a particularly rugged set of scissors. On the right, the modern style tends to provide more leverage and is easier to use for cutting curves and edges. It also has a lock to prevent the jaws from opening unintentionally.

To cut metal, these tin snips should be kept extremely sharp and should be used very carefully. Although they might appear like scissors, they cut far more quickly and are therefore far more dangerous.

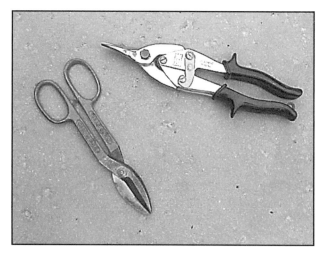

FIGURE 2.3 *Two types of tin snips.*

Cordless drill

An essential set tool for most departments, a cordless drill (see figure 2-4) is used for everything from driving in screws to stirring paint to drilling holes. A high-quality cordless drill can solve many problems on the set. Be sure, however, to keep a close eye on your portable tools as they can be used by nearly everyone and are therefore the most common target of thieves.

With tools, the general rule is that the more expensive the tool, the higher the quality. Nowhere does this rule prove more true than with battery-powered drills. More expensive drills have more power, variable speeds, multiple speed ranges, faster battery charging, and longer battery life. Some have jackhammer features and many are

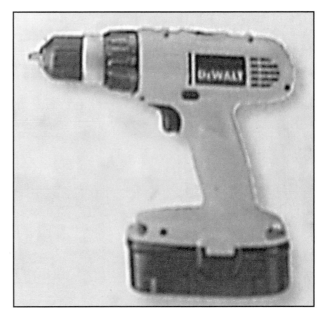

FIGURE 2.4 *Cordless battery-powered drill.*

reversible. Make sure to buy at least one spare battery for the drill, as it is likely you'll end up filming somewhere where no power is available. Having the extra battery can save your skin.

Materials

The materials you choose can make a large difference in the flexibility and durability of the projects you construct. In some places, for example, PVC pipe can be substituted for iron pipe to make the project lighter and waterproof. In other places, iron pipe can be substituted for PVC pipe for more strength and extended life.

Throughout the book I've chosen the materials that I consider will work best for each project. If you have more experience with a particular type of item, you may choose to substitute a material you know would work better. At the time of this writing, all the listed items are widely available even at a small hardware store. If your local store doesn't carry a particular item, ask a salesman what part might provide a suitable replacement.

Metal pipe nipple

Threaded metal pipe is generally labeled as pipe nipple regardless of whether its length is $3''$ or 3 ft. In figure 2-5, you can see three lengths of metal pipe nipples (3, 12, and $24''$) with a diameter of $\frac{1}{2}''$ (the diameter of pipe used in this book). This pipe is available either in the electrical or in the plumbing sections of the hardware store.

Metal pipe is generally available as standard iron pipe (painted black) or

FIGURE 2.5 *Lengths of steel pipe with threaded ends also called metal pipe nipples.*

galvanized pipe (appears silver). While galvanized pipe is more resistant to the elements (specifically rust resistance), it is often substantially more expensive. For this reason, all the projects in this book use simple iron pipes.

Be aware that if the threads on the iron pipes are exposed to water and not cleaned, they can rust and corrode. The corrosion can either make the threads unusable or it can bind two screwed together items (such as a pipe and a joint) permanently. You might consider oiling the threads from time to time to prevent this sort of corrosion.

PVC pipe

Schedule 40 PVC pipe is a significant construction material for the guerilla filmmaker. It's light, waterproof, cheap, easy to cut, easy to drill, and semi-rigid. In figure 2-6 you can see a short length of $\frac{3}{4}''$ (on the left) and $\frac{1}{2}''$ pipe. You can use PVC for thousands of applications and even re-use lengths from an older project.

Most of the PVC used in this book has a diameter of $\frac{1}{2}''$. If you feel this size isn't strong enough for a particular project, in most cases you can substitute $\frac{3}{4}''$ pipe since identical fixtures (unions, T-joints, etc.) are available in the larger size.

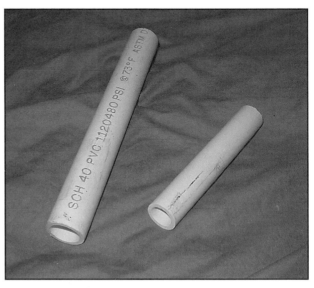

FIGURE 2.6 *Lengths of PVC pipe with diameters of $\frac{3}{4}''$ and $\frac{1}{2}''$.*

TIP ▶ *When you have to cut PVC pipe, you'll invariably be left with various small lengths of pipe. Don't throw these little extras away. Start a scraps bag that holds them as you'll find numerous times when you need either a small extension or a piece of scrap pipe for testing a technique.*

Flange

A flange (see figure 2-7) provides a threaded metal socket with mounting screw holes. Galvanized and ungalvanized versions are available in the plumbing section in the $\frac{1}{2}''$ diameter size. You'll use flanges extensively in the book to secure metal or PVC pipes (with a threaded adapter).

Flanges are used in conjunction with conduit hangers in the C-stand chapter to create a stand head. After you purchase a flange, be sure to try placing the proper screw size through each screw hole. Unfortunately, the outer coating process that occurs during manufacturing can partially fill-up the holes on a frustrating percentage of flanges. If you discover this problem, you can either widen the holes yourself with a heavy-duty file or take the flange back to the hardware store to exchange for an acceptable one.

FIGURE 2.7 *Galvanized pipe flange.*

Union

A union is a tremendously useful pipe connector available in the plumbing section of the hardware store. In figure 2-8, you can see a galvanized union. Behind the union are the three separate pieces that are screwed together to make up the union. Unions are available in iron, galvanized steel and PVC plastic versions. The unions used in this book are made for the $\frac{1}{2}''$ pipe size.

A union consists of three separate pieces: a threaded coupling, an unthreaded coupling, and a housing. The threaded coupling screws into the housing and secures the unthreaded coupling. When the housing is loosened, the unthreaded coupling spins freely.

FIGURE 2.8 *Assembled union and three disassembled union pieces.*

TIP ▶ *Whenever you have to mount a union for one of the projects, pay close attention to the figures that go with the instructions. While both ends of the union may appear the same, the orientation of the union will determine which direction the tightening ring will fall when it is completely loosened. The orientation also determines the direction (clockwise or counter-clockwise) that will tighten the union. In nearly every assembly, I've placed the union where the orientation is the most effective. Therefore, I would suggest you place your unions as shown for the best performance.*

90° elbow bend

This piece of pipe provides a 90° bend or corner joint (see figure 2-9) and is available in PVC, iron, and galvanized versions. A bend is used to connect two pipes together at a right angle. Bends are generally available in three types: threaded, unthreaded, and single end threaded. In this book, all three types are used.

If your hardware store only carries the unthreaded type, you can easily glue together a short length of pipe with a threaded adapter to create your own threaded corners.

T-joint

This piece provides a junction where three pieces of pipe can be attached together (see figure 2-10). A T-joint allows two pipes to connect together along a single axis and a third to intersect at a right angle to this axis. This piece is

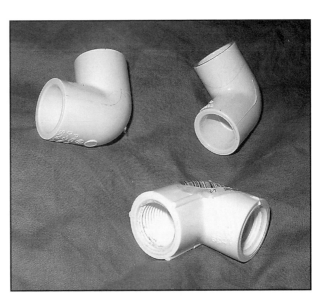

FIGURE 2.9 *Threaded and unthreaded 90° PVC elbow bends.*

available in iron, galvanized steel, and PVC plastic versions. The T-joint used in this book is primarily the $\frac{1}{2}''$ size.

T-joints are available as unthreaded, single-opening threaded, and all-threaded. Most commonly, the projects in this book use unthreaded joints for PVC requirements and all-threaded for metal pipe construction.

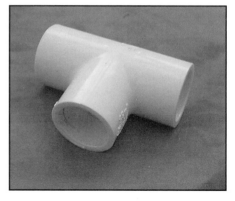

FIGURE 2.10 *PVC T-joint.*

Four-way joint

The four-way joint provides a junction where four pieces of pipe can be attached together (see figure 2-11). Four-way joints allow pipes to connect together along a two axis' at right angles to each other. This piece is available in iron, galvanized steel, PVC plastic threaded, and PVC plastic unthreaded versions. The joint used in this book is primarily the $\frac{1}{2}''$ size.

Corner joint

This piece provides a junction where three pieces of pipe can be attached together (see figure 2-12). A corner joint allows each of the three pipes to approach from a different axis and intersect. The joint used in this book is primarily the $\frac{1}{2}''$ size. The PVC version of the joint has two unthreaded openings and one threaded opening. To accept three unthreaded pipes, you'll need to use a threaded adapter on the threaded opening.

FIGURE 2.11 *Galvanized four-way threaded pipe joint.*

Threaded adapter

This PVC piece converts a standard unthreaded male pipe end to a threaded male end (see figure 2-13). This adapter is extremely useful when connecting PVC pipe to iron or galvanized steel fittings. It is also

FIGURE 2.12 *PVC three-way corner joint.*

FIGURE 2.13 *PVC threaded adapter.*

very useful when a pipe joint must be secure, but still easy to disassemble. The pipe used in this book is primarily the $\frac{1}{2}''$ size.

Conduit hanger with speed thread

This crucial little piece of hardware is used in a bunch of the projects including the C-stand, softbox, hi-hat, camslider, and others. Since it grips a $\frac{1}{2}''$ pipe, it provides the ideal part to allow rotation around the pipe's diameter. It is also very cheap per unit and comes in bags of 5–10 units.

For many applications in this book, you will be replacing the central bolt with a threaded eyebolt (see figure 2-14). An eyebolt provides the ability to hand tighten or loosen the grip of the hanger. Be sure to put a nut at the base of the eyebolt before placing it into the conduit hanger. The nut will prevent the hanger from being warped and damaged by the tightening of the bolt.

Eyebolt

An eyebolt (see figure 2-15) is the best substitute I've found for a threaded tightening knob. Knobs that are used in professional equipment from light stands to camera mounts can be prohibitively expensive. They can also be difficult to find in specific needed sizes. In contrast, a simple eyebolt is available inexpensively in nearly every hardware store.

The eyebolt provides a fairly good gripping surface for tightening. Dip the eye in rubber or plastic (available in most hardware stores for coating tool handles) for an excellent handhold.

Conduit clamp or two-hole strap

These clamps (see figure 2-16) seem to come under a variety of names and are available in metal or plastic form. They can usually be found in the electrical section since their primary purpose is securing electrical conduit to a wall.

Be sure to examine the type of clamp closely before you buy it. Some

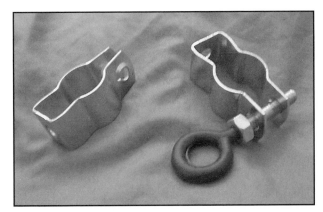

FIGURE 2.14 *Conduit hanger and conduit hanger with eyebolt for tightening knob.*

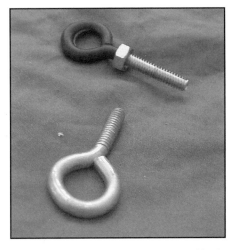

FIGURE 2.15 *Eyebolt and eyebolt with coated head for easier handling.*

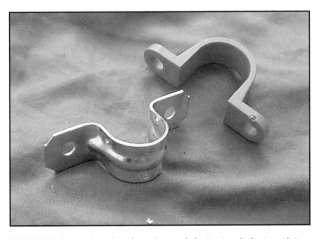

FIGURE 2.16 *Steel conduit clamp (or two-hole strap) and plastic conduit bracket.*

clamps are made to be bent around the conduit to secure it. These clamps can't be used for applications such as holding the softbox frames to the panels. Take a small piece of PVC pipe to the hardware store with you and make sure that the clamps you buy extend easily and firmly around the pipe.

Malleable coupling

These couplings (see figure 2-17) are used to hold two threaded pieces of pipe together. The coupling is generally found in the plumbing section of the hardware store and is available in galvanized and ungalvanized versions. In this book, the $\frac{1}{2}''$ size is primarily used.

FIGURE 2.17 *Galvanized and steel malleable pipe coupling.*

Locking nut

A locking nut (see figure 2-18) functions just like a traditional nut except it doesn't loosen. This is critical for some applications where the bolt that the locking nut is placed upon acts as a pivot point. The rotating motion of the item on the pivot would loosen a normal nut, but a locking nut remains securely in place.

Galvanized shingle or shingle flashing

These simple sheets of shingle flashing are generally available in 8″ squares. They can be cut with a pair of tin snips and are excellent when thin sheets of metal are needed for a project.

FIGURE 2.18 *Lock nut.*

Hyco bar or erector set brackets

The multiple holes in these brackets (see figure 2-19) reminder me of a toy I had as a kid that was called an erector set. The hyco bar brackets are found in the plumbing section of the hardware store. They are generally used to secure pipes and other fixtures to a ceiling, a board, or a wall. The brackets are available in a variety of gauges (thicknesses) with the most common being 26 gauge, although 14 gauge is also widespread.

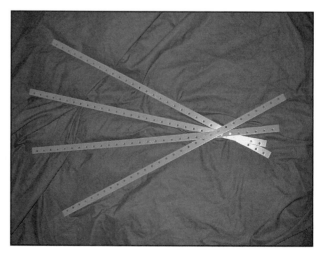

FIGURE 2.19 *Four lengths of hyco bar.*

By placing machine screws in the holes, brackets can be secured together and easily taken apart again. Additionally, the brackets are flexible enough, so they can be easily bent into nearly any desired shape or curve.

Bendable wire

When I began writing this book, I assumed that I would use wire coat hangers as a standard material for bendable wire. Surprise! I went down to the store and could only find plastic hangers and designer metal ones. I knew I could search somewhere and find wire hangers, but the fact that this major retailer no longer carried those types of hangers told me that they aren't as common as they once were (and getting rarer still).

Fence wire (see figure 2-20) provides an excellent substitute. It is available in several different diameters (or gauges) and is fairly cheap. You'll find it near the fence frame and joint materials at the hardware store. Wire seems to be stored in a variety of places based on the individual store, so you might ask at the front counter before spending too much time in your search.

FIGURE 2.20 *12-gauge hanging wire.*

Suggestions

Here are a few suggestions to find the best materials:

- *Ask the salespeople* In this chapter I sought to not only cite the various parts, but also to include descriptions of where each part is traditionally found. If you can't locate a part, you can often ask a salesperson and, by describing the part's function, avoid a blank stare. Further, you may be able to locate a replacement part if the desired part is no longer available.

- *Check the Internet* If you can't find a part or material, odds are good it is available somewhere. I needed a specific clamp a couple of years ago and to my great surprise, several people were selling them on eBay. When you begin your search, try various key words and descriptions because another industry may use that type of part, but it may be available under a different name.

- *Ask a construction contractor* If you have any friends that are construction contractors, they might be able to obtain these materials for much cheaper than the prices listed at the hardware store. When I asked a construction friend of mine, he gave me dozens of free PVC joints that he'd purchased for pennies when a hardware distributor went out of business.

Preproduction Introduction

Applications

At the beginning of a venture, the preproduction staff is generally chiefly you – the filmmaker. Whether you'll be the director, producer, writer, or make-up person on the actual shoot, a guerilla film almost always begins with one person. To assure success in the endeavor, spending time on preproduction planning is a must.

Preproduction time is perhaps the one huge advantage guerilla filmmakers have over large Hollywood productions. Big-budget films are often launched during a short crunch time window when the green light decision, the actor's schedules, and the director's vision all coincide. Preproduction is often kept to a bare minimum in order to get the film off the ground. Sometimes shooting begins without even having a completed script! Most guerilla productions, however, aren't made until the desired outcome comes into clear focus. That means that there is usually time to think things through.

The following chapters are meant to help you maximize your preproduction time. Whether you're storyboarding or location scouting, the time spent in these areas can result in tremendous savings of time and money to the production. Guerilla filmmakers need to get the most out of limited and precious resources to make great films.

Writing a production statement

At the very beginning of your project, perhaps before the script is even complete, you should write a production statement. This statement is a brief description of what the production is actually about. It doesn't even need to contain a plot summary. A production statement might read like one of these:

- This 35-mm film will be a claustrophobic psychological murder mystery with gothic overtones.

- This commercial spec will provide a demonstration of the cutting edge compositing technology available from our effects house.

- This DV romantic comedy will be a light, surreal romp through the highways and byways of employee relationships in the banking system.

Each of these single sentence abstracts tells the reader a great deal about the production. The camera department will know the general feel of the lighting that's needed; wardrobe and make-up will be able to start thinking about the appropriate looks of the character types; post-production will have an idea whether the film will be effects-heavy; and so on. The point of the production statement is to provide a general overview that describes the destination of the project.

Begin organizing

Organization is really the only way you can accomplish a movie effectively. I've worked on many disorganized shoots and it always takes its toll on the final on-screen results. The less organized a shoot, the less likely you'll be able to get the quality you want. While studio-backed productions can (often) afford the waste instigated by on-the-spot decisions, I'm assuming you don't have a spare couple of million sitting around to cover overruns.

Organization, while not glamorous, can set a professional tone from the beginning of the project. The amount of information that must be collected and organized for a film is simply staggering. Therefore, the first thing you should do when beginning preproduction is set aside a drawer in your file cabinet to centralize all the information you collect.

Some important documents you should keep in your file cabinet include:

- *Crew list* This list should contain the names, general positions, phone numbers, and emails of all principal members of the crew. If one crew member needs to be able to obtain information from another crew member, this list will make communication much quicker and easier.

- *Copies of the storyboards* Storyboards are often kept by the director, so notations and instructions can be made on them. You should try to keep a copy of the panels in the file cabinet both for reference and security against the loss of any material.

- *Legal release forms* All legal releases should remain in a secure location. The loss of a release could cause tremendous problems for distribution in the future, so be sure to keep them out of harm's way.

- *Location scouting reports* Be sure to keep reports of scouted locations even if you don't plan to use them. Discarded locations can be like gold when planned locations unexpectedly fall through.

Creating a preproduction deadline list

Principal photography may be a long way off and you might think that setting deadlines is premature. Although it's usually never too early to start setting at least tentative deadlines, the preproduction deadline list should record the critical path required before you begin your production.

There are immutable time periods and requirements that mean that some dates must precede others. For example, if a location permit is required, it may take the issuing city 2 weeks from the time of the request before the permit is granted. You need to know this! Any problems that create time delays that can't be immediately resolved should be added to a list.

Some of these deadlines might include:

- *Construction times* If a stage, set, or prop needs to be constructed, you'll need a time estimate of how long this will take. That way, when you begin actually scheduling dates, you can either allocate the time before production begins or push the dates of the scenes that require the constructed item to the end of the shooting schedule.

- *Permit issuing time* How long does it take for the city to issue a permit? What documentation is necessary to obtain the permit? How long will it take to obtain this documentation? These questions should be answered on your deadline list.

- *Location, cast, and crew availability* Scheduling around actors can test the patience of nearly everyone – especially the first assistant director. Although all the schedules can change at the drop of a hat, begin planning early.

- *Loan of equipment* Does your brother-in-law say you can borrow his boat for filming in March? This may be an important consideration in your schedule – especially if he'll be using it himself all April. Anything that needs to be borrowed, even wardrobe, should be determined for availability.

- *Seasonal items* Finding Halloween decorations in the beginning of February may be difficult even for well-funded productions. Begin to consider where and when you can obtain any seasonal items needed for the shoot.

Suggestions

Here are a few general suggestions to help you get the most out of your preproduction time:

- *Get an organizer or project folder* For any film, you'll have to organize a million details and record a million requests before you shoot one frame. Keep names, phone numbers, ideas, and dates close at hand. Whether you keep a well-planned folder or a notebook with a bunch of random notes, keep this information together in something you can carry with you.

- *Take note of other movies* There are many occasions where something you'll observe in a film will be something you can use in your own. Don't focus on big-budget productions – rent B-movies. B-movies and independent films are places you can really see where ingenuity was used to find ways of solving film problems even if the film itself is terrible. Everything from faking big locations to successfully implying offscreen carnage can be learned by paying close attention and guessing how they were accomplished. Likewise, make it a point to listen to DVD commentaries (preferably by someone other than the movie star) for tips on production procedure.

- *Don't listen to criticism* It seems sometimes like everyone feels the need to offer discouraging advice or commentary just to help you "keep things realistic." I don't know what it is about making a film that seems to induce people with the need to criticize the script, the premise, the budget, the actors, the locations, the authenticity of the props, or even the likelihood the movie will ever be shown. Ignore everyone. If you want to make your movie, make it.

Storyboarding

Applications

Storyboarding tells the story of a film visually in a series of comic-like panels. Unfortunately, many filmmakers approach the process of storyboarding with a sense of dread. Some believe that they don't have the artistic talent to draw the storyboard panels correctly. Others think that storyboarding hampers spontaneity and flexibility on the shoot. Among A-list filmmakers, there seems to be a constant argument on this topic, so I'm not about to address the pros and cons of each viewpoint here.

One thing that is definitely true – the use of storyboards on a film can drastically reduce the time necessary for prepping shots while on set. Some big-budget filmmakers can afford to take hours to figure out a shot during principal photography and then communicate it to the actors and filmmaking staff. Few guerilla filmmakers can afford to fritter away valuable time and energy "winging it" on a production day. A thorough set of storyboards can help focus the filming activities for each day of the shoot.

General Instructions

Storyboarding is essentially a form of planning that enables a filmmaker to understand and recognize exactly what footage needs to be obtained to tell the desired story. Time is taken in preproduction to create the storyboards from a shooting script. Once the storyboards have been created, the panels can be re-arranged and augmented. Like the script, a storyboard is not the movie itself, but instead a blueprint or a guideline from which the movie can be dynamically created.

Concrete shot understanding

It takes many, many years of experience to read a script and know the shots, inserts, and reverses that will be needed to create a coherent scene. To an inexperienced filmmaker, the translation from script to screen on the surface appears straightforward. However, whether you're framing shots or describing the performance that should be given by the actors, a great deal of work is required to comprehend exactly the footage that's needed.

For example, filming a car chase down a suburban street might seem like a simple process of setting up the camera in various positions and shooting. Later close-ups of the actors and the necessary dialogue are filmed. But wait . . . have you made sure that when the cars race past that they're moving in the same direction through the frame in each shot, say left to right? Does the angle you've chosen to film the actors match the exterior footage? Does an actor point off to the left side of the street for a driveway that's located on the right side in the exterior shot? Will both cars fit in frame given the camera angle you intend to use?

The process of storyboarding forces the director to think precisely about how a scene needs to be constructed. This construction process can often reveal shooting problems and sticking points that would normally have been overlooked. The points usually revealed in storyboarding are continuity problems, shot-matching problems, logistical problems (such as the presence of unwanted immovable background objects such as water towers, billboards, etc.), and framing problems where multiple items (actors, props, scenery) are poorly composed. Once identified these problems can be minimized or resolved.

With a storyboard, proper shot angles, reversals, inserts, and ambient footage can all be pre-planned. The concrete understanding of each shot allows everything from lens choice to set decoration to be considered before the pressures of shooting are upon you.

A method of communication

Guerilla filmmakers often rely on free workers to serve in positions as varied as PAs, grips, gaffers, and actors. These individuals may not have any previous experience on a film set. Attempts to instruct them on what is needed for a scene can be difficult and time-consuming. A simple storyboard frame can be used to immediately communicate the desired shot to the entire staff.

Even examining the storyboard panels for the day's shot list can help everyone. Wardrobe can know whether shoes will be seen, so the actress can take off her 3″ stilettos. Make-up can see when a wide shot will not pickup fine details of the eyeliner; the production designer can recognize when the left set wall will need to be removed for proper positioning of the camera; the prop master can see that certain props will be needed in the background; the lighting crew can work faster because everyone understands the illumination goal; and so on.

A budgeting tool

The most difficult estimation problem on a shooting schedule is determining how much can be shot in a single shooting day. Outside of your lead actor refusing to come out of his trailer, re-lighting for each new shot is probably the most time-consuming process that takes place in a shooting day.

A storyboard can help you determine how many shots you can make. A scene may only take up a single script page, but if you want to shoot it from 18 different angles, a dozen or more lighting set-ups may be required. Since each storyboard panel would show you a different angle, you can more accurately determine what is and isn't possible in your shooting schedule.

Storyboarding allows you to see what props need to be rented for a shot or what locations can be faked or "cheated" to minimize expensive locations. The storyboards allow for much more accurate time and financial budgeting than a script alone.

A useful checklist

Films are generally shot over very long hours under very stressful conditions. This environment can make it difficult to obtain all the footage needed. On guerilla films, there are very limited opportunities to come back at some later date and re-shoot missed scenes. Locations disappear, crew members are unavailable, or actors have changed their look (cut their hair or got a new tattoo).

A storyboard can provide a visual checklist for an accurate idea of how much of the film is in the can. On a shotlist, every item can be checked off and yet there may still be missing reaction shots, inserts, and other easy-to-overlook footage. The storyboard provides a common foundation checklist between the director, the director of photography, and the script supervisor. Often late into a night of shooting, even a director who is excellent at remembering desired shots and framing new ones may have his attention flag enough to miss a crucial setup.

NOTE→ On a short film I made, I had storyboarded the entire movie except one critical dialogue scene which I felt that I could easily handle. Due to a scheduling conflict, however, one of the actors had to leave early. We quickly shot his part of the dialogue early in the evening. Since I didn't have a storyboard, I just positioned him where I thought it best.

At hour 14 of the shooting day, when we reached the other actor's part of the dialogue, I realized that the positioning of the first actor was all wrong to make the scene work. We had the location for 1 day only, so there was no possibility of a re-shoot. It took forever in editing to make this scene work and it taught me the extreme value of storyboarding everything.

Construction

Making storyboards can be as simple as sketching a quick frame on a piece of paper and drawing stick figures inside. The following sections contain a number of suggestions for materials, methods of construction/drawing, and means of presentation. These ideas can help you make better storyboards or aid you in using them more effectively. However, the key to making storyboards is to do them – however you can. Don't procrastinate. Ugly or neat, organized or messy, get them done by whatever method you find most useful.

3″ × 5″ cards

You can begin creating your storyboards with simple 3″ × 5″ cards. The 3″ × 5″ card has a height to width ratio of 1.66 that closely approximates the HDTV standard and Super 16 mm negative proportions (Standard/matted 35 mm is 1.85, DV is 1.5, 16 mm is 1.33, and Television is 1.3). These cards are convenient since you can buy them anywhere, take them anywhere, sort them, color code them, paste them to posterboard, pin them to a corkboard, and mark the edges for filing. They're even available for feeding through laser or ink-jet printers.

You can get started by creating a simple sketch of the frame on the blank side (see figure 3-1). If you're shooting for television, you can draw a line down the right side (a little more than 1″ from right) to obtain the proper frame proportions. You can draw action arrows and necessary frame directions on the surface.

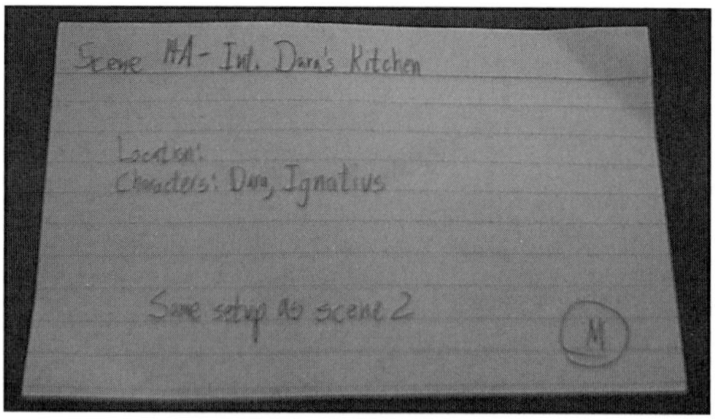

Script notes and scene explanations can be written on the lined side (see figure 3-2). At a minimum, usually the scene number is written on the card. You

FIGURE 3.1 *A simple sketch of a frame on the blank side of a 3″ × 5″ card.*

FIGURE 3.2 *Script notes and scene explanations written on the lined side of a 3″ × 5″ card.*

might also include a shot number (within the scene), the names of the characters involved, and the location if known. Leave room to scratch out and rewrite this information in case it changes.

Once you have a few cards, you'll want to begin organizing them. You can use a hole punch and affix the cards to a ring (see figure 3-3) which I find very effective to present the storyboard like a flip book. These rings are available inexpensively at most office supply warehouses. You can also put the storyboard cards in a card box and number them in shot order.

While working on a scene, you could pin them to corkboard, although it's impractical to keep an entire movie up on

FIGURE 3.3 *Cards affixed to a loose leaf binder ring.*

the board because of the number of cards involved. You might create a number of posterboards although when you tape them to the board, just do it along the top or you'll be unable to look at the notes on the back.

One of the disadvantages of the 3″ × 5″ card method is the difficulty in duplicating the cards. I haven't seen a copy machine that can accept a stack of cards, so the cards would have to be fed through the machine by hand. Drawing the storyboards on a standard 8.5″ × 11″ sheet of paper has many advantages in this area.

Basic templates

Using paper, pen, and ruler or a computer, you can easily create a template for a storyboard that provides the proper proportions for the medium you'll be filming on. The type of medium you will be shooting will determine the size of your storyboard panel. In figure 3-4 you can see templates for the most common film and video types.

Even the drawing tools in the popular word processor Microsoft Word can be used to create the template. If you don't have easy access to a computer, you can draw the templates by hand and use a copier to make duplications. Depending on the size of the storyboard you desire, a template could include several panels on a single page.

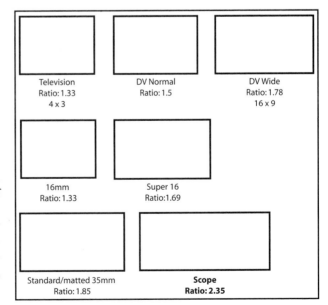

FIGURE 3.4 *Templates for the most common film and video types.*

Thumbnail sketches

Filmmakers often see the professionally rendered drawings used by directors such as Steven Spielberg or Ridley Scott and feel that they don't have the artistic skill to draw a storyboard. Professional storyboards are really works of art created by trained, full-time artists. Few filmmakers need this level of detail to understand, visualize, and communicate a shot.

Stick figures are the favored method of panel drawing among filmmakers who have to draw them themselves. In figure 3-5, you can see some stick-figure actors and actresses in a scene. For thumbnail sketches, stick figures are perfect for the first pass to try and decide how the scene will be framed.

Try to always include the horizon line which appears in figure 3-5. It can usually tell the camera operator if you're shooting above or below the actors. Shooting above the actors will make the horizon line rise (see figure 3-6),

FIGURE 3.5 *Thumbnail sketches of stick-figure actors in a scene.*

FIGURE 3.6 *High horizon line framing.*

while below the actors will make it drop (see figure 3-7).

You might also want to write the shot you intend to shot directly on the frame and use the abbreviation CU for close-up, M for medium, MCU for medium CU, ECU for extreme CU, and W for wide. You might consider other directions as well such as 2S for two shot when both actors are in scene, I to indicate an insert, and so on.

Don't worry about making the backgrounds too detailed. Each panel is meant to help understand the actions of the scene, not represent the scene itself. Here are the typical steps that are taken to draw a storyboard.

1. Draw the horizon line first to provide a guideline for the rest of the picture. Note that with most CUs, the horizon line will be out of the frame, so it doesn't need to be drawn at all.

2. Draw circles for the heads of your actors. Don't put in any features yet.

3. Draw a drop line from the head to show the angle of the bodies. If an actor is standing, you can drop it straight down. Bent over, draw a curve.

4. Draw the nose to show the direction and inclination of the head.

FIGURE 3.7 *Low horizon line framing.*

5. Draw the shoulder line to indicate the direction of the torso.

6. Draw the remaining facial features such as the eyes, ears, hair, and eyebrows.

7. Connect the hip line to indicate the direction of the hips.

8. Add arms and legs.

9. Add any necessary scenery.

Quick thumbnail sketches may help you get started with storyboarding but don't let it stop you from creating the full panels. You may not be familiar enough with basic drawing conventions to advance beyond the stick figures. For this reason, I've created Adam Actor and Amy Actress.

Adam Actor, Amy Actress

To properly frame a scene that will show people, you need to make sure that the people are correctly proportioned. For example, you can see in figure 3-8 that the entire length of the body of a simple cartoon figure and his twin can fit within the frame. The figure is not correctly proportioned for a human, however, so this shot will not actually be possible with most cameras.

The same shot with Adam Actor shows that only his upper torso will appear in the frame (see figure 3-9). Adam Actor is constructed to correspond to the proportions of a human being, so he can be used to accurately estimate how a shot will look.

FIGURE 3.8 *Simple cartoon character with improper proportions.*

FIGURE 3.9 *Adam actor is a simple character for fast storyboarding.*

FIGURE 3.10 *Amy actress is 6.5 heads tall.*

For simplicity, both actor and actress are proportioned using head size as the standard unit of measure. Adam Actor is 7 heads tall while Amy Actress is 6.5 heads tall (see figure 3-10). You can use a ruler to draw in the head and then measure off the rest of the body. However, this provides precision that's not necessary for most panels.

I use the fingertip-measuring method. Since most of your figures in the panels are small, you can easily hold together your thumb and your index finger, and use the edges of your fingernails to approximate the measurement of the head (see figure 3-11). Keep your fingers together at that angle and you can use that distance to quickly measure further spaces of the panel. With a pencil in your other hand, you can mark distances as you measure.

Figure 3-12 shows the heads of Adam and Amy from all eight primary angles (each turn of 45°). You can use these heads as templates that you can copy into your panels. If the head of one of your actors is tilted (perhaps bent over), rotate this book to the proper angle and then copy the head.

In figure 3-13, you can see some common facial expressions. Notice that only the eyebrows, eyes, and mouth really change to alter the expression. Try other variations of these facial features to obtain different expressions. Remember that these shouldn't be works of art. You're just looking for a representative picture to understand the scene.

If you have problems sketching your own poses, buy a flexible doll or action figure. Draw a proper head, so you can get the proportions correct and then use a stick-figure body modeled on the position you've placed the action figure (see figure 3-14).

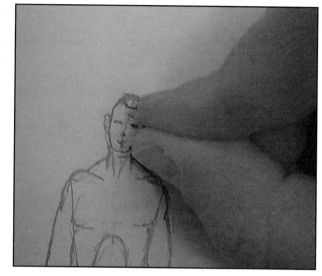

FIGURE 3.11 *Thumb and index figure measurement approximation.*

FIGURE 3.12 *Heads of Adam and Amy from the eight primary angles.*

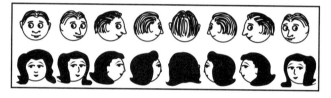

Happy   Angry   Sleeping   Disbelief   Conceit   Laughing

FIGURE 3.13 *Some common facial expressions.*

FIGURE 3.14 *Overdrawing an action figure photo.*

Sketch a few storyboard panels of movies that you know. Below are four famous movie scenes that I used Adam Actor to illustrate (see figure 3-15). Do you recognize the movies these are from? Storyboarding existing material will help you to learn how excellent directors framed a scene.

Photographic storyboarding

If you don't want to draw the storyboards, you can always use a camera instead. With dolls or stand-ins actors and a few toy props, a complete storyboard can be made of all the key scenes.

The advantages of using photographic storyboarding include:

FIGURE 3.15 *Framing of four famous movie scenes.*

- *Simple to begin* You can start immediately without worrying about your drawing talent or ability to accurately project the scenes. You can also usually use many of the pictures that have already been taken on the location scout.

- *Provides actual color photos of the scenes* You can take the pictures at the time of day and the place where you think you might want to shoot the actual scenes. Lens filters, diffusion, and camera angles can all be used to make the storyboard pictures appear close to the intended final picture of a scene.

- *Determining focal lengths* If your camera has interchangeable lenses or a wide-ranging zoom lens, you can determine the general focal length that might be needed for the shot. While a drawn storyboard can easily show a close-up or wide-angle shot of a scene, it won't provide a good idea of how the frame will actually look through the camera.

Disadvantages of the method:

- *Expense* Developing all the film or printing to an ink-jet for a digital camera can be very expensive. While pen and paper costs almost nothing, each photo may stretch your budget to the breaking point.

- *Availability of resources (human and otherwise)* Stand-ins may get tired of acting out every shot in the scene. Dolls or action figures may not provide the flexibility or emotional drama needed to communicate the key aspects of the scene. Additionally, a critical prop or set may be difficult to procure for the picture.

- *Tedium* Standing somewhere with a camera and taking every single shot needed for the storyboard can be incredibly tedious. It can also be time-consuming since making a simple sketch typically requires a few moments, but each picture needs to be setup, framed, and shot.

In figures 3-16 through 3-18, you can see a few storyboards I've created using an action figure and a doll. The male action figure is excellent because of the wide range of movement for the limbs as well as the head and neck. Can you see how the difference in lighting between figures 3-16 and 3-17 makes a difference in the tension of the scene? These type of lighting effects are often difficult to represent in sketches, but are fairly easy to accomplish using a small light in a photograph.

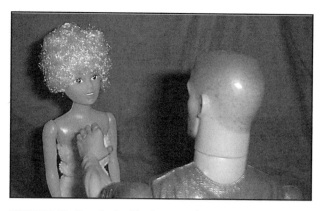

FIGURE 3.16 *Over-the-shoulder shot using photographic storyboarding with two action figures.*

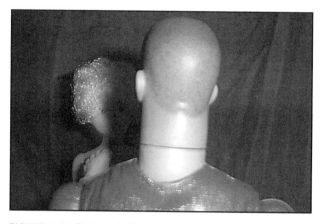

FIGURE 3.17 *Casting a shadow using photographic storyboarding.*

FIGURE 3.18 *Medium shot using photographic storyboarding.*

For those who want to spend the money, there is a program called Poser that allows you to position computer-generated people, change their expressions and poses, alter their hairstyles, add scenery, and so on. It even lets you choose the camera angle, set and modify lights, and render out the final image in high resolution.

I thought this sounded great, so I bought Poser and found myself wasting a great deal of time. Though no fault of the program itself, I couldn't abandon a frame that wasn't quite perfect. I spent hours and hours tweaking the actors or the camera angle to achieve the shot I really wanted. Each storyboard panel must have taken at least an hour. The program gives you so much control you almost can't resist becoming a director of the moment.

Of course when I went to shoot the scene, the logistics and actor's decisions rendered these panels no more accurate than the quick 5-min sketches I'd made for the rest of the film. If Poser works for you, that's great, but try and prevent yourself from wasting time making the panels hyper-accurate.

> **TIP** ▶ *You can also combine the photographic storyboard with your own drawings. If you're using a traditional film camera, you can take the pictures and either draw on an acetate overlay of the picture or sketch on the picture itself with a marker. With a computer, you can use features such as the layer options in Adobe Photoshop to draw representations of the characters over the scenery pictures.*

Presentation storyboarding

Whether your storyboard panels are photographed or hand-drawn, presentation software can be used very effectively to help develop your movie. Common programs such as Microsoft Powerpoint, Lotus Freelance, Macromedia Director, or other presentation software can be used to turn your static storyboard panels into a dynamic presentation.

The software can be used to set up timing of the movie, put in a sample soundtrack, or create an automated presentation. The flexibility of presentation software allows you to rearrange panels instantly. Additionally, the presentation can be output to a CD, DVD, or even the web for easy distribution. Viewer software for the presentation files is free and available on most computers in most formats.

Most presentation software also has excellent printing capabilities. Presentations can be printed to standard paper sheets, 3″ × 5″ cards, or tiled summary slides. Further, most programs feature the ability to add speaker notes to each slide. These notes can be used for a number of uses including important narration, prop lists, lighting notes, and transition information.

Suggestions

Here are a few suggestions relating to creating useful storyboards:

*   *Be sure to storyboard your inserts* When you're creating your storyboards, include a number of inserts or cutaways (general scenery, the clock ticking on the wall, children playing in the park, etc.) for each location. If you make sure to shoot different cutaways, editing becomes a much easier task. Cutaways are also often the shots that are forgotten on the shooting day in the thrill of the moment or end of the day trudge.

*   *Use corkboard or posterboard to mount the panels* You can easily mount 12 or more panels, so an entire scene may be viewed at once.

*   *Do a little storyboarding at a time* Storyboarding can be extremely tedious, so don't do it all at once. Break the task up into blocks of scenes or time. I generally sit down, start my stopwatch, and work for 20 min. This block of time seems long enough to get something done, but not long enough to create drudgery. Just make sure you do more than one 20-min block per day or you'll never get your storyboard done!

Script Supervisor Template

Applications

The role of a script supervisor (often known as a scriptee or continuity clerk in Europe) is to monitor what is actually shot during principal photography. Continuity, line readings, and length and quality of each take are all recorded. Notes on hair, make-up, costumes, and props are also kept. The log of the script supervisor forms a critical picture of what actually occurred on the set and is used extensively by the editors to organize the raw footage. The script supervisor position takes an eye for detail and unwavering attention.

If you think you can dispense with the services of a script supervisor on a guerilla production, you'll find out how high the cost can be in continuity errors, dramatically extended editing times, and additional re-shoots. Even if you're editing the film you shot yourself, you'll find that simply organizing and cataloging the shots in post-production to be tedious and frustrating. All this unpleasant labor could have been avoided by having a scriptee on staff during the shoot.

Even if the takes are catalogued in post-production, how would you know which take was considered best (by the director, DP, or actor)? Script notes can minimize time wasted sorting through the shoot footage. A feature film may have 150,000–200,000 ft of exposed film. Sorting through all this footage to find a small take is a poor use of resources when a script log can be examined and the shot instantly located.

I have often heard of the script supervisor position described as a continuity safety net. Note that the various departments should all do their part for continuity. The script supervisor should only be relied on to provide an overview of the entire continuity rather than being viewed as a crutch that other departments expect to catch their mistakes.

> **NOTE→** There are often continuity problems that seem difficult to reconcile. For example, in a scene shot one day the actor might be wearing a tie. A week later, another contiguous scene was shot without the tie. A month later a scene in between those two needs to be shot, but someone has noticed the tie mistake. In the new scene, an action is added where the actor removes the tie, thereby justifying its absence in a later scene.
>
> If there is a continuity mistake, don't immediately assume that a re-shoot is necessary. Consider the ways that previous or subsequent scenes can be augmented to explain the continuity difference. The script log can help you make these decisions.

General Instructions

Script supervisors are asked to play many roles. Sometimes they read off-camera dialogue while the actors relate and respond to it. Sometimes they run through lines with actors before a take, especially if the actor didn't prepare beforehand. However, the script supervisor's primary responsibility is for taking notes of what happened on the shoot.

This role is performed through two key tasks: lining the script and keeping a script log. "Lining the script" means to literally draw a line through each piece of action and line of dialogue after it has been captured on film. With a lined script, it only takes a moment to determine whether specific dialogue or action sequences have already been shot. The script log contains all the basic information and notes that will help continuity during the shoot and editing in post-production.

Script supervisor equipment

Compared with most other departments, the script supervisor requires little equipment. At a minimum, the scriptee can get away with having only a script, a notebook, and a pen. However, to get the best results and make yourself most comfortable, there are a number of items you can include in your kit.

A script supervisor generally has the following key pieces of equipment:

- *Script notebook or log* Your most important item. The notebook will hold your script and all the script notes you take.

- *Stopwatch* For timing the length of each take. Make sure you can turn off the start/stop beeper! Angry stares will be directed at any novice scriptee who disturbs the actors and the sound department with the noise of a stopwatch. If you love a stopwatch you have, but are unable to stop it beeping, take it to a jeweler who can disable the sound.

- *Many pens or sharpened pencils* Script supervisors seem to differ on the advantages and disadvantages of pen versus pencil. Choose whichever you feel comfortable using, but make sure you have spares.

- *Small folding chair* The script supervisor spends a majority of the time sitting. In addition to the long shoot hours that are required, having to juggle a script, a script log, and a stopwatch makes using a chair almost a necessity. Also, make sure that your chair is comfortable and light. A padded, aluminum, folding chair seems just about perfect.

- *Rugged bag* To carry your notebook and supplies. It will get kicked and knocked around, so avoid using anything dear to your heart.

- *Camera* To take continuity pictures, typically a Polaroid or other instant photo camera is used. Generally take pictures immediately before or just after the first take. Make sure film for the continuity camera is included in the film budget.

- *Office supplies* Whiteout, a hole punch, highlighters, and scratch paper while not strictly necessary, can come in very handy.

- *Water bottles* Be sure to drink sparingly as frequent trips to the bathroom are frowned upon.

Preproduction info

When there is time in preproduction for preparation, a script supervisor should make a personal script breakdown. The breakdown will contain details that will help make tracking continuity easier and will substantially reduce the amount of preparation required on the morning of each shoot day.

How you format a preproduction list is up to you. Some people use individual form pages to break-down each scene. More commonly, notes are made or highlighted directly on the script for easy reference.

Some of the information for each scene that should be noted during preproduction includes:

- Scene number;

- Location;

- Interior or exterior scene;

- Brief description of the action;

- Time of day the scene takes place;

- Estimated shooting hours;

- Characters in the scene;

- Extras;

- Props used by actors;

- Costumes.

Working through the script ahead of time will make your work much easier. A quick review of these items can let you know what you need to watch closely. For example, if at the end of a long scene, a character named Winona discretely slips a watch from the coffee table into her purse, you can note the position of the watch at the opening of the scene. Later you can ensure that the watch is returned to the proper position for the next take.

Basic log information

In the script log you'll have to construct, there are a number of basic items that need to be recorded for each take. This log information is especially important if there is a mis-slate before the scene or simply no slate at all. No matter what type of shoot you're working, this basic information will provide the foundation for the editor's work. For this reason, log information should always be coordinated with the items written on the slate. Having the log and the slate footage in sync will allow the editors to easily match the notes to each take.

> **TIP** ▶ *Be sure to put a circle around the takes that the director likes the most. That way the editor can know instantly that for Scene 17B, the 4th take (on camera roll 19 and sound roll 17) was the best.*

The basic items tracked include:

- Take number with take 1A, 1B, etc.;

- Start time of take;

- Length of take;

- Lens used;

- Camera and sound rolls;

- MOS or not;

- Abbreviated shot type such as CU, MCU, ECU, or WA;

- Director's comment such as "soft focus," "beautiful light," or "excellent dolly move;"

- Take flaws such as NG sound, NG camera, or incomplete dialogue.

In addition to this information, the script log should record the time when first shot of the day occurred, when lunch was called, when wrap called, and the total number of pages shot. This information will be needed by the production office to track how the shoot is going.

On a professional set, all this basic information is summarized at the end of every shoot day in the "daily wrap report." The numbers of camera and sound rolls used, setups, scenes, minutes shot, and pages shot should all be totaled and included in the report. If the basic information of the script log is kept accurately, it takes very little time to complete this report.

Log notes

In addition to the basic information contained in the log, a good script supervisor takes many notes for continuity and clarification. Continuity is especially important in time lapses or flashbacks, so be sure to pay close attention to the scenes that bookend the time transitions.

Some of the most important pieces of information to record are:

- Any ad-libs to the dialogue including any changes, additions, or deletions;

- Violations of the 180° line;

- Changes in the eyeline direction of the actors watching something off-screen (such as Mary looks RT-LT) or eyeline for reversals in a dialogue scene;

- Blocking and action matching such as which side of the actor's face was punched, so the make-up bruise can be applied correctly;

- Comportment of make-up and hair such as the color of lipstick or whether hairdo was up or down;

- Comportment of clothes such as a spaghetti strap that is fallen down or whether the jacket open or buttoned;

- Comportment of accessories such as glasses on or off or shoved up into hair;

- Arm on-hip or off-hip;

- Burning cigarette length and which hand-held it;

- Height of burning candles;

- Liquid levels in drinking glasses;

- Point in dialogue when an item (such as a glass) was set down on table;

- Order that people enter or leave the room;

- Position of actors in a group shot;

- Doors open or shut.

Construction

The following template provides all the basic information that should be taken down by a script supervisor. Some scriptees take down this information directly on the script rather than keeping a separate log page. On a professional production, I don't know how the production company finds this acceptable. On a guerilla film, do it any way you like as long as the information gets recorded. Try to discuss with the editors the form that will help them most. If you can reach some sort of agreement, that would be best for everyone involved.

Use a spreadsheet or the table function within a word processor. Create the following form:

Scene	Take	ST	L	CamR	SndR	Page	Description	Notes/continuity

Depending on your taste, you might set the page orientation to landscape to have more room on each line. However, portrait orientation is sometimes easier to use if you're keeping the script in the same folder. Make sure the scene, take, and start time (ST) are coordinated with the camera department and the slate. The camera roll (CamR) and sound roll (SndR) should also match those currently in use. The length (L) of the take you should determine with your stopwatch.

In the header of the form page, you should also provide spaces for shoot information such as when the first shot of the day occurred, when lunch was called, when wrap called, and the total number of pages shot for the day. That way you can easily record this information and keep it with the notes that relate to that shooting day.

When you begin a new shoot day and also when you switch locations (this can include moving to another room in the same location), draw a bold line through one of the rows and then note the new location information. Items such as the location number, location type, interior or exterior, and time of day when location filming begins are all important factors.

Suggestions

Here are a few suggestions to help you as script supervisor:

- *Study before you scriptee* Make sure you know what you're getting into before you volunteer for the script supervisor position. This chapter provides a fairly good overview of the responsibilities of the position. For explicit information, check out *Continuity in Film and Video* by Avril Rowlands (Focal Press Media Manuals Series, 1989) and *Script Supervising and Film Continuity* by Pat Miller (Focal Press, 1990).

- *Learn to let go* Many times you will make the director or DP aware of a continuity mistake you know will cause problems in the edit, only to be completely ignored. Don't take it personally and don't harp on it or you'll find yourself ignored in more instances. Just shrug it off and move on.

Location Scouting

Applications

Location scouting is more of an art than a science. To be able to interpret the director's desired vision and find a location that properly communicates the story is a difficult skill. It's simple enough to pick a place and declare "I want to shoot there!" It's much harder to take into account whether it's practical to obtain permission for shooting, where lighting and camera equipment can be placed, how expensive it will be to rent the location, and so on.

By first learning the logistics of scouting, you can spend more time being creative in thinking of places and areas that might photograph well. At the end of the chapter is a form that can be used when going on a location scout. It contains blanks and checkboxes for all the most important factors to record about a site.

Even if you have the locations for your film chosen, I would recommend filling out the form for each place anyway. This process can highlight and identify problems or difficulties you may experience while shooting there. You can then plan around any obstacles you recognize.

General Instructions

Before you begin scouting, you'll need to generate a location list. This list should contain all the sites listed in the script. If you have an electronic version of the screenplay, most screenwriting programs will automatically generate a location report. The following table contains a sample report generated by the screenwriting program Final Draft from a short film script:

Location	Occurrences
EXT. – HILLTOP	1
EXT. – OLD TRAIN STATION	2
EXT. – PARK PLAYGROUND	2
EXT. – NEW TRAIN STATION	1
INT. – LIVING ROOM	5
INT. – MATTHEW'S BEDROOM	1

In addition to listing all the unique locations, this report contains the number of times that each appears in the script (the Occurrences column). This number can aid you in planning how long you'll need to use a location. It can also give you an idea of how important each place may be to the overall story.

> **WARNING→** Be careful to check this report against the actual script. If the person that wrote the script didn't properly mark an element as a Scene Heading, it won't show up in the location report. You don't want to be missing any locations when you begin scouting.

Once you have a location list, you're ready to begin scouting. Be sure to bring a map, a compass, and a long tape measure. The map will allow you to mark down the locations and see their proximity to major highways and landmarks. The compass will help you determine the direction individual parts of the building are facing. The direction will be important in determining the sun's location at the various times of day for any daylight exterior shoots. You'll use the tape measure for everything from determining the distance from the buildings to the curb to measuring the width of a room to gauging the height of hedges that surround a house.

You should also carry at least one still camera to record the location for "show-and-tell" later. Digital cameras are great because you can take many pictures without worrying about the expense of each shot. You can also see the shot on the small color screen to make sure you got all of the detail you needed. If the shoot requires an entire building or street, you might do well to bring a camcorder. Full motion video can help you to record the neighborhood and the surrounding environment to give the director an idea of the general area.

The factors of interior/exterior and day/night are going to be the primary considerations in determining when and where you'll be scouting. It seems that seldom do the ideal exteriors having corresponding ideal interiors. Therefore, you're better off grouping your scouting expedition to inspect all the interior days/nights, all the exterior days, and all the exterior nights together. By grouping of the potential locations into these three categories, you can maximize the use of your time.

Artistic Considerations

After availability, the artistic considerations are the most important factor when considering a location. Problems of parking, power, and other obstacles can typically be addressed, but if the location doesn't look appropriate to the story, then the quality of the film is compromised.

When you look at a location, what does it say to you? What is your first impression? Does it say wealth or poverty? Hope or despair? Dream or nightmare? Modern or provincial? Is your impression determined by the neighborhood and the houses around it? If you ignore the direct environment and imagine shooting only that particular location, does it say something different?

Location scouting takes thinking like a director, because great locations advance the story or reflect elements of the plot or a character in the script. While interiors can and generally are modified by the Art Department, exteriors are far more difficult. For exteriors, try to find locations that closely match the vision of the script.

You will need to take photos of all the locations that you visit. Even if you think it's inappropriate, take a photo. If later the director describes the ideal location of something you've rejected, you won't immediately have to head back out. Photos are a quick and excellent way for a number of people to examine a variety of sites that may be in many different locations. Once the list of possibilities has been narrowed down, it's much easier to create an inspection-driving plan for the principals.

> **TIP ▶** *If you are roaming all over scouting for locations, it's often useful to note the page number or grid designation from a Thomas Bros. guide or map on your location report. That way, it's easy for you to find again if you need to guide someone to the location and you can easily fax them a map of the area.*

Visual Considerations

After the artistic concerns, the location needs to be evaluated in terms of lighting and shooting. As far as a production is concerned, the only reason a location exists is the ability to catch it on film. If the location is perfect except it's impossible to light or a film crew can't fit inside the available space, then the site has no value.

For example, an exterior night shoot in the woods is one of the most difficult locations to use even if it is easily accessible. Not only is a huge amount of light needed since there is generally no ambient light available (in a downtown shoot, city light often just has to be augmented), how is any light source motivated to the viewer? That is to say, why in the story would there be a bright light in the woods at night? A forest that's brightly lit at night will generally look fake unless a visual cue is given to the viewer (such as a large nearby campfire). Aspects of obtaining a good exposed image are an important consideration when examining a location.

Some of the most important visual considerations include:

- *Ambient light* Is there too little? Too much? Just right? If a romantic night interior is needed, a street lamp just outside the window may be hard to work around. Filming in a factory with dozens of suspended lamps that can't be properly adjusted for light level may be a problem since they may be in the frame and would look odd if turned off. Note all existing light sources that will be present at the time of the shoot.

- *Immovable objects in frame* Will objects in frame need to be hidden? Power lines can ruin an otherwise perfectly framed exterior shot. A shot that requires an open sky can be a problem if there are telephone poles everywhere. High trees, bushes, mountains, or buildings block the sun earlier than sunset which may cause other problems. For interiors, a large oak bed that can't be moved or a safe bolted to the floor are examples of problem objects.

- *Level ground* Level ground is very important for quickly setting up a dolly track. Soft ground, mud, hills, and dunes can all make a dolly shot very difficult and time-consuming. When the ground isn't level or hard, be sure to record this in your location notes.

- *Match the interiors and the exteriors* If the actors will enter one location (such as a house), but another location will be used for the interior (such as a soundstage), what number of doors and windows must be duplicated? A location with vast windows over an ocean view may be difficult for the DP and Art Department to replicate on a stage.

Sun tracking

For the exterior location that you are considering, it's critical to examine how the sun will move across the sky. Shadows from other buildings alone may make the Director of Photography declare the location unworthy. For daylight exteriors, determine how the sun is positioned during different times of the day and how this will affect the shadows of surrounding landscape objects (buildings, poles, mountains, etc.).

The sun generally moves at 14° per hour, though it moves faster around noon. Put a piece of tape on the ground facing east/west. Use your arm to describe the arc of the sun. This will help you visualize where the shadows will be cast in relation to the locations you will be shooting.

You might also get a sun location calculator. Some programs that do this are available on the Internet for free download. Check out what's available and see if you can find a program that can be used with your computer platform (Palm, iBook, etc.).

Logistical Factors

Once you've found a location that seems like it might work for the script, there are numerous practical implications that must be considered. Generally these are not the factors that make or break the use of a location, but determine the difficulty and cost of shooting there.

Can you get permits to shoot at a particular location? Many guerilla filmmakers have a cavalier attitude about permits because of the difficulty and expense of obtaining them. Some locations, such as the New York subway, can levy astronomical fines if you're caught filming there. Others will confiscate your equipment. Some might do both. Be sure to understand what you're up against before you decide to risk it.

Be aware that even if you're not explicitly caught without permits, you can poison the well for future shoots there. A disgruntled neighbor or employee can make excessive noise, call the police, prohibit convenient parking, and generally make things very difficult. Never forget that you may have later pickup days at that location. Woe be it to the filmmaker that abuses the surrounding inhabitants.

Make sure the area around the location is safe! It's wonderful if you want to shoot a ghetto-based gangland drama, but often gangland is not a good place to find locations. It is the film production's responsibility to assure the safety of the cast and crew, so filming in a dangerous spot is a no-no. Also, problems of equipment theft must be considered. Even if the location is perfect and the rent for it is cheap, think carefully before filming in a very poor neighborhood.

Surroundings

Shooting even a simple movie can be taxing on the neighborhood around you. Lack of parking for the necessary cars and equipment can turn an ideal location into a nightmare. You should always consider the placement of necessary vehicles and facilities when examining a location.

Some of the most important factors include:

- *Rest rooms* Are there rest rooms for the crew nearby? There is no better way to alienate cast and crew than by having too few bathrooms or locating them too far away. Make certain that the proper number of rest rooms are located at an appropriate distance from the set.

- *Crew parking* Working in Los Angeles, finding appropriate parking for the crew can be a difficult task. Check to make sure that there aren't scheduled street sweepings during your days of filming, otherwise an already difficult parking situation can become impossible. Also you don't want the car of your lead actress towed away during the shoot, so try and plan ahead where parking is acceptable and where it isn't.

- *Camera/grip truck or van* At the very least, make sure that there is a close place to park during loading and unloading. Hauling heavy grip and camera equipment long distances is exhausting and time wasting. Half of the shooting day may be wasted just getting equipment to and from a distant set.

- *Make-up location* Don't count on the actors to make themselves up before they arrive. Since the talent usually spend a good deal of time waiting for the shot to be ready, the make-up location is usually the place where they can wait comfortably. You'll benefit in better performances if you ensure that the make-up location is nice. It may require the rental of a tent or a make-up bus (often called a honey wagon).

- *Generator location* If the generator must be close to the shooting location, this can cause serious problems for the sound department. Any location that has a space near the set that's shielded by a barrier (brick wall, dense hedge, etc.) is definitely a plus for that site.

- *Prop truck* The art department may have to unload furniture, curtains, framed pictures, lamps, and any number of props. Parking might be required the day before if they need to prep the set.

- *Craft services* The craft services (snacks, water, etc.) should be easily accessible by the set. People often like to chat at craft services, so a location that has a sound barrier to the shooting set is ideal.

- *Room for administration* If you will need the producers or other administration on set, be sure to have a location to park their van or other working vehicle. They may need electrical and phone hookups as well for computers, fax machines, and printers.

Even if you're combining vehicles (one van carries the talent, camera equipment, and lighting), you will need to locate this vehicle close to the shooting location. Is there available room? Can you take up five parking spaces without angering the neighbors? Make sure these factors are considered.

Is power available at the location? Unless you have a generator, you will need power for the lights at a minimum. Although the camera department generally has charged batteries, they may need power to recharge if the shoot is long. Also note if the power outlets at the location have two or three holes (three means the plug is grounded). A location wired with two hole outlets is older (since the ground plug outlet has been standard for at least the last 15 years), so the internal wiring may have less available power capacity.

Is there shade if it's hot or warmth if it's cold? Extremes in temperature can destroy a film schedule. Try to make sure the location has protection from the elements for the cast, camera, and crew. Filming inside an abandoned building may seem like a great idea until the temperature drops and the location has no available heat source.

Sound concerns

The sound department will thank you if you can include notes relating to the sound conditions of the location. Although the principal players in a production rarely consult the sound crew on location selection, any sound-related notes will help them prepare for the conditions they'll face. The sound crew can adjust their selection of microphones and recording equipment to suit the area.

For exterior shots, is the location next to a freeway? An airport? Other sources of loud noise? Is there construction going on one street over? Power lines, dogs, etc. can all make problem noises for the soundtrack.

For interior shots, is there central air conditioning? Can it be turned off if too loud during the shoot? What about refrigerators? Does the apartment have thin walls where the neighbors will be heard? Do the existing lights give off any humming sound? Can they be switched off?

One location scout I know uses a decibel level meter he bought at Radio Shack. He says that our ears too quickly accommodate themselves to ambient noise. What subjectively sounds OK to a location scout may be very loud to the microphones. Therefore, he records the objective decibel sound level at each location.

Make sure you take some type of notes about the sound landscape for both exterior and interior locations. Information provided in advance can even help to determine whether certain microphone types (such as a boom mic) can be used at all.

Special Day/Date Considerations

As you draw close to generating a shooting schedule, you will need to consider the days and the dates on which each shoot day occurs for particular locations. I've had the unlucky experience of working for a production that schedules entirely around actor and location availability and ignores the presence of holidays. On one shoot, a location that had previously been fine became a nightmare because of the holiday traffic and parking.

Take into account any holidays that fall within the shooting schedule and how they might impact your location. Will the street you're shooting on become the site of a St. Patrick's Day parade? Is the restaurant next door to the location advertising a Mecca for Mother's Day brunch? Is a heavy dialogue scene scheduled on the 4th of July when firecrackers will make the soundtrack unusable? On the positive side, will Easter Sunday keep most of the traffic away from downtown where you're shooting?

Even if the script calls for the event to take place on a holiday, it's usually better to shoot background footage on the holiday itself or maybe just record an audio track of authentic noise for mixing in post-production.

The day of the week can also cause problems. Is your location next to a hip dance club? Shooting Friday night at 8 p.m. can create traffic problems as well as the sounds of drunken revelers. Scheduling call time at 9 a.m. Monday morning for a downtown location is asking for everyone to be late.

Although these special considerations are not necessarily part of the location report, it is a good idea to consider them. Note any potentially glaring conflicts on your report. This is one of those little details that a good location scout tries to address, so the production company can take them into account.

Location Layout Templates

There are often times when locations need to be diagrammed for various reasons. For example, often a low-budget shoot is limited in the shoot range. A car may need to be shot driving down a small town street, turning around and parking. By creating a quick street layout template, the director can determine where to place the camera.

If geography is important to the scene, make a little map drawing of the area. It's much better to make this sketch and not need it, then to need it and not have made it.

Location Scouting Form

In figure 5-1 you'll see a sample location form. I've found this form to be extremely useful when scouting for myself and worth its weight in gold when looking for someone else.

The small drawing space supplied in the left corner labeled "Location layout and orientation" is provided to allow you to make a quick sketch of the location. The "N" direction provides an indicator to show you the direction North, so lighting considerations can be made. This area is also available to staple a polaroid or other location photograph.

This template has all the primary information necessary for most location scouts. However, everyone has different needs. Feel free to modify the form to include any particular considerations that might be important to your particular shoot.

Suggestions

Here are a few suggestions to help you with location scouting:

- *Make a location flyer* You may need a location (such as a house) and find an entire street of the ideal type. If you have a location flyer that describes your needs and contact information, you can put it on doorknobs and post it on lampposts. The people that are most interested will contact you. You can usually get two or three potential locations this way and that will allow you to choose which location is best based on your shoot considerations such as price, accessibility, etc.

- *Check the web for locations* Websites such as www.cinemascout.com will sometimes show pictures as well as have links to information on permits and the rental cost per day. At the very least, check the website of the city where you'll be shooting for information on permits. Also, it's generally a good idea to locate the nearest hospital and fire department just in case anything unpleasant happens on set.

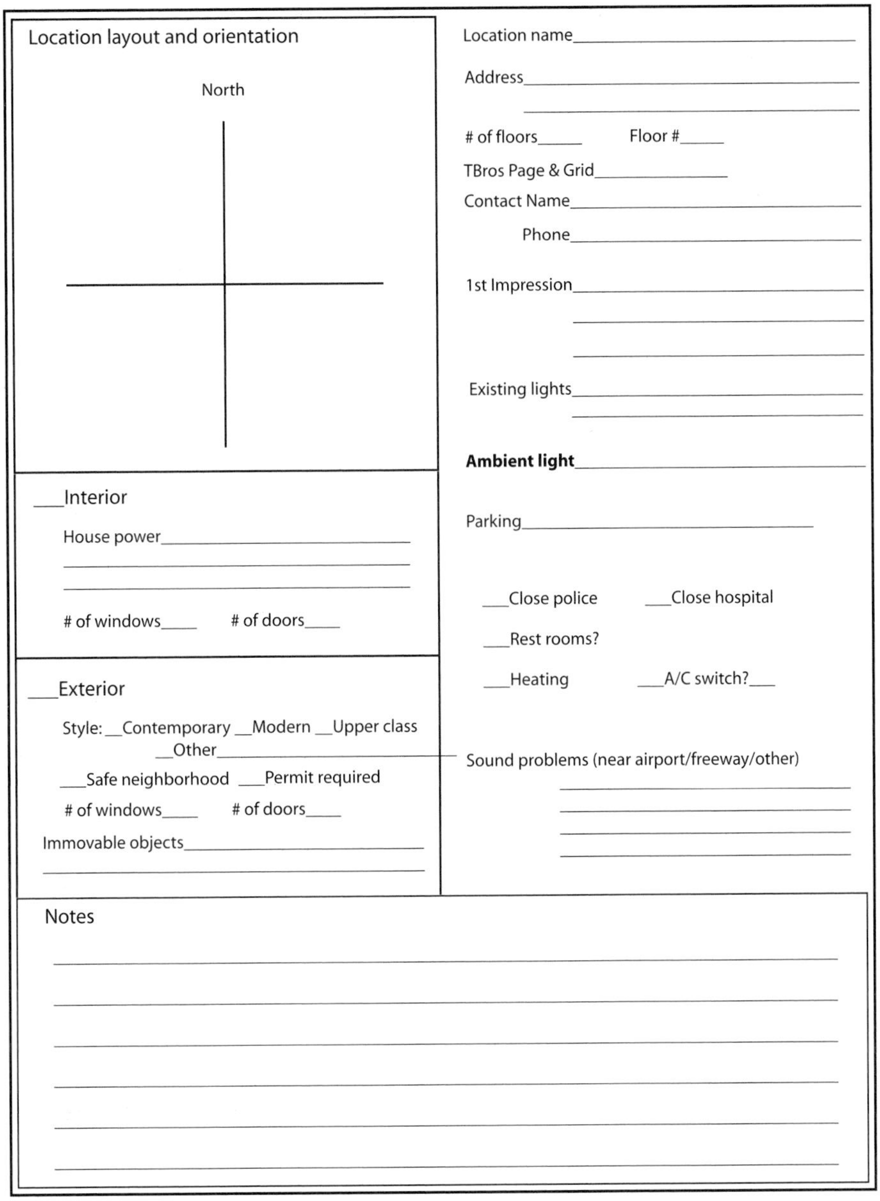

Location layout and orientation	Location name_____

Location layout and orientation

North

___Interior

House power_____

# of windows_____   # of doors_____

___Exterior

Style: __Contemporary __Modern __Upper class
          __Other_____
___Safe neighborhood ___Permit required
# of windows_____   # of doors_____
Immovable objects_____

Location name_____

Address_____
_____

# of floors_____   Floor #_____

TBros Page & Grid_____

Contact Name_____

      Phone_____

1st Impression_____
            _____
            _____

Existing lights_____
            _____

Ambient light_____

Parking_____

___Close police   ___Close hospital
___Rest rooms?

___Heating   ___A/C switch?___

Sound problems (near airport/freeway/other)
      _____
      _____
      _____

Notes
_____
_____
_____
_____
_____
_____
_____

FIGURE 5.1 *An example location form for performing location scouting.*

- **Ask a real estate agent** Many times a real estate agent can point you in right direction for a location you're seeking. The agent might even suggest a seller who has a house on the market that wouldn't mind earning a few extra dollars before they've moved out. Additionally, real estate agents know all about areas and can generally warn you about things such as local dangers or new construction that might take place at the time of your shoot.

- **Check if a location be used multiple times** Often a single office can be transformed using angles and set decorations to appear as two or more offices. Check if you can adapt a single location to represent multiple locations on film. This process of redressing can save a great deal of time and money.

Legal Release Forms

Applications

Considering the legal aspects of film production may be unpleasant, but a very necessary evil. Even if you're making a short film, you need to protect yourself legally regarding any work or film materials that appears within the movie. Legal forms are even more critical if you're even considering any type of distribution. Guerilla filmmakers ignore legal safeguards at their own peril.

Since your budget is probably limited, you can't expect to have a high-profile attorney making sure that each step of film production is legally protected. Instead, be sure that you have a basic level of legal shelter. This means having basic documents that give you permission to film at a location, incorporate acting performances into your film, and use works of art (such as a musical soundtrack) in your production.

The following three releases have been included thanks to Eve Light Honthaner. She has written a valuable book named "The Complete Film Production Handbook" (ISBN 0-240-80419-8). The book includes legal forms, reference materials for producers and production managers, in-depth examination of film planning, basic accounting procedures, sample breakdowns and schedules, and lots more information. It's a must-have if you're participating in the logistics of production.

Because I think you'll find information in the handbook that you won't find anywhere else, I've included an abbreviated table of contents here:

- The production team and who does what;

- Basic accounting;

- From script to schedule;

- Pre-production;

- Insurance requirements;

- Making good deals and saving money;

- Deal memos;

- Unions and guilds;

- Principal talent and extras;

- Clearances and releases;

- Locations and foreign locations;

- Industry survival tips;

- Tear-out blank forms.

The first release, the Personal Release (see figure 6-1), grants permission to use an actor's performance and likeness in your film. It's critical that you gain this permission before any footage has been recorded. If you don't obtain this permission in advance, the actor may have you over a barrel when you ask for it days into principal photography.

The Use of Artwork release (see figure 6-2) grants the rights to include a copyrighted work within your film. Be careful to understand the limits of this agreement. A copyright holder can only grant rights that he or she actually owns. Therefore, if a musician grants the rights to use a song he's written and performed, yet the song includes samples to which no license has been obtained, he doesn't have the right to grant the use of the song in your film.

PERSONAL RELEASE

Film _____

Production Company _____

Address _____

_____   Date _____

Ladies and Gentlemen:

I, the undersigned, hereby grant permission to _____
("Producer") to photograph me and to record my voice, performances, poses, acts, plays and appearances, and use my picture, photograph, silhouette and other reproductions of my physical likeness and sound as part of the _____ _____ tentatively entitled _____
_____ (the "Picture") and the unlimited distribution, advertising, promotion, exhibition and exploitation of the Picture by any method or device now known or hereafter devised in which the same may be used, and/or incorporated and/or exhibited and/or exploited.

I agree that I will not assert or maintain against you, your successors, assigns and licensees, any claim, action, suit or demand of any kind or nature whatsoever, including but not limited to, those grounded upon invasion of privacy, rights of publicity or other civil rights, or for any other reason in connection with your authorized use of my physical likeness and sound in the Picture as herein provided. I hereby release you, your successors, assigns and licensees, and each of them, from and against any and all claims, liabilities, demands, actions, causes of action(s), costs and expenses whatsoever, at law or in equity, known or unknown, anticipated or unanticipated, which I ever had, now have, or may, or shall hereafter have by reason, matter, cause or thing arising out of your use as herein provided.

I affirm that neither I, nor anyone acting for me, gave or agreed to give anything of value to any of your employees or any representative of any television network, motion picture studio or production entity for arranging my appearance on the Picture.

I have read the foregoing and fully understand the meaning and effect thereof and, intending to be legally bound, I have signed this release.

Dated _____

_____
Signature

_____
If a minor, Guardian's Signature

_____
Please Print Name

AGREED AND ACCEPTED TO

_____
Address

_____

By _____   (___) ___ - _____
Phone Number

A Location Release (see figure 6-3) is good to obtain as soon as a party agrees to allow you use of the location. Although getting this release is no guarantee that a location owner won't renege at the last minute (this happens often, so be prepared with an alternate), a signed agreement has much more weight than a verbal guarantee. That said, once you obtain the location release, be sure to instill in your film crew respect for the location they'll be using.

USE OF ARTWORK
(RELEASE FROM COPYRIGHTED OWNER)

Film _____

Production Company _____

Address _____

_____ Date _____

Ladies and Gentlemen:

For good and valuable consideration, receipt of which is hereby acknowledged, I, the undersigned, grant to you, your agents, successors, licensees and assigns, the non-exclusive right but not the obligation to use my artwork (as described below) in the _____ tentatively entitled _____ (the "Picture"), and to utilize and reproduce the artwork in connection with the Picture, without limitation as to time or number of runs, for reproduction, exhibition and exploitation, throughout the world, in any and all manner, methods and media, whether now known or hereafter known or devised, and in the advertising, publicizing, promotion, and exploitation thereof.

I hereby release you, your agents, successors, licensees and assigns from any claim of any kind or nature whatsoever arising from the use of such artwork, including, but not limited to, those based upon defamation (including libel and slander), invasion of privacy, right of publicity, copyright, or any other personal and/or property rights and agree that I will not now or in the future assert or maintain any claims against you, your agents, successors, licensees and assigns.

I represent that I am the owner and/or authorized representative of the artwork, and that I have the authority to grant you the permission and rights herein granted, and that no one else's permission is required with respect to the rights herein granted.

In granting of the foregoing rights and licenses, I acknowledge that I have not been induced to do so by any representative or assurance by you or on your behalf relative to the manner in which any of the rights or licenses granted hereunder may be exercised; and I agree that you are under no obligation to exercise any of the rights or licenses granted hereunder.

Title of Artwork: " _____ "

Very truly yours,

_____
Signature of Owner and/or Authorized Agent

_____
Please Print Name

_____
Title/Company

AGREED AND ACCEPTED TO

_____

_____
Address

By _____   (   )   -
_____
Phone Number

LOCATION RELEASE

Property Owner _____ Location _____

Property Address _____ Set Number _____

_____

Production Company _____ ("Producer")
Address _____

_____

Re: _____ (the "Picture")

To the Producer:

Owner hereby acknowledges that the Property as referred to in the LOCATION AGREEMENT between Producer and Owner dated _____ , (the "Agreement") has been returned to Owner in substantially the same condition as it was in prior to Producer's use thereof.

Owner hereby acknowledges that

(a)   All payments required under the Agreement have been paid;

(b)   No additional restoration work is required in connection with the Property;

(c)   Owner, and any individual who entered the Property at the invitation or on behalf of Owner, suffered no personal loss or damage in connection with the use of the Property by Producer; and

(d)   Producer has no other responsibilities in connection with the Property other than to continue to hold Owner harmless from any and all third-party suits, claims, or loss or liabilities directly resulting from Producer's use of the Property.

Owner hereby releases and forever discharges Producer, its parent, subsidiary, affiliated and associated companies and its and their officers, employees and agents, and their successors and assigns of and from any and all claims, debts, demands, liabilities, obligations, costs, expenses, damages, actions and causes of action of whatsoever kind or nature, whether known or unknown, which Owner has ever had, now has or which Owner or any of its successors or assigns hereafter can, shall or may have against Producer based on or arising out of, relating to or in connection with the Agreement.

Producer may assign, transfer, license, delegate and/or grant all or any part of its rights, privileges and property hereunder to any person or entity. This Agreement shall be binding upon and shall inure to the benefit of the parties hereto and their respective heirs, executors, administrators, successors and assigns. This Agreement and Owner's rights and obligations hereunder may not be assigned by Owner.

ACCEPTED AND AGREED TO

_____   _____
Owner   Date

Suggestions

Here are a few suggestions to help you:

- *Have releases signed well ahead of need* People change their minds constantly. You don't want to show up at a location on the day of the shoot and be denied clearance or be required to give an actor a better credit just to get his release signature. Your best friend may decide that you can't use his soundtrack the week before the final cut is due. The unthinkable happens often in the movie business. Make sure you're protected.

- ***Document location conditions*** When filming at a location, it's important to document the condition of the site *before* you start filming there. I can't tell you the number of times people have demanded cleaning and repair on conditions that existed before the film crew arrived. The one time I saw a location manager confronted with a Polaroid that contradicted his claims, he immediately withdrew his other illegitimate demands.

- ***Carefully weigh legal advice*** Lawyers are paid to make sure you're completely protected, so they tend demand safeguards that may not be practical when things need to get done. It's up to you to decide whether some unprotected risks are appropriate. I met a producer, trying to get a film made, who was partnered with a lawyer. The producer consulted the lawyer before making any moves. Needless to say, the movie they were trying to make never got past preproduction. Remember that in the end, you have to rely on your own judgment.

Camera Introduction II

Applications

The camera department generally has the most prestige of any department on a shoot. That means that it often has the most people vying for positions, so people that want to work in camera will need to master a great amount of technical information to excel. While the director makes the executive decisions and works with the actors, camera's responsibility is capturing the intention of the scene by "painting with light," as it is famously described. The head position in the camera department is the Director of Photography (aka DP, DoP, or cinematographer) who must obtain the desired image through a careful balance of lenses, film speed, shutter speed, aperture, and light.

The information in this section of the book describes the creation of equipment used by the camera department, but contains very little technical information on specific cameras, camera accessories (lenses, French flags, etc.), or camera use. Cameras are precision equipment and are vastly different from model to model. Although tinkering with the internals of a camera is a time houred hobby, it's beyond the scope of this book.

At the time of this writing, the camera world is going through an amazing upheaval. Digital cameras are storming the castle of traditional celluloid photography. Some filmmakers have embraced the new technology. Others testify that the technology is not mature enough to be taken seriously. Traditional camera manufacturers are addressing the digital challenge by upgrading and adding fantastic new features to existing cameras.

Any written book that provides extensive details of particular cameras will be quickly outdated in these turbulent times. Therefore, I have chosen to include little information concerning specific cameras. I've included some information on MiniDV techniques and DV cameras since this format is so popular and looks like it will be with us for quite a few years. It is also a very popular choice for guerilla filmmakers because of inexpense, widespread availability, and flexibility.

If you want to work in a professional camera department, be sure to purchase "The Camera Assistant's Manual" by David E. Elkins (ISBN 0240804015). It provides essential technical information on cameras, film, camera magazines, and so on and is regularly updated to reflect the newest improvements and technical advances in camera equipment. This book provides a clear and concise introduction for someone learning camera as well as supplying all of the basic information needed to be a first or second AC. For a more complete survey of the camera world, consider picking up "The Camera Assistant: A Complete Professional Handbook" by Douglas C. Hart and Mary Mortimer (ISBN 0240800427).

Suggestions

Here are a few general suggestions for working in the camera department:

- ***Make sure your compressed air is made for camera applications*** Bottles of compressed air are used to clean camera mechanisms, lenses, and a variety of other items. On a professional set, every camera position below the DP carries a bottle for fast cleaning of camera components. Some compressed air will leave a slight residue when used on a surface. Check the bottle and avoid compressed air labeled not for use with camera mirrors or parts. Often compressed air bottles available in computer stores carry such a warning.

- ***Don't take advice, test*** There is so much information that you must know in relation to cameras, exposure, mediums, etc. that it's tempting to ask for advice in solving a problem and use that advice without proper testing. Older camera operators can become entrenched in a specific way of doing things and will sometimes pass on advice that, while tried-and-true in the past, has been outdated by technology or fashion. Although there is never enough time, make the time to test and verify advice you've received.

- ***Everyone starts at the bottom*** Camera magazine or mag loading, the lowest task in the camera department, is where nearly everyone starts. It's tedious, boring, thankless, and yet the position demands a substantial amount of responsibility. On a professional film, no one starts as a camera operator because there is too much on the line if the operator fails. Recognize that if you don't want to start at the bottom, you don't want to do camera badly enough.

Matte Box

Applications

A matte box is a black hood that fits over the front of a camera lens (see figure 7-1). The matte box prevents unwanted light from entering the lens by keeping the actual optics of the camera within its shadow. This prevents unintended overexposure of the film and minimizes artifacts commonly known as lens flares. It's very rare to work on any professional exterior shoot where a matte box isn't being used.

A common filming problem known as lens flare can be prevented by a matte box. A lens is made up of several layers of glass elements. When a light source (such as the sun) shines directly into the lens, the light hits each layer of glass causing circles that appear in the final footage (see figure 7-2).

FIGURE 7.1 *Matte box mounted on the front of a camera lens.*

Occasionally, lens flares are used for artistic reasons (such as in the movies Die Hard or Legends of the Fall). But generally, flares are a signature of amateur filmmaking. Flares make editing a film difficult because some shots in a sequence will have the flare and others will not. The appearance and disappearance of the flares between cuts (such as cutting between two people having a conversation) is very distracting to the viewer.

In this chapter, you'll construct a simple matte box for a camera. Professional matte boxes can be incredibly expensive because they include custom accordion bevels. The bevels can be expanded and collapsed to accommodate different lens sizes and also provide slots to hold various filters. However, since a matte box doesn't generally take a lot of abuse, a simple hood that will last a long time can be made from materials such as foamcore.

A matte box must be able to adjust to wider or narrower field of vision depending on the lens or the zoom of the lens. For example, if the lens is zoomed to the

FIGURE 7.2 *A lens flare in the picture of an author before his morning coffee.*

maximum magnification (large focal length) and the light source is near the subject, the matte box will be narrowed to protect the lens against flare. If the next shot is a wide angle with the lens zoomed out, the unadjusted matte box would be visible in the frame. Therefore, the matte box must be expanded to accommodate the increased viewing area.

Most mid-ranges DV cameras (VX-1000, VX-2000, GL1, GL2, etc.) have a small plastic shield on the front of the camera that looks almost like a mini-matte box (see figure 7-3). While this piece of plastic provides a rudimentary level of shade for the lens, it doesn't prov-

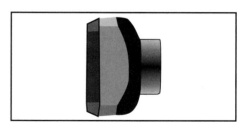

FIGURE 7.3 *Mini-matte box included with many cameras.*

ides nearly the coverage needed to shoot professional footage on a bright day.

In figure 7-4, you'll see a diagram of a light source, that with only the standard plastic shield, will surely create a lens flare. With a proper matte box, the source comes nowhere close to directly hitting the lens.

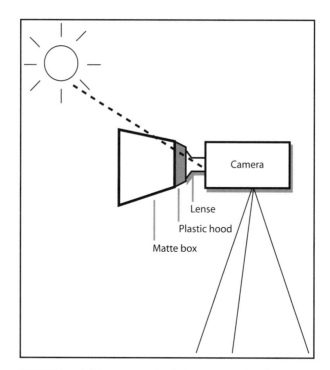

FIGURE 7.4 *A light source entering the lens to create a lens flare.*

PARTS	Qty	Item
	1	18″ × 22″ (46 cm × 56 cm) piece of foamcore
	2	Binder clips
	1	Piece of heavy black cloth
	1	Bottle of matte black spray paint

General Instructions

The following instructions explain how to make a matte box for a round lens since this type is the most difficult. The instructions can be easily adapted to match the type of camera you'll be using. The mounting of the matte box should be solid enough that doesn't move when the wind is blowing.

This matte box is constructed from foamcore. You can use lighter material as long as it's sturdy enough to withstand the abuse it will suffer during shooting. Make sure whatever material you choose is painted with a matte black. You don't want to create any new reflections in the lens.

Construction

In figure 7-5, the template for the matte box is shown. The solid lines indicate where cuts should be made while the dashed lines indicate places where the material should be scored.

To create the matte box, follow these steps:

1. Enlarge the template to fit the front of your lens or plastic hood. A copying machine is excellent for producing the enlargement or you can do it by hand. Notice where the lens opening is specified on the template. The lens opening show is designed for mounting on a circular lens. If you have a lens hood, simply alter the template to use a rounded rectangle.

2. Transfer this template to foamcore.

3. Cut along all the black lines to create the matte box. I would suggest cutting the foamcore with an exacto knife, but a utility knife will work fairly well. Don't cut out the circle for the lens opening. Instead, cut along the starburst lines and bend the triangles backward. These triangles will encircle the lens and help prevent light leaks.

4. Score the foamcore along the dashed lines indicated by the template.

5. Paint the silver parts of the binder clips with the matte black paint. Note that in the following pictures, I haven't painted the binder clips so they would show up better in the photographs.

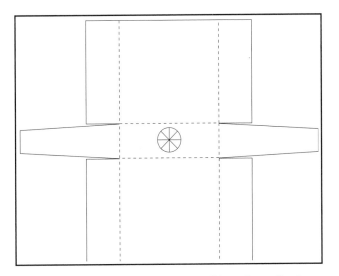

FIGURE 7.5 *Template for the matte box that will be cut from cardboard or foamcore.*

6. Mount the hood on your camera lens.

7. Attach the binder clips to the matte box flaps as shown in figure 7-6.

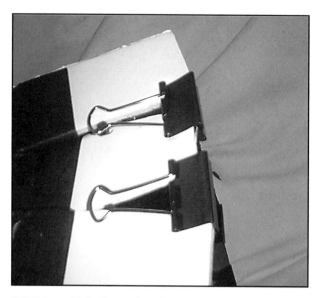

FIGURE 7.6 *Binder clips to adjust the viewing angle of the matte box.*

8. Look through your viewfinder and adjust the flaps until they're out of the viewing area (see figure 7-7).

9. The mounted matte box now be properly adjusted for use and should appear as shown in figure 7-8.

10. Tape the heavy black cloth to the back of the matte box and drape it over the area where the box attaches to the lens in order to prevent light leaks. Also, use black tape to cover and white edges that you notice inside the hood to prevent possible artifacts in your picture.

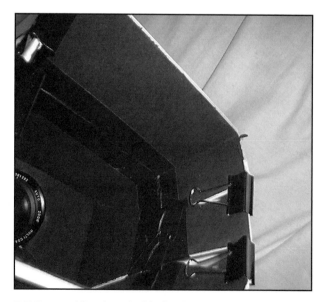

FIGURE 7.7 *Adjust the angle of the flaps by looking through the viewfinder.*

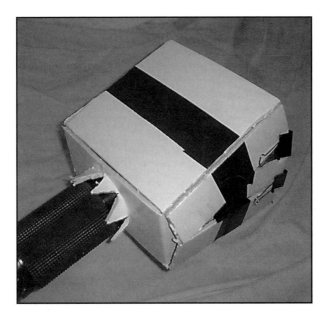

FIGURE 7.8 *Properly mounted matte box.*

It is a good idea at this point to check the parameters of the matte box. Close down the flaps to their smallest opening and zoom out on the camera to the maximum viewing area. Do you see the side of the box? If so, you'll have an idea of the bounds within which you'll have to work. Remember that this template is just a guideline. You can make the hood as big or as little as your needs.

Suggestions

Here are a few suggestions for using the matte box most successfully:

- *Check the parameters of the matte box* Make sure that the matte box doesn't infringe on your image area. If you make the hood too narrow or use the zoom to make the shot wider, you may not notice that the edge of the box is now in the frame. Look through the viewfinder and poke your fingers into the frame from all four sides (top, bottom, left, and right). When you see your finger, you will know the limits where you can collapse the matte box to be. A test commonly used to see if the matte box will be in frame is to move your finger around the outside of the frame. If the first knuckle of your finger is below the side of the matte box, you know the box is too close.

- *Take off the matte box when you store the camera* Since the matte box and the frame can be so easily bent or damaged, remove it from the camera when not in use. You'll avoid potentially having to make a new one the next time you take your camera out.

- *Use the matte box in addition to a flag* If you have a flag for keeping the camera in shadow, use that in addition to the matte box. There are many potential slivers where light can leak through into a camera. Keeping it in shadow will help in avoiding exposure problems. It will also keep the camera (and the camera operator) cool and functioning better.

Camera Hi-hat

Applications

While a beanbag is excellent for very low mounts, it's not secure enough when a high camera position is required. Raising a tripod can be difficult and cumbersome, and since most high shots are only brief walk-ins or other snippets, creating a raised tripod platform is usually overkill. However, going hand-held has its own disadvantages including possible shake, inability to lock down a position (for blue screen or camera matching), and general camera safety. The hi-hat mount (see figure 8-1) solves all these problems.

The hi-hat is essentially a flat board with a camera mount on it which can be strapped onto a flat surface. Most often, the hi-hat is ratchet-strapped to a tall ladder. By using the hi-hat, you can securely place a camera on almost any stable platform. The hi-hat mount you'll learn to construct in this chapter provides a stable camera mount that can also tilt and pan.

FIGURE 8.1 *Completed hi-hat mount.*

> **NOTE→** A professional hi-hat is just a single board with a metal bracket on top. The bracket is made to accept a standard camera tripod head. Since tripod heads are very expensive at the high end and aren't standardized at the low end, the nuts-and-bolts hi-hat serves the purpose traditionally filled by both the head and the hi-hat.

PARTS	Qty	Item
	1	$\frac{1}{2}''$ union
	2	$\frac{1}{2}'' \times 1''$ threaded steel pipe
	1	$\frac{1}{2}'' \times 8''$ steel pipe
	2	$\frac{1}{2}''$ pipe clamps
	8	$\frac{1}{4}''$ 20 nuts

	Qty	Item
PARTS	4	$\frac{1}{4}''$ 20 lock washers
	2	$\frac{1}{2}'' \times 6''$ PVC pipe
	2	$\frac{1}{4}'' \times 2''$ 20 machine screws
	2	$\frac{1}{4}'' \times 1''$ 20 machine screws
	3	$2\frac{1}{2}''$ eyebolts, $\frac{1}{4}''$ 20, 2″ shaft
	2	$\frac{1}{2}''$ threaded 90° bends
	2	$\frac{1}{2}'' \times 3''$ threaded steel pipe
	8	$\frac{1}{4}'' \times \frac{1}{2}''$ wood screws
	4	$\frac{1}{2}''$ flanges
	1	$2' \times 2'$ mounting board
	1	$3\frac{1}{2}''$ diameter circle of non-slip material

The mounting board can be out of any solid type of wood that you would trust to secure your camera. I would recommend a board that is at least $\frac{1}{2}''$ thick. In my case, I had a $2' \times 2' \times \frac{1}{2}''$ slab of particle board in the garage that worked perfectly.

Construction

You can begin construction by preparing the camera mount itself. Glue some type of non-slip pad onto the top of a flange (see figure 8-2) that will be used to hold the camera. The non-slip surface will prevent the camera from moving on top of the mount. Once the glue is dry, punch a small hole on the material where one of the flange holes is located. The camera mounting screw will come through this hole into the bottom of the camera.

FIGURE 8.2 *Glue a non-slip pad onto the top of a flange.*

Creating the mounting screw

For many of the projects in the camera section, you will be using this type of mounting screw. Therefore, if you plan to build more than one project, it may save you some time to create several mounting screws at the same time.

The mounting screw will screw into camera-mounting thread insert on the bottom of the camera. The length of the mounting screw is very important. If the length is too long, the screw will not tighten down properly and the camera may spin on the mount. If the length is too short, you might overtighten the screw and harm the camera. Some camera-mounting thread inserts have a breakaway feature, so the camera itself is not destroyed if the body of the camera if stressed. Tightening down the screw too much may pull out this breakaway feature.

Place your camera on top of the flange with the non-slip surface. Push the mounting screw through the screw hole in the flange and turn it until it is tight in the camera-mounting insert. Take a marker and make a mark on the threads of the mounting bolt at the point that it enters the flange. This will be the place where a blocking nut will prevent further tightening.

Remove the mounting screw from the camera. Take a $\frac{1}{2}''$ nut (which we'll call the holding nut) and screw it all the way to the bottom of the mounting screw. Take a second nut (we'll call the main nut) and screw down until to top of the nut sits just below the mark you made on the threads.

Turn the holding nut counter-clockwise until it rests against the bottom of the main nut. You will need two wrenches now. With one wrench, hold the main nut. With the other wrench, turn the holding nut counter-clockwise until it's tightly butted up against the main nut. Both nuts should now be solidly held in place by the other and they're located at the proper distance from the top of the screw to make a tight hold when screwed into the camera-mounting insert.

Your mounting screw is now complete (see figure 8-3). From the figure, you can see that I used a small piece of cord to tie the screw to the mount. That way when it isn't secured to a camera, the screw is kept with the hi-hat.

You might make one final improvement to the mounting screw by coating it with rubber. I used Performix Plasti Dip (www.plastidip.com) that I bought at the local home improvement store. It's generally used for coating the handles of tools. I find it produces a good and non-slippery coating for all of my eyelet screws.

Creating the swivel flange

FIGURE 8.3 *Completed mounting screw attached to hi-hat with a length of cord.*

Since the hi-hat is generally mounted to a flat surface, it's critical that the camera can tilt to reach the proper viewing angle for the desired shot. The swivel flange connects to the mounted hi-hat bar and allows the camera to tilt (see figure 8-4).

To begin creating the swivel flange, take a bolt and put it through one of the holes in the flange. Then take a conduit hanger and fit the base hole onto the bolt and tighten the nut into place with your fingers. Don't completely tighten the nut yet because you may need to align it in a moment. Follow the same

FIGURE 8.4 *The swivel flange mounted on the hi-hat bar for camera tilt.*

procedure to attach the second conduit hanger in the hole opposite the one with the first bracket.

You'll want to replace the conduit hanger screws with eyebolts so that you can loosen or tighten the swivel at will. I've found that adding a nut at the top of the bolt (see figure 8-5) helps secure the bolt for better tightening.

Now take an 8″ iron pipe and put it through both conduit hangers as shown in figure 8-6. The pipe will properly align both brackets. Now tighten the nuts and bolts on the brackets. If you can't get a wrench into the bracket to hold the nut steadily, simply wedge a screwdriver between the head of the nut and the side of the bracket. Then tighten the screw.

FIGURE 8.5 *Adding a nut at the top of the threads helps secure the bolt.*

Creating the head

To complete the head, you need to connect the mounting flange (the one with the non-slip surface) to the swivel flange (see figure 8-7). This connection is made by placing a union between the two flanges. The union provides a way for the camera to be panned. By simply loosened the union connecting nut, the camera can easily be turned from side to side until the desired angle is reached.

First, screw the 1″ threaded pipe into the flange that you glued the non-slide surface. The other end of the pipe screws into the top of the union. There are two threaded ends of the union, so you could use either end. However, it's best to standardize on how the union end mounts. That way, you could unscrew the top of the hi-hat with the camera still attached and mount it on top of the tripod's union or the camera glider or any other mount.

Take the bottom part of the union and screw a 1″ threaded pipe into it. The other end of the threaded pipe is then screwed into the swivel flange (see figure 8-8).

Next, screw each end of the pipe into a 90° elbow. Into the elbows, screw the 3″ threaded iron pipes. To the ends of each of these pipes, attach a flange. Each side of pipe should look like the one shown in figure 8-9.

At this point, you should have your mounting board ready, as well as the wood screws you will need to mount it. However, don't screw it into the board yet.

The weight of the camera could potentially spin the 8″ pipe within the fittings of the 90° elbows. For this reason, I would suggest that you use a glue compound such as Liquid Weld that is available at

FIGURE 8.6 *The 8″ iron pipe slid through the conduit hanger holes.*

FIGURE 8.7 *Completed head with two flanges joined by the union.*

FIGURE 8.8 *Threaded pipe screwed into the swivel flange.*

your local auto supply store. Auto supplies have many different types of glue and epoxy that can be used to permanently join two pieces of metal together. Pick one that provides the most permanent bond.

Remove the 90° elbows (and the 3″ pipes and flanges with them), so you are left with the 8″ pipe with the head affixed to the top. Smear some of the compounds on the threads of the pipe and then re-screw the elbows into place. The compounds typically take 3–4 hours to dry, but some set within 15 min. That's why you have the mounting board ready. You can set the flanges on the board and make sure they sit flat.

Place the flange legs on the mounting board. Using the wood screws, attach the flanges to the board (see figure 8-10).

Once attached, don't use the hi-hat until you are sure the compound securing the 8″ pipe has dry and set.

Safety bars

Although you can use the hi-hat as it is, I would recommend that you put safety bars on it. When you unscrew and ease the tension on the lower screws, you should be holding onto the camera. If you slip or are not paying attention and not holding the camera, the camera may freely swing down and hit the mounting board or whatever's located under it. In the same circumstances, with the safety bars in place, the camera will swing but the safety bar will hit the mounting board and stop any forward or backward progress before the camera is damaged.

Safety bars can be made of any material that will accept a $\frac{1}{4}''$ screw to be mounted on the front and/or the back of the swivel flange. In figure 8-11, you can see the metal bracket I used for one of my safety bars.

FIGURE 8.9 *90° elbow bend attached to the threaded pipe.*

FIGURE 8.10 *Flanges attached to the mounting board with wood screws.*

FIGURE 8.11 *A front safety bar created from a "found" bracket.*

You can use a metal bar of about 6″ long or you can simply drilled holes in a couple of $\frac{1}{2}$″ PVC pipes and mounted them. Only use plastic, though, if your camera is light. You don't want the weight of the camera snapping the bars, thereby defeating their purpose.

The only drawback to the safety bars is that they place a limit on the amount that a camera can be tilted if an extremely steep tilt is required. However, it is far easier on those special occasions to loosen the bolt on the safety bar and swing it out of the way than to risk your camera a majority of the time.

With the safety bars in place, your hi-hat is complete. Ratchet straps are the traditional way of attaching the hi-hat to a surface. These straps can be purchased at nearly any home warehouse. Note that it is usually worth the money to buy the more expensive straps. In the cheaper ones, the ratchet tends to jam making their use far less pleasant.

Inside Car Mount

Applications

Movie footage taken from inside a car is a staple of contemporary films. Taking these car shots is problematic for guerilla filmmakers. Most car mounts are expensive, difficult to configure and use, somewhat distracting for the driver (resulting in safety issues), and may scratch the outside paint or ruin the interior. As a result, holding a camera by hand is the most commonly chosen solution. However, this method generates shaky and less than optimal footage. Using an in-car camera mount (see figure 9-1) can create ideal, smooth footage since the camera is essentially held static to the movement of the car.

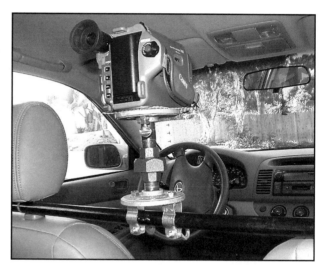

FIGURE 9.1 *Completed and positioned in-car camera mount.*

The in-car mount described in this chapter is simple to construct since it consists primarily of a threaded iron pipe that is attached to the bars of the headrest with standard tie-wraps. On this pipe, the same camera head you created for the hi-hat will be used to mount your camera. The head provides the ability to swivel and tilt the camera to allow nearly any capture angle.

	Qty	Item
PARTS	1	$\frac{1}{2}''$ union
	2	$\frac{1}{2}'' \times 1''$ threaded steel pipe
	2	$\frac{1}{2}''$ conduit hangers
	8	$\frac{1}{2}''$ 20 nuts
	3	$2\frac{1}{2}''$ eyebolts, $\frac{1}{4}''$ 20, 2″ shaft
	1	$\frac{1}{2}'' \times 36''$ threaded steel pipe
	1	$3\frac{1}{2}''$ diameter circle of non-slip material
	2	$\frac{1}{2}''$ four-way joints
	8	Plastic tie-wraps

General Instructions

Whenever you're shooting within a car, selecting a proper exposure setting is difficult. The interior and the exterior of the car will generally have extremely different lighting levels that will result in a contrast ratio far beyond the limits of most cameras. Further, if the automobile is moving, the light levels will change based on the direction of the car in relation to the current position of the sun. If the camera is shooting out the front window, you'll need to even more precisely control the exposure.

The simplest way to dim the outside light is to affix neutral density film to the windows. This will bring the outside light levels closer to the level of the interior. Because of the brightness of daylight, usually an ND6 or an ND9 level diffusion is needed. If you're mounting the ND film on the exterior, you'll probably need the special ND film that has an adhesive side. It's difficult to use snot tape to fix the ND to the exterior without wind causing sound problems or acceleration creating enough pressure to rip the ND from the outside of the window.

Alternately, you can use an in-car light to increase the interior light level to more closely approximate the exterior exposure. Interior lights are problematic because the amount of light required could generate a lot of heat in the small enclosed space of a car. These lights also require quite a bit of power. Interior lights (particularly portable fluorescent) are sometimes used in combination with ND gels on the windows to obtain the desired light levels.

FIGURE 9.2 *Exposure setting selected to photograph the exterior scene.*

Even with these techniques, most often you'll have to decide whether you want to sacrifice the detail of the interior or the exterior. In figure 9-2, you can see that an exposure setting has been selected to properly photograph the exterior of the car. My reflection in the rearview mirror is underexposed to the point of being a dark gray blob. Additionally, the controls on the car dashboard are lost in shadow. Setting the exposure for the exterior can provide a very dramatic silhouette appearance of the actors inside the car.

In contrast, figure 9-3 shows the exposure set to properly expose the interior of the car. In this figure, my reflection is clear and the dashboard controls (including part of the speedometer) are clearly visible. The exterior, however, is fairly blown out and lacks crisp detail.

FIGURE 9.3 *Exposure setting selected to properly photograph the interior of the car.*

> **TIP ▶** *Before you begin construction of the in-car mount, make sure that your camera has a small enough focal distance to obtain the footage you need. Hold the camera in approximately the spot where it will sit when mounted. Zoom the lens all the way out and look at your viewing area. If this area is too small, you'll either need to get a wider lens (such as a fish-eye lens) or, if possible, attach the mount to the headrests of the back seats.*

Construction

Aside from the camera head, there is very little actual construction on the car mount. The mount is essentially a bar tie-wrapped to the headrests where it can be easily put into place and later removed. The bar can be attached to the headrests of the front or back seats. It can swivel a full 360° for flexibility to photograph the front or back seats. Make sure when you use the mount to bring a pair of scissors or wire cutters to remove it once you're through.

Creating the mounting bar

The mounting bar will hold the camera head and will secure it to the car frame, thereby ensuring minimal jiggle in your final footage. This bar also provides the flexibility that will allow you to easily slide the camera to the left or right to dramatically change the angle that will be shot.

Before you begin construction, you'll need to measure the distance between the headrest bars. In my car, each headrest is supported by two bars (approximately $\frac{1}{4}''$ in diameter). There was a distance of 34″ between the outside bar on the driver's side and the outside bar on the passenger headrest. This distance was perfect for a 36″ threaded steel pipe since that bar length covers the proper distance with a couple of inches to spare. If your headrest bars are farther apart (40″ is common in an SUV), you will probably need to use a coupling joint to attach two bars (say a 36″ and a 6″ bar) to extend the mounting bar to the proper length.

To make the mounting bar stable, screw a four-way joint onto each end of the bar. These joints will rest against the top of the back seat and will prevent the bar from tilting forward or backward. Once the four-way joints are in place, the threaded steel pipe (or camera-mounting bar) will be attached behind the headrest bars, positioned for safety. If for any reason the tie-wraps should come undone, the bar is in no danger of hitting the driver or front passenger.

Raise the passenger headrest and use a tie-wrap to secure one end of the mounting bar to the outer headrest bar (see figure 9-4). Run the tie-wrap through the middle of the four-way joint and then cinch it around the headrest bar. Pull the tie-wrap tightly to minimize the amount of movement that is possible from the mounting bar.

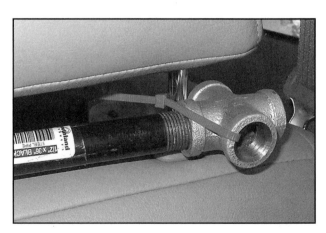

FIGURE 9.4 *A tie-wrap is used to secure one end of the mounting bar to the outer headrest bar.*

Take another tie-wrap and secure the length of the steel bar to the inner headrest bar (see figure 9-5). The one end of the mounting bar should be fixed firmly. When you have the tie-wraps cinched tight enough, lower the headrest so it will wedge the mounting bar securely in place.

On the other side of the mounting bar, secure two tie-wraps in the same fashion (see figure 9-6). When the tie-wraps are secure, push down this headrest as well. Pull and lightly twist the bar to make certain that the entire structure is firmly in place.

FIGURE 9.5 *Another tie-wrap secures the length of the steel bar to the inner headrest bar.*

T I P ▶ *Although tie-wraps are very strong and can carry a great deal of weight, if you have a heavy camera you should use multiple wraps to ensure that the mounting bar stays in place. You don't want to risk your expensive and fragile camera gear in order to save the pennies that an extra tie-wrap or two would cost.*

If necessary, you can secure the mount on only one of the headrests. However, this is not advisable since it will produce much shakier footage. A single headrest mount is also more likely to be unstable with a heavier camera since the mounting bar will act almost like a diving board with the camera weight at one end and no weight at the other.

Creating the head

The head will match the one used for the hi-hat in Chapter 11. If you already have a hi-hat, you can simply use that

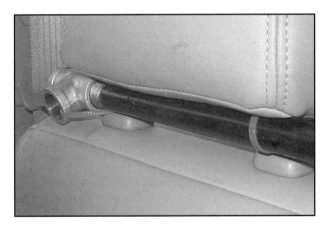

FIGURE 9.6 *On the other side of the mounting bar, secure two more tie-wraps.*

head when a car mount is needed. The head uses two flanges mounted opposite to each other with a union in the middle to allow the camera to swivel 360°. The swivel flange will attach to the mounting bar with two conduit hangers. The other flange, the camera flange, will provide the platform on which the camera will sit.

Begin by gluing a non-slip pad onto the top of a flange that will be used to hold the camera. The non-slip surface will prevent the camera from moving on top of the mount. Once the glue is dry, punch a small hole on the material (see figure 9-7) where one of the flange holes is located.

The camera-mounting screw will come through this hole into the bottom of the camera.

To begin creating the swivel flange, take a bolt and put it through one of the holes in the flange. Then take a conduit hanger and fit it onto the bolt and tighten the nut into place with your fingers. Don't completely tighten the nut yet because you may need to align the conduit hanger in a moment. Follow the same procedure to attach the second bracket in the hole opposite the one with the first bracket (see figure 9-8).

You'll want to replace the conduit hanger screws with eyebolts so that you can loosen or tighten the swivel at will. I've found that adding a nut at the top of the bolt (see figure 9-9) helps secure the bolt for better tightening.

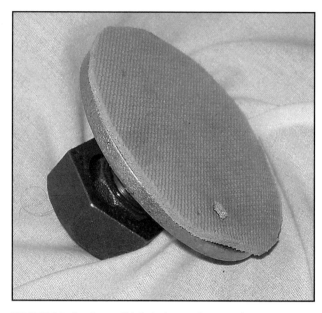

FIGURE 9.7 *Punch a small hole in the non-slip material.*

Connect the mounting flange (the one with the non-slip surface) to the swivel flange (see figure 9-10). This connection is made by placing a union between the two flanges. The union provides a way for the camera to be panned. By simply loosened the union-connecting nut, the camera can easily be turned from side to side until the desired angle is reached.

First, screw the 1″ threaded pipe into the flange you glued the non-slide surface. The other end of the pipe screws into the top of the union. There are two threaded ends of the union, so you could use either end. However, it's best to standardize on how the union end mounts. That way, you could unscrew the top of the hi-hat with the camera still attached and mount it on

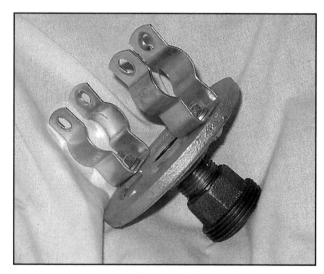

FIGURE 9.8 *Attach the second bracket in the flange hole opposite the first one.*

top of the tripod's union or the camera glider or any other mount. Take the bottom part of the union and screw a 1″ threaded pipe into it. The other end of the threaded pipe is then screwed into the swivel flange.

With the eyebolts removed, bend the ends of the conduit hangers outwards enough so they may be slipped over the mounting bar. Replace the eyebolts into the holes of the conduit hangers and tighten them (see figure 9-11). The mounting bar will properly align both the conduit hangers. Now tighten the nuts and bolts on the hangers. If you can't get a wrench inside the hanger to hold the nut steadily, simply wedge a screwdriver between the head of the nut and the side of the bracket. Then tighten the screw.

FIGURE 9.9 *Add a nut at the top of the bolt to help secure the bolt.*

FIGURE 9.10 *Connect the mounting flange to the swivel flange.*

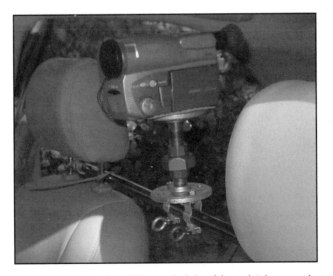

FIGURE 9.11 *Place the eyebolts into the holes of the conduit hangers and tighten them.*

Suggestions

Here are a few operating suggestions to help you get the best use from the in-car mount:

- *Bring extra tie-wraps* Because you cut the wraps off when you're finished, make sure to bring extras. You may believe you've completed the shot, but later decide on a re-shoot.

- *Set manual focus and manual exposure* Automatic focus and exposure settings on a camera are excellent for home photography, but terrible for professional filmmaking. A driving car makes the camera adjust so often, the brightness fluctuates rapidly and creates unpleasant and unprofessional footage. Setting the focus and exposure manually will allow you to control how the footage will appear.

- *Do a dry run* To prevent wasting the actors' time, make a dry run of the shot at the exact time of day that you plan to take principal photography. You'll find that much of your imagined framing will have to be modified to fit the reality of the light and surrounding setting.

- *Bring gaffer tape* If you do any lighting inside the car, you'll probably need to secure your fixtures in places where it won't be convenient to use a clamp or other attaching device. Gaffer's tape holds nicely and won't leave much residue.

Camera Glider

Applications

Achieving fluid camera movement has bedeviled filmmakers since the first moving picture was produced. While hand-held camera shots are ideal for some situations (brief sequences or getting the "reality feel"), they often generate a wobbly recording as soon as the camera operator starts moving. Since extended shots with this type of footage can cause motion sickness in some viewers, most filmmakers do their best to avoid it.

The camera dolly is the oldest and most common method of getting a camera moving smoothly. While a dolly may be perfect for many situations, moving on uneven terrain, navigating stairs, or traveling over medium to long distances can be a problem. Even setting up the dolly track can require a substantial amount of time that you could be using to get the perfect shot!

Steady-cams were invented to solve many of these problems. A steady-cam uses a system of balances and counter-balances to soften the camera movement. Unfortunately, the cost of a steady-cam unit is outside the budget of most small filmmakers. Additionally, the complexity of the system makes it difficult to construct on your own. In contrast, the camera glider is simple to use and inexpensive to create.

The camera glider is a camera-mounting post with balancing counter-weights (see figure 10-1). Essentially, the weight on the bottom of the glider dampens tilting and side-to-side motion. The arm of the operator then steadies the overall movement of the entire rig.

Mastering the camera glider can take some practice. Once you've learned to use it, however, you can get graceful shots that would be impossible without it. I've used this very glider to follow an actor through a wheat field. The footage turned out beautifully.

FIGURE 10.1 *Camera glider with balancing counter-weights.*

	Qty	Item
PARTS	1	$4'' \times \frac{1}{2}''$ pipe
	1	$24'' \times \frac{1}{2}''$ pipe
	1	$\frac{1}{2}''$ steel flange
	1	$\frac{1}{2}''$ steel union
	1	$\frac{1}{2}''$ steel cap
	1	$\frac{1}{4}'' \times 2''$ bolt
	4	$\frac{1}{4}''$ steel nut
	1	$\frac{1}{4}''$ washer
	2	2 lb steel weights

General Instructions

There are essentially two parts to the camera glider: the head and the body. You'll mount your camera on the head while the body will hold the counter-weight. The head is connected to the body with a piece known as a "union." As with all the parts in the camera glider, a $\frac{1}{2}''$ union is available at nearly any hardware store. The advantage of employing a union between the head and the body is that it allows you to quickly and easily separate the camera from the dead weight without disassembling the whole glider.

You'll need to select the length of pipe for the body shaft of the glider. At your local hardware store, there are typically a number of sizes of threaded iron or steel pipe available including: 12″, 24″, and 36″. Since it's easy to swap out the body pipe, you can buy more than one length and simply use the one that best fits a given situation.

As a rule of thumb, the longer the body pipe, the steadier the camera will be. However, a longer pipe also adds more weight and makes the glider harder to maneuver. This may increase the chances that the bottom of the glider will bump into objects close to the ground, ruining your shot.

The amount of weight on the bottom should match the weight of the camera. The counter-weights balance the glider and provide the most commonly desirable shot. However, if you want footage that is not "common," you can put a greater weight on the bottom. This unbalanced configuration creates a form of pendulum swing with the camera that can be useful for showing psychedelic or disoriented movement.

Construction

To begin construction, acquire the supplies shown in the parts list. Be sure to wash the pipes with simple soap and water and then dry them thoroughly. Pipe is often dirty when you buy it, so cleaning the material once will save you from cleaning your hands numerous times during assembly and use.

Assembling the head

Begin the assembly by putting together the head which will actually attach to the camera. Drill a $\frac{1}{4}''$ hole in the top of the cap (see figure 10-2).

You can use a plastic cap or a steel cap (see figure 10-3). The steel cap is highly recommended because it is stronger and therefore provides a greater safety margin. However, not everyone has the drill bits to easily go through a metal cap. I've used a plastic cap with cameras of various weights without any problem, but just for safety's sake I've recently switched up to a steel one.

FIGURE 10.2 *Drill a $\frac{1}{4}''$ hole in the top of the cap.*

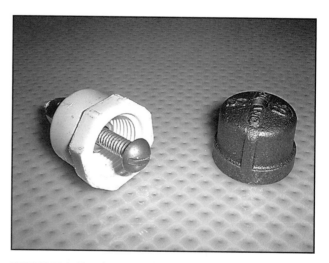

FIGURE 10.3 *One plastic cap and one steel cap for the head mount.*

You will need to assemble the bolt that holds the camera to the cap. Since we don't want the camera to come loose under any circumstances, a strong "platform" is needed on both the inside and the outside of the cap. We can accomplish creating a "platform" by placing two nuts next to each other on the bolt and then tightening one down on the other. This creates a solid, largely immovable position on the bolt.

First, adjust the nuts so the bottom one is positioned about $\frac{7}{8}''$ from the end as shown in figure 10-4. This length makes the bolt protrude the proper distance from the cap, so it will seat perfectly in the threaded mounting socket of your camera.

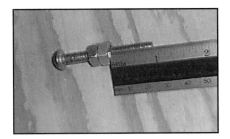

FIGURE 10.4 *The nuts positioned about $\frac{7}{8}''$ from the screw end.*

Take two wrenches (see figure 10-5) and place them over the nuts. Hold the bottom nut steady and tighten the top nut down onto it. They should be tightly butted up against each other as shown in figure 10-6.

Now insert the bolt into the cap as shown in figure 10-7 and push it as far as you can through the hole you drilled earlier.

Use the same double-nut binding technique on two nuts above the cap (see figure 10-8). Before you use the binding technique, make sure the lower nut is tight against the cap. This will prevent the bolt from spinning in the cap which could cause the camera to turn.

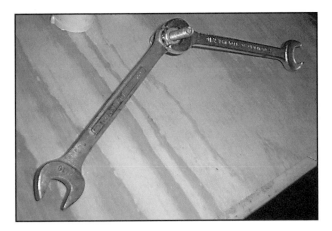

FIGURE 10.5 *Use two wrenches to turn the nuts in opposite directions.*

FIGURE 10.6 *The two nuts tightly butted up against each other.*

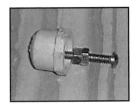

FIGURE 10.7 *Insert the bolt with the nuts into the mounting cap.*

Once the bolt is securely in place, you only need to the place the washer on the end of the bolt to have a complete cap (shown in figure 10-9). The rest of the assembly of the head is simple.

The 4″ pipe length shown in figure 10-10 will form the main part of the head. You can use a shorter length if you want, but the 4″ length allows you to easily use the head as a small hand-held mount if necessary.

When you purchase a union at the hardware store, it comes as a single unit. However, it is actually made up of three separate pieces (see figure 10-11).

When assembled (figure 10-12), the union has two threaded female ends. One end will be attached to the body pipe and the other to the head.

Screw the 4″ pipe into one end of the union. Then screw the cap onto the other end of the pipe. Your complete head should look like the one shown in figure 10-13.

Screw the protruding bolt into your camera mount socket to test it. Don't forget the washer between the top nut of the head and the bottom of the camera. Some cameras have a breakaway socket to prevent damage to the camera. If there is a shock to the camera or too much pressure placed on it,

FIGURE 10.8 *Use the same double-nut binding technique on two nuts above the cap.*

FIGURE 10.9 *Place the washer on the end of the bolt to have a complete cap.*

FIGURE 10.10 *The 4″ pipe length will form the main part of the head.*

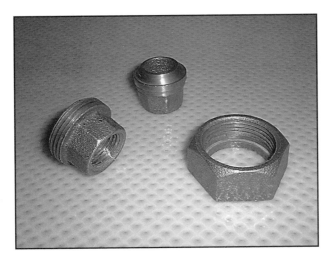

FIGURE 10.11 *The three separate pieces of a union.*

FIGURE 10.12 *An assemble has two threaded female ends.*

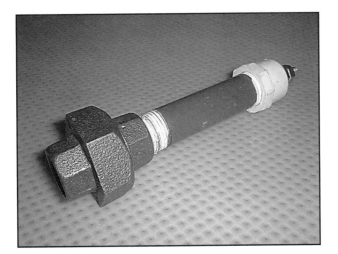

FIGURE 10.13 *A complete camera glider head.*

the socket will release and may drop your camera, so be careful. The washer will help stabilize the camera and spread the pressure over a wider area. You should be able to hold the camera as shown in figure 10-14.

FIGURE 10.14 *Holding the head of the glider.*

Assembling the body

The body doesn't require much construction; it's mostly assembly of the various parts. First, slide the proper amount of weight to counter-balance your camera onto the body pipe.

> **TIP** ▶ *The camera glider can get awfully heavy for the camera operator. It's a good idea to plan glider shots for the beginning of the day when the operator will be most rested. Also, since the glider shots are often difficult to get right, they're good to get in the can early.*

Take the flange (like the one shown in figure 10-15) and screw it to the bottom of the body pipe.

The flange should be positioned under the weights as shown in figure 10-16. The iron weights will sit on top of the flange when you're using the glider. If the center holes in the weights are much bigger than the diameter of the body pipe, wrap the top of the flange and the body pipe with duct tape. This will help prevent the weights from sliding. It will also silence them when you're moving, so they don't end up on the soundtrack.

Finally, screw the bottom of the union onto the top of the body pipe and you're ready to go! By using a union, you can

FIGURE 10.15 *Flange that will be attached to the bottom of the body pipe.*

FIGURE 10.16 *Screw on the bottom flange after the weights have been placed on the body pipe.*

easily remove it from the body and re-attach it moments before filming must begin. Figure 10-17 shows the head and the body separated at the union.

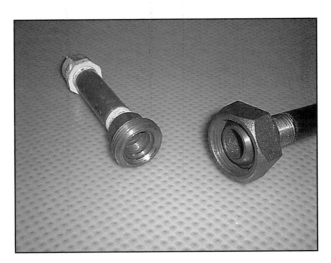

FIGURE 10.17 *The head and the body of the glider separated at the union.*

Using the Glider

Once you have the glider completely assembled and the camera mounted on the head, you're ready to go to work!

Grasp the body pipe about one-third of the way down from the top. When you walk, your objective is to walk as smoothly as possible. Because of the weight, you may need to grasp the holding arm with your other hand to keep it steady. Try to avoid using both hands on the body of the glider. Holding both hands on the body pipe limits the amount of pivot that is possible to soften movement. This generally leads to footage that is less fluid than the single-handed technique.

For safety, always walk the intended path before you're carrying the weight of the camera. This will help you understand how best to approach the path. It will also give you time to remove obstacles that could cause you to trip.

Suggestions

Here are a few operating suggestions to help you get the best use from your new camera glider:

- *Glue rubber to the top of the support washer* This will help the washer grip more effectively to the bottom of the camera. You can glue on a rubber washer or simply cut a piece of a disposable wash glove to the proper size and use that.

- *Practice, practice, practice!* Don't wait for the day of the shoot to practice how the shot will be made, do it in advance. The type of terrain you need to move over will have a great effect on the best method of holding the glider as well as helping you decide which length of body pipe will be best suited to the situation.

- *Create a grip on the body pipe to prevent your hands from slipping* Layers of duct tape can be built up to create a makeshift grip. Better yet, cut up a disposable wash glove up and tape it around the pipe. Rubber provides an excellent gripping surface.

- *You can also create a grip using an electrical clamp* These clamps are available in the electrical supply area of most hardware stores. The advantage of the clamp is that once the screw is loosened, the half of the clamp head can be pivoted to take it off or move it along the length of pipe. See Chapter 11 on the tripod glider for a complete example.

Weighted Tripod Glider

Applications

Although the cam glider introduced in the last chapter is probably the most effective means of obtaining a smooth camera shot, you can use an ordinary tripod if your time and/or finances are extremely limited. Turning your tripod into a glider is as easy as affixing a number of weights to the tripod (see figure 11-1) such that the weight pulls directly down on the center of the tripod. This weight will steady the tripod as it's moved around.

Aside from convenience, there is an added advantage of using a tripod since the camera can be easily tilted and swiveled on the tripod head. However, the tripod will generally not provide as balanced a shot as a device specifically created for this purpose.

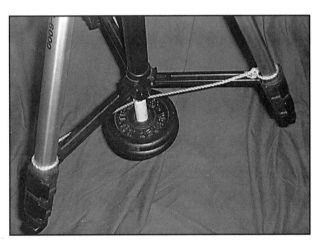

FIGURE 11.1 *Affixing weights to a tripod turned it into a glider.*

> **WARNING→** Tripods are not deliberately built to carry weight in the manner shown in this chapter. The weight puts a great deal of strain on the tripod itself. Test the weight first on the tripod and see if you can determine where exactly wear points and points of stress will occur. One point is usually on the restraining bolt on the neck of the tripod. If this point fails or slips, what happens to your camera? Be certain there is a final catch of some sort that even under circumstances of failure that the camera remains safe.

PARTS	Qty	Item
	1	Tripod
	3	24″ pieces of rope
	2	2 pound weights
	1	4″ length of $\frac{1}{2}$″ PVC pipe

General Instructions

Make sure the rope you use has very little stretch in it. The weights need to be as steady as possible. If the rope is stretching and retracting like the end of a bungee cord, not only will your shot most likely have problems, but also the apparatus will be far less maneuverable. With rope that stretches, you'll also have to make sure that the weight doesn't hit you in the shins!

To create the weighted tripod, follow these steps:

1. Tie each of the three pieces of rope around one leg of the tripod (see figure 11-2). You can use a double half-hitch to ensure each knot will tighten on the leg. Once the knot is tied, drape the end of the rope in the same direction (say the right side) for each leg. There are a large number of tripod types available, so you may have to modify the tying technique shown here to properly balance the tripod you'll be using.

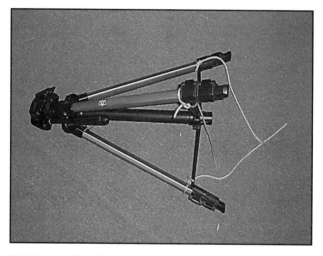

FIGURE 11.2 *Tie each of the three pieces of rope around one leg of the tripod.*

2. Make sure the lengths of the rope are mostly even (see figure 11-3). If not, re-cut or re-tie the ropes until they are even.

3. Cut a PVC pipe to a 4″ length.

4. Draw three evenly spaced dots (for the rope holes) near the base of one end of the pipe. I've found that the easiest way to obtain these evenly spaced holes is to wrap a small sheet of paper around the pipe. On the paper, place a mark on the paper where the wrapping overlap occurs. Unroll the paper and you should have a mark that indicates the complete diameter of the pipe. Use a ruler to measure this diameter and divide the value by 3. Make two marks on the paper at the appropriate distances to indicate thirds (the end of the paper will indicate the first third). Wrap the paper around the pipe again and mark on the pipe where the holes should go.

5. Drill the three holes large enough so that each hole can accommodate one of the ropes.

6. Feed the ends of the ropes through the central holes of the weights.

7. Feed the ropes through the center of the PVC pipe and push one rope through each hole (see figure 11-4). To accomplish this process, I had to tie a piece of string to a rope, feed the string through the hole, and then pull the rope through.

FIGURE 11.3 *Make sure the lengths of the rope are mostly even.*

8. Tie a stopper knot in the end of each rope (see figure 11-5). You can use the figure-8 knot that is demonstrated in Chapter 49.

9. Hold the tripod by the neck and make sure the weights hang directly under the center of the tripod (see figure 11-6). If the weights hang off to the side, adjust the position of the stopper knots until the weights hang even.

When you carry the tripod, you'll grasp it around the neck. To retain a firm grip on the neck (since it is usually slick metal or plastic), wear a latex glove. These gloves are available cheaply in dollar stores for dish washing. It is usually a good idea to keep the neck at full extension, so the weight rests on the neck stopper rather than the neck-restraining bolt.

FIGURE 11.4 *Feed the ropes through the center of the PVC pipe and push one rope through each hole.*

FIGURE 11.5 *Tie a stopper knot at the end of each rope.*

FIGURE 11.6 *Hold the tripod by the neck and make sure the weights hang directly under the center of the tripod.*

Suggestions

Here are a few operating suggestions to help you:

- *Make a cam glider if you have the time* A tripod glider may seem more convenient since you don't have to create and transport a completely separate apparatus. However, the cam glider is a specialized piece of equipment that will provide you with the best footage. And getting the best footage is what it's all about, isn't it?

- *Weigh the material of the tripod* Although a metal tripod may seem like a much better choice for a tripod glider because of the sturdy material, the weight of a metal tripod may quickly fatigue the glider operator. That will result in the later shots suffering. A plastic glider, while not as sturdy, may have a tremendous weight advantage for the user. Aluminum tripods are excellent because they're light although they're often far more expensive than the equivalent metal or plastic tripods.

- *Take some test footage* Evaluate if the glider will give you the results you want. If not, find you'll know before you waste time on the set.

- *Gliders require special care in set dressing and lighting* Realize that with the added freedom of any glider comes added responsibility. Even a wide panning shot, when taken on a stationary tripod, is very controlled and can be limited to see specific areas of the set. Gliders and steady-cams tend to look around the scene in a much more uncontrolled way. That means that undressed areas, light stands, and dark areas might all be captured (even briefly) and ruin the entire take. Plan your glider shots carefully.

- *Light your scene evenly* Obtaining the correct exposure with variations in lighting are much harder to control when using a glider. Lighting the entire shooting area evenly can help prevent over- and underexposure while taking glider footage.

Wheelchair Dolly

Applications

A dolly is critical to nearly any film that wants to appear like a professional production. Occasionally you see a film with lots of energy that has almost no dolly shots (the original Star Wars comes to mind), but most filmmakers use dollies extensively to provide their films with extra emotional power. While several dolly construction designs are provided in this book, the simplest and in some cases most effective requires not assembly at all – the wheelchair dolly.

Since the dawn of hand-held cameras, filmmakers have been using traditional wheel chairs (see figure 12-1) as a cheap and effective method of obtaining moving shots. Wheelchairs are small (so they can fit through doorways and tight spaces), light and collapsible (for easy car transportation), and smooth riding (thanks to their large rubber wheels). They're inexpensive to rent, comfortable to sit in for several hours, and give a camera operator a great deal of flexibility in movement.

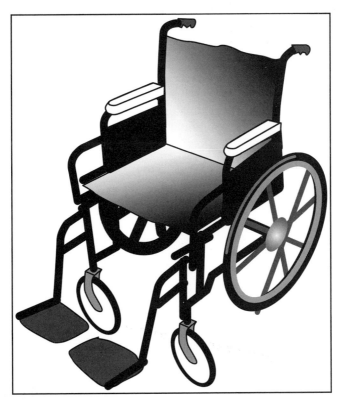

FIGURE 12.1 *Use a traditional wheel chair as a flexible dolly.*

General Instructions

Wheelchair rentals generally run about the price of a portable CD player for a week rental. This makes them a bargain in the world of film equipment rental. On a small film with good planning, you can usually schedule all of your dolly shots to be performed within that week.

Be sure to schedule the rental at least one day before its needed in principal photography. You may go to pickup the wheelchair only to find that the rental place has provided one in terrible condition (this has happened to me). A poorly maintained chair won't provide the smooth ride that you need for a steady picture. The extra day provides time to have the rental place obtain a better one or for you to find an alternative rental location.

The effectiveness of using the wheelchair dolly begins and ends with the skill of the dolly grip pushing it. Football players seem to be the most ideal type of person to use for an untrained dolly grip. The dolly grip must be able to push the weight of the rider easily, start and stop smoothly, and push the chair consistently in either a straight line or through a curve.

Set aside some time before the day of the shoot to practice with your dolly grip. An hour of practice the day before can literally save the entire shooting day. An untrained dolly grip will be intimidated by the pressure of the shoot and the impatience of the actors. It can result in worse and worse results until you have to eliminate desires shots just to obtain the critical footage you need. Pushing a dolly is not an easy task and the more experience your dolly grip has, the better off you'll be.

> **TIP** ▶ *No matter what dolly you use, recognize that dolly shoots substantially limits the possibilities of editing. With still shots, an editor can be easily cut away from the scene or to different parts of it. Dolly shots, on the other hand, generally need to be continuous. For this reason, you'll need to schedule extra time for every dolly shot because a single mistake will require you to start the whole shot again.*

I recommend against a motorized wheelchair because I've attempted to use one on a shoot with fairly poor results. Most problematically, the motorized chair produces a slight jerk when stopping or starting. While nearly unnoticeable to the rider, the camera captures the jerk almost without fail. Secondly, the wheels on a motorized wheelchair are much smaller than the large wheels on a traditional chair. While this is not a problem on carpeting or smooth concrete, it almost eliminates use on rough surfaces – something a traditional wheelchair handles like a champ.

Suggestions

Here are a few operating suggestions to help you get the best use from the wheelchair dolly:

- **Don't remove the footrests** In beginning practice, the footrests always seem to get in the way as you stand up and sit down again. It seems natural to remove then. Don't. Over several hours of using your legs to hold your feet off the ground, you'll be desperate for them back.

- **Bring a tape measure** Most dolly shots occur in a straight line. It is often difficult, especially with an untrained dolly grip, to keep the dolly rolling over a straight path. A tape measure with a tape lock can be laid on the ground as a quick and simple guide by which the dolly grip can judge a straight path. Be sure the camera doesn't see the ground with the tape measure or your shot will be ruined.

- **Never set the camera in the chair** You'll find that an empty chair on a set is a temptation to all to take a seat. Even if you're careful to avoid mistakenly sitting on the camera, someone else may not be.

Tripod Dolly

Applications

The tripod dolly (see figure 13-1) is a smooth rolling platform where a tripod can be mounted and perform dolly shots. This type of dolly is extremely useful because it's lightweight, portable, and easy to use. Moreover, with it you can obtain professional-looking dolly tracking shots that are the hallmark of a polished film.

With the tripod dolly, only the tripod and the camera move along the track – unlike a professional dolly where the camera operator rides on the dolly with the camera. The advantage of this dolly design is that it allows the track to be made of lightweight PVC pipe that can be easily transported. Additionally, the camera will ride more smoothly given the uncertain tolerances of consumer-grade wheels and track. The only real disadvantage is that manual focus pulling is difficult since the camera is moving separately from the operator.

> **TIP** ▶ *Rack focus on the tripod dolly is possible with an external manual focus control. Varizoom (http://www.varizoom.com/) manufactures a popular control for DV cameras that I have heard many good things about. External controls use an electronic interface to the camera to control the zoom and focus of the camera. While these controls can sometimes seem expensive, the added flexibility they provide can help you obtain exceptional footage.*

PARTS	Qty	Item
	3	L-bracket $1\frac{1}{2}''$ wide with $3''$ strut lengths
	6	Roller blade wheels
	3	$4\frac{1}{2}'' \times \frac{1}{4}''$ bolts
	6	$2\frac{1}{2}'' \times \frac{1}{4}''$ bolts
	1	$6'$ 2×6 board
	2	Frame-mounting brackets
	2	$12'$ $\frac{3}{4}''$ PVC pipe lengths
	4	PVC T-joints
	1	$4'$ length of $\frac{3}{4}''$ PVC pipe
	3	Tennis balls
	3	$1''$ wood screws w/washers
	12	$\frac{1}{4}''$ nuts

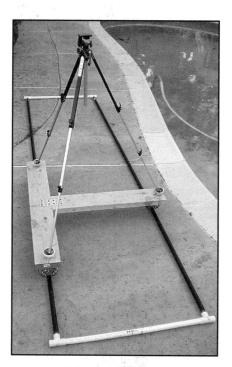

FIGURE 13.1 *The tripod dolly is a smooth rolling platform where a tripod can be mounted.*

General Instructions

When you use the tripod dolly, the camera operator must move along with the dolly. This generally requires a fair amount of practice since the dolly should begin smoothly and come to a stop in the same manner. Luckily, the lightweight of the tripod dolly makes this process much simpler than with a traditional dolly. It is a bad idea to push on either the camera or the tripod while performing the dolly move as this will produce shaky footage.

> **NOTE→** While PVC pipe is much lighter and works well for the tripod dolly track, I've used two 12′ steel pipes for the rails. I did this so I could later mount the wheel assemblies on the doorway dolly (see next chapter) to have a complete dolly platform. I feared that the PVC pipe would break under the weight of the dolly and the camera operator standing on top of the platform. Use whatever material best fits your application.

Construction

You'll begin construction by creating the wheel assemblies. There are three assemblies needed for the tripod and each assembly uses two wheels apiece. The wheels I used came from a pair of roller blades I found at a discount store for less than the price of a music CD. You can buy the wheels in packs of four as replacement rollers for an existing pair of roller blades. Alternatively, you could use the wheels from a pair of roller skates, but be aware that you may have to use washers or some other form of standoff to elevate the wheels the proper distance, so they will effectively grip the rail.

Wheel assemblies

To construct a wheel assembly, you'll need to drill the wheel-mounting holes in the steel L-bracket. To drill these holes I found it easiest to mount each bracket in a small vice (see figure 13-2). Since metal is much more difficult to bore through than wood, the vice will hold the piece firmly in place and allow you to exert more pressure on the drill.

Mount an L-bracket in your vice and use an ice pick or a center punch to create a pit to allow the drill bit a firm place to begin. You should make the pit and a point $\frac{3''}{4}$ from the bend and centered horizontally on the bracket (see figure 13-3). Punch another indentation on the other side of the bend in a matching location.

FIGURE 13.2 *Mount each bracket in a small vice to drill the holes.*

FIGURE 13.3 *Make a pit and a point $\frac{3''}{4}$ from the bend and centered horizontally on the bracket.*

The point you just made will act as a guide, so you can drill a $\frac{1''}{4}$ hole that will accept the wheel shaft. In figure 13-4, you can see three of the L-brackets. In the first one on the left, I've drilled an $\frac{1''}{8}$ pilot hole on each side of the bend. Since the metal of the bracket is so thick, the pilot hole acts as a guide to make it easier to drill the final hole properly. The middle bracket in the picture shows the finished holes drilled on either side of the bend. Finally on the right, you can see the properly mounted wheels.

Mount the wheels temporarily to make certain that they fit properly. Use a $\frac{1''}{4} \times 1\frac{3''}{4}$ length bolt and matching nut for each wheel. When you do mount the wheels, recognize that the wheel has a standoff with a long side and a short side. Make sure that you mount the longer side of the standoff inward, so the wheel stands the maximum distance away from the surface of the bracket.

Try holding the assembly and rolling it over one of your rails. The wheels should move smoothly. There should also be a fair amount of clearance between the peak of the bend and the rail. You will need to drill another hole in the bracket at the peak of the bend (to hold the wheel assembly to the dolly) and place the $4\frac{1''}{2}$ bolt in it. The head of the long bolt should have enough clearance so that it touches neither the wheels nor the rail.

If you can see this is already a problem, your wheels may be larger or smaller than the one I used. You may need to determine the proper distance from the bend to fit your wheels and drill a new $\frac{1''}{4}$ hole. Once you have determined the proper distance, drill the $\frac{1''}{4}$ holes in each of the three L-brackets.

Now you'll need to drill a $\frac{1}{4}''$ hole on the peak of the bend. In figure 13-5, the bracket on the left has the pilot hole drilled in it while the bracket on the right has the finished $\frac{1}{4}''$ hole. Make sure you center punch to make a pit first or the drill will slip. I found it easiest to mount the bracket in the vice (so the $1\frac{1}{2}''$ width is clamped) and then drill the hole from the backside. Drill these peak holes in all three brackets.

When you complete construction of all three wheel assemblies, they'll look as shown in figure 13-6.

FIGURE 13.4 *Three L-brackets in various stages of completion.*

FIGURE 13.5 *The bracket on the left has the pilot hole while the bracket on the right has the finished $\frac{1}{4}''$ hole.*

FIGURE 13.6 *Completed construction of all three wheel assemblies.*

T-board platform

The platform that the tripod will ride on is simply two 2 × 6 boards attached together. To make these boards the proper length, you'll need to extend the legs of your tripod and measure them. The long board will be 2″ longer than the distance between two extended tripod legs (I cut a 36″ board). The short board will be the distance between one of the extended legs and an imaginary point halfway between the other two legs (my short board was 26″).

Use two strut-mounting brackets (one on each side) to hold the boards together in a T shape (see figure 13-7). You can see one of the brackets in the figure while the other is on the opposite side facing down against the pavement. I also put a few 1″ wood screws into the mounting bracket to increase stability. This is not absolutely necessary, however, since only the weighted tripod will be sitting on the platform.

Next, mount the wheel assemblies on the corners (see figure 13-8) of the platform. You'll need to drill $\frac{1}{4}$″ holes for the assembly bolts. Use the $4\frac{1}{2}$″ bolts and matching nuts to secure the assemblies to the board. When you drill the holes, make sure that the two assemblies that are mounted on the top of the T are exactly the same distance from the long edge of the board. This will make them parallel and

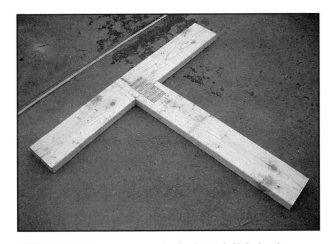

FIGURE 13.7 *Use two strut mounting brackets to hold the boards in a T-shape.*

they will ride properly on the rail. Making sure all the wheel assemblies are pointing the same direction.

Rails assembly

Assemble the rail structure as shown in figure 13-9. If you're using $\frac{3}{4}''$ PVC for the rails, you'll want to glue the T-joints to the tops of each pipe. Since I've used steel pipe, threaded T-joints were screwed onto each of the four ends. The two lengths of PVC pipe that are used to complete a rectangle will keep the rails perfectly parallel. These end bars, therefore, will need to be cut to exactly the same size.

FIGURE 13.8 *Mount the wheel assemblies on the corners of the platform.*

To determine the size of the end bars, place the rails on the ground. Put the dolly platform on the rails and you can measure the proper length between the T-joints. Remember to measure the distance between each set of T-joint ends. This distance should be identical or your tracks are not running parallel. Move the rails until you make sure they are parallel and then cut the end bars to the proper size.

Once you have the rail assembly completed, test the tripod dolly by rolling it all the way from one end to the other (see figure 13-10). If any of the wheels come off the rail during the push, measure the distance from the outside end of one T-joint to the outside end of the T-joint on the other side of the PVC pipe. Take the same measurement from the other PVC assembly. If these lengths don't match, one set of T-joints may not be pushed all the way onto the PVC pipe.

FIGURE 13.9 *Assemble the rail structure.*

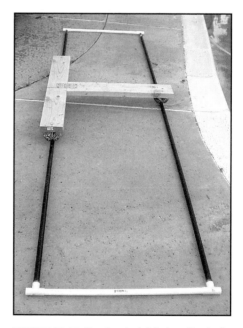

FIGURE 13.10 *Test the tripod dolly by rolling it all the way from one end to the other.*

FIGURE 13.11 *Place a washer onto a wood screw and drill it through a tennis ball into the T-platform.*

Once you have the rails properly adjusted, you can create cups to steadily hold the legs of your tripod. Set up your tripod on the T-platform. Mark where the legs can rest solidly. Cut three tennis balls in half. At one of the locations you marked, place a washer onto a wood screw and drill it through a tennis ball half into the T-platform (see figure 13-11).

Do the same for the other two tennis ball halves and place the tripod on the tripod dolly (see figure 13-12). Your tripod dolly is now complete! I've found mounting a rope on the front and back of the tripod dolly allows you to perform the smoothest starts and stops once you become accustomed to using it. You could also mount a push bar such as the one used with the doorway dolly in the next chapter.

To steady the tripod, be sure to weigh it down with sandbags or another method. Weight will ensure the tripod stays steadily anchored to the platform for the smoothest footage. You might consider creating a weighted tripod as demonstrated in Chapter 18 to use standard dumbbell weights to hold the tripod solidly on the platform. Additionally you might put some sandbags or other barriers at the ends of the rails to make sure the tripod dolly is never pushed beyond the rails onto the ground.

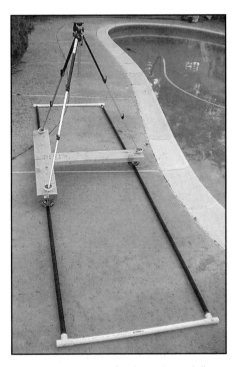

FIGURE 13.12 *Mount the other two tennis ball halves and place the tripod on the tripod dolly.*

TIP ▶ *On a professional set, a dolly grip will endeavor to avoid having the wheels of a dolly ever touch the ground. This prevents the wheels from picking up dirt or rocks that might mar the wheels (or the rail) and prevent a smooth camera movement. You should try to keep the wheels clean and free from any ground debris.*

Suggestions

Here are a few operating suggestions to help you get the best use from the tripod dolly:

- *Use the heaviest tripod available* A sturdy tripod will prevent rocks and jiggles that result in poor footage. A sturdy tripod can also accept more sandbags or other weight to make certain the shots are steady.

- *Create bent track for special shots* PVC pipe can bend to a limited degree without breaking. You can bend a medium-length PVC pipe into about a 15° curve and hold it there using 2 × 4s that can sit under the rails (like railroad ties). Simple glue or screw the bent pipe onto the ties.

- *Use 4-wheel assemblies and a board* You can easily modify the instructions provided in this chapter and create 4-wheel assemblies and mount them on a solid piece of plywood. That structure would allow you to create a platform where the camera operator could ride on the dolly. While not nearly as portable or convenient as the tripod dolly, such a platform does provide more flexibility in the types of dolly shots that may be performed.

Doorway Dolly

Applications

While the tripod dolly is excellent for uneven terrain or light camera equipment, a doorway dolly is ideal for general use. A doorway dolly (see figure 14-1) provides a platform where you can place a camera, cameraman, and necessary film equipment. It works best when operating on a smooth or soft surface such as a hardwood floor, a concrete slab, or shallow carpet.

This doorway dolly is constructed using a couple of furniture dollies available at nearly any hardware store. These dollies provide the ideal backbone to creating a rugged and useful dolly which can carry a great deal of weight and operate smoothly. Furniture dollies are readily available and fairly inexpensive (each costing about the price of a DVD disc). Each dolly is rated to carry 1000 pounds, so equipment and personnel weight is not a problem.

Qty	Item
2	Furniture dollies
2	$\frac{3}{4}''$ unions
2	$\frac{3}{4}''$ flanges
2	$\frac{3}{4}''$ 90° bends
2	$\frac{3}{4}'' \times 2''$ threaded steel pipe
2	$\frac{3}{4}'' \times 36''$ threaded steel pipe
1	$\frac{3}{4}'' \times 24''$ threaded steel pipe
16	$1\frac{1}{2}''$ drywall screws
8	$\frac{1}{4}'' \times 2\frac{1}{2}''$ hex head bolts
24	$\frac{1}{4}''$ washers
8	$\frac{1}{4}''$ wing nuts
1	$2' \times 4'$ sheet of $\frac{3}{4}''$ plywood
4	Tennis balls

PARTS

General Instructions

The doorway dolly is designed for easy disassembly and transportation. The push bar is mounted with union joints that allow for easy removal, so the dolly can be stored flat. For further breakdown, the board holding together the furniture dollies is secured with bolts and wing nuts. Remove the bolts and the individual pieces of the dolly can be stored separately.

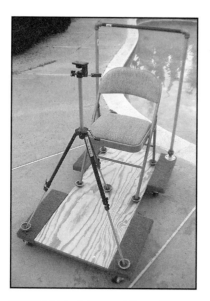

FIGURE 14.1 *A doorway dolly provides a platform for a camera, camera man, and film equipment.*

Once you've constructed the dolly, be sure to practice with it for best use. In my experience, placing the camera on a tripod produces the smoothest footage if the surface the dolly rolling over is flat and even. When moving over a surface such as a sidewalk with cracks, holding the camera yourself will take out a great deal of the jarring since your body will absorb most of the shock. However, since your grip will not be rock steady, the frame will move around slightly and give your footage a more subjective feel than the steady glide of a mounted dolly movement.

Using a "dance floor" is another solution to getting a smooth tracking shot while operating over rough surfaces. A dance floor is a smooth path created for the dolly to move across. It usually consists of a number of flat $\frac{1}{2}''$ plywood boards that are placed end to end for the desired length. The dolly can travel smoothly over the dance floor surface.

TIP ▶ *High-end commercial dollies have a small laser attached to the side of the dolly. When turned on, the laser shoots a red point directly onto the ground below it. To plan a tracking shoot, a line is drawn (usually in pencil or chalk) with a straight edge onto the surface being traversed (street, carpet, etc.). Making sure the laser point remains on the line, the dolly grip can precisely maneuver the dolly using the line as a guide.*

If you can find a cheap laser pointer with an on–off switch, you should consider mounting it to the rear side of the dolly. Using the pointer can help you get a move precise shot. The red dot is also useful when pushing the dolly near a wall since so you can keep the distance between the wall and the dolly the same for the entire tracking move.

Construction

The key components of the doorway dolly are the furniture dollies (see figure 14-2) that will be used for the platform. When you buy them, check to make sure that the wheels are smooth and undamaged. Also make sure that the boards that make up the dolly are straight. The better the quality of the dollies that you purchase, the smoother the final footage will be.

FIGURE 14.2 *Furniture dollies used for the platform.*

To construct the doorway dolly, follow these steps:

1. Mount a flange on one carpeted end of the first furniture dolly (see figure 14-3). Pre-drill the four holes and then use drywall screws to secure the flange to the surface. Make sure that the screws are snug because each flange will have to withstand a fair amount of pressure as the dolly is pushed.

FIGURE 14.3 *Mount a flange on the carpeted end of the first furniture dolly.*

2. Screw a 2″ pipe nipple into the flange (see figure 14-4). Just screw it in with your fingers. When you tighten the union, it will subsequently turn the nipple down tightly into the flange.

3. Take apart a union and screw the bottom half (with the tightening ring) onto the nipple (see figure 14-5). Use a wrench to tighten the bottom half of the union onto the nipple.

4. Put together push handle (as a U shape) by screwing together the 36″ pipes as the sides, the 24″ pipe as the bottom, and the 90° bends to hold them together. Assembling the push handle will allow you to determine the position to mount the second flange.

FIGURE 14.4 *Screw a 2″ pipe nipple into the flange.*

FIGURE 14.5 *Take apart a union and screw the bottom half onto the nipple.*

5. Take apart the second union and screw the bottom half (with the tightening ring) onto the second nipple.

6. Screw the union/nipple combination into the second flange.

7. On the open ends of the 36″ pipes, screw the top pieces of the unions.

8. Screw the second union back together (see figure 14-6), seat the other side of the U in the first union, and find the proper place to mount the second flange.

9. Mount the second flange (see figure 14-7) securely on the dolly. The unions allow you to easily remove the push bar for transportation.

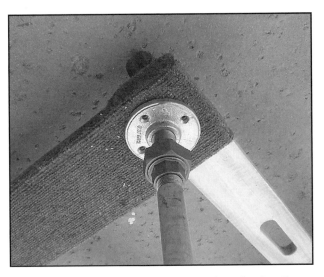

FIGURE 14.6 *Screw the second union together and seat the other side of the U in the first union.*

FIGURE 14.7 *Mount the second flange securely on the dolly.*

10. Now that you have the first furniture dolly prepared, put the second dolly against the front (see figure 14-8) and compare the widths between the carpeted boards. One of my dollies was $\frac{1}{2}''$ narrower than the other. The narrower width will determine how wide you should cut the 4′ platform board.

11. Cut the platform board to fit the width of narrowest dolly. Be sure to cut the 2′ side of the board, so you retain the entire 4′ in length.

12. Lay the platform board between two dollies (see figure 14-9) and check to make sure that the width is right. The board should fit snugly between the carpeted boards of the narrower dolly.

13. Drill eight holes for the $\frac{1}{4}''$ hex bolts to hold the platform board. You'll need to drill the holes in both the platform and the uncarpeted dolly boards. I found it easiest to drill the two holes at the front end of the front dolly (the one without the push bar) and slide the bolts in the holes to retain proper alignment. Then I drilled the two holes at the back end of the back dolly and

FIGURE 14.8 *Align the second dolly against the front.*

FIGURE 14.9 *Lay the platform board between two dollies.*

seated two bolts. That allowed me to safely drill the remaining four holes without any further worry about alignment.

14. Put the eight bolts in the holes using washers (see figure 14-10) to allow them to more securely hold the board in place.

15. On the bottom end of each bolt, use a washer and a wing nut (see figure 14-11) to hold the bolt securely in place.

16. When all the bolts are in place, the dolly is complete in its basic form (see figure 14-12). This doorway dolly can be used to stand on or place a tripod.

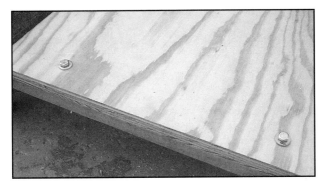

FIGURE 14.10 *Put the eight bolts in the drilled holes using washers.*

FIGURE 14.11 *On the bottom end of each bolt, use a washer and a wing nut.*

For someone planning to use the doorway dolly extensively, you might wish to make a few refinements. It's very useful to have secure sites where you can position a seat and secure the tripod. Fixed positions make setup faster and provide an added level of safety for the camera operator and the camera itself.

Before you decide on the final placement of the chair and tripod, test the positions of each (see figure 14-13). You'll find that you'll have to re-position them several times before you find the most comfortable location. On the tripod, use a combination of leg spread and head elevation so you can obtain the desired height while maintaining a comfortable margin between the ends of the legs and the edges of the platform. Try sitting in the chair and having someone push the dolly. Do you feel comfortable? Can you reach all of the camera controls? Would you feel comfortable in this position if the shoot lasted 14 hours?

Mark the seven locations of the leg placements (three for the tripod and four for the chair). Cut the four tennis balls in half so you have eight pieces. I used a hacksaw that was fast and accurate. The tennis

FIGURE 14.12 *Completed dolly in its basic form.*

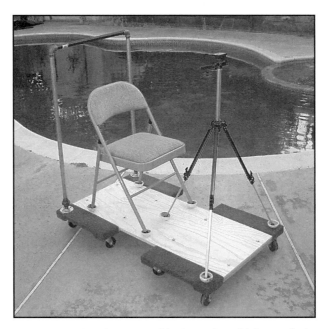

FIGURE 14.13 *Test the positions of the chair and tripod before you decide on the final placement.*

ball halves provide the perfect cups to hold the ends of chair and tripod legs. The rubbery material of the tennis ball provides some shock absorption as well.

Mount a tennis ball half by placing it over one of the marked points and drilling a hole through the ball into the board. Drive a drywall screw (see figure 14-14) through the tennis half into the board to secure it. You can make it more secure by adding a washer so the screw can't pull through the tennis ball.

Add the other cups for the tripod (see figure 14-15) and then mount the ones for the chair. Put the chair and the tripod in place and test again. Are the positions comfortable? If not, move the tennis ball halves to new locations.

Once completed, your dolly should look like the one shown in figure 14-16. Since the wheels are free spinning, be sure to make a short push in the direction you'll be moving before the take begins. This push will align the wheels properly so you won't have any delay once the director shouts "Action!"

FIGURE 14.14 *Drive a drywall screw through the tennis half into the board.*

FIGURE 14.15 *Add other cups for tripod and the ones for the chair.*

FIGURE 14.16 *The completed dolly.*

Suggestions

Here are a few operating suggestions to help you get the best use from the doorway dolly:

- *Replace the flange drywall screws with bolts* When using the dolly on carpeting, recognize that it takes a lot more energy to push the dolly across this type of surface. That means that there will be a great deal of more pressure on the flanges securing the push bar. If you'll be doing a lot of on-carpet shooting, you might consider replacing the drywall screws that hold the flanges to the dolly surface with hex bolts, washers, and nuts. Using bolts will more securely anchor the flanges to the dolly and prevents the possibility of the flanges tearing free (as they might given enough pressure on the drywall screws).

- *Use bigger wheels* The bigger the wheel on the dolly, the smoother the ride. At an industrial liquidation store, I found some larger wheels with good mounts that I intend to use to replace the furniture dolly wheels. Since I had to scrounge to find these wheels, I didn't want to make them a part of the project. However, if you can find bigger wheels, you might consider using them.

- *Sandbag the tripod onto the platform* To diminish any jiggling of the tripod (and therefore the camera) and to secure the tripod to the platform, add the appropriate number of sandbags to the tripod legs. The dead weight will hold the tripod to the platform and provide better shots and more safety for your camera.

- *Use the dolly for transportation* Although you want to be sure to keep the tires in best condition, you can use the dolly to transport equipment to and from the set. Most commonly a doorway dolly is used to move sandbags or the heavier lights.

Underwater Cam Stand

Applications

Shooting below the waterline is one of the more difficult filming tasks you can attempt. Underwater enclosures are expensive and generally have to be obtained specifically to fit a particular model of camera. Controlling the camera through the enclosure is not very convenient.

While it doesn't give you the flexibility of a sealed underwater camera, placing your camera inside a fish tank (see figure 15-1) can allow you to film below the surface of the water. It will even allow you to move from the surface of the water to just below it – a technique used to obtain excellent effect in the classic movie Jaws.

In this chapter you'll build a frame that will secure an aquarium to a stable platform that rests on the bottom of a pool. Placing a fish tank under the water may seem rudimentary on first glance, but it's actually fairly involved. To force the bottom of the tank under the water's surface, a fairly large volume of water needs to be displaced. To achieve the proper amount of displacement, a significant amount of downward pressure (supplied by dead weight) can be required.

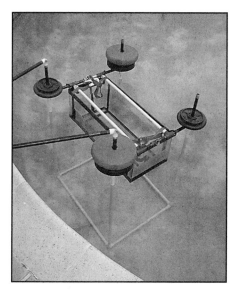

FIGURE 15.1 *Placing a camera inside a fish tank allows filming below the surface of the water.*

	Qty	Item
PARTS	1	Fish tank larger than your camera
	2	Ratchet straps or ratchet tie-downs
	10	$\frac{1}{2}''$ steel T-joints
	4	$\frac{1}{2}'' \times 3''$ threaded steel pipe
	8	$\frac{1}{2}'' \times 8''$ threaded steel pipe
	12	$\frac{1}{2}''$ PVC to threaded adapter
	4	$\frac{1}{2}''$ PVC corners
	4	$\frac{1}{2}'' \times 10'$ PVC pipe
	8	Dumbbell weights

General Instructions

The underwater cam stand is a frame made from lengths of iron pipe and PVC pipe. PVC is an excellent building material for such a stand because it won't rust or absorb water. It also won't scratch the bottom surface of the pool while resting on it.

The exact measurements of the PVC lengths will be determined by the size of your fish tank and the height of the water in your pool. A good general level is to adjust the height of the stand so that half the tank is above and half is below the waterline.

Any fish tank or aquarium that is large enough to hold your camera can be used effectively. While a tall thin tank can provide the greatest viewable distance under water, it may not be wide enough to avoid getting the edges of the tank in the camera frame. Test your camera in the aquarium before you even consider using it for the underwater cam setup.

With a tall enough tank, you can take footage simultaneously above and below the surface. Figure 15-2 shows a picture of a pool thermometer taken from within the tank. You can see that the difference in diffraction between the above surface and under water provides an interesting split effect.

Once you've selected a tank that you believe will fit your purposes, you should test the tank to make sure it doesn't have any leaks. This should be done before you put your camera in harm's way. You can test for leaks by filling the tank with water and placing it on a solid dry surface such as a table. Leave it for half an hour and then move it. If the tank is in watertight condition, there shouldn't be any water deposited on the surface.

Once you're confident that the tank is well sealed, you can begin to prepare it for filming. You'll build a frame that will be secured to the tank and will hold mounted weights to force the tank below the water line.

FIGURE 15.2 *Diffraction differences between above surface and under water.*

> **WARNING→** Be *extremely* careful whenever your camera is near water. In the process of taking the photographs for this chapter, I wasn't paying attention and dipped my digital still camera about an inch into the pool water. The camera died a quick and vocal death. I hope my expensive mistake can serve as a lesson to help you make sure that you pay strict attention anytime your equipment is in close proximity to a body of water.

Construction

To achieve underwater filming, you'll be creating an empty space in the water with the aquarium where your camera can be safely positioned. Being no physicist, it surprised me how much weight it took to push the tank below the water line. In the end, the tank you see in the photos took more than 90 pounds of dead weight to keep it solidly anchored to the bottom of the pool. Therefore, it's better to overestimate the amount of weight you'll need than underestimate. Be sure to have extra weights on hand.

There are two primary structures to the frame: the top and the base. The top is the frame that will be secured to the top rim of the tank with ratchet straps. The base is an open-ended box of PVC pipes that will sit on the bottom of the pool and structurally keep the tank at the proper level.

Constructing the top frame

Before you begin creating the top frame, you'll need to take the measurements of your tank. The goal is to have the top frame rest securely on the rim of the tank. In figure 15-3, you can see a diagram of the top I constructed to fit my tank. The tank measured 12.25″ × 24.75″ × 12.5″. That meant that the central pipes of the top frame that span the width of the tank would be 25.75″ long after taking into account the added length of the joints.

The central PVC pipes have threaded caps attached to allow them to be screwed into the metal T-joints. Each of the central pipe ends feed into a T-joint (see figure 15-4) to extend across the width of the tank. You'll then need two other PVC pipes to complete the rectangle and span the length of the tank. In figure 15-4, you can see that I used two smaller threaded pipes that are fed into a T-joint to form the proper length. These T-joints are placed at each end. They're then rotated downward on each side to somewhat "sandwich" the tank between the joint on the top frame.

Once you have the primary rectangle together, you'll add the weight-carrying extensions. These are formed by screwing an 8″ iron pipe into each of the T-joints. Then add another T-joint to the end of the new pipe with the two open ends of the joint facing up and down. To the top of the joint, add another 8″ pipe (see figure 15-5).

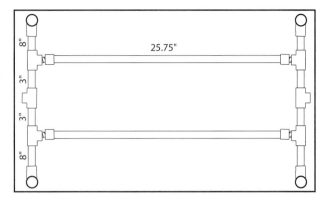

FIGURE 15.3 *A diagram of the top frame.*

FIGURE 15.4 *The central pipe ends each feed into a T-joint to extend across the width of the tank.*

FIGURE 15.5 *Add another 8″ pipe to the top of the joint.*

To complete the weight-carrying member, screw a threaded PVC adapter into the final open socket of each T-joint. These adapters will convert the threaded socket into a normal PVC socket (see figure 15-6). The converted sockets will allow you to slide the four PVC pipes from the base frame into the open PVC end.

The top frame itself is now complete. You need only to use the two ratchet straps to secure it to the top of the tank. Be careful to make sure that the primary stress from the straps lies on the metal parts of the top frame rather than the frame of the tank. You want to hold the top frame to the tank, but not unnecessarily stress the tank.

Also make sure that the top frame has a solid anchor on the rim of the tank before ratcheting it down. I accomplished this by sizing the central pipes such that the lip of each T-joint sat inside the rim and the rest of the joint sat outside (see figure 15-7). Placing the joints in this way ensures that the top frame doesn't slide back and forth, even without the ratchet straps to hold it in place.

Once the top frame is strapped to the tank (see figure 15-8), you'll have essentially a single piece. From now on, lift the tank using the top frame to avoid any danger to the tank itself.

FIGURE 15.6 *Adapters convert the threaded socket into a normal PVC socket.*

FIGURE 15.7 *Size the central pipes so the lip of each T-joint sits inside the rim while the rest of the joint sits outside.*

Constructing the base

Once you have the top frame complete, you can easily determine the measurements of the base. Use a tape measure or long ruler to obtain the length and width distances between the T-joints at the weight-bearing extensions (see figure 15-9).

When you have these distances, cut four lengths of PVC pipe to the proper lengths to allow you to construct a rectangle frame that will match these edge sizes. Assemble the four lengths with corner joints (see figure 15-10). The rectangle should be precisely the same size as the rectangle created by the top frame's T-joints.

The foundation of the base frame is now complete. Before you continue, you'll need to know the desired elevation for the tank in the water. Use a tape measure to determine the distance from the bottom of the pool to the water line. Then determine the amount of tank you want above the water line and add this to the measurement. By adding these together, you'll have the length of the support poles that you'll need. For example, the shallow end of my pool was 4-ft deep and I wanted 8″ of clearance at the top of my tank. Therefore, I cut the poles to 4′ 8″.

Cut four poles to the proper lengths and attach threaded converter caps to a single end of each PVC pipe (therefore four caps will be needed). Screw the threaded ends into the corners of the base frame (see figure 15-11). You should do another measurement to make sure that the height will hold the top frame at the proper level.

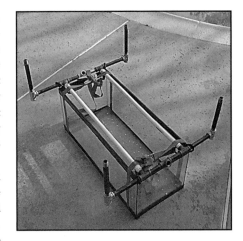

FIGURE 15.8 *Strap the top frame to the tank.*

Once you've obtained the tank and completed the top and base frames, you'll need some type of weight to push the buoyant structure to the bottom of the pool. Dumbbell weights will be placed on the weight-bearing 8″ pipes attached to the top frame. The weights shouldn't be in place until the tank and the frame are in the water. Be sure to keep them handy because once the structure is lowered into the pool, you won't be able to release it until the weights are in place. If you don't want to use weight, you can use some of the sand-bag alternatives listed in Chapter 44.

FIGURE 15.9 *Use a tape measure or long ruler to obtain the length and width distances.*

Lower it into the pool

You're now ready to use the underwater cam stand. Note that the next step requires two people to accomplish safely. Since the stand is only meant to be used in the water, the flexible PVC pipe is unstable on land and the tank should not be left unattended once mounted on the base (see figure 15-12). Have two people lift the top frame with tank attached and push it onto the tops of the base poles. Once this is complete, you should have the entire underwater cam structure in place.

With a person holding each end of the top frame, lower the structure into

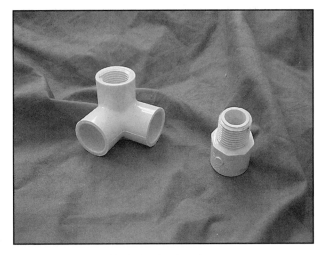

FIGURE 15.10 *Assemble the four lengths with corner joints.*

FIGURE 15.11 *Screw the threaded ends into the corners of the base frame.*

FIGURE 15.12 *Don't leave the tank unattended once it's mounted on the base.*

the pool. It's best if there is a third person (perhaps the cameraperson) already in the pool to guide it down properly. Note that without any weight on the frame, when the bottom of the aquarium reaches the water line, the structure will float above the bottom.

The person in the pool should position the stand in the desired position for shooting. Begin adding weights to the weight-bearing poles. Distribute the weights evenly around the four corners. Little by little, the weights will force the base to the bottom of the pool. When you have enough weights to hold the frame securely to the bottom, continue to have someone gripping the stand to make certain that it doesn't tip over because of a wave or someone bumping into it.

Now you need to perform a safety check to make sure that the tank is tall enough so that the agitation of the water (by the actors) won't splash over the rim of the tank. Have someone make a wave at the position desired for the actors. Start small and progressively make larger waves. Stop before water is actually splashing into the tank. This test will give you the parameters of how much splashing is possible before placing the camera in danger.

Finally, I would recommend taking a large plastic bag (a trash bag will do), cutting a hole large enough for the lens of your camera, and keeping the camera inside for the duration of the underwater cam shoot. The plastic bag will prevent any random splash of water from reaching the camera. Keep in mind that if you use a black bag, on a sunny day the temperature within the bag might rise and pose a danger to your camera. Make sure you always operate the camera within the parameters specified in the manual.

Suggestions

Here are a few operating suggestions to help you get the best use from the underwater cam:

* ***When not in use, remove the camera from the tank*** Under no circumstances should your precious camera be left in the tank unattended. That's just asking for someone to unintentionally knock over the stand or splash water into the tank possibly causing damaging.

- ***Whenever the camera isn't in use, power it down*** Typically, water only damages electronics when power is running through the circuitry. If the camera is powered off, even if it gets slightly wet, no harm will occur as long as you're sure to completely dry the camera before attempting to power it back on.

- ***Determine the white balance before shooting*** Water filters most wavelengths of light and let's through light mostly in the blue/green spectrum. Since audiences are accustomed to seeing an underwater picture with a slight blue/green tinge, it is usually a good idea to white balance the camera to the above water picture. Just make sure that whether you white balance above or below the water, lock it before you shoot.

Gray Card Incident Meter

Applications

Light meters are critical for proper lighting whether you're shooting on video or film. While instructions for properly using a light meter are beyond the scope of this book, it is important to describe why a meter is necessary. The growth of digital technology, monitors, and video assist has convinced some filmmakers that using a meter is unnecessary. Only after they've shot poorly lit footage or gone dramatically over the shooting schedule that it becomes apparent that a light meter is an investment well worth making.

The most basic lighting for scene simply makes everything important visible. Most notable films, however, use lighting to create a mood or further a theme. Lighting is used to separate the actors from the background and highlight parts of the background for specific effect. Light meters allow you to determine and thereby precisely control the level of each light in the overall scene.

Have you ever driven your car in the darkness when there are very few other cars on the road? A single car following two car lengths behind you with their headlights on can be incredibly distracting and annoying in your rearview mirror. However, those same headlights at the same distance in daylight are virtually unnoticeable. The difference is the level of contrast between the headlights and the surrounding environment. In daylight, headlights are lost because the ambient light level is so high (thanks to the sun). At night, the headlights become a spotlight in a pool of darkness. The difference between these situations is the level of light contrast.

Using a light meter can help you determine and adjust the light contrast to mold the environment within the frame to highlight particular actors or set decoration. Since a light meter will allow you to quantitatively determine the light level at any spot on the set, you can control explicitly what needs to be emphasized in your film.

Many low-budget filmmakers avoid using a light meter because of the expense. A good light meter can cost as much as a low-end DV camera! However, you can use an inexpensive reflected meter in conjunction with a gray card to obtain the same readings provided by an expensive incident meter. Whether shooting on film or video, you'll quickly learn that using a meter will save you both time and money. A meter will also minimize the amount of unusable footage that you'll shoot.

Shooting on film

When shooting on film, you don't really have much choice – you have to use a light meter. Since the final negative image is determined by a large number of factors (film type, ASA/ISO, exposure latitude, filters, etc.), proper lighting is based on using your experience to guesstimate how all these factors will affect the final image. A light meter provides the information the cinematographer (DP) needs to make a proper assessment of factors such as contrast ratios, blow-out levels for highlights, and detail levels in shadow areas.

Shooting video

Some videographers believe that they can just look at the monitor and light the scene properly without a meter. Having worked with a number of professional cinematographers, it has been my observation that lighting a scene with the monitor generally is much slower than using a meter. Using a meter seems to allow the DP to take in the entire lighting scheme and balance accordingly.

When a monitor is used, the DP tends to focus on individual areas in the scene. Just as one area is perfectly lit, adjustments are made to another area that throws off the entire picture. While it is entirely possible to light a scene well using only a monitor, in real life it seems to burn a great deal of time.

Reliance on a monitor also creates problems if the monitor is not properly tuned. I myself have shot footage based on the monitor image, only later to discover that the monitor brightness or contrast was set improperly. Frustratingly I discovered this while examining dailies and all of my footage was too dark due to underlighting.

Types of Meters

There are two primary types of light meters: incident meters and reflected meters. Incident meters are the kind most commonly used on film sets. Reflected light meters (including spot meters) are generally used more often in still photographs.

> **TIP** ▶ *If several people on the shoot have meters (typically the DP and the gaffer), check the meters against each other. If there is any variation between them, you can choose one of the meters as the standard and make adjustments to the other meter readings so they match. Most current digital meters provide a feature that allows slight adjustment to allow for meter synchronization. With older meters, you just have to mentally make the calculation (e.g., add a third of a stop).*

Incident meters

I use Minolta Flash Meter IV as shown in figure 16-1 for most of my current film work. There are many other popular brands including Sekonic, Gossen, and others. The problem with digital incident meters is that they are very expensive. Even older used meters can run a couple of hundred dollars, so they are not within the financial reach of many low-budget filmmakers.

General practice of using an incident meter involves placing the meter where your subject will be and pointing the meter toward the camera (see figure 16-2). The reading will tell you how much light is falling on the subject. By taking a reading in the highlight area and another in the shadow area of the frame, you can get a good idea of whether both the highlights and the shadows will retain detail. If the range between light and dark is too great for the media (film, video, etc.), detail in a portion of the image won't be captured.

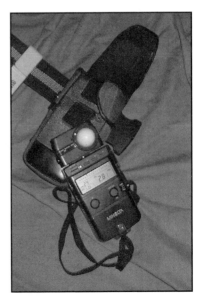

FIGURE 16.1 *The Minolta Flash Meter IV.*

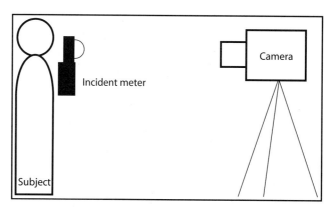

FIGURE 16.2 *Place the meter where your subject will be and point the meter toward the camera.*

The specifics of using incident light meters are beyond the scope of this book. For an excellent and complete explanation, see the "Exposure" section of Blain Brown's "Cinematography Theory and Practice" (ISBN 0-240-80500-3).

Reflected meters

Older light meters used for still photography are called *reflected light meters*. In contrast to incident meters (which read light falling on a subject), a reflected meter is pointed at the subject and it takes a reading of how much light bounced-off of or was reflected back from the subject. Reflected meters can be obtained at many pawnshops or on Internet auction sites generally for less than the price of a pizza.

> **TIP** ▶ *Whenever you buy a used meter, be sure to check it against one that is known to be tuned properly. Digital meters can generally be adjusted if they aren't correct.*

The problem with reflected meters is that the meter reading is meant to be an average of everything in the picture. Think of taking all the white and blacks of a picture and averaging them together. Generally, you would get a gray. That is the intent of the reflected meter. If everything taken together and averaged is a gray, then the exposure is at the right level.

This works out great for pictures that are generally balanced in light such as a family standing in a lit living room or in the backyard. However, if you don't want this average "good enough" picture, the reading becomes a problem. Most movies are made so and they have broad contrast ranges in frame. That keeps the picture interesting. Foreground and background are often separated by light levels.

Further, the averaging doesn't work well in conditions such as taking footage with a background of white snow. Since the reflected meter is trying to average the whole picture to gray, that is generally what the photo will show – gray snow. That's where a gray card comes in.

General Instructions

A gray card is available at most photo stores for under $10. A gray card is made to reflect 18% of the light that hits it. Therefore, if you point a reflected light meter at a gray card (see figure 16-3), the reading will tell you the amount of light hitting the subject – the same as an incident meter.

FIGURE 16.3 *Point the reflected light meter at a gray card.*

Simply place the gray card where you want to take a reading (see figure 16-4) and trigger your reflected meter. Be sure not to get in the way of the light source or your reading will be incorrect. While using the gray card with a reflected meter may seem a little cumbersome, the ability to cheaply meter a scene is well worth the trouble. It also provides an excellent learning tool allowing you to examine various lighting situations long before principal photography begins.

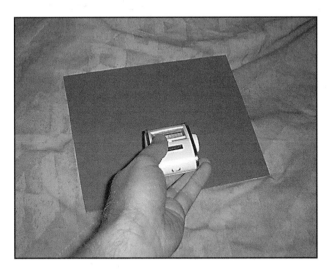

FIGURE 16.4 *Place the gray card where you want to take a reading.*

Lux Incident Meter

Applications

While using a gray card is an excellent way to obtain light readings, there is a way to obtain a light level measurement with a little more precision. Inexpensive digital lux meters (see figure 17-1) are available that measure the total amount of incident light and return an absolute numerical reading in units known as lux. A lux unit is a measurement of the amount of light striking the incident meter.

Lux meters are fairly cheap (about the price of an inexpensive microwave) and yet very accurate. These meters, used by farmers and gardeners, are employed to determine the amount of light striking a particular area of land. Additionally, art galleries use them to make sure that the light level is low enough to protect paintings from fading. Because of their intended use, a lux meter has an incident area larger than the ball on a meter made for film production. While the larger area is not as exact as the point reading on a film meter, it handles most cinematic situations perfectly.

You can obtain a lux meter through some garden supply outlets or look on the Internet. A couple of years ago a friend recommended I buy one from the company Family Defense Products (www.familydefense.com).

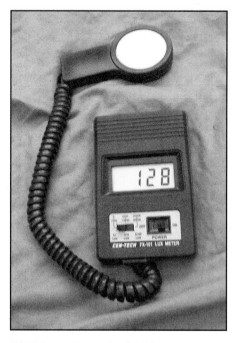

FIGURE 17.1 *Inexpensive digital lux meters measure the total amount of incident light.*

It's worked perfectly since I got it. Other manufacturers include Extech Instruments (www.zefon.com) and University Products (www.archivalsuppliers.com).

> **NOTE→** In the past, absolute light meters were actually the industry standard in movies and tele-vision. Many cinematographers still use these meters (particularly the meters made by Spectra) because they can obtain a precise value (instead of a calculated value such as an f/stop) indicating exactly how much light is striking an area. When I had the honor of working with Janusz Kaminski (the Oscar-winning cinematographer), he used an analog Spectra Professional light meter to take his meter readings.

	Qty	Item
PARTS	1	Lux incident meter
	1	Spreadsheet program such as Microsoft Excel or Quatro Pro
	2	Sheets of paper

General Instructions

The unit lux is the measure of the amount of light emitted by a single candle that is exactly 1 m away. In other words, 1 lux is equal to 1 lumen per m^2. Similarly, you might hear of light measured in foot-candles. The foot-candle (fc) measurement unit is the amount of light emitted by a single candle that is exactly 1 ft away. Converting between lux and foot-candles is a simple process, as approximately 1 foot-candle equals 10 lux. Therefore, multiplying an fc value by 10 will result in a lux value.

> **NOTE→** To be precise, 1 foot-candle equals 10.76 lux. The breadth of the light scale makes this level of precision generally unnecessary. However, if you need a specific value and you have a cal-culator handy, use the 10.76 value.

While you may be used to working in f/stops, lux values have several advantages. Since it is an absolute light value, a lux reading exists apart from the lens and film speed being used. f/stops depend on a number of variables including film stock ISO/ASA rating, camera filters, frame-rate, etc. A lux value pro-vides a single number that states how much light is falling on the light meter.

With practice, the lux reading can be intuitively understood to determine the proper exposure. Of course, lux values can be converted into a working f/stop value with a simple table. Using a conversion ratio along with the factors of film ISO/ASA and shutter speed, exposure can be calculated.

One of the practical reasons to use absolute lux values is the suitability of the measure's use with video cameras. Although some cameras attempt to simulate f/stop settings, there can be a wide range in how closely these settings approach reality. On lower-end cameras, f/stop settings aren't even included. Instead an "exposure value" scale specific to each camera type indicates an increase or decrease in exposure.

Because the lux meter provides a single objective light value reading, it is much easier to learn proper exposure for a given video camera with the lux meter scale. Attempting to manually convert the f/stop and ISO/ASA charts to match the specifics of a particular camera can be complicated and frustrating.

Lux values are also excellent in understanding light source levels and placement. It's far easier for a gaffer to learn how much light will be provided by a particular source at a particular distance when a sim-ple absolute value is used. After learning how changes to a light source will alter the lux value, an experi-enced gaffer can very intuitively add or remove lights to reach a desired lighting level.

Table 17-1 shows lux values for common light sources and situations. Briefly studying this chart should provide a basic understanding of the ranges of lux readings.

Value	Source
100 lux	Standard art gallery
270 lux	Normal office
400 lux	Bright office
450 lux	85 W spotlight at 5 ft
750 lux	500 W halogen at 5 ft
800 lux	Typical shot on single room set
1000 lux	500 W halogen at 4 ft
1600 lux	500 W halogen at 3 ft
2800 lux	In shadow on sunny day
3000 lux	500 W halogen at 2 ft
9600 lux	500 W halogen at 1 ft
55000 lux	Direct sunlight on sunny day

TABLE 17.1 *Lux values of common situations.*

Testing video cameras

If you are using a camcorder (Hi-8, MiniDV, etc.), check the technical specifications in the camera manual. Most likely the minimum amount of light required for shooting will be provided as a lux value. With a lux meter, you can test to see how close the stated minimum level is to reality.

To perform a light level test, you'll need a small flashlight to read the meter display and a light facing a white wall. When you sit in a completely darkened room and face away from the light, you should have a zero meter reading. Slowly turn toward the light until the meter shows the stated camera minimum value. Place an object (preferably an item that is fairly detail) at the point where you obtained the reading.

Point the camera at the object and record a small segment. In playback, do you see any detail? Raise the light level until you can make out the object and you'll have the practical minimum lux value for filming. To perform this test more easily, you can build the squeezer described in Chapter 35. That will allow you to manually increase the light level by turning the dimmer dial.

Finding the minimum light level with your camera is fine, but not especially useful. When you watch the playback, you may have noticed a large number of small gray or white flecks in the picture. This picture noise is caused by circuitry in the camcorder that digitally boosts the signal under low light conditions. This signal boost is a terrible technology for professional filmmaking as it makes the picture look very amateurish.

Therefore, use the process described above for testing the low light level, but instead, keep increasing the light until these noise artifacts are no longer present. Write down the lux number of this minimum no-noise level. When the light levels fall below this number on a shoot, you can know that you'll be introducing noise artifacts into the footage. You can then take steps to increase the light level and prevent these unsightly artifacts.

Lux to f/stop chart

If you are using film or a camera that has f/stop settings, you'll need to convert the lux values into settings you can use. Table 17-2 provides the lux values and their equivalent f/stop numbers. You'll need to know the speed of the film you're using to convert one value to the other.

ISO	f/1.4	f/2	f/2.8	f/4	f/5.6	f/8	f/11
25	1000	2000	4000	8000	16000	32000	64000
50	500	1000	2000	4000	8000	16000	32000
64	400	800	1600	3200	6400	12500	25000
100	250	500	1000	2000	4000	8000	16000
125	200	400	800	1600	3200	6400	12500
160	160	320	640	1250	2500	5000	10000
200	130	250	500	1000	2000	4000	8000
250	100	200	390	800	1600	3200	6400
320	80	160	320	640	1250	2500	5000
400	64	130	250	500	1000	2000	4000
500	50	100	200	400	800	1600	3200

TABLE 17.2 *Lux values to f/stop conversion chart.*

To use the chart, find the ISO/ASA of the film in the first column and that will indicate the proper row of lux readings. Take a meter reading and, using the proper film speed row, locate the column with the approximate lux value. The heading of that column will provide the equivalent f/stop value. If your value falls between the values given in two of the columns, you'll have to approximate the f/stop value just as if you had a traditional digital light meter that returned a setting such as f/1.4.

Suggestions

Here are a few operating suggestions to help you get the best use from the lux meter:

- *Measure the contrast range on your camera* Since the lux meter provides a single precise lux value for a particular area, it's perfectly suited to determining the exposure range of a camera. This is particularly effective for testing digital cameras. Start with a nearly dark room and obtain a lux reading. Try to photograph for detail. Check your footage. Did anything record? Continue raising the light level until you determine the real minimum lux for the camera. Do the opposite to determine the high end of the scale.

- *Keep spare batteries* As with any light meter, keep spare batteries close by on the set in case your meter stops working.

- *Determine the minimum level when digital gain begins* Most DV cameras have an automatic gain control that, if the light level is too low, the gain kicks in and brightens the image to provide detail. Unfortunately this gain creates a great deal of picture noise that looks like little fireflies throughout the image. This signal noise is unacceptable for most dramatic footage. By using the meter testing techniques described in the last suggestion, determine the lowest lux level that does not engage the gain circuitry.

Depth of Field Spreadsheet

Applications

For many filming setups, a cinematographer (DP) will want to decide explicitly the degree of focus necessary to tell a story with a particular shot. Deep focus may be preferred or at other times the choice is made to blur the background while the actors remain in sharp focus. Depth of field (DoF) calculations allow the DP or cameraperson to determine the size of the field of focus based on a given lens size and aperture setting.

On a professional set, you will often see the Assistant Camera people (ACs) use a tool called a Kelly Wheel (or Guild Kelly Wheel or Mark II Calculator) to determine the DoF. Unfortunately for the average filmmaker, these devices cost over $100, so they're too expensive for easy purchase. Fortunately, many ACs find that carrying pocket-sized tables for the lenses they'll be using is just as functional and some-time more convenient. By creating a simple spreadsheet, you can generate these tables yourself.

The DoF tables provide the hyperfocal, near-focal, and far-focal distances in both meters and feet. This information will be calculated for a given lens and aperture setting (or f/stop). Figure 18-1 shows the completed table of a 50-mm lens (listed in the top-left corner) for f/stops 2, 2.8, 4, and 5.6.

Once you've generated a set of tables, they can be easily kept in the camera pouch or your pocket for easy reference. It can also be very informative to simply study the tables and examine the way that changes in the aperture setting and distance factors affect the DoF.

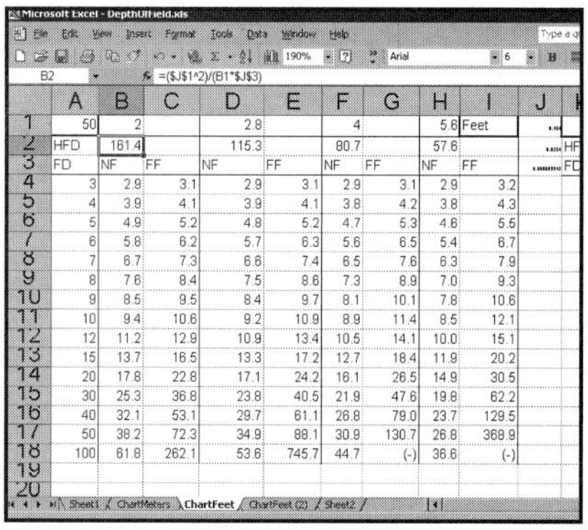

FIGURE 18.1 *A completed table of a 50-mm lens for f/stops 2, 2.8, 4, and 5.6.*

> **TIP ▶** *A PDA or hand-held device equipped with a spreadsheet can be used as a portable depth of field calculator. Even if your PDA doesn't have a spreadsheet, the Internet has many DoF applications that are available for free download. These applications allow you to enter any lens focal length and will instantly make the necessary calculations. This can be especially convenient when you operate zoom lenses where the focal length can vary. Although I have a PDA with this type of program, I still prefer using my small printed tables because of convenience, unbreakability, and ease of reading even in low light conditions.*

Be aware that no table will be exact for a particular camera. While the distances presented are excellent guides for determining what image will be recorded, it is always recommended to perform camera tests before principal photography to ensure a practical understanding of the camera limitations.

PARTS	Qty	Item
	1	Spreadsheet program such as Microsoft Excel or Quatro Pro
	2	Sheets of paper
	1	Wallet/ID card protector or laminator

General Instructions

You undoubtedly have a general understanding of focus since you're reading this book. However, film-making requires that focus be understood very precisely in relation to the image you're trying to capture. Focus is more than a point at a set distance which is sharpest to the camera, it's the range of distances in focus that are nearer and farther than that point.

This range of distance is called the *depth of field* (DoF). Objects within the DoF will appear to be nearly indistinguishable focus-wise from the object exactly at the focal point. To properly use a DoF table, you must understand how depth is affected by the various aspects of the camera and lens. Here are three general rules to help you manage DoF:

The greater the...
> *focal distance,*

The shorter the...
> *focal length,*

The greater the...
> *f/stop number,*

> *...the greater the depth of field*

All three of the above factors will increase DoF. Likewise the opposite of these rules will decrease the DoF. To increase the focus distance, you need to move the camera farther away from the subject (without changing the lens). If the camera is moved closer, there will be less depth of field. To decrease the focal length, a wide-angle lens (such as an 18-mm lens) will provide more depth of field than a telephoto lens (125 mm). An increase in the f/stop number (i.e. f22) means a smaller aperture and therefore greater depth of field.

> **TIP ▶** *To easily remember the last two DoF rules, think of a pinhole camera. A pinhole camera has almost unlimited DoF. The tremendous DoF is caused by the camera's very short focal length and perhaps the smallest aperture (largest f/stop number) of all!*

Recognize that it usually isn't practical to increase the DoF by simply changing to a lens with a smaller focal length. There is often a particular framing desired for a shot – an actor's head, for example. If a wider lens is used, there will be more DoF. However, to get the same framing of the shot, the camera must be moved forward, eliminating the DoF gains from the lens size! The same is true if you move the camera away from the subject and cancel those gains by using a longer lens. To solve this problem, change the light level on the subject, so a specific f/stop can be used to match the desired DoF.

When there is too much depth of field, you can decrease the f/stop number to fit your needs. If the smallest f/stop number is too bright for the desired look, use a neutral density filter on the lens. This will allow you to use a smaller f/stop and achieve the limited DoF you desire.

Terms

To properly use a DoF table, you will need to have a basic understanding of four terms: near-focal distance, far-focal distance, hyperfocal distance, and circle of confusion. The near- and far-focal distances simply specify the near and far limits of the depth of field.

Hyperfocal distance is the nearest distance in sharp focus when the lens is focused on infinity. The hyperfocal distance will provide the greatest DoF for a given lens and f/stop. When focused on the hyperfocal distance, everything half the distance to the camera to infinity will be in focus. The hyperfocal distance remains the same for a given lens and f/stop setting regardless of the current focal distance setting.

The *circle of confusion* (CoC) defines the acceptable level of focus for a given media (35 mm negative, 16 mm negative, DV CCD, etc.). I've found that the easiest way to remember the meaning of CoC is to think of a point source of light traveling through the lens of the camera. The CoC value defines the out of focus limit where your eye would be confused and see the point of light as a circle on the imaging medium (negative, CCD, etc.).

To properly create a DoF table, a specific value for the CoC must be used to determine at what point an object is in or out of focus. The COC values for common camera types are listed below:

Imaging medium	CoC value (mm)
35 mm motion picture	0.0254
35 mm still camera	0.025
16 mm motion picture	0.016
$\frac{2}{3}''$ CCD video	0.021
$\frac{2}{3}''$ CCD HDTV video	0.008
$\frac{1}{2}''$ CCD video	0.016
$\frac{1}{3}''$ CCD video (XL1, VX2000)	0.011
$\frac{1}{4}''$ CCD video (GL1, GL2)	0.008

When you construct the tables with the provided instructions, the CoC value for a 35 mm motion picture will be used (0.0254 mm). You can easily change this value to the one that represents the camera you will be using.

Mathematics

If you don't want to understand the equations behind the DoF tables, you can skip this section. It's not critical that you understand the equations to use the tables. The information provided allows you to evaluate the limitations of the formulas. Since there are a large number of real-world factors that affect DoF (lens precision, camera mounting, etc.), there are more complex equations available that have special case calculations to add precision. However, that higher level of precision is generally more important for optical professionals than filmmakers.

To calculate DoF, the hyperfocal distance must first be computed. Hyperfocal distance is the distance that for a given lens and f/stop setting provides the greatest DoF. The equation for calculating this number is listed in the American Cinematographers Manual, 8th edition, as:

$$h = f^2 / (a \star c)$$

In this equation, f is the focal length of the lens, a the aperture setting (f/stop), and c the circle of confusion. The formula for the near-focal plane distance of the DoF is

$$nf = (h\star d)/(h + (d - f))$$

In this equation, h is the hyperfocal distance, d the distance to the point of focus, and f the focal length of the lens. The formula for the far-focal plane distance of the DoF is nearly the same:

$$ff = (h\star d)/(h - (d - f))$$

Using these three equations, all the values needed for the DoF table can be calculated. For a complete account of the background of optics, characteristics of camera optics, and an in-depth explanation of depth-of-field as it relates to cinematography, see the excellent description in the "Optics" section of "Cinematography Theory and Practice" by Blain Brown.

DV cameras

For DV cameras, there are some special considerations with regards to DoF. In contrast to the size of a 35-mm film negative, DV cameras have a small CCD chip that records the video image. Smaller chips have more depth of field than larger chips. This means that limiting the amount of DoF for DV cameras can be tricky. However, achieving deep focus on the average DV camera is a snap!

TIP ▶ *Note that the image quality of the small chips suffers from a loss of resolution caused by diffraction at small aperture sizes (large f/stop numbers). Therefore, even if you want the optimal deep focus image, try to avoid having an f/stop greater than 11.*

Table 18-1 shows some of the most common DV cameras and the sizes of their CCDs. Note that the professional-grade cameras have the largest CCD sizes, therefore allowing them to have the smallest depth of field. Since professional cameras all have interchangeable lenses, they have even more latitude in the choice of DoF.

CCD size	Camera type
$\frac{1}{4}''$	Canon GL1/GL2, Sony TRV900, Sony PD100
$\frac{1}{3}''$	Sony VX2000/DSR-250/PD150, Canon XL1/XL1S, JVC GY-DV300U, Panasonic AG-DVC15/AG-DVX100
$\frac{1}{2}''$	Sony DSR-370L, JVC GY-DV500U/550U/5000U, Panasonic AG-DVC200
$\frac{2}{3}''$	Professional-grade video cameras (dimensions close to a 16-mm camera): Sony DSR-570WSL, JVC GY-DV700WU, Hitachi Z-V1A, Panasonic AJ-D610WA/AJ-D810A/AJ-D900W, AJ-SDX900

TABLE 18.1 *The CCD sizes of popular DV cameras.*

Limiting DoF is one of the key ingredients to giving a DV image the "film look." Most commercial films use DoF very specifically in order to blur background details to let the audience focus on the actors. Consumer-grade DV cameras, constructed primarily for taking family or vacation footage, seek to provide the largest DoF possible, so everything will always be in focus.

There are two practical methods of limiting the DoF with a DV camera: increasing the focal length and decreasing the f/stop. When I shoot DV, I typically use a Sony VX2000 and by zooming in as much as possible, the DoF can be minimized. Unfortunately, this also means that you must back away from your subject which cancels some of the advantage. By using a combination of zooming in and decreasing the f/stop number, decent results can usually be achieved.

While the DoF tables are primarily for use with prime lenses, they're still very useful if your camera has a built-in zoom lens. Check your camera manual and you'll find the upper and lower limits of the zoom lens. Print the proper DoF tables for the upper limit, the median, and the lower limit of your camera.

Construction

The final DoF table will contain a list of hyperfocal distances for each lens and f/stop as well as the near- and far-focal plane distances cross-referenced with focal distances. Since the common camera lenses are listed using the metric system, the table that provides the distances in meters is slightly simpler because no measurement conversion is necessary. The English system tables will be adapted from the metric tables to show the distances in feet.

All the instructions for table construction are presented for use in Microsoft Excel. If you're using another spreadsheet, you may have to make some adaptions. I've tried to use only standard mathematical functions, so they may be adapted to simple spreadsheets that are available on a PDA.

Metric DoF table

Since each table is specific to a single lens and four f/stop values, you'll be probably duplicating the same table across the different areas of the sheet. I find that I can use a 6-point font and it will still be legible. At that point size, eight tables can be fit on a single page with each table having the dimensions of less than a business card. By making each table the size of a business or credit card, you can use a standard clear wallet protector to hold your tables.

Feel free to use the table in a large point size to fit your needs. For easier reading, it is usually best to use a large font size until you've finished construction.

To make a DoF table, follow these steps:

1. Create a new spreadsheet in your spreadsheet program. The default Excel cell designations will be used here with rows numbered (1, 2, 3, etc.) and letters for column headings (A, B, C, etc.).

2. In the top-left cell (A1), enter the number 50. This cell will hold the focal length of the lens that is used in the table.

3. In the next columns, enter the f/stop values of 2, 2.8, 4, and 5.6 while leaving one empty cell between each. Therefore, the value 2 will appear in cell B1, 2.8 in cell D1, and so on.

4. Enter the text "Meters" into cell I1. This text is useful since you can quickly glance at the table and know all the focal distance measurements are denoted in meters.

5. Enter the formula "=A1/1000" in the cell J1. This formula will convert the current lens size into meters (from millimeters) to simplify calculations.

6. In cell J2, place the value of 0.0254. This value is the default CoC value for a 35-mm motion picture. You can change it later to the value required for your camera. For now though, use this value so you can verify the sheet is working properly with the supplied information.

7. Starting the second row, enter the text "HFD" for hyperfocal distance into cell A2.

8. Enter the formula "=(($A\$1^2)/(B1*J2))/1000" into cell B2. This formula calculates the hyper-focal distance by squaring the focal length supplied in cell A1 and dividing it by the current f/stop times the CoC value in cell J2. The cell should show a value of 49.21259843.

9. Select the cell B2 and use the Copy item in the Edit menu.

10. Paste the formula into the cells D2, F2, and H2. You might wonder about the function of the "$" symbol in the formula. Any cell reference preceded by the dollar sign doesn't change when pasted into a new cell. Cell references that don't include the dollar sign automatically adjust to their new location. Therefore, when you pasted this formula into the new cells, the f/stop references changed to use the value above them, while the focal length and CoC references remained constant.

11. Format the cells to display a number with a single decimal place. In Excel, use the Cells . . . option in the Format menu. The formatting options only effect the display and not the actual stored precision, so the calculations will remain accurate. You should now have a row of hyperfocal distances that read 49.2, 35.2, 24.6, and 17.6.

12. Enter the text "FD" for focal distance into the cell A3.

13. Enter "NF" for near focus into the next cell (B3) and "FF" for far focus into the cell after that (C3).

14. Repeat the "NF"/"FF" pattern in the cells D3–I3.

15. Enter the following values (one per cell down the column) in A4–A18: 0.5, 0.75, 1, 1.25, 1.5, 1.75, 2, 2.5, 5, 6, 7, 8, 10, 15, 25.

You've now completed the basic template of the DoF table. It should appear approximately like the one shown in figure 18-2.

All that remains is entering the formulas for the near- and far-distance calculations. Follow these steps:

1. Enter the formula "=(B$2*A4)/(B$2 + (A4−J1))" into cell B4. This is the near-distance equation.

2. Enter the formula "=(B$2*A4)/(B$2 − (A4 − J1))" into cell C4. This is the far-distance equation.

3. Enter the following formulas into the cells D4–I4. Each of these formulas represents the near- and far-distance equations customized to each cell location.

$$=(D\$2*A4)/(D\$2 + (A4-\$J\$1))$$

$$=(D\$2*A4)/(D\$2 - (A4-\$J\$1))$$

$$=(F\$2*A4)/(F\$2 + (A4-\$J\$1))$$

$$=(F\$2*A4)/(F\$2 - (A4-\$J\$1))$$

$$=(H\$2*A4)/(H\$2 + (A4-\$J\$1))$$

$$=(H\$2*A4)/(H\$2 - (A4-\$J\$1))$$

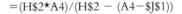

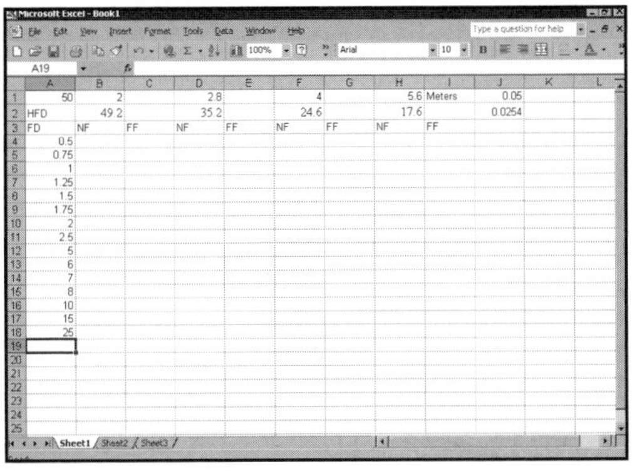

FIGURE 18.2 *Basic template of the DoF table.*

4. Select all the formula cells in that row (B4–I4).

5. Format the cells as numbers that display a single decimal place (see step 11 in previous section).

6. Select the square dot in the bottom-right corner of the selection and drag it downward until the selection area extends to row 18. This should fill all the necessary table cells with the proper variations of the near- and far-distance formulas (see figure 18-3).

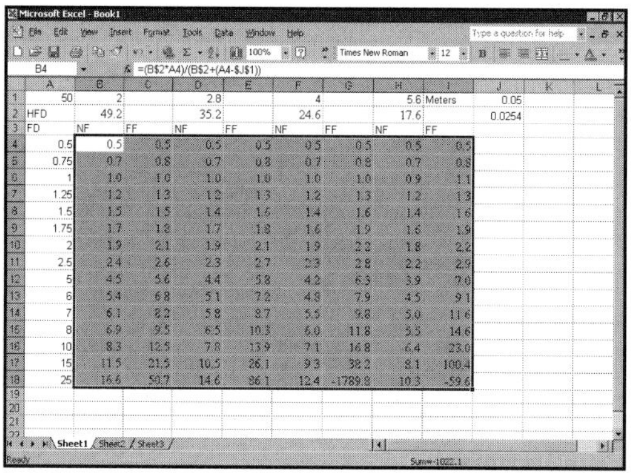

	A	B	C	D	E	F	G	H	I	J
1	50	2		2.8		4		5.6	Meters	0.05
2	HFD	49.2		35.2		24.6		17.6		0.0254
3	FD	NF	FF	NF	FF	NF	FF	NF	FF	
4	0.5	0.5	0.5	0.5	0.5	0.5	0.5	0.5	0.5	
5	0.75	0.7	0.8	0.7	0.8	0.7	0.8	0.7	0.8	
6	1	1.0	1.0	1.0	1.0	1.0	1.0	0.9	1.1	
7	1.25	1.2	1.3	1.2	1.3	1.2	1.3	1.2	1.3	
8	1.5	1.5	1.5	1.4	1.6	1.4	1.6	1.4	1.6	
9	1.75	1.7	1.8	1.7	1.8	1.6	1.9	1.6	1.9	
10	2	1.9	2.1	1.9	2.1	1.9	2.2	1.8	2.2	
11	2.5	2.4	2.6	2.3	2.7	2.3	2.8	2.2	2.9	
12	5	4.5	5.6	4.4	5.8	4.2	6.3	3.9	7.0	
13	6	5.4	6.8	5.1	7.2	4.8	7.9	4.5	9.1	
14	7	6.1	8.2	5.8	8.7	5.5	9.8	5.0	11.6	
15	8	6.9	9.5	6.5	10.3	6.0	11.8	5.5	14.6	
16	10	8.3	12.5	7.8	13.9	7.1	16.8	6.4	23.0	
17	15	11.5	21.5	10.5	26.1	9.3	38.2	8.1	100.4	
18	25	16.6	50.7	14.6	86.1	12.4	-1789.8	10.3	-59.6	

FIGURE 18.3 *Fill the table cells with the proper variations of the near- and far-distance formulas.*

You now have a complete DoF table with measurements in meters. You may have noticed that some of the cells contain negative numbers. This indicates that the focal distance for that combination of parameters is infinity.

To make the chart easier to read, I've used a custom cell format to display negative numbers as the "(-)" text. To use this technique, select all the distance cells in the table. Open the Format dialogue and select Custom for the category. Now type "#, ##0.0; (-)" into the Type text box.

You may also want to add borders and other formatting to make the chart easier to read. You can look at figure 18-1 to see the formatting I find most legible. Be sure to save your spreadsheet when you're done!

English measurement DoF table

Now that you have the tables constructed, adapting them to use feet instead of meters is fairly straightforward. Because the lens size and CoC measurements are given in millimeters, the table has to first convert these values to feet (or fractions of a foot) before the computations can be completed.

To adapt the metric DoF table to display the distances in feet, follow these steps:

1. Open the metric DoF table and Save As . . . to store it as a new file. You don't want to corrupt your original.

2. Enter the text "Feet" into cell I1.

3. Enter the formula "=(A1*3.28)/1000" in the cell J1. This formula will convert the current lens size into feet (from millimeters).

4. Enter the formula "=J2*0.00328" in the cell J3. This formula will convert the CoC value held in J2 into feet (from millimeters).

5. Enter the formula "=(J1^2)/(B1*J3)" into cell B2. This formula calculates the hyperfocal distance. The cell should show a value of 161.4.

6. Select the cell B2 and use the Copy item in the Edit menu.
7. Paste the formula into the cells D2, F2, and H2.
8. Enter the following values (one per cell down the column) in A4–A18: 3, 4, 5, 6, 7, 8, 9, 10, 12, 15, 20, 30, 40, 50, and 100.

That's it! Your table should appear like the one shown in figure 18-4.

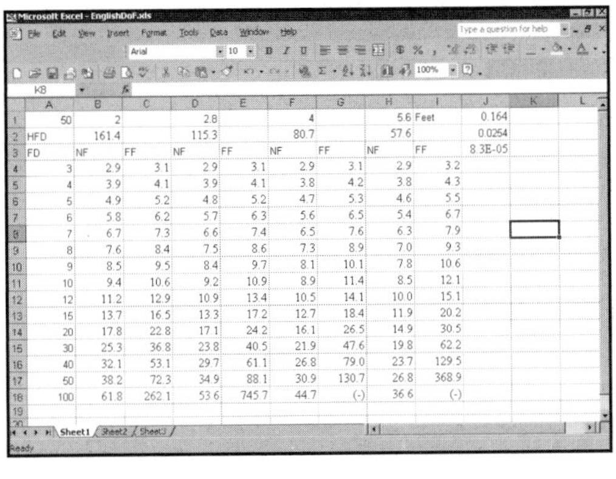

	A	B	C	D	E	F	G	H	I	J
1	50	2		2.8		4		5.6 Feet		0.164
2	HFD	161.4		115.3		80.7		57.6		0.0254
3	FD	NF	FF	NF	FF	NF	FF	NF	FF	8.3E-05
4	3	2.9	3.1	2.9	3.1	2.9	3.1	2.9	3.2	
5	4	3.9	4.1	3.9	4.1	3.8	4.2	3.8	4.3	
6	5	4.9	5.2	4.8	5.2	4.7	5.3	4.6	5.5	
7	6	5.8	6.2	5.7	6.3	5.6	6.5	5.4	6.7	
8	7	6.7	7.3	6.6	7.4	6.5	7.6	6.3	7.9	
9	8	7.6	8.4	7.5	8.6	7.3	8.9	7.0	9.3	
10	9	8.5	9.5	8.4	9.7	8.1	10.1	7.8	10.6	
11	10	9.4	10.6	9.2	10.9	8.9	11.4	8.5	12.1	
12	12	11.2	12.9	10.9	13.4	10.5	14.1	10.0	15.1	
13	15	13.7	16.5	13.3	17.2	12.7	18.4	11.9	20.2	
14	20	17.8	22.8	17.1	24.2	16.1	26.5	14.9	30.5	
15	30	25.3	36.8	23.8	40.5	21.9	47.6	19.8	62.2	
16	40	32.1	53.1	29.7	61.1	26.8	79.0	23.7	129.5	
17	50	38.2	72.3	34.9	88.1	30.9	130.7	26.8	368.9	
18	100	61.8	262.1	53.6	745.7	44.7	(-)	36.6	(-)	

FIGURE 18.4 *The completed DoF spreadsheet.*

Multi-table pages

While you can print out the individual tables for each lens and set of f/stops, I've found it most convenient to create a page with eight tables on a single page. Note that when you copy and paste the table into a different section of the spreadsheet, you'll have to adapt the formulas to reference the proper cells.

In figure 18-5, you can see the general layout that I've used. Make the first two tables on the left side (A1 and A2) for the same lens size (18 mm) with the full range of necessary f/stops. For example, have table A1 include f/stops 2, 2.8, 4, and 5.6 while table A2 includes f/stops 8, 11, 16, and 22. Do the same with tables B1 and B2, only this time use a different lens size (i.e. 35 mm).

Follow this same pattern with tables A3 and A4 for the 25-mm lens and tables B3 and B4 for the 50-mm lens. When you have the page filled with the eight tables, print them out. Cut the page into four rows and fold them in half so, for example, tables #1 and #2 are back to back (see figure 18-6).

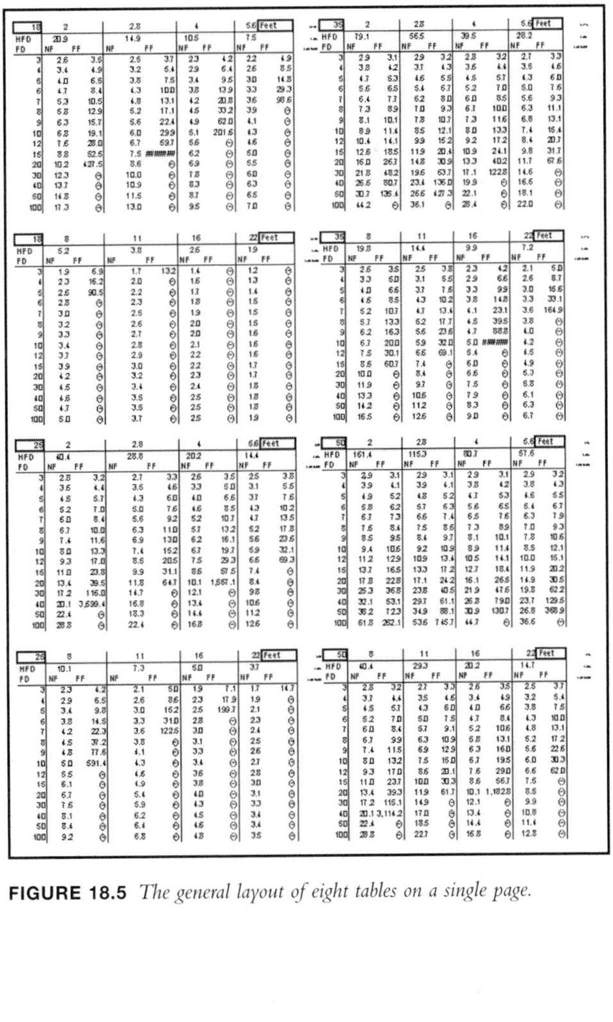

FIGURE 18.5 *The general layout of eight tables on a single page.*

Each set of back-to-back tables can then be slid into a clear plastic wallet ID protector slot. When complete, you have a wallet protector with a full range of lens sizes for easy reference. For more loose-leaf reference, you can use clear ID badge protectors that are available at office supply stores.

You can customize the tables based on the camera kit you will be using. It's been my experience that a low-budget 35-mm shoot will have a lens package that includes around six prime (see Glossary) lenses. The focal lengths of a standard 35-mm kit may include 18, 25, 35, 50, 85, and 135 mm lenses. If you find out what lenses will be part of your camera package, you can print out the necessary tables to fit the ones you'll be using.

FIGURE 18.6 *Cut the page into four rows and fold them in half.*

The focal distances that I've suggested to put in the table have been very useful in my experience. If you have access to the lenses you'll be using, however, you can make tables that are customized to the lens distance markings. For the feet table, these markings may include the distance (in feet) of 2, 3, 5, 6, 8, 10, 15, 20, 25, 30, and 40.

Suggestions

Here are a few suggestions when dealing with focus:

- **Get a fiberglass tape measure (see figure 18-7)** These inexpensive measures are the same type used by professional ACs to determine the distance from the camera to the focal point for focus pulling. There is usually a small metal bolt or flange on the camera where the end of the tape is hooked on.

FIGURE 18.7 *Use a tape measure and test focus at specific positions.*

The other end is run out to the actor's mark. If your camera doesn't have such a bolt or flange, measure from the general location of the image plane – in a DV camera that would be the CCD. Check your manual for the approximate location of the CCD within the camera body.

- *While professional-grade prime lenses use a linear focus scale so that you may change the focus between one spot and another evenly, many zoom and consumer-grade lenses do not* Manufacturers of consumer-grade lenses often provide greater control of focus at the near end of the focus scale. The focus settings are more closely clustered where the lens focuses near infinity. Be sure to do tests with the lenses you will be using before the shoot.

- *It's a good idea to perform focus tests prior to a shoot* Set up the camera at one end of a long hall. Place an object such as a chair (with its back facing the camera) in the hallway at a specific distance. Set the camera so that lens is at the same height as the back of the chair (any up or down tilt will affect the distance to the lens). Focus the camera on the top back of the chair. Using a tape measure, test focus at specific positions as you move the chair away from the camera. Match the focal distances that you have used for your DoF tables.

Slate

Applications

Whether you've ever been on a professional set or not, I'm sure you've seen the boards that snap together before yelling action. The slate or clapper is almost an icon of moviemaking. You can easily construct a slate (see figure 19-1) for your own use whether you'll be recording to film or direct to video.

While there are many reasons a slate is used, a few of the most important include:

- **Editing information** Written on the slate is information specifying the film roll (or DV cassette number), the scene number, the take, and other information that can be imaged for later use during the post-production process.

- **Start and end of a take** On a continuous roll of film or tape, clapping the slate provides a way to designate the separations between takes. Without it, there's often confusion when a take begins and ends.

- **Audio track alignment** The loud clapping sound generated by the slate puts a distinct audio spike on the sound track. This spike can be aligned with the frame that shows the slate boards coming together in order to properly synchronize the audio and the image.

When shooting using film, audio isn't recorded on the film itself. The slate provides the invaluable service of allowing the sound to be synced to the film. With the standardized use of DATs, a digital slate actually synchronizes with the sound equipment and displays a digital readout of the proper SMPTE time code for the rolling tape. Although a digital slate can be expensive to rent, the use of such a slate can save time (and therefore money) in the post-production phase of the film.

FIGURE 19.1 *Construct a slate for film or video.*

On DV production, I've found using a slate to be critically important. You may wonder why it's necessary, since DV records sound directly onto the tape with the video. I can't tell you the number of times that the import processing for DV footage messes up the sync between the sound and the picture. Without the slate image and clack, you can spend many tedious hours re-aligning the audio track to your picture. With the clack, it's a simple process to adjust the timeline until the audio spike from the slate aligns with the proper frame of the clacking action.

> **NOTE→** If the director wants to start a new take immediately and there's no time to do the slate, then it's common practice to do a *tail slate*. When you tail slate, it means that you clack the slate after the take is complete. To be able to recognize a tail slate, the slate is held upside-down thereby making it obvious to the editor that the slate information is related to the scene just completed. After you do the tail slate, you might want to quickly turn the slate over and hold it for a second, so the editor can easily read the information.

It's traditionally the job of the second AC (assistant camera) to use the slate to designate the take. On a smaller film, try to assign the slate to a single person. If the job is given to anyone that's available at a given moment, you'll find that often a fair amount of the slate information is inaccurate. A large amount of invalid information can make editing more difficult than no slate information at all.

PARTS	Qty	Item
	1	Dry-erase board
	2	Pieces of hardwood 11″ × 2″ × 1″
	1	Dry-erase marker
	1	Piece of duct tape
	1	Piece of cheese-cloth
	1	Small hinge

Construction

To make a slate, you'll need a small dry-erase board. The board provides a useful surface where you can clearly write the necessary filming information and update the details between takes.

Cut the dry-erase board to the proper size with a saw. The board I used already had a frame, so I simply cut it in half. This provided me with two slates, each with the top was left open.

Measure and cut two pieces of hardwood board to match the length of your dry-erase board frame. One piece will be mounted on top and the other will be attached to the first one with the hinge. You can use softer wood if it is more available (or your budget is limited). Hardwood is nice because it creates a crisp, clear sound when the two pieces are clacked together.

Mount the first piece of hardwood board to the top of the dry-erase board (see figure 19-2). With the frame of the board, I used two wood screws (one on each side) to affix the hardboard. You might notice that since I didn't pre-drill the holes, the hardwood split when I screwed into it. I suggest you learn from my mistake and pre-drill the holes where the screws will be used.

Once the basic frame is complete, add stick-on letters and lines to record the necessary information for each take. In figure 19-3, you can see the proper placement of the various data. The stickers provide convenient slots where the proper details can be recorded.

The details recorded actually vary from slate to slate. However, the most standard information includes the film roll (or DV cassette number), scene number, take, current director and DP, date, designation of day or night shoot, and whether the scene is MOS (without sound) or not.

FIGURE 19.2 *Mount the first piece of hardwood board to the top of the dry-erase board.*

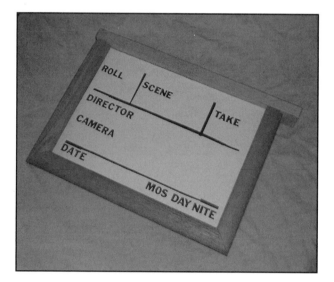

FIGURE 19.3 *The proper placement of the various slate information.*

NOTE→ The famous legend behind the term "MOS" is that the German director Erich Von Stroheim would say "Mit out sound" when he didn't need the sound recorded. The word "mit" meaning "with" in German. The initials MOS began as an industry joke, but quickly became the standard through use.

Mount the hinge on the first and second boards (see figure 19-4). You can see that I chose to mount the second board perpendicular to the first board. This makes it much easier to grasp the top board and avoid painfully trapping your fingers when you clack the slate.

Before you mount the second board onto the hinge, try a test clack. The arm should swing freely and easily. If not, you may have to change the mounting of the hinge until it works properly.

FIGURE 19.4 *Mount the hinge on the first and second boards.*

Once the slate is complete, you'll want to tape a small piece of cloth to the back end of a dry-erase marker. Like an eraser on a pencil, this small piece of cloth is very convenient to wipe away old details on the board. The slate information needs to be quickly and constantly updated. I've found that facial swab pads are the most effective, but you might try cotton balls or a small piece of cloth (such as cheesecloth) for more flexibility.

Suggestions

Here are a few suggestions to help you make a better slate:

- ***Add striped contact paper to the top and bottom boards*** You've probably seen the diagonal striped pattern on professional slates. These stripes make it much easier to see the exact frame where the slate clacks together. You can add these stripes with contact paper or even strips of white tape.

- ***Add color bars*** Many slates have color bars that allow the post-production staff to precisely calibrate the color palette to the original footage. I couldn't find a cheap source of these special color bars, so I didn't include it in the basic construction. Use professional renderings of the color bars; otherwise any hand-printed bars would cause more problems and confusion than clarity.

Gaffer Introduction

III

Applications

The gaffer, also known as the chief lighting technician, is responsible for setting up the lights to achieve the visual effect desired by the Director of Photography (DP). A gaffer is also responsible for providing the electricity (via generator if no house power is available) and controlling it on set. The gaffer manages one or more electricians under him to achieve these ends.

The gaffer is essentially the head electrician. Electricians are also commonly known as juicers or sparks. Their responsibilities include placing and focusing lights, setting up distribution of electrical power, and often providing power for other departments such as make-up lights, wardrobe irons, etc.

On a guerilla shoot, the positions of gaffer, key grip, electrician, and grip may all be rolled into one. For the purpose of this book, the following chapters will provide tools and information to fulfill the tasks of gaffers and electricians. You'll learn the items that go on an electrician's tool belt. You'll construct various lights and light controllers. You'll learn techniques used to achieve particular lighting effects.

Even if you have access to professional equipment, you'll find that some hand-made items, such as the soft box, have advantages over their professional equivalents. Even if you don't intend to build your own lighting equipment, I would suggest that you at least skim the following chapters. I've included many lighting and electrical techniques that I've learned in my working time in Hollywood. This information will probably help you if you are at all involved with the lighting aspects of moviemaking.

> **NOTE→** It is important to recognize that a set electrician is *not* a fully qualified electrician such as those who perform house wiring. A movie electrician knows all about power distribution relating to solving filming problems and rarely does he need to know the theory and general knowledge behind use, installation, and maintenance of general power systems. Likewise a certified electrician typically has no training in the specialty equipment used by a film crew.

Suggestions

Here are a few general suggestions for working as a gaffer:

- *Test all your equipment* Whether you're obtaining your equipment from a rental house or building it yourself, be sure to test every important piece before production begins. With rental houses, you're responsible for everything being brought back in working order. You don't want to find out when you return it that an item never worked – and you have to pay for it. With your own equipment, you need to make sure that the time in storage since its last use has not rendered it inoperable.

*   ***Obtain spare bulbs before the shoot*** Bulbs burn out. Make sure you're not caught empty handed when they do.

*   ***Label bad equipment immediately*** If a cable burns or a light stops working, label it as "BOL" or burn out. If you don't do this when it happens, you may forget to do it later. That means you'll either attempt to use the bad unit again (dangerous or simply counter-productive) or you'll have to search for it when it's time to replace it.

*   ***Treat electricity with respect*** Late at night after a long day, activities of plugging and unplugging power tend to become cavalier. It's at this time that most accidents happen. Using electricity is perfectly safe if handled properly. Regularly remind yourself and your crew to pay attention and work in a safe manner.

*   ***Ask your DP about the film's look*** All the neat lighting effects in the world will be worthless if they don't show up in the final footage. You have to know what the final desired effect must be in order to accommodate this. Maybe the DP is using a special post-production technique or special lenses (such as anamorphic lenses) and you have to overlight each shot. You need to know about this, so the light and electrical packages you choose will be able to handle the extra load.

*   ***Carry extra C47s clipped to your shirt sleeve*** C47s, otherwise known as clothespins, are generally used to hold gels or other diffusion to the barn doors of lights. You won't look like a professional electrician if you don't have at least a few of these hanging from your shirt sleeve at all times.

*   ***Buy the handbook*** If you're serious about working in the movies, whether as a gaffer or an electrician, buy Harry C. Box's "Set Lighting Technician's Handbook" (ISBN 0-240-80257-8). It provides complete information on everything from lighting equipment to generators and is considered the electrician's bible on most sets. This book is very well written and bursting with real-world information and advice.

Electrician's Belt

Applications

A lighting technician or "electrician" manages all the power requirements and lighting on the set. To be effective, an electrician must carry a number of tools and items with him/her at all time. Most commonly, these tools are secured on a belt (see figure 20-1), so they are conveniently available to the electrician, but don't get in the way. Simply knowing the use of all the items on a professional electrician's belt will help you evaluate what you do and don't need for your own equipment.

Typically, an electrician or grip assembles the items on a belt over time, swapping out less useful items for more useful. Weight of individual tools is an important consideration since a belt that is too heavy won't be worn. If you have a heavy item on your belt that you seldom use (such as a color meter), it's better to keep this item in your car or somewhere generally handy rather than toting it around with you all day.

FIGURE 20.1 *Tools secured to the electrician's belt.*

> **TIP ▶** *When I wear my electrician's belt, I always wear a normal belt through the loops of my jeans. All the weight of the belt tends to pull down on the top of your pants and the tool belt typically doesn't stay well positioned on your hips. The normal belt holds your pants in place and generally makes wearing the electrician's belt much more comfortable.*

Belt Equipment

Many of the items are attached to a belt with belt loops, clips, and carabineers. The items you use most often are located on the side of the belt of your pointing hand (if you're right-handed, then your right side). Commonly, the most used tools are the multi-tool, flashlight, work gloves, permanent marker, and circuit tester.

Leatherwork gloves

A good pair of leatherwork gloves is perhaps your single most important piece of equipment. Electricians often handle hot lights and powered electrical lines, so a pair of gloves provides basic insulation from heat and electricity. They also keep hands clean when coiling numerous dirty cables. Grips likewise use good work gloves since they are constantly lifting, moving, and re-positioning equipment – often fairly heavy.

Gloves serve the following primary purposes:

- Prevents your hands from slipping on equipment when your hands are sweaty or when the equipment is slick.

- Allows you to save wear and tear to your hands. Gloves can prevent cuts, pinches, and abrasions that make continuing to work with your hands difficult or unpleasant.

- Prevents buildup of grime and dirt. Coiling cables that have been sitting on the ground can be one of the dirtiest jobs on a set. By wearing a simple pair of gloves, you can avoid several hand washings per day.

- Provides basic insulation against heat and electricity.

When shopping for a pair of gloves, it's best not to skimp on the price. While you don't need the most expensive ones, a cheap pair of gloves will wear out quickly and you'll have to replace them anyway. Also, avoid buying gardening gloves as they will never fit your hands snugly. They make a task as simple as tying a knot in thick rope with your gloves on nearly impossible. At the time of this writing, a good pair of leather gloves can be purchased for about $15–20.

Multi-tool

Multi-tools are prized by electricians and grips alike. A multi-tool (see figure 20-2) has numerous tools that fold out from the handles. They generally provide a pliers, a knife, a saw, a small ruler, a lanyard, a Phillips head and flat screwdriver, and, of course, the ever important bottle opener.

With multi-tools, you'll thank yourself later if you invest in a decent one. Cheap multi-tools are the lowest price unbranded tools and are often included in a set with other tools or even given away free with such things as electric razors. These tools use low-grade metal, so the blades never sharpen well and can even bend or break off (which I know from experience). Also, a decent multi-tool features a lock for the individual implements when you fold them out of the handle. You don't have to worry about the screwdriver folding in when you get it at the wrong angle. Almost none of the cheap tools include this locking feature.

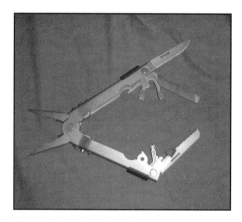

FIGURE 20.2 *A multi-tool has numerous tools that fold out from the handles.*

Use your best judgment when purchasing a multi-tool. Usually the middle of the road in the price range is ideal. Remember that you're going to be carrying this around all day long. The top-of-the-line models usually have a large array of features you'll never use and suffer from bulk and weight inconveniences.

Both Leatherman and Gerber are excellent brand names for a multi-tool. Most electricians that I know prefer Gerber because the pliers of the tool can be opened with a single hand. For example, if you're standing on a ladder and need to remove a hot scrim from a light, you can keep a solid hold on the ladder with one hand while opening the pliers for use with the other.

6″ or 8″ crescent wrench

A crescent wrench is very useful since there are constantly bolts that need tightening on equipment, scaffolding, and other various frames. A small crescent wrench doesn't add too much weight to your belt but comes in very handy. The best choice is to find the smallest crescent wrench that can still fit a $\frac{3}{4}''$ bolt.

Screwdriver

Carrying a flat and a Phillips head screwdriver can be very handy, especially when you need to open a light housing to change a bulb. I often use the tools built into my multi-tool, but the handle and the length of the screwdriver makes a full screwdriver a godsend for difficult-to-reach places and stubborn screws.

Instead of two full screwdrivers, you might carry a single driver with a reversible tip. These lighten the amount of weight you need to carry and some electricians swear by them.

Small portable flashlight

A small light that takes two AA batteries can be a lifesaver. If the sun goes down and you haven't finished packing your equipment and have no work light, the light can guide your way. There are often times even on a sound stage when you need to examine something such as a cable route or dimmer setting when you can't turn on the house lights.

Utility knife

Cutting material as varied as rope, foam core board, or diffusion gels can sometimes seem like a full-time occupation. Having a handy utility knife can make these chores a snap. The one I use has blade that can be broken off when the current blade gets dull.

Needle nose pliers

Most commonly a part of pliers can be used to adjust a hot part on a light such as barn doors or a scrim. If you have a multi-tool, you'll already have a pliers. If not, make sure you're carrying one.

Tape measure

Electricians are always cutting gels or bounce boards to fit a particular size. With a tape measure, you can quickly measure the area and cut to an exact length. Likewise, grips often have to construct custom-sized rigs or determine whether a piece of equipment can fit within a limited amount of space. A 10–15-ft tape measure is plenty for most jobs, so you can buy a small plastic one for lightweight and ease of handling.

Scissors

You might wonder with a knife in the multi-tool and a utility knife, why you want need to carry a scissors. It's actually more of a convenience than a necessity. However, when you need a straight edge cut on a gel and you're in a hurry, there's nothing better than a trusty scissors.

To make a straight cut with a knife, you typically need a flat surface such as a desk while with a scissors, no accessories are necessary. Scissors are also excellent for cutting a good edge on a piece of mason line so that it doesn't fray before you seal the end.

Permanent marker

A permanent marker is excellent for labeling cables, writing on gels, marking lengths for cutting, and a million other uses. The standard medium-tip Sharpie pens are the most popular. The only real disadvantage to carrying a marker is that once people know you have one, they'll be constantly borrowing it from you!

Pen and paper

Carry a pen for writing things down. You never know when you'll suddenly be sent down to the expendables store to get a long list of supplies that the gaffer rattles off the top of his head. There are also numerous times when you have to record a list of numbers for a task such as balancing a generator where it's easiest to perform the calculations on paper to prevent any mistakes.

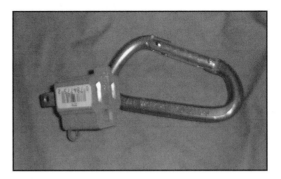

FIGURE 20.3 *A cheater adapts a two-prong groundless wall or cable outlet to receive a three-prong grounded cable.*

Cheater or ground plug adapter

This little device (shown with a carabineer in figure 20-3) will adapt a two-prong groundless wall or cable outlet to receive a three-prong grounded cable. Very useful if you're shooting in a location such as old house or business where you need power.

Cube tap

You'll find that you use cube taps constantly on small films. A cube tap (shown with a carabineer in figure 20-4) splits a single outlet into three. Carry two or three of these with you. Try to find the compact ones as they are much more convenient to carry with you. You may have to search a few different stores to find them, but it's definitely worth it.

    I usually carry a cheater, a cube tap, and a circuit tester stacked for convenience (see figure 20-5).

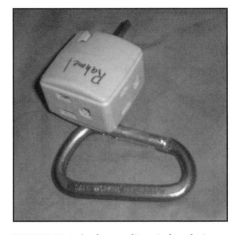

FIGURE 20.4 *A cube tap splits a single outlet into three.*

Gaffer's tape

Gaffer's tape is a special type of tape made by Permacel. It is a matte black (non-reflective) that has a strong sticking surface that generally doesn't leave a bunch of gunk behind (like duct tape).

    Gaffer's tape can be quite expensive (around $9 per roll at the time of this writing). If you're working on someone else's production, let the production supply it. With your own production, you can substitute duct tape (disadvantages: shiny surface causes reflections and leaves gunk behind) or black paper tape (disadvantages: tears easily and weaker sticking surface).

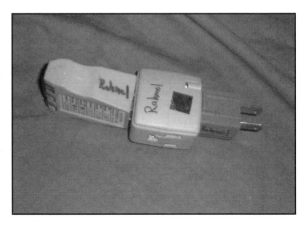

FIGURE 20.5 *A cheater, a cube tap, and a circuit tester stacked for convenience.*

The roll of tape is usually attached to your belt with sash cord or medium size rope. I found this item called Speedclip at the local home improvement warehouse that's really great (see figure 20-6). If someone needs tape, you can just pull it off your belt and hand it to them.

Wire cutter/stripper

Essential if you're wiring for a light that will seen in the frame (called a practical) or doing a re-wiring job on something like a light. Some electricians can easily strip a wire with a pair of cutters. I prefer to carry a separate stripper where you can set the gauge of the wire and then quickly and perfectly strip as many pieces as you need.

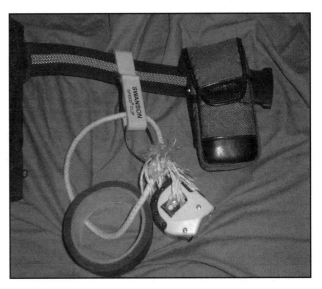

FIGURE 20.6 *A SpeedClip attaches a roll of tape to your belt.*

3/8″ wrench

This wrench is optional unless you'll be working a lot with generators. Some older generators use connectors called lug adapters for hooking the cables to the generator. A $\frac{3}{8}''$ wrench is the standardized size of the bolt that tightens the lug adapter to the generator bus bar.

Allen wrenches

Allen wrenches are optional unless you'll be working on a professional set. These wrenches are used to tighten the screws in junior stands and spider boxes.

Baseball cap

The baseball cap is an optional piece of equipment that you can easily clip to your belt. If you're working in the sun all day, it can provide your head with much needed shade. When you're rigging a gel or diffusion to a really bright light, you can pull down the bill of the cap to shield your eyes from most of the glare.

Multimeter/continuity tester

A typical multimeter has several functions. It can be used to test the voltage on a line. It can also test if the line is live. Typically a meter is used to check voltage (120, 208, or 240 V) or voltage drop. You can also use it to test for broken connections of flipped circuit breakers.

The continuity tester is used to check for shorted connections and determine if a light bulb or fuse is dead. The tester generally provides an audible beep when a connection is completed.

A clamp-on meter allows the meter to read the existing amperage that is running through a power line.

A generator has several power phases (usually three). These phases must be kept within 50 A of each other. If the power drain difference is greater than this for any length of time, the generator may malfunction and long-term damage can occur. It is traditionally the responsibility of the Best Boy Electric to make certain the generator remains in balance.

In figure 20-7, you can see the Amprobe multimeter that I use. Sitting next to it is the optional clamp-on, so when I'm assigned to regulate the generator I can check it easily. There are much more inexpensive meters available, but this meter is really nice because it's small and light making it easy to carry around.

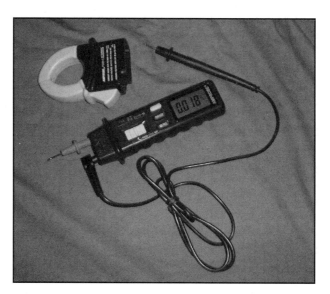

FIGURE 20.7 *A multimeter used to test the voltage on a line.*

Circuit tester

A circuit tester (see figure 20-8) is a small piece of equipment that's plugged into a wall socket or extension cord (stinger) and will tell you if the cord is live and/or wired properly. If the tester tells you that the neutral and hot leads are reversed, plugging an item into the socket may electrify the item housing which can result in a socket to some who touches it.

A circuit tester is essential if you work on location. Often you will be plugging lights into wall outlets that you've never used before. If the light goes out, it could be the light, a failed extension cord, or a circuit breaker that's tripped.

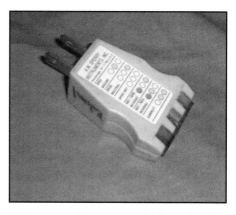

FIGURE 20.8 *A circuit tester will tell you if a cord or socket is live and/or wired properly.*

TIP ▶ *When on location, the first thing an electrician usually does is locating the circuit breaker. That way if any of the breakers flip, they can be quickly reset and shooting can continue.*

I've found that once I locate the breaker box, I quickly jot down on my pad of paper any of the switches that are set to the off position. When a breaker trips, I can go right to the breaker box and check my pad. Immediately I can then determine which switch now in the off position was tripped.

Light meter

Of the electricians, typically only the gaffer (head lighting technician) carries a light meter (see figure 20-9). However, if you are on a small set or if you want to learn to use a light meter, it's a good idea to have one. Be careful, though, not to get in the way when metering or upset the gaffer by your metering.

The light meter usually has its own pouch to keep in safe. Many gaffers also carry a spot meter (such as a Minolta Spot Meter F) as well. My meter has a spot attachment that I can use if spot metering becomes necessary.

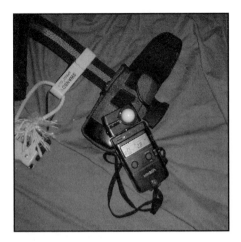

FIGURE 20.9 *A light meter.*

Color meter

It is unusual for anyone but a gaffer to carry a color meter (see figure 20-10) because they are specialized and often fairly expensive. The color meter tells you the color of the light from a particular light source (for more information on color of light, see Chapter 24).

The color meter typically provides readings of two different color types: blue/red and green/magenta. The blue/red reading is most commonly used. It will tell you the blue (daylight) or red (tungsten) of the current light. The meter will indicate what type of filter can be used on the camera lens to correct for a type of film (if shooting daylight with tungsten film or vice versa).

Old analog blue/red meters can be purchased inexpensively. If you buy one of these meters, check if a local photo store will rent you a full digital meter for a day. At the time of this writing, a meter could be rented for $20 for a day. Since color meters tend to drift over time, this will help you check your analog meter and make sure it's providing the correct information.

The green/magenta reading is the reading I've seen most often used on a set. Fluorescent lighting has a green spike that can show up as a greenish cast on your film footage. By checking the green/magenta of the light source, a magenta gel can be placed on the source to eliminate the green tint.

FIGURE 20.10 *A color meter measures the color of the light from a particular light source.*

Line sensor

The line sensor is handy, but optional. It's a small device that if held next to a cable will tell you if there's live current running through it. It detects this by the cable's magnetic field. There are two instances where

I find this tool very useful. If you have a bunch of extension cords (stingers) lying in a straight run, you can quickly determine which are being used and which are inactive.

The other place it's useful is around generators. A surprising number of older generators have the circuit breaker on a different side of the generator than the electric bus bars. They also have no indicator light to tell you that they're live! A quick sweep with the line sensor can assure you that the breaker has been cut before you reach into disconnect any high-voltage cables.

Suggestions

Here are a few suggestions to help you:

- *Don't leave your belt lying around* You've got a lot of expensive equipment on your belt – equipment other production people might love to have. Theft on a set is hardly unknown, so be careful. Equipment that is portable enough to be easily carried is also easy for someone to lift and hide.

- *More pockets are good* With the military belt I'd also purchased a rifle clip pouch/grenade holder. I used to carry my light meter in it, but now carry a small digital camera and use the clip of one of the grenade holders to hold a pair of a scissors. I can't tell you the number of times I've been stopped on a set by an ex-member of the armed forces who wants to share an interesting story about when they used a similar pouch in the service – so the pouches are also a good conversation piece.

Softbox

Applications

Soft or diffused lighting is one of the most natural and warmest ways to light actors. Soft light wraps around facial features for a sensual, glowing look. Hard or direct lighting, the opposite extreme, creates angular shadows that can highlight facial blemishes. Outside of stylized effects lighting (such as in horror or film noir movies), hard lighting is rarely used for illuminating actors. Figure 21-1 shows how traditional direct light is very harsh and unforgiving.

In figure 21-2, I'm sitting in the same position, but the hard light has been replaced by a soft one. Shadows are less distinct, so the face looks smoother. Soft light is more in line with how we see people in real life. A type of light fixture called a softbox provides the warm, soft light. The softbox is another one of those tools used extensively by professionals to achieve a film "look" while many guerilla filmmakers are unaware of its importance in creating attractive footage.

The softbox you'll build in this chapter uses up to six standard light bulbs cast through diffusion material to cast soft light. Most softboxes are constructed as a large solid box that can be thrown on the grip truck for transportation. Since I don't own a grip truck and I assume you don't either, I've made this softbox (see figure 21-3), so it can be folded up and transported in a car. It can then be quickly re-assembled on location for use.

FIGURE 21.1 *Traditional direct light is very harsh and unforgiving.*

FIGURE 21.2 *A softbox provides warm, soft light flattering to actors.*

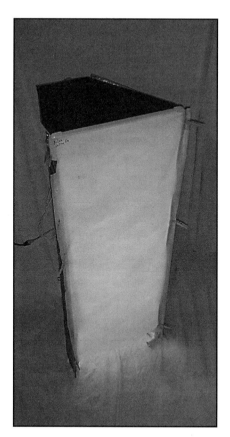

FIGURE 21.3 *This softbox can be folded up and transported in a car.*

When I had the privilege of working on a film with Janusz Kaminski (the cinematographer of such beautifully lensed films as Saving Private Ryan, AI, Schindler's List, Minority Report, etc.), I watched him extensively use a pair of softboxes for a majority of his close-up work. Observing him arrange and position the softboxes demonstrated to me the critical importance of effective use of a softbox in achieving superior footage.

PARTS	Qty	Item
	6	Ceramic light sockets
	4	$\frac{1}{2}''$ pipe clamps
	4	$2\frac{1}{2}''$ length eyebolts, $\frac{1}{4}''$ 20, 2″ shaft
	2	$\frac{1}{2}'' \times 1''$ threaded steel pipe
	1	$\frac{1}{2}'' \times 8''$ steel pipe

General Instructions

The softbox operates on the simple principle of placing multiple light sources behind a large piece of diffusion material to make a single, large light source. The more a light source approaches a single point, the sharper the shadows. For this reason, a spotlight uses a single point source bulb to create very direct light and sharp shadows. A long fluorescent tube, on the other hand, casts very soft shadows (although fluorescent light doesn't generally look very good on film).

Construction

Before you begin construction of your softbox, you'll need to carefully select the materials to achieve the results you desire. The diffusion material and the bulbs are the two most important pieces of the softbox since together they will determine the type of light your softbox will shine.

The diffusion can be chosen from any number of materials. I know a DP who uses a very thin table-cloth on his softbox to great effect. Note that the thicker the material used the less light that can escape to light your scene. Some of the mostly commonly used materials include white silk, bleached muslin, or plastic diffusion such as rolux (see Chapter 28 for a large list of possible diffusion materials).

WARNING→ Since the distance from the light bulbs to the material is about 2 ft, creating a fire hazard is unlikely. However, make sure that you don't use any diffusion material that is flammable since there is the heat of six light bulbs involved.

The light bulbs you use depends on your budget, the power limitations of your set, and the availability of different types of bulbs. Ideally, it would be best to use 100 W, tungsten-balanced, film-grade photofloods. These bulbs are specifically made for use on film and are light balanced for the specific tungsten frequency in Kelvin degrees. The problem with these bulbs is that they are expensive and short-lived when compared with other bulbs.

Because of budget limitations, I usually outfit my softbox with 75 or 85 W spotlight bulbs (see figure 21-4). The extra heat generated by the 85 W bulbs makes me avoid them unless I really need the extra light. Using the 75 W bulbs gives me about 450 W of lighting power before it's reduced by the diffusion. These bulbs

FIGURE 21.4 *My softbox is outfitted with 75 or 85 W spotlight bulbs.*

are in the same section as the floodlight bulbs at a hardware store. In contrast to floods, these lights direct all the light forward rather than diffusing before even hitting the softbox.

NOTE→ When you buy the bulbs, be sure to check the amount of lumens listed on the box. The lumen figure tells how much light is actually emitted from the bulb. You'll find that all bulbs are not created equal. A soft white bulb will put out far fewer lumens than a clear bulb. Since we are going to put diffusion on the front of the softbox, using soft white bulbs would put the light through diffusion twice. While you won't get softer light, you will waste a large amount of your electricity without any better results.

The most important aspect of choosing a bulb is to make sure that all the bulbs are of the same type. Like fluorescents, incandescent bulb color temperatures will vary dramatically among various manufacturers. Make sure that all the bulbs are of the same type and brand so that, whatever the color temperature, it will be consistent for all the light emitted from your softbox.

Additionally, pay special attention to the wattage of the bulbs you use. The light bulb sockets are generally rated to only handle a particular level of bulb. Also remember that all the bulbs will be going through a single power strip so the draw will be cumulative. Therefore, if you were to use 250 W bulbs, 1500 W would be drawn through the power strip – generally more than it could handle.

Light-socket board

The backbone of the softbox is the light-socket board that contains six wired light sockets (see figure 21-5). In addition to holding the lights, this board will provide the support to mount the reflection panels and the diffusion material.

For the power cords that you'll need for each light, you can buy the plugs and wires and create them by hand. I found that it was cheaper to buy an extension cord that could handle the power I needed. It was then a simple process to cut off the electrical socket end, strip the wires, and connect them to the light socket. You should make the cords short so there isn't a great deal of excess cord hanging that will get in the way or might be tripped over. As you can see from figure 21-6, each light socket has a separate plug that is routed into the power strip.

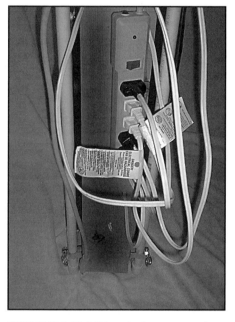

FIGURE 21.5 *The light-socket board contains six wired light sockets.*

FIGURE 21.6 *Each light socket has a separate plug that is routed into the power strip.*

Using the power strip in this manner has several advantages over wiring a switch for each light:

- *Electrical hazard reduction* The light sockets only include two leads (neutral and hot) without a ground. If during construction the builder were to reverse these leads and a switch was put in line, a potential electrical hazard would be created since the housing may carry the current even while switched off. Since all power is cut at the properly wired and grounded power strip, this isn't a problem.

- *Much cheaper than individual switches* Putting a switch box on every light socket can quickly become expensive. Using the power strip, one or more lights can be simply unplugged from the strip.

To construct the light-socket board, follow these steps:

1. Drill six holes down the board, each about $\frac{3}{8}''$ in diameter or large depending on the size of the power cords that will have to go through them (see figure 21-7). To know the proper horizontal position to place the holes, take a light bulb socket and see where the hole will have to be so that the power cord can be attached to the light socket, yet the socket can sit flat against the board. For the sockets I used, this meant that the center of the hole was 1″ from the edge of the board. Vertically, these holes should be evenly spaced, although you should leave extra space on the bottom so a light bulb is not sitting too close to the floor.

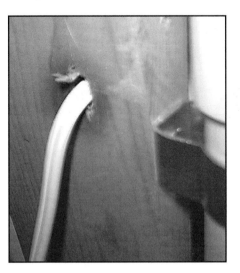

FIGURE 21.7 *Drill six holes down the board, each about $\frac{3}{8}''$ in diameter or large.*

2. Feed a power cord through each hole.

3. Attach each power cord to a light socket. You should be able to simply screw the leads of the wires into place in the light sockets.

4. Screw the two mounting screws on each light socket into the board to fix the socket in place.

> **NOTE→** Before unplugging any of the individual lights, make sure you first turn off the power strip. Then you may remove the desired plug and turn the power strip on again to re-strike the remaining lights. Failure to turn off the strip before removing a plug can result in potentially dangerous electrical arcing.

Reflector panels

The reflector panels can be made out of a variety of materials. For my panels, I used foamcore board since it's stiff but also light. If foamcore is too expensive, you can use standard cardboard. Go to a store that sells appliances and ask if they have any spare washer/dryer or refrigerator boxes that you can have. The sheets from those boxes will be large enough to create the necessary panels.

Cut two panels, each with a size of 51″ × 23″. Once the panels are cut, you need to affix sheets of aluminum foil (shiny side out) to act as the reflecting material (see figure 21-8). I've found that the easiest method of attaching this material is to staple it right to the cardboard. Since the foil will be on the inside of the softbox, you don't have to worry much about the foil getting beat up or ripped once it's in place.

Reflector panel frames

With the panels complete, you'll need to create the frames to which you'll attach them. These panel frames are special because they provide most of the structural integrity for the softbox. Each frame will be made out of a rectangle of PVC pipes.

First, you'll need to cut two pieces of PVC to the length of 50″ and two more pieces to the length of 22″. The long pieces will be used to give the panel height; the short ones will provide width. Use three 90° bend joints for the top-right, the bottom-right, and the bottom-left corners. For the top-left corner, use a T-joint with the open end of the T facing vertically.

Once you have one panel frame complete, use the same instructions to construct the second panel. Make sure you use PVC cement on the joints of the panel frames. Since the softbox will be moving around a great deal, people generally tend to lift the box by grasping the panels. Without the joints cemented, the box will come apart under the weight when lifted.

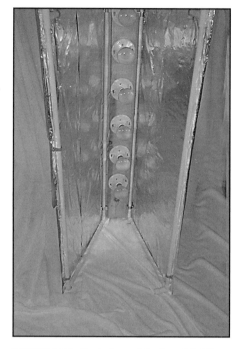

FIGURE 21.8 *Attach sheets of aluminum foil (shiny side out) to the panels to act as the reflecting material.*

Attaching the panel frames

You'll need to mount the panels to the panel frames. You'll want to mount the panel to the frame such that the bottom of the panel is nearly flush with the bottom of the frame. This will allow the light fixture to sit on the frame instead of the bottom of the panel. The front of the panel should overhang the frame about 1.5″ as shown in figure 21-9 so that the diffusion material can be attached to it. Note that the panel on the second frame is mounted in the opposite way, so the two reflector panels face each other.

Mount two of the $\frac{1}{2}$″ brackets along the top (see figure 21-10). Mount the third $\frac{1}{2}$″ bracket on the side PVC pipe near the bottom of the frame. To attach the final corner, I simply punched a hole in the panel and used a piece of

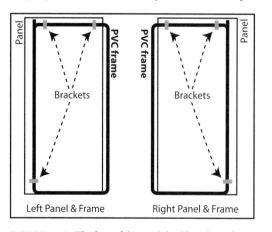

FIGURE 21.9 *The front of the panel should overhang the frame about 1.5″.*

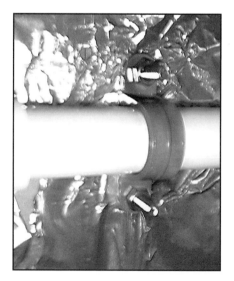

FIGURE 21.10 *Mount two of the $\frac{1}{2}$″ brackets along the top.*

wire to bind it to the frame. You may use a piece of rope or whatever is thin and small enough such that the frame is boosted.

Once the panel frames are complete, you'll need to attach them to the light-socket board. This is accomplished by screwing conduit hangers into the light-socket board (see figure 21-11). Two hangers should be mounted 4″ away from the top of the board and two mounted 4″ away from the bottom of the board.

Once the conduit hangers are in place, spread each hanger open and slide the back PVC pipes of the panel frame into it. Replace the bolts that come with the conduit hangers with the eyebolts so that they may be tightened and released by hand (see figure 21-12).

FIGURE 21.11 *Screw the conduit hangers into the light-socket board.*

FIGURE 21.12 *Replace the conduit hanger bolts with eyebolts.*

Creating the frame stabilizers

Although the panel frames are attached, they are like unstable wings that can open and close to any angle. Since you'll be cutting your diffusion material to an exact size, the panels need to remain a precise distance apart. For this reason, you'll need a frame stabilizer (see figure 21-13). After you've transported the softbox, you'll simply need to spread the panel frames to the proper width to snap the stabilizer in place to have the perfect size for the diffusion material.

Create two frame stabilizers: one for use and another for transportation (see figure 21-14). The smaller one will hold the panel frames apart the proper distance, so they don't collapse on the light bulbs during transport.

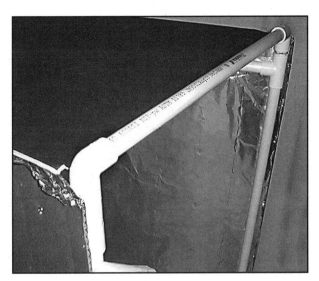

FIGURE 21.13 *The frame stabilizer will ensure that the panels remain a precise distance apart during transportation.*

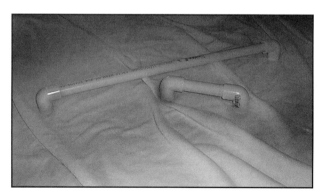

FIGURE 21.14 *Create a long frame stabilizer for light for use and another short one for transportation.*

Before you create the stabilizers, you will need to make the PVC stubs that the stabilizers will be placed onto. Simply cut two lengths of PVC pipe to 2″. Use PVC cement to cement one length into each open T-connector on the ends of the panel frames (see figure 21-15). To create the stabilizers, follow these steps:

1. Cut lengths of PVC pipe to 19″.

2. Use PVC cement to glue the 90° bends onto each end of the PVC pipe. Note that the bends on each end of the pipe should be pointing in the same direction, so they can properly snap into place on the panel frames.

3. Repeat the above steps on a PVC pipe with a length of 4.5″. When you're finished, you'll be able to use this stabilizer to make the softbox transport-ready (see figure 21-16).

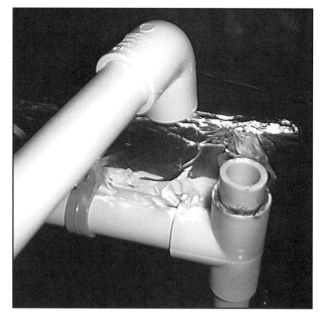

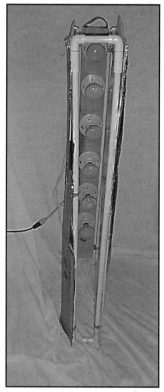

FIGURE 21.15 *Use PVC cement to secure a length into each open T-connector on the ends of the panel frames.*

FIGURE 21.16 *The stabilizer makes the softbox transport-ready.*

Adding the top reflector

With the panels in place, you can now cut a piece of cardboard or foamcore for the top reflector. Put the long frame stabilizer in place and then position a piece of cardboard over the top of the softbox. The cardboard should extend from just behind the top stabilizer to just short of the light-socket board.

Use a pen to mark the lines along the bottom of the cardboard. Now cut the cardboard along the marked lines. You should now have a piece that fits over the top of the softbox (see figure 21-17). Attach aluminum foil to the panel using the same method that you attached it to the side panels.

With the panel complete, it's a good idea to attach it to one of the side panels so it can be easily swung into place. Punch two holes in one side of the top panel, one at the front and one at the back. I then used small pieces of wire to attach it to the top of the panel. You can use fishing line, twine, or whatever is most convenient.

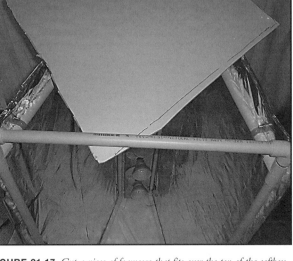

FIGURE 21.17 *Cut a piece of foamcore that fits over the top of the softbox.*

Adding the diffusion material

Your softbox is almost ready for use. The diffusion material is really the easiest part to attach. You'll need a piece that measures 24″ × 50″. Simply use six clothespins (three per side) to attach the material to the overhang lip at the front of the softbox (see figure 21-18). This arrangement makes it easy to setup and break-down the softbox.

This arrangement also allows you to have several different types of diffusion material and choose the best one for a particular job. You can even stack the materials or add a gel to change the color of the light, although you'll be cutting down the amount of output illumination.

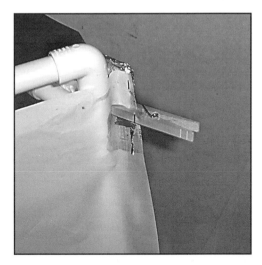

FIGURE 21.18 *Use clothespins to attach diffusion material to the overhang lip at the front of the softbox.*

Suggestions

Here are a few operating suggestions to help you get the best use from your softbox:

- **Set the softbox on a table** Since the softbox is so light weight, if you need higher placement, simply set it on a table. I've found that end tables are about the right height to boost the soft light if your subject is standing.

- ***Buy spare bulbs***   Since it is important for all the bulbs to match, it might be a good idea to buy two spare bulbs at the time you purchase your primary bulbs. That way you're assured that the spares are the same type and brand, and might even come from the same production lot.

- ***Use the softbox on objects***   The soft light put out by this fixture is ideal for caressing the curves of numerous objects from guns to glasses of wine.

- ***Adjust your color balance***   Recognize that normal tungsten light bulbs put out light that generally has a slightly yellowish tint. If you're working on film, you might consider putting a $\frac{1}{4}$ CTB gel over the front of the light to bring the light a little more into the range of tuned tungsten (3200 K). If you're working with video, make sure to adjust your white balance for the proper color capture.

Coffee-can Spotlight

Applications

A spotlight can provide an interesting visual separation of an object from the background. Most guerilla filmmakers don't have access to sophisticated light fixtures such as those made by Dido. Perhaps the flood to spot settings on a Fresnel light is just what you need, but rental or purchase of these lights may be too expensive for your budget. Using a combination of a spotlight bulb and a cylinder to limit the angle of the beam (see figure 22-1), you can create a fixture that is essentially a low–budget spotlight.

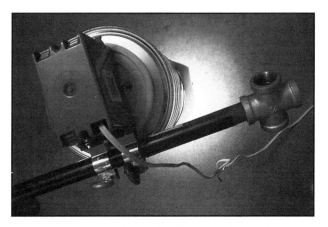

FIGURE 22.1 *A spotlight bulb and a coffee-can cylinder limit the angle of the beam.*

> **NOTE→** A Fresnel lens is actually no different in its function from a magnifying glass. The Fresnel pattern was discovered to have the same focusing capabilities of a traditional magnifying lens, but comparatively uses only a small fraction of the glass. Therefore, a Fresnel lens provides the same functionality, but is lighter, more durable, and can be manufactured more cheaply than a traditional lens.

The spotlight can be used against a dark background for a master-of-ceremonies type presentation or the distinct circle can highlight one particular item by making it brighter than the ambient environment. A spotlight can provide elegant accent highlights to shiny props and scenery. Numerous shots can be enhanced with the little extra polish a well-deployed spotlight can bring.

	Qty	Item
P A R T S	1	85 W spotlight bulb
	1	Empty 3-pound coffee-can
	1	Electrical box
	1	Electrical cord
	1	Ceramic light socket
	2	$\frac{1}{2}''$ conduit hangers
	2	$2\frac{1}{2}''$ eyebolts, $\frac{1}{4}''$ 20, 2″ shaft
	2	$1\frac{1}{2}''$ 6–32 bolts w/nuts
	2	$1\frac{1}{4}''$ bolts w/nuts
	1	Small roll of 18″ aluminum flashing
	3	1″ wood screws

General Instructions

Spotlights generally provide the most benefit when they are contrasted with a darker background. This may require you to substantially lower the ambient light level to allow the outline of the spotlight to be distinct. Multiple spotlights can be focused on a single point to create dramatic exposure blow-outs and visual distinction.

The spotlight bulbs (see figure 22-2) are found in the same lighting section as floodlights. Even the packaging often appears nearly identical with the exception of small labels that indicate "Spot" or "Flood". Even the bulbs themselves appear almost identical, although a floodlight produces a diffuse wide-angle cast of light, while a spotlight projects most of the light forward in a narrow cone.

FIGURE 22.2 *Spotlight bulbs are found in the same lighting section as floodlights.*

For best construction, I recommend using a ceramic light socket. While they're heavier than the plastic sockets, they're much better at insulating the heat. Since the housing of the light can get fairly hot, you don't want the plastic melting and creating a potential fire hazard. The ceramic is also better at insulating the electrical connections in a variety of extreme conditions.

> **NOTE➔** Although track lighting fixtures can be used for inexpensive spotlights, these fixtures generally lack the lighting power required because of the low level of the maximum-watt bulbs they can use. However, if used judiciously, track lighting can be effectively mounted on a lighting stand (or C-stand) for excellent portable accent lights.

Construction

An empty 3-pound coffee-can will provide the main body of the spotlight. A coffee-can provides a good foundation for a light fixture because it is cheap, easy to cut with tin snips, and offers the proper size to fit a light bulb inside without danger of touching the sides.

Begin construction by turning the coffee-can over so the closed end is facing up. Take the light socket and place it head down on the bottom of the can. Use a marker to draw a circle around the socket. This will be your guide to cut a hole large enough to insert the head of the socket into the can. Remove the socket and then use a marker to indicate a point approximately at the center of the drawn circle (see figure 22-3).

Take an ice pick and punch through the marked center point. Make several other holes surrounding it (see figure 22-4) in order to allow you to easily use tin snips to cut out the hole. Use whatever pattern you think will be most convenient.

Use tin snips to cut from the center outward until you have the entire circle open (see figure 22-5). The hole should be large enough for the head of the light socket to be inserted. Test it and widen the hole if necessary. Don't worry about sharp edges since they won't be exposed once the light socket is mounted in place.

The electrical box will be used as the mount for the spotlight. Run the

FIGURE 22.3 *Use a marker to make a point at the center of the drawn circle.*

FIGURE 22.4 *Make several other holes surrounding the center point.*

bare wire ends of the electrical cord into the box using one of the exterior holes. Attach the leads of the cord to the light-socket terminals (see figure 22-6). I've cut off one end of an extension cord here to create an inexpensive electrical cord.

FIGURE 22.5 *Use tin snips to cut from the center outward until you have the entire circle open.*

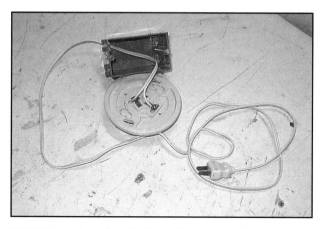

FIGURE 22.6 *Attach the leads of the cord to the light-socket terminals.*

Insert the head of the light socket into the hole of the can. Push an ice pick through each of the two smaller screw holes on the light socket and punch holes into the can (see figure 22-7). These holes will be used with nuts and bolts to secure the socket to the can. Make sure that the holes aren't too close to the edge of the cut-out circle or there may not be enough metal to support the light mount.

Since the electrical box will become the foundation of the spotlight, we'll need to attach conduit hangers to the box to provide a swivel mount to put the light on a stand or bar. In the top of the electrical box close to the edges, drill two $\frac{1}{4}''$ holes (see figure 22-8). You can hold a conduit hanger in the proper place and use a marker to determine where to put the holes.

Use the $\frac{1}{4}''$ nuts and bolts to secure the two hangers to the electrical box (see figure 22-9). Make sure that the bolts are tightened well because they will be inaccessible once the light socket has been mounted on the box.

FIGURE 22.7 *Push an ice pick through each of the two smaller screw holes.*

FIGURE 22.8 *In the top of the electrical box, drill two $\frac{1}{4}''$ holes.*

Secure the light socket to the electrical box by tightening the top screw on the box in the outer hole of the socket (see figure 22-10). If your electrical box is the right size to properly fit the light socket, insert and tighten the second screw as well.

Put the head of the socket through the hole in the coffee-can bottom. Insert a $1\frac{1}{2}''$ screw with a washer into each of the two holes you punched in the can earlier (see figure 22-11). The washers prevent the screws from pulling through the thin coffee-can metal.

FIGURE 22.9 *Attach two conduit hangers to the electrical box.*

FIGURE 22.10 *Secure the light socket to the electrical box with the top screw in the outer hole of the socket.*

Place nuts on the outside ends of the screws and tighten them (see figure 22-12). Once you have these nuts secure, there should be no play between the electrical box and the coffee-can. It should feel like a single solid light fixture.

To make sure that everything is working properly, screw the light bulb into place (see figure 22-13). Plug the fixture in and see if the spotlight works. The spotlight should create a clear, if wide angle, beam of light.

FIGURE 22.11 *Insert a $1\frac{1}{2}''$ screw with a washer into each of the two holes.*

FIGURE 22.12 *Place nuts on the outside ends of the screws and tighten them.*

The spotlight should shine properly, but the length of the coffee-can does little to acceptably limit the angle of the spotlight. You'll need to add an extra length of flashing to provide enough shield length. The longer the length of the shield, the smaller the angle of the light cast.

The best material for the shield is aluminum flashing. You'll find it in the roofing and insulation section of the hardware store. Thin rolls of flashing are widely and cheaply available (see figure 22-14). I've found that flashing with a width of 18" provides a good, fairly intense beam. Much wider flashing is available, however, if you need a narrow light angle.

Unplug the electrical cord and remove the light bulb from the fixture so it won't be damaged during the shield construction. Wrap a length of flashing around the coffee-can and mark it so there is approximately 1" overlap (see figure 22-15). Use tin snips to cut the proper length along the marked line.

Wrap the flashing around the can making sure that end of the flashing extends a few inches beyond the top of the can. The can will act as structural support for the flashing while you use a wood screw to

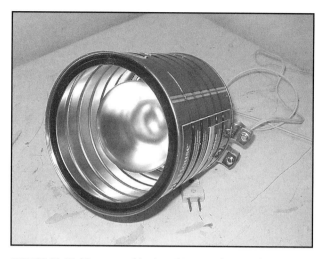

FIGURE 22.13 *To test everything is working properly, screw the light bulb into place.*

FIGURE 22.14 *Thin rolls of flashing are widely and cheaply available.*

FIGURE 22.15 *Wrap a length of flashing around the coffee-can and mark it, so there is approximately 1″ overlap.*

secure the outer end. Use a threaded wood screw to drive through both ends of the sheet at the overlap (see figure 22-16) making sure that the screw doesn't pierce the can.

Slide the flashing cylinder to the end of the coffee-can and screw another wood screw through the flashing into the can (see figure 22-17). Put another wood screw on the opposite side to firmly hold the flashing to the can. If the flashing seems at all wobbly, use two more screws on the perpendicular axis to make sure that the flashing is completely secure.

The spotlight is now basically complete. Put the conduit hangers around the C-stand arm (see figure 22-18) constructed in Chapter 32 or to any $\frac{1}{2}″$ PVC or steel pipe. Add eyebolts to secure the fixture to the stand and allow you to tilt it as needed.

FIGURE 22.16 *Use a threaded wood screw to drive through both ends of the sheet at the overlap.*

FIGURE 22.17 *Slide the flashing cylinder to the end of the coffee-can and screw through the flashing into the can.*

FIGURE 22.18 *Put the conduit hangers around the C-stand arm for mounting.*

Suggestions

Here are a few operating suggestions to help you get the best use from the spotlight:

- ***Create a vent on the light*** The amount of heat generated by even a 75 W lamp can be substantial if left on for a long period of time. You might consider drilling a few holes in the rear of the can that will act as vents for the heat. Having vents will extend the life of the light bulb and ensure that the housing remains cool.

- *Change the distance to change the light circle* The distance of the light from the subject it's casting upon will determine the diameter of the light circle. Increasingly the distance will increase the size. If you wish to increase the distance of the light but decrease the size, extend the front shield to contain the spread. Likewise, for a large diameter, decrease the length of the shield.

- *Carry an extra flange and short length of pipe* Spotlights are often needed on film to shoot down onto a subject. Stands that can obtain the proper height are difficult to come by and transport. It is, however, often possible to drill wood screws into an overhead beam. That would allow you to quickly mount a flange with a screwed $\frac{1}{2}''$ pipe that can act as a simple stand for your spotlight.

- *Paint the inside of the can and flashing* The spotlight presented doesn't have a completely sharp edge to the cast light. One of the reasons for this blurriness is the reflectivity of the coffee-can and the flashing. While this reflectivity makes the light more powerful, it also somewhat blurs the cast edges. Therefore, if you want a sharper cast outline, paint the inside of the light with matte black paint to eliminate the reflections. Use the paint available for BBQ grills, so you can safely avoid any fire hazard.

Projector Spotlight

Applications

A common slide projector (see figure 23-1) provides a brilliant, focused light source that's excellent for cinematic effects. The projector can be used in a film for a variety of uses from spotlighting a master of ceremonies at a circus to "beaming-up" a human being to the alien ship. The sharp edges of the projected light can give a scene a very distinctive look.

Slide projectors are excellent tools for the guerilla filmmaker because they are available inexpensively. You can find used slide projectors on various online auction sites (such as eBay) for about the price of a portable CD player. The projectors often include one or more spare bulbs. I found a working projector at a thrift store for less than the cost of a single music CD. Camera equipment stores carry slide projectors as well, but they tend to be more expensive.

FIGURE 23.1 *A common slide projector provides a brilliant, focused light source.*

Before you buy a projector, be sure to determine the brightness of the light that will be projected. Most common slide projectors use a 300 W bulb, although 750 W projectors are available. As with most light applications, the brighter the light, the more flexible it will be for your use. You can always place a scrim or diffusion filter to lower the level of a bright light, but you can't augment the level of a light that's too dim for your needs.

General Instructions

Adapting the slide projector for interesting effect can be an extremely creative challenge. You'll have to use the light in conjunction with the rest of your lighting package for the best results. Then you'll have to decide if you want to modify the pattern of light thrown by the projector. You can experiment with these dynamics until you achieve interesting and compelling visual results.

Using the spotlight

A spotlight light source will be distinctive only if it is surrounded by contrasting darkness (see figure 23-2). Therefore, think about how the rest of the in-frame objects and scenery will need to be lit. Generally you'll want to use the slide projector when the ambient light in the surrounding areas of the frame is low enough to allow the camera to clearly pick up the distinction.

However, you'll probably want to be sure that the surrounding areas have at least a minimum level of ambient light. Otherwise your spotlighted subject will appear surrounded by a sea of blackness. Setting a slight level of ambient light can provide a low-contrast image of the background that is often more pleasing for the frame.

While a sea of blackness may be suitable to your artistic considerations, your camera may frustrate your intentions. Most MiniDV cameras do a poor job of capturing black as black and instead

FIGURE 23.2 *A spotlight will be distinctive only if surrounded by contrasting darkness.*

render black as a washed out dark gray. Be sure to shoot test footage to determine if you can achieve the effect you want before the time during principal photography when the spotlight will be used.

TIP ▶ *While it is difficult to obtain a sea of blackness in-camera with a MiniDV camcorder, it isn't difficult to obtain these results in post-production. You can use the Levels filter in a product such as Adobe After Effects to crush the blacks. For more information, see the information regarding crushing blacks in Chapter 54.*

When making adjustments to the camera, remember that the color temperature of a slide bulb will be in the range of a standard incandescent bulb. Your white balance should be tuned to the area of projected light to make sure that the images are recorded in the proper color range.

Creating projected shapes and cookies

A slide projector casts a frame of light that has the same horizontal/vertical ratio as a slide. You can change the projected shape by creating slides that you've custom made to show a particular shape (such as a circle). Creating these custom slides is as easy as cutting the desired shapes out of white and black cardboard.

To create projection shapes, first you'll need a 35 mm camera. Just about any 35 mm camera will work, although a camera that allows you to manually control the exposure settings works best. By manually setting the exposure, high-contrast pictures can be taken to provide more distinct shapes on the final slide.

Slide film is available at most stores, including discount vendors such as Target and Wal-Mart. Slide film developing is less common, so you may have to go to a specialty film-processing store that can send it out.

To create the best slides, recognize that when placed in a projector, white areas of the slide will allow light to shine through, while black areas will block the light. Therefore, a white circle against a black background will generate a slide that projects a focused light circle. Create a variety of patterns so that you can use all the frames on a roll of 24 exposures. Once you have the slide film processed, you can test to see what shapes work best for your desired application.

Beyond simple shapes to change the shape of the light beam, you can make a slide to simulate a cookie or gobo. I've created several slides to represent the shade of leaves from a tree. Any shapes or designs used for a cookie can be replicated by a slide. When you make your slides, take two or three pictures of the same design so that when one slide becomes damaged or faded, you can switch to another without having to retake the picture.

Textures for cookies work best if they consist of high-contrast black and white shapes. A simple black and white texture can be made by placing texture material (such as pinto beans) on white poster board. A 35 mm camera with automatic exposure settings may have problems getting this type of slide to photograph properly. If there is a setting for photographing against a background of snow (for outdoor pictures), that setting will probably work best. For optimum results when using the snow background setting, photograph your texture outdoors using natural light.

Suggestions

Here are a few suggestions to help you get the best use of the slide projector:

- *Bring extra bulbs* The bulbs of a slide projector burn very hot and therefore have a relatively short life. If you are going on location, be sure to bring extra bulbs in case the bulb you're using burns out.

- *Don't leave a single slide showing for a long time* There can be a huge amount of time between takes when the slide is just burning in the projector. Use this time to shut off the slide projector and rest the slide. Long exposure to the bright projector bulb can fade your slide or worse – burn it. Therefore, when not filming, either turn off the projector or change slides at regular intervals.

- *Load a carousel by similarity* Most slide projectors have a carousel that holds all the slides. Load the slides in order of similarity. For example, the oval light shape slide follows the circle slide. With this ordering, you can advance between the different slides to quickly test a variety of effects.

Rotating Socket Light

Applications

Movie lights can be challenging to obtain and difficult to transport. When shooting documentary or guerilla style, lights are also time-consuming to handle and put into place when needed. On the other hand, using lights that are already at the location may prove frustrating to control since they are not made to be directional. That's where this little trick comes in handy.

By using two simple twin light sockets (see figure 24-1), you can instantly turn almost any standard lamp fixture into a directional light. You can then control the lighting quickly even in difficult locations.

FIGURE 24.1 *Using two simple twin light sockets to turn a standard lamp fixture into a directional light.*

	Qty	Item
PARTS	2	Bulb splitters
	1	Light bulb
	1	Lamp fixture

General Instructions

Get two twin light sockets (see figure 24-2) that split a single socket into two. These are inexpensive and can be found at almost any home warehouse or hardware store. Use tape such as gaffer tape to seal up one socket on each splitter. Covering the sockets with tape will prevent anyone from accidentally sticking a finger or other object into an open, unused socket. Twist one socket into another and add the light bulb to the top socket (see figure 24-3).

You can now screw the base socket into any ordinary lamp fixture and you have a fully directional light. By twisting one socket within the other, you can position the direction of the light at a wide variety of angles without having to move the lamp. This twin socket light can be particularly effective when used as a rim or backlight in a ceiling light socket.

WARNING→ Make certain the lamp fixture where you're placing the socket is rated to handle the wattage of bulb that you plan to use. Many fixtures can only safely handle 60 W bulbs and lighting a bulb of greater wattage can pose a fire hazard risk.

FIGURE 24.2 *Get two twin light sockets.*

FIGURE 24.3 *Twist one socket into another and add the light bulb to the top socket.*

Squeezer

Applications

A squeezer is a small box that has a dimmer control combined with an on/off switch (see figure 25-1). Squeezers are excellent for light control situations since they can be set to a particular light level and turned off and on while retaining that selected level. A squeezer can be used with most incandescent lights and many other electric devices (such as barber poles, old tape players, etc.).

The most common use of a squeezer is to control the light levels of practical lights (lights seen by the camera). This can be particularly useful to adjust the level of a practical to minimize lens flare. Since practicals are typically more for set decoration than determining the general light level of the scene, the squeezer can help adjust the practicals to match the ambient light level provided by the rest of the lighting package.

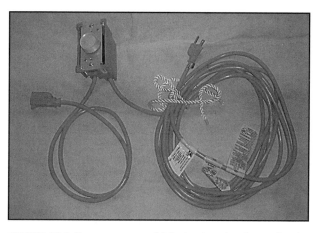

FIGURE 25.1 *Squeezers can control light situations since they regulate the illumination level of an attached light.*

	Qty	Item
PARTS	1	Dimmer control
	1	Extension cord
	1	Wall mount socket box
	4	Twist-on electrical caps

General Instructions

A squeezer works by increasing resistance (thereby decreasing the voltage) on the power being sent to the device. The decrease in voltage results in a dimmer light or a slower motor movement (in a barber pole, for example). To be confident the squeezer to work properly, make sure the device that it's attached to is a direct AC device. If the device converts the AC current (coming from the wall outlet) into DC current, the effects of decreasing the voltage may be uncertain.

> **NOTE→** A squeezer cannot be used on fluorescent lights because of the nature of the fluorescent design. To dim a fluorescent light, you will need a special type of dimmer known as a *variac dimmer*. Variac dimmers are available for rent from most film equipment rental houses and generally come in types that handle a maximum load of either 1000 or 2000 W.

For incandescent lights, the general rule is that for every 10 V decrease in power, the color temperature will decrease 100 K (see Chapter 38 for an explanation of lighting temperature). Therefore a 120 V tungsten light that provides a color temperature of 3200 K will shine at 3100 K when the voltage is dimmed to 110 V. Likewise, the light will shine at 3000 K when the voltage is decreased to 100 V and so on.

A squeezer can be used dynamically within a scene for a variety of effects. Manually rotating the dimmer back and forth quickly with a light gelled to yellow or orange can effectively simulate the flicker of a campfire. Gelled to blue, it can simulate the flicker of a television. After you've created a squeezer, you'll find numerous uses for everything from simulating lighting flashes to imitating the passing of car headlights.

Construction

A squeezer can be assembled in less than half an hour with a screwdriver and a pair of wire-cutters. Since none of the parts require soldering, be sure that the various wires are securely mounted to provide good connections. Be aware that generally a dimmer comes with three twist-on caps to secure the wires and this project requires four. Therefore, you'll have to obtain an extra cap to properly complete the project.

The complete wiring diagram is shown in figure 25-2. The extension cord and dimmer should use the industry standard color scheme for the wires (green = ground, white = neutral, and black = hot). If the wires in your equipment don't follow this standard, make sure that you wire the box properly, so you don't have any electrical problems.

> **TIP ▶** *When building new equipment that uses electricity, it is usually a good idea to test them on an outlet with a breaker already on it. That way, electrical problems don't throw a distant breaker, blow a fuse, melt cable, or cause other problems. You can usually find an electrical outlet with a built-in breaker in your bathroom. These outlets have two buttons (usually one black and one red) labeled "Reset" to reset the breaker when it gets thrown. Also, there are some power strips that have breakers included.*

To create a squeezer, follow these steps:

1. Cut the extension cord into two pieces. Cutting the cord will create two cords: one with a plug end (we'll call the plug cord) and another with a socket end (we'll call the socket cord). I always cut my cord in uneven pieces with the socket cord being a length of about 2′ and the plug cord taking up the rest. That way the squeezer can be kept close to the item it will be controlling and the rest of the cord becomes an extension. Some people prefer the socket cord to be longer, so the item can be controlled distantly. The choice is yours.

2. Strip the wires on the cut sides of each cord.

3. Feed the stripped ends of each cord through the input holes into the wall outlet box (see figure 25-3).

4. Wind the white (neutral) lead of the plug cord to the white lead of the socket cord and twist on the cap (see figure 25-4). Be sure to twist the wires together in the clockwise direction and then twist the cap on in the same direction. Matching the twist directions will help the cap be most secure.

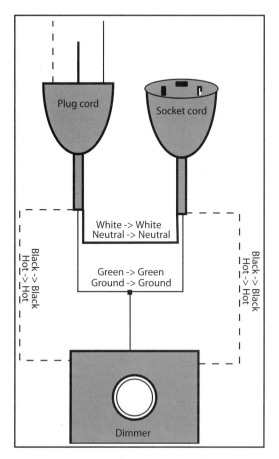

FIGURE 25.2 *The complete squeezer wiring diagram.*

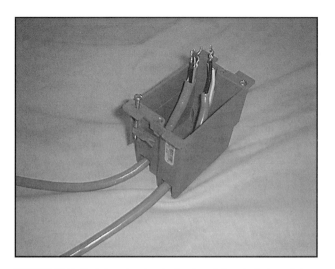

FIGURE 25.3 *Feed the stripped ends of each cord through the input holes into the wall outlet box.*

5. Twist together one black (hot) lead of each cord to a black lead on the dimmer and put on the cap. The black lead is the hot lead, so this wiring puts the power through the dimmer for control of the voltage. Be sure to screw the caps on the twisted leads to bind the connection and insulate it from the environment.

6. Twist together all three green (ground) leads and twist on the cap.

7. Push all the wire down and screw the dimmer plate to the wall outlet box (see figure 25-5). There should be two screws included with the dimmer that will hold the plate firmly in place.

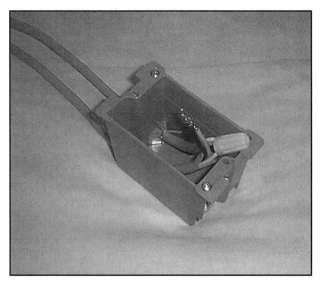

FIGURE 25.4 *Wind the white lead of the plug cord to the white lead of the socket cord and twist on the cap.*

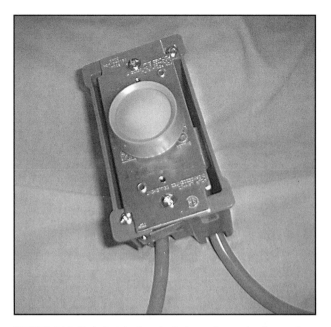

FIGURE 25.5 *Push the wire down in the box and screw the dimmer plate to the wall outlet box.*

To use the squeezer simply plug the plug cord into a wall outlet or powered extension cord. Plug the controlled device (such as a light) into the socket cord. Have fun!

Suggestions

Here are a few operating suggestions to help you get the best use of the squeezer:

- *Label the maximum wattage of the dimmer* Dimmers are certified for a maximum amount of power they can handle by a rating in watts (a normal household dimmer is rated at 600 W). It is a good idea to place a label right on the faceplate to indicate the maximum number of watts that can be drawn through the dimmer. This will prevent someone from using a light or other device that exceeds the rating which might create a fire hazard or other problems.

- *Use the squeezer only on accent lights* Any change in voltage will alter the color frequency of the light emitted from the bulb. Therefore, you don't want to use the squeezer on a key light as it may change the color balance of the entire scene. Try to limit the use of the squeezer to accent lights.

- *Mark the minimum and maximum positions of the dimmer* Place a mark on the dial of the dimmer. Then turn the dial and mark the lowest possible point on the faceplate. Turn the dial the opposite direction and mark the highest possible point on the plate. If you want, mark a few positions in between. These markings will help you when the DP indicates that the light level should be varied between two points.

Flashpan

Applications

You've undoubtedly seen movies that have a moving light pattern on the ceiling to indicate a body of water such as a pool or a house on the beach. This effect is typically generated with a flashpan. There are two primary reasons that a flashpan is used instead of lighting the water itself: the flashpan allows control of where the moving pattern will appear and it also uses far less power than it would take to create the reflections off an actual pool of water. Additionally, it's possible to do the master shots with a real pool of water present and later use the flashpan to do any close-up or pick-up shots on a sound stage with the water pattern providing the visual connectivity.

Sometimes the water pattern is used strictly for effect by a cinematographer. If you want to see this in action, check out the movie Basic Instinct that was DPed by the great Jan de Bont. About half way through the movie when Michael Douglas' character confronts Sharon Stone's character in the house, notice the numerous wave patterns on the walls. Although there's apparently no indoor pool in the room, the patterns seem to be everywhere for great cinematic effect.

	Qty	Item
PARTS	1	Baking pan
	1	Fan
	1	Glass bottle
	1	Mirror
	1	Roll of aluminum foil

General Instructions

A flashpan uses a light reflecting off a small enclosed pool of water such as a baking pan. The pan's bottom is covered with a mirrored surface to maximize its reflectivity. A fan is used to make waves in the water's surface. Broken glass in the water breaks up the uniform waves generated by the fan. Although difficult to show in a small black and white picture, figure 26-1 shows a flashpan being used in a bathroom to reflect water patterns onto the wall.

One of the most effective reflective surfaces you can use for your flashpan is a traditional mirror. If you have a mirror that matches the size of the baking pan, that can be used. Otherwise, most hardware stores stock mirror tiles that are inexpensive, function well, and can be easily cut to size. If you have a large pan, just use multiple tiles, as the lines between the tiles won't appear in the reflected pattern.

FIGURE 26.1 *A flashpan reflects water patterns onto the wall.*

> **TIP ▶** *I've tried different fluids, but water seems to provide the most satisfactory results for clear, bright, white light. However, if you are looking for a different effect, feel free to experiment with different liquids. Oil typically gives the reflected light either a yellow or orange hue and the patterns move much more sluggishly. This effect may prove ideal for summer day reflections off a pond.*

Placement of the flashpan often requires some creative experimentation. Generally the reflected pattern is required on the ceiling, so the pan is often placed behind or beside the actors for reflection overhead. If you need to tilt the pan to get the patterns to show in the right place, make sure the splash level does not allow the contents of the pan to spill on the surface where it sits. If the patterns need to be reflected onto the face of one or more actors, consider using a mirror or reflector to reflect the image generated by the pan rather than tilting the pan too far.

> **TIP ▶** *When you use water reflections, you'll most often want to use a wide shot to establish the source (such as a pool) of those reflections. If the source water is not throwing any reflections by itself, be sure to make the shot with a low camera angle, so the audience won't notice.*

Construction

To construct the flashpan, you'll need a cake pan, a medium-sized mirror, and an oscillating fan. Put the aluminum foil on the bottom of the pan. It will create reflections on any surfaces not covered by the mirror. In figure 26-2 you can see my flashpan with a mirror that roughly matches the pan's proportions. Although I've tilted the mirror up so you can see it in the picture, it generally sits right at the bottom of the pan.

A baking pan is a good container for several reasons. It's made to withstand heat, so no matter how close the light is positioned to the pan, there will be no worry of it melting (as could take place with a plastic container). A baking pan is also opaque because you'll want to control exactly where the reflection occurs. With a clear container, light leaks would fill the room.

You'll want to put broken glass that sits atop the mirror to break up the wave pattern and create a more realistic light cast. To break the glass, rap a glass bottle completely in a towel. Keep your hands clear and smash the bulge in the towel with a hammer. The towel should effectively contain any glass shards. Discard all but the largest fragments. These large shards will most effectively break up the wave pattern.

FIGURE 26.2 *The mirror roughly matches the pan's proportions.*

WARNING→ Be very careful handling the glass shards as they may be sharp enough to cut you. I would love to recommend a safer material to generate the proper light effect, but I haven't found anything nearly as effective. Just be sure to handle it carefully and make sure to keep track of it at all times. You don't want the glass to be accidentally knocked to the floor on the set where someone can step on it.

Note that you can use aluminum foil instead of a mirror for the reflector at the bottom of the pool. However, aluminum foil is much less reflective and as such you'll need a more powerful light source to achieve the same effect. If you're worried about the weight or the possibility of cracking the mirror, Mylar would be an excellent, although slightly expensive, replacement.

Now that you have your flashpan ready, you'll have to decide how it will be used. If you have an extra assistant that can provide the rocking motion for the whole scene, this generally works best. You avoid regular patterns since it will be rocked slightly differently each time. Additionally, having a person rock the pan will keep the whole process completely silent.

However, most guerilla shoots don't have an extra person to spare, so you'll need to use a fan. A fan pointed into the flash pan will produce a nice regular wave pattern. Try and obtain the quietest fan available to minimize the noise on the soundtrack.

Point the fan down into the flashpan. You may have to set the pan on some type of pedestal to bring it to a place the fan's air can reach it. Having a variable speed fan is essential because the size of the pan will determine how much agitation is required to generate the desired effect.

Finally, you'll need to point a strong light into the bed of the pan. I generally use a Sylvania Sun Gun that I purchased on eBay for less than the cost of a music CD. Keep in mind that the Sun Gun produces daylight-balanced light (see Chapter 38), so any other lights you use sound match this color temperature.

In figure 26-3 you can see a top-down picture of the setup I commonly use. The light is mounted on a tripod so I can easily adjust the angle that the light hits the fan. The fan sits perpendicular to the light, so the waves bounce the length of the pan. The fan has three speed settings to create whatever atmosphere I might need.

FIGURE 26.3 *A top-down picture of a common flashpan setup.*

Suggestions

Here are a few operating suggestions to help you get the best use from the flashpan:

- *Use a low ambient light level* As in real life, the water reflections are most obvious under low light conditions (such as at night). Since the light has to travel a great distance (from the light source to the pan and then to the ceiling), much of the light output is lost along the way. Therefore try to minimize other ambient sources during the scene and shoot with the aperture wide open.

- *Try coloring the water* For a different look, you might consider adding food coloring to the water to provide a specific mood or effect. I've seen this used effectively when the fluid is colored red for the reflection from a murder in a pool. Use your imagination.

- *Be sure to bring a clean-up materials* On set, people seem to have a knack for tripping on, knocking into, and kicking over flashpans. Therefore, it's important that you bring paper towels and whatever overcleaning items you might need in case the contents of the pan is spilled.

Barn Door Mount

Applications

Barn doors (see figure 27-1) are perhaps one of the most efficient methods of controlling the throw pattern of a light. While light control with flags and diffusion is more exact, barn doors can be adjusted instantly right at the source. Additionally, barn doors provide an easy mounting platform to attach gels, diffusion, or other light-modulating materials.

While most professional lights for film production include barn doors, few consumer-grade lights do. The size and form factors vary so much from light to light, so you can't purchase generic barn doors that will fit any lighting fixture. The construction of barn doors, however, is not very complicated. With a little work and ingenuity, you can construct a set for each of your lights.

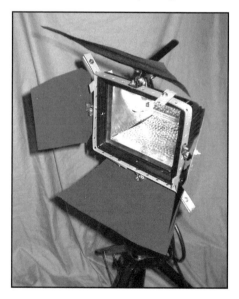

FIGURE 27.1 *Barn doors are one of the most efficient methods of controlling the throw pattern of a light.*

	Qty	Item
PARTS	3	24″ Hyco metal bar 14 or 26 gauge
	4	Sheets of galvanized metal flashing
	1	Can of BBQ Grill black spray paint
	18	$\frac{1}{2}″$ 8–32 machine screws with hex nuts
	4	Locking nuts
	8	Small L-brackets
	1	Pair of tin snips

General Instructions

The barn doors you'll construct in this chapter are made up of two parts: the doors themselves and the frame on which they're mounted. Both the doors and the frame may have to be modified to fit the front of the light you'll be using. The instructions provided here describe doors meant to fit a standard construction work light available at most hardware stores (see figure 27-2).

The front of a construction work light is rectangular, so the barn door frame is also rectangular to match the light's face. Since the chassis of lights vary dramatically, you may need to make modifications to the frame for it to mount properly. If the front of your light is circular or oval, you can bend the brackets of the frame to fit an irregular shape. Although you'll have some light leaks, these can be masked with blackwrap or simply ignored (if the light doesn't fall into the scene).

FIGURE 27.2 *These barn doors are meant to fit a standard construction work light.*

NOTE→ Lights can get very hot, so under no circumstances would you want the barn doors to fall or be knocked off once they've been heated by the light. Therefore, if you make modifications to the frame mount, pull on the frame before you use it to make sure it is mounted securely in place.

Remember that blocking light close to the source makes soft shadows, while close to the destination makes hard shadows. The close proximity of barn doors to the light source creates a very soft border on the shadows, so if you want a harder cut, you'll need to use a flag to create the sharp line.

Besides directing light, the other primary purpose of barn doors is to serve as a mounting edge where professional gels and diffusion can be attached with clothespins as shown in figure 27-3. Multiple layers of gels may be used to achieve the exact lighting results desired. These gels have been fabricated to withstand the heat of very bright lights, so most lights available to the guerilla filmmaker present no fire risk. However, realize that by putting gels on barn doors, a great amount of the light's heat energy will be confined within the fixture. This constriction will make the light fixture run much hotter and will reduce the working life of the bulb.

WARNING→ You should only use professional gels and diffusion material on a barn door frame. These professional gels have been specially heat-treated to ensure they won't catch fire or burn. The close proximity of the barn doors means that the material is extremely close to the heat of the light. Putting any material not explicitly made for such use is very dangerous, so *don't do it.*

Gel material can be fairly expensive and I've talked to a number of guerilla filmmakers who planned to locate cheap cellophane that matched the gel colors and simply keep the material far enough away from the light to avoid a fire hazard. While this plan is fine to introduce color for lighting effects, it won't work very well for color correction (see Chapter 38).

Any type of translucent material looses some color and fades when light passes through it. Cellophane is not made to withstand the high-intensity light blasting that takes place on a movie set. Therefore, while the color may be close to the desired correction at the beginning of a shoot, it will quickly fade and lose its color. That means that the light coming through the low-grade cellophane will be a different color gradient at the end of the film than at the beginning. The use of cellophane would be terrible news to the post-production people who will have to attempt the color correction.

Professional gels are produced to minimize the color shift even under the strongest lights. If you can't afford a full set of professional gels, you can often find a fairly inexpensive "starter pack" online. These packs provide you with square gels in various color correction levels at a reasonable price.

FIGURE 27.3 *Barn doors serve as a mounting edge where professional gels and diffusion can be attached.*

> **TIP ▶** *At the conclusion of principal photography of a film, I often ask for any gel scraps that the production crew had planned to throw away. Once a gaffer handed me hundreds of dollars in barely used gels. When I first started working in film, I did a lot of volunteer work to learn the ropes and obtained the equivalent of a free starter gel kit this way. If there's any filming in your area, you might do the same.*

Construction

For the barn door construction, you'll only need a few tools including tin snips, a drill, a screwdriver, and a few wrenches. The materials are very inexpensive, so you should be able to make a set of doors for every light you have in your arsenal.

After you've completed a set of barn doors and mounted them, be sure to take the light outside, turn it on, and leave it for half an hour. The coating from the paint will need some time to bake and solidify. While it does, it produces a distinct and sometimes strong odor. By running it outside for a while, a majority of the smell will be burnt away, so you won't have to worry about it polluting your set when you use the light for interior shots.

The doors

Before you begin construction, you'll need to figure out exactly the size of the barn doors you'll need. Figure 27-4 shows a rough pattern for barn doors that will fit on the utility work light. If you have a similar light fixture, measure the face frame to make sure the dimensions approximately 7″ (18 cm) by 5.5″ (14 cm).

If your light is not the same as this one, I recommend you scale the template accordingly and then cut sample doors out of cardboard. Tape the cardboard mock-ups to the sides of your light (while it's turned off) and see if the size you've chosen will work properly. Adjust the mock-up doors until you have the proper cardboard cut-out size to use as templates for your doors.

The barn door panels are made with the metal shingle flashing that is available in the roofing section of most hardware stores. Metal flashing is inexpensive, made to withstand heat, and easy to cut (with tin snips) yet firm enough to resist being easily bent.

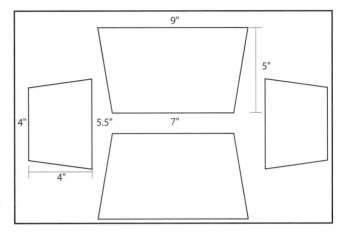

FIGURE 27.4 *A rough pattern for barn doors that will fit on the utility work light.*

Use tin snips to cut the panels to the proper size. You'll be surprised how easily the snips can cut through the tin panels – so be extra careful. While tin snips may appear like a pair of large scissors, they are many, many times sharper. Tin snips can be dangerous if used carelessly.

Once you have the doors cut, you'll need to spray paint each door to matte black. Since flashing is normally silver, without painting it would reflect the light at various angles creating odd light spots on your set. When I first constructed these barn doors, I didn't paint them and within moments of turning on the light, I could see my mistake glaring on the floor and ceiling.

Use barbeque grill spray paint to paint the panels. This paint is especially made to handle extreme heat levels which makes it perfect for use around lights. Be sure to sand the panels before you paint them. Flashing is generally very smooth, so the sanding will roughen the surface, so the paint will hold better.

The grill spray paint can take some time to dry. Once it has dried, you should add a second coat. After the second coat has dried, the surface will have thin coat of black dust on the surface. Wash each door with water and a sponge or toothbrush to remove the dust. Otherwise the dust will get all over your hands during the shoot.

Creating the frame mount

The frame mount will be secured to the face of the light and provide a surface where the doors will be attached. The frame will be constructed from hyco bar brackets that are traditionally used to hold plumbing pipes (see figure 27-5). These strips are perfect for many applications in project construction since they're inexpensive, malleable, and have holes at regular intervals that can accept screws of various sizes.

Bend the end of the first length of hyco bar to a 45° angle. The end should have a single hole available to insert a

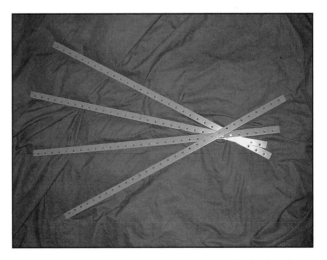

FIGURE 27.5 *The frame will be constructed from hyco bar brackets that are used to hold plumbing pipes.*

screw. Make a right angle bend at the corner of the light frame so the bar fits two sides of the light. The corner bend should be tight enough to hold the frame snugly over the front housing of your light. At this point, cut (or bend) off the remaining length of bar, so there is one hole available at each end (see figure 27-6). The bar you have should cover two sides of the light.

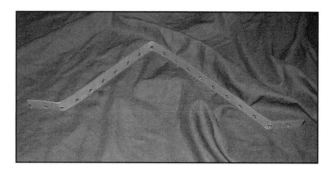

FIGURE 27.6 *Cut off the remaining length of bar so that there is one hole available at each end.*

TIP ▶ *To obtain the proper lengths of the hyco bar, you can use a cutting tool such as a hacksaw. I've found that it's much easier to take two pliers (see figure 27-7) and bend the metal back and forth until one side shears off. For the least work, perform the bending at one of the holes where the metal is weakest. I've found that it generally takes six bends before the metal gives. If you have a mounted vise, place the bar in it for the easiest bending. Be sure to cover the sheared ends with tape to prevent anyone from getting a metal sliver or being cut by a sharp edge.*

Create a matching bar to fit the other two sides of the light and secure them to each other with a pair of machine screws and nuts (see figure 27-8). If the holes punched in your hyco bar are not centered in the middle of each bar, before you start bending check to make sure both of your brackets will match so they're not offset from one another.

Now that you have a frame, you'll need to create some brackets that will hold the frame onto the front of the light. These brackets will be in the form of a lopsided U. One side will be longer than the other since it has to reach the back of the light faceplate fixture. For me, one bracket per side of the frame (four in total) was enough to safely secure the frame, although you can feel free to use more to create a firm hold.

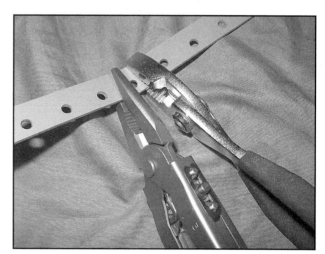

FIGURE 27.7 *Take two pliers and bend the metal back and forth until one side shears off.*

Create the lengths for the U-brackets from small pieces of hyco bar. On my hyco bars, a length that had two holes was just about perfect. Secure these short lengths to the frame (see figure 27-9).

Slide the frame onto the light (see figure 27-10). Mark the place in the front and back of the U-brackets with a pen where you will make the bends to secure the light.

Remove the barn door frame and make the bends to the front of the U-brackets. With only the front part of the bracket bent, the frame can still slide on and off the light. Only after everything is ready and mounted will you bend the back of the U-bracket to solidly fix the frame to the light.

Mounting the doors to the frame

Now you'll need to create the pivot mounts that will attach the barn doors to the frame. Each pivot will use a lock nut opening and closing the barn doors repeatedly will not rotate the nuts loose.

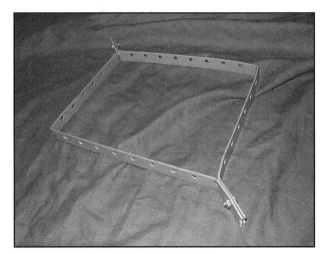

FIGURE 27.8 *Create a matching bar to fit the other two sides of the light.*

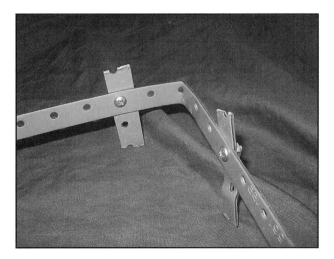

FIGURE 27.9 *Secure the short bar lengths to the frame.*

Create the top mount pivot by following these steps:

1. Attach an L-bracket to the frame with a screw and a nut. Tighten the screw, so it won't move when you swivel the barn door.

2. With the lock nut, attach the second L-bracket to the first (see figure 27-11). Tighten the lock nut until the bracket is secure, but moves smoothly.

3. Hold the top barn door panel up to the second L-bracket and mark the spot where a screw will hold the panel centered over the light's face.

4. Using the marked spot as a guide, drill a hole that is wide enough to accept a screw.

5. Mount the barn door panel on the pivot of the frame (see figure 27-12) with a screw and a nut. The barn door should pivot smoothly, so the panel can be placed flush with the face of the light.

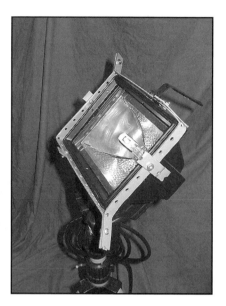

FIGURE 27.10 *Slide the frame onto the light.*

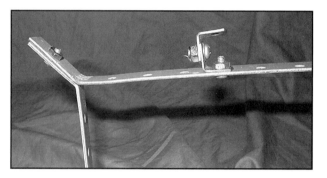

FIGURE 27.11 *With the lock nut, attach the second L-bracket to the first.*

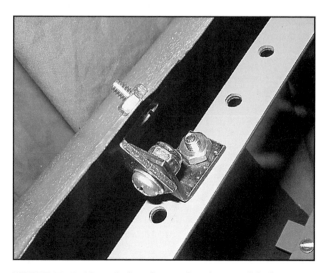

FIGURE 27.12 *Mount the barn door panel on the pivot of the frame.*

Repeat the above steps for the other three barn door panels, so they allow the barn doors to shut out the light. Having the barn doors closed is the traditional way that a light is wrapped for storage. The doors provide protection for the glass they cover.

Slide the frame onto the light and bend the backsides of the U-brackets down to secure the frame into place (see figure 27-13). You might find bending the short lengths of bar to be difficult. To make it easier, before you place the frame on the light, bend the bars to the proper U-shape and then bend them back. That will slightly weaken the metal and make it easier to bend later.

FIGURE 27.13 *Slide the frame onto the light and bend the backsides of the U-brackets down.*

Your barn doors are now complete. If you find that the panels that you made have some light leaks, cut pieces of cardboard to larger sizes and attach them to the existing panels. When you find a shape that accomplishes what you want, construct a new set of panels.

Suggestions

Here are a few operating suggestions to help you get the best use from the barn doors:

- ***Give the barn doors time to cool*** There is always pressure when you wrap for the day to get off the set and go home. However, if you've been shooting all day (or night), both the barn doors and the light will most likely be hot. Turn off the light and give them time to cool. You don't want to burn your hand or set a hot surface on carpet.

- ***Re-cut the doors if necessary*** The flashing material and spray paint are cheap. Therefore, if you didn't cut the doors properly in the first place and you have light leaks, re-cut new ones. The small inconvenience of re-doing the doors is nothing compared to the aggravation that can be created on set when light leaks.

- ***Barn doors will cut the life of the light*** Almost invariably, work lights are constructed with poor ventilation. When you add the barn doors that hold in the extra heat, the life of the light bulb will almost certainly be shortened. Be sure to bring extra bulbs. Also you may consider drilling a few ventilation holes in the light housing as long as these holes do not create additional light leaks.

- ***Add safety wire or chain*** On a professional set, barn doors are secured to the light itself with a safety chain. If they ever come loose or are knocked off, there is no chance then will fall away from the light and hit anyone. I would suggest that you create a safety chain or use some thin wire to securely attach the frame of the barn doors to the housing of your light.

Light Diffusers and Gels

Applications

The number of materials that can be used for light diffusion, reflection, or modification is bounded only by your creativity and imagination. Once you start looking, you will find items everywhere that can reflect and diffuse light in unique ways. Whenever you find an interesting material, you should try to take a picture of the effect it creates. Keep a scrapbook of these effects for later use. You'll find that you can look through this book before a shoot begins and you will instantly recognize particular scenes or shots that could be enhanced by using one.

The point of using any of these materials with light is to change the light with a particular goal in mind. This goal may be as simple as casting a cool pattern on the back wall or may change the color of the light, so the scene will photograph correctly. Try to experiment extensively with all materials you planned to use as many can have unexpected consequences on your final image.

> **WARNING→** Any material that will be placed in front of a hot light can be a fire hazard. Make sure that you don't use any materials that are flammable under the conditions you use them.

General Instructions

Modifying light is more of an art than a science. You have to subjectively determine the results that you want to achieve. Deciding on the plan to achieve the look you desire can comes from planning and logical thinking. One of the most important steps to methodically creating a lighting scenario you've devised comes from studying how light actually works and what modifications actually affect the final image on your medium.

Color temperature

All light contains a range of frequencies. For film, these frequencies are denoted as temperatures which are measured in terms of kelvin (K). In table 28-1 you can see a list of common light sources and their temperatures. Our eyes automatically adjust to these color ranges. Film and video, however, don't adjust easily and have far more limited ranges than our eyes. For this reason, every filmmaker must understand how the color temperature will affect the final image you capture – whether on film or video.

To understand how to effectively use light in your film, you need to know that most light, film, and video settings are divided into two main categories. The two main guideline temperatures of light you need to know are:

3200 K for artificial light

5600 K for daylight

Temperature (K)	Description
1000	Candles, oil lamps
2000	Early sunrise
2500	Household light bulbs
3200	Tungsten studio lights, photofloods
4000	Clear flashbulbs
5200	Daylight, electronic flash
5500	Noon daylight
6000	Bright sunshine
7000	Overcast sky
8000	Hazy sky

TABLE 28.1 *Color temperature in kelvin.*

If you use daylight-balanced film or the daylight settings (for white balance) in your digital camera, you are attempting to photograph in the daylight temperature range. If you are using tungsten-balanced film or the indoor settings in your digital camera, you are attempting to photograph in the artificial light temperature range. Daylight temperature in the color spectrum tends to be bluer. Artificial light tends toward yellow/red/orange.

What happens if you use daylight settings to photograph artificial light? In a room with a window with daylight coming through and a single lamp, all of the objects lit by the daylight will look normal, while items on which the lamp shines will look extra red/orange. Likewise, if set for tungsten settings, the lamp items will look perfectly fine. Any objects outside the window or those lit by daylight will appear almost a monotone shade of blue.

> **NOTE→** Not all artificial lights generate light within the artificial light range. HMI and xenon lights in particular are made to generate daylight temperature light. Likewise, daylight temperature tubes are available for most fluorescent fixtures such as Kino-Flo lights.

Why is light temperature important to you? One of the primary uses of gels is not to change the visible color of light, but instead to change the light temperature. Blue gels (CTB) can be placed over a tungsten light and filter out all the color temperatures but those within the daylight range. That can allow you to use tungsten lights to augment daylight scenes without adding an orange cast. Likewise, orange gels (CTO) can be used to filter daylight so that it shows through only in the tungsten color temperature range.

Therefore, whenever you use any type of colored gel or diffusion, be aware that it may have an unexpected effect unless you take into account the color temperature range of both the light source and the setting for your recording medium.

Color temperatures can be determined with the help of a color temperature meter (see figure 28-1). These meters can take a temperature reading from a light source and even suggest what type of gel or filter would be needed to bring that source into the desired temperature range.

Traditional diffusion

Diffusion is used for a variety of reasons. Perhaps the light needs to be softened. Maybe the actress needs a warm glow on her face. It is up to the skills of the DP to choose the right diffusion to achieve the lighting effect that is desired for the scene.

FIGURE 28.1 *The temperature of a light source can be determined with a color temperature meter.*

Realize that reflectors, diffusion, and other light-modifying materials all cut the amount of light that hits the subject. Therefore, a light source that may be bright enough when uncovered may be too dark once diffused or reflected. For example, lights with lenses (such as Fresnel lights) can project up to 50% less light than an equivalent light without a lens. Always take into account light loss when setting up a diffusion or reflective light scheme.

Almost anything can be used as diffusion material. Guerilla and professional filmmakers regularly use household items. Some household diffusion materials include:

- *Sheet* A normal bed sheet can be used as a white reflector or a fairly dense diffusion material. Simply hanging a white sheet opposite a well-lit window can change the entire light feel of a room. Watch for white sales and discount coupons to purchase sheets inexpensively.

- *Window sheers* The translucent material called sheers that is often placed behind curtains provides excellent diffusion. It is available in a variety of white and off-white colors and may be purchased in silk or polyester varieties. If your city has a garment district, this material can be obtained inexpensively. Generally try to purchase silk sheers as the polyester sheers reflect a good deal of light and as such make poorer diffusion material.

- *Silk blouse* Often old silk blouses provide excellent diffusion and can be found cheaply at thrift and used clothing stores. You may need to sew several together to cover the entire frame.

- *Satin sheets* Available in white and other colors, satin sheets provide excellent soft light reflection.

- *Tracing paper for diffusion* Warning! Tracing paper, like all papers, is very flammable. Although tracing paper is regularly used for diffusion in professional sets, it is commonly used to cover an outside window when the lighting is either supplied by the sun or with a distantly located powerful light. Make sure you don't place your light source close to this paper.

- *Aluminum/tin foil* Fix aluminum or tin foil to cardboard or foamcore. I find the easiest way to attach the foil to the board is to staple it directly to the cardboard.

- *Mylar* Mylar is a fantastic material for lightweight yet extremely reflective applications. The major drawback with Mylar is the expensive price. Watch for it on sale at local party stores.

- *Colored cellophane* Typically available at party stores, colored cellophane is available in a variety of colors for various light effects. While you can't effectively use colored cellophane as a gel (such as CTB or CTO) it can be used for general mood coloring of light.

- *Window tinting* Window tinting material is available at home improvement stores as well as automotive supply stores. At the home improvement stores, you can find a variety of levels of tinted material that is meant to be stuck to a household window with static cling. I found this material to be cheap and perfect as a diffusion or scrim-like material. Be aware that it is generally shiny and may create a reflection of other lights.

- *Window screen* You can buy this screen material without the frame at a hardware store. It's perfect to cut to size and use as a large scrim.

- *White or black trash bags* Can be cut open and attached together to create a nice shiny plastic reflector similar to a professional griff (or griffolyn). Most often you'll use this as a bounce material to create fill light.

- *White or black foamcore* Foamcore is probably one of the most used materials in the film industry. It provides excellent backing material for another material. Foam core is often used with the white side for a reflector or the black side as a flag. It can also be easily painted for a simple backdrop or a blue screen background. Generally available in $4' \times 8'$ sheets.

- *Foam insulation board* Although they're flammable, so they're only really suitable to reflect sunlight, foam insulation panels are extremely cheap, available in large and small sizes, and provide effective reflectors. Available at almost any hardware store, these panels are made of lightweight rigid foam with one side white and the other side dull silver. I use these all the time.

- *White van or truck* More than once have I seen this trick used to great effect. Placing the large white side of a truck or a van at the proper location can provide an excellent bounce surface for fill light. It can also increase privacy to minimize spectators.

- *Acrylic light panels* Available at any hardware store, acrylic light panels made for fluorescent light fixture can be obtained cheaply and provide a wide variety of diffusion types.

- *Chrome spray paint* Available at any auto parts store and most hardware stores, chrome paint can be used to create an excellent reflective surface on nearly anything. Generally also available in gold color.

Special effects diffusion and reflection

Special effects diffusion and reflection is much more difficult to use properly. Not only does the effect look excessive if not used cleverly, but many lighting effects break the light into patterns. These patterns are difficult to control and may fall unattractively on the face of an actor or actress.

Here are some examples that I have seen used effectively on sets:

- *Tape on frame to simulate window slats* A simple cross design on a frame can provide an excellent simulated window if used in front of a light source and cast onto a white wall.

- *Bicycle tire to simulate television* Attach strips of blue clothe or gel on a bicycle tire. Placing a light source behind the tire and then turning the tire can cast a flickering reflection onto an actor's face. Use this technique with orange or red gel strips and fire may be simulated.

- *Stained glass* Using a variety of cellophane, you can effectively simulate the light patterns of stained glass windows. I saw this used to simulate such a window on the back wall of a "nunnery" and I was stunned by the final footage. What was a bland little room became an expensive holy room using this simple effect.

- *Kaleidoscope* A few of these toy kaleidoscopes and a number of spotlight bulbs can be used together to create an interesting psychedelic/rave party environment.

- *Matching color light* This technique can create fantastic results, but I've only seen it used a couple of times. Take a surface such as a red wall and place a red gel over the light shining on the wall. The light will supersaturate the color of the wall for magnificent effect. Used carefully, the same technique can even be used for smaller surfaces (i.e. use a red gel on a light hitting a red dress).

- *Rope weave cookie* A rope weave can create a fantastic, natural-looking, and portable cookie.

- *Aluminum/tin foil with cutouts* Cutouts in aluminum foil can create interesting reflective effects including simulating broken glass reflected onto an actor's face.

Suggestions

Here are a few suggestions to help you with light modification:

- *Be frugal with your lighting effects* Setting up a light effect properly can take a great deal of time and using too many effects in one film can make it look cheesy. Be reserved in the effects you use to achieve the greatest dramatic impact when they are seen.

- *Match your mediums* If you are using a digital camera for your film, use a digital still camera for your tests. Likewise, if you're going to use film to record your movie, use a real film camera to perform any light tests. Digital encoding and film exposure record images in very different ways. It is important that all the lessons learned from your experiments will correctly translate to your final medium.

Blue Screen

Applications

Compositing, a technique used to superimpose footage onto other footage, is used extensively in movies from Star Wars to Titanic to Spider Man. Actors are filmed in front of a solid blue or green colored background (see figure 29-1).

In post-production, this background is eliminated and substituted with other footage (such as a miniature set or CGI rendering) with special software (see figure 29-2). The process is known by many names including blue screening, green screening, chroma-keying, and compositing. For simplicity, in the remainder of this chapter I'll refer to this process as compositing.

Professional blue screens contain a specific hue of the color blue that's known as Chroma Blue. Human skin contains none of this shade of blue, so when this color is removed from the final image, none of the actor's skin is made transparent. Green has become more dominant because blues are more often desired than greens in sets, make-up, and wardrobe. Additionally, the color of an actor's blue eyes may overlap the tonal range of the blue screen.

FIGURE 29.1 *Actors are filmed in front of a solid blue- or green-colored background.*

> **TIP ▶** *If you know of a local TV station, you may want to visit and ask if you can use the screen normally used by the weather person. A friend of mine talked a local station into letting him use their screen (in the off hours) and obtained excellent footage – primarily because the station already had the screen perfectly setup and lit.*

Unfortunately, the shade of green used for a green screen is difficult to obtain in everyday items. In contrast, a blue color near the range of Chroma Blue is available in everything from tablecloths to tarps. For this reason, the project in this chapter will use a blue screen for a background.

PARTS	Qty	Item
	1	100′ × 40″ roll of blue table cover
	1	Thumbtacks
	1	Double-sided tape

FIGURE 29.2 *The background is eliminated and substituted with other footage.*

General Instructions

Proper setup and photography of footage (video or film) is much more important to the realism of your final image than the software you use for compositing (Final Cut Pro, Adobe Premiere, Adobe After Effects, etc.). With this in mind, here are a few general suggestions to help you maximize the quality of your final image:

- *Underexposure should be avoided* It is better to overexpose your image which will provide the color range necessary to make the compositing screen transparent in post-production. Underexposure forces shadows into closer color proximity to the compositing screen.

- *Avoid low-contrast lighting, fog, and smoke* Low-contrast images make removal of the background more difficult. Fog and smoke make it nearly impossible. Effectively creating a believable composited image with a smoking cigarette is only possible with high-end equipment.

- *Test the lighting* Light up the blue screen and leave the actors in darkness. This will allow you to see if there is any spill onto the hair or shoulders of the actors in the scene. If there is spill, try to move your actors farther away from the screen.

- *Highlight with the opposing color* To minimize the effect of spill, you can cast colored light at the opposite end of the spectrum onto your actors to cancel some of the effect. Use magenta light to cancel spill for green screens and orange light for blue.

- *Use mirrored surfaces for the actors to stand on* If you need to do a wide shot and show the actor's feet, have them stand on a mirrored surface (such as Mylar) rather than material with the composite color. The mirrored surface will reflect the surrounding composite color, yet minimize the amount of color spilled onto the actor.

- *Eliminate reflective surfaces* Surfaces such as chrome steel armrests on a chair can reflect the compositing screen color and will disappear when the background color is removed. Use colored tape or dulling spray (or hairspray) to reduce and eliminate the reflective surfaces of items.

- *Light the compositing screen as uniformly as possible* Having uniform lighting on your screen will be one of the more challenging tasks of compositing. The background should be lit uniformly across the surface. Any shadows or highlights make compositing much more difficult.

- *Avoid finely stranded objects* Did you notice that everyone had slicked hair in the Matrix movie? Sure the slicked hair looked cool, but it had a more important technical aspect – it minimized compositing artifacts. Fine, frizzy hair is one of the most difficult subjects to composite. Try to avoid hairstyles, wardrobe, or props that have fine strands including fur, splayed fiber-optic cable (such as those fiber effects lamps), angora sweaters, and trolls.

- *Use light cues properly* There are a variety of small cues that will tell the audience that the background is fake. The most obvious cues are the light sources and the shadows. If the background picture will show the sun streaming down from behind, a lack of backlight on the actor will make it obvious that he and the background have been shot separately.

- *Match background to composite color* If you composite a black background into the scene, fringing around the actor (in the color of your composite screen) will be difficult or impossible to avoid. To minimize the visibility of the fringe, make your background match the color range of your blue screen. A background scene that contains blues will make it harder to see any blue screen fringe. Likewise a green background will help footage shot using a green screen.

- *With a green screen, use fluorescent lights* Fluorescent lights are perfect for properly and evenly lighting the compositing screen. Green screens generally require less light to generate a solid hue, so the lower fluorescent output is not a problem. The light output is also a flat light that will reduce any highlights. Additionally, fluorescent lights have a slight green tinge, so they won't muddy your screen color (as orange tungsten lights might).

Following the above guidelines should help you obtain better compositing footage. Keep in mind that besides lighting, the other primary determining factor in the quality of the footage is the grade of the camera. Unfortunately, DV cameras are one of the worst types of cameras to shoot compositing footage.

The reason for the poor DV performance is not resolution, but color space. The compression used by the MiniDV format loses a significant amount of the color information from the picture. Most of the compression takes place in the color space, meaning that information that can help produce a crisp composite is lost as the image is recorded to the MiniDV tape. Because the color information is used to separate the picture from the background, this loss is catastrophic for good blue screen work.

If you have a small amount of compositing work in your film, try to rent a DigiBeta or BetaSP camera to record those scenes. The results are substantially better than those you'll create using a DV camera.

Construction

The needs of a compositing screen are different for different people. Guerilla filmmakers are getting advanced with their compositing work and the software technology is falling in price so rapidly that I'm already surprised at the fantastic quality of some no-budget work. Therefore, I've organized the following sections to provide you with a variety of construction methods.

Advanced compositing goes well beyond simply standing in front of a colored screen. Now even low-budget films are using props and actors that contain compositing color (famously Sgt. Dan's missing legs in the movie Forest Gump). You can mix and match some of these techniques and color matching to fit most of your needs.

Getting the right color

It is important to realize that compositing colors of Chroma Blue and Chroma Green are not the only colors or tints that can be used for compositing. In fact, any color or even no color can be the composite color. In the old days, something called ultra-black provided a color that stood apart from the normal footage spectrum that allowed it to be dropped for compositing. The Chroma colors are simply colors that have maximum reflectivity and minimize the tones that might be found in other materials.

That said, there are a large number of ways that you can create a compositing screen and you should use any material that you have available that will meet your needs. Since exact coloration in particular hues is not a prerequisite to the screen working properly, here are a few suggestions on materials that can be used for the blue screen application:

- **Fluorescent green or blue posterboard for close-ups or small items** These colors are actually very close to the Chroma colors. Making a large wall with this posterboard is problematic, however, because of expense and the shadows created by the seams between the board sheets.

- **Shower curtains or tarps** I've found shower curtains and tarps that almost match the hue of Chroma Blue. The shower curtain I have has the color specified as electric blue. The biggest problem with these surfaces (aside from the expense) is the semi-gloss finish. You want to try to avoid highlights of any type off the compositing screen itself.

- **Custom mixed paint** At your local paint store, you can have paint mixed that comes really close to the Chroma colors. Get a behind-the-scenes book (such as one on the movie Titanic) and take that to the paint store and have them mix to match that color. Sometimes a color close to Chroma Green can be found as Ultra Key Lime Interior Latex Flat. Check the swatches they have in the paint store to see if they have something pre-mixed that is close.

Setting up a compositing wall

One of the most difficult problems to avoid with compositing screen is shadows from the actors. Shadows cast by the actors onto the background screen are almost impossible to remove in post-production. Further, any spill light from the screen onto the actors will produce fringing around the actor in the final footage. Therefore, the actors must be a reasonable distance away from the screen. That in turn means that the compositing screen must be fairly large so that camera can get far enough away to capture the actor and the screen.

On a professional set, a large, lightweight frame is often used to host a large compositing cloth. Despite numerous tries, I haven't been able to find an inexpensive and effective substitute for this frame. Therefore, I've found it easiest to temporarily dedicate a wall to holding the screen. This method works perfectly and can be setup temporarily and taken down without any major damage to the wall.

First, you'll need the blue screen material. With the help of a Smart & Final (a food service and restaurant supply store) salesman, I found an excellent blue screen material. Restaurant supply stores and party stores sell rolls of blue matte plastic (see figure 29-3) that are

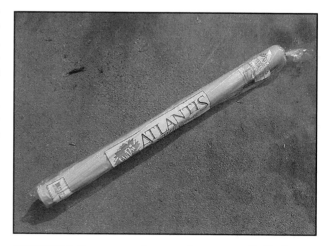

FIGURE 29.3 *Restaurant supply stores and party stores sell rolls of matte plastic table covers.*

used for covering tables at banquet-type events. A roll of this blue plastic table cover roll contains 100 ft of the material with a 40 ft width, all for less than the price of an audio CD!

Check out your local stores to see if they have these rolls in blue (see figure 29-4). The color green at my local store was much to dark for use. If you can't find it locally, check the Internet where it is often available under the brand name of Masterpiece. You'll also need a box of about 100 thumbtacks and a roll of double-stick tape.

Since the roll is very long, but not very wide, make the runs horizontal. Therefore, cut two or more sheets that will cover the width of the wall you've chosen. Two sheets will provide a height of 6.5 ft, while three sheets will give you a 10-ft screen if your ceiling is high enough.

To construct a two-sheet (6.5 ft) blue screen, start by using two thumbtacks at the top corner of the lowest sheet. Place the tacks all along the top of the screen and make sure the length is tight. Don't forget that any folds will create shadows that are terrible for compositing. Therefore, the sheet should be as tight as possible without tearing it. After you've tacked the top completely, do the left side. Progress to the right side of the sheet, pulling out any slack in the sheet. Finally tack down the bottom.

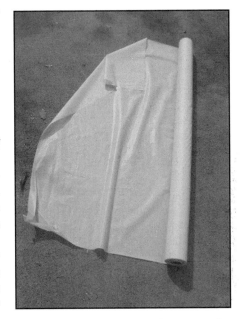

FIGURE 29.4 *Check out your local stores to see if they have these rolls in blue.*

For the next sheet, you'll probably need a ladder to put it up. If you can get someone to give you a hand, that will make placement much easier. Before you put in the first thumbtack, make sure at the bottom that there is enough overlap to cover the thumbtacks of the other sheet. When you have the top of the second sheet tacked up, get out the double-sided tape. Run a length of tape over the thumbtacks on the bottom sheet. Pull the bottom of the second sheet tight and push it onto the double-stick tape. Finish by tacking down the left and right sides of the second sheet.

You should now have a screen that is almost 6 ft tall with only a single minor seam. Add as many other sheets using the same method until you have the size of screen that you desire. When filming is complete, you can take down the screen and the only damage to the wall will be the thumbtack holes.

Using still camera backgrounds

You are already aware of the fact that MiniDV severely compresses the color space for each frame. DV also has limited resolution. Many people have digital still cameras that have much greater resolution and do an excellent job of preserving the color space of a picture.

If you're using a blue screen with a still subject (such as a miniature or model) and you have a good digital camera, you might consider taking the image against the blue screen with the still camera. This image will most likely have better color range and therefore have a better chance of properly dropping out when using compositing software. This is especially true with fine details such as fur or small antennas.

Gaffer Techniques

Applications

Since the gaffer is responsible for all lighting on the set, there are a number of techniques that can be used to best manage lights and electricity. The gaffer also has to be a sort of light magician and often needs to simulate light events. The gaffer is responsible for accomplishing both practical and artistic goals relating to electricity and lighting.

General Instructions

Many guerilla filmmakers have little experience with electricity outside of plugging a cord into a socket. If you've been given the position of electrician or gaffer on a small film, you'd best know some electrical calculations and lighting techniques. A gaffer has a great deal of responsibility and often must solve problems under intense time pressure. For this reason, having an understanding of basic principles can dramatically increase the effectiveness of a new gaffer.

Electrical calculations

Some people unfamiliar with electricity may fear the math involved with calculating the basic figures. This fear is unfounded since most of the important day-to-day calculations are very simple and can be done in your head.

One of the most important calculations you'll make is the amperage load. Electrical cords, power strips, sockets, and electrical circuits are all rated by the number of amps of power that they can handle. For example, cheap extension cords are rated to handle 10 A. What does this mean? To figure out what size lights can be put on the extension cord, we need to know that amperage draw of each light.

There is a shorthand method of figuring out the number of amps used by a light. It is: Amps = Watts/100. Using this formula, a 100 W bulb will use approximately 1 A. That means that a single extension cord could handle 10 lights that use 100 W bulbs. Or the cord could power one light that has a 1000 W bulb. Since lights are generally the largest use of power on a set, this simple calculation can help you ensure that you don't have any safety or fire risks by overloading your electrical equipment.

To determine the maximum amp capacity of electrical devices, look on the device itself. Almost every piece of electrical equipment (including extension cords) will state the maximum power draw that they can handle. Some common limits for consumer-grade electrical equipment include:

Item	Limit (A)
Power strip	15
Ungrounded extension cord	5
Grounded extension cord	10
Cube tap	15

Many times you will be shooting inside an office or residence and using "house power" as opposed to power from a generator. Wherever there are power outlets, there are generally different circuits. Power comes from the street as a single power source and is divided into different circuits inside the house. House circuits each have a separate breaker (see figure 30-1).

The circuits of a house can be located in a seemingly haphazard manner, but generally they are created to minimize the amount of cable that needs to be run. For this reason, often the opposite wall sockets in a room are on different circuits. This layout is great advantage to a film crew as they may have access to 100 A of power in a single room.

Each circuit has a breaker with a maximum amp rating. Generally, modern residential homes install 20 A breakers for each circuit (see figure 30-2). Like the extension cord rating of 10 A, that means that the maximum amount of amperage that can be pulling through the breaker is 20 A. If you were to plug one 1000 W light into one socket and two 2000 W lights into another socket on the same circuit, you would reach the limit immediately.

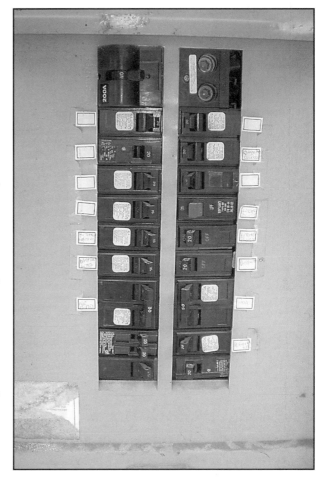

FIGURE 30.1 *House circuits each have a separate breaker.*

FIGURE 30.2 *Modern residential homes generally install 20 A breakers for each circuit.*

It's generally best to avoid coming even close to the limits of the breakers. An electrician seldom knows all the power drains plugged in line on the circuit. Maybe a refrigerator is plugged into the circuit in the next room.

TIP ▶ *If you're using any but the simplest lighting scenario, you will probably overload the breaker at least once on a location. Therefore, it is important to always locate the breaker or the fuse box immediately upon arriving at the location. Make sure if the location has a fuse box that extra fuses are readily available.*

General lighting

Keep in mind when lighting that film and video are lit in the opposite manner. Since how video and film handle over- and underexposure differently, scenes need to be lit to play to the strengths of the particular medium.

Follow these guidelines:

- Negative film should shoot for shadows and let highlights take care of themselves. Blown out highlights on film is not generally visually distasteful and this effect is often used intentionally. Therefore, most film shoots focus on setting the camera and lighting to obtain the shadow details.

- Video or reversal film should shoot for highlights and let shadows take care of themselves. Blown out areas on video tends to look horrid, therefore overexposure should be avoided. Most video cameras provide a feature called the "zebra pattern" that will show areas of overexposure in the eyepiece. It is much easier to turn up the brightness of video in post-production to lighten the underexposure than regain the detail lost in overexposed areas.

Keep in mind that at the time of this writing, film has a much greater exposure range than video. Film has nine f/stops range from black to white while video generally only has 4–5 f/stops. Meanwhile the human eye has about 13 f/stops, so use a light meter to supplement your visual judgment.

Lighting layers

While generally the decision of the DP, the gaffer always looks for ways to suggest using light to best present the scene. Often this requires pre-planning on the part of the gaffer so that suggestions, if taken, are possible to rig within the given shoot time. One of the most dramatic uses of light can be creating layers of light within a scene. By using variations of light and dark, the scene can almost pop into 3D reality for the audience.

Light layers are created by alternating light and dark. Therefore, in a medium shot, the foreground objects might be lit in a particular way. Then the ambient level is lower in the space between the foreground and the actors. The actors are then lit with the greatest amount of light in the frame. Another layer of darker ambience follows. Finally a few background objects are highlighted. When I've seen it used well, this technique can produce absolutely stunning effects in the final footage.

Sometimes you don't even have to use much light to create the layers. Particularly on background objects, you might place white tape on edges of the objects to make them pop. The slim white tapeline can catch even a small amount of light and provide an interesting effect. Also, negative fill can be achieved with flags or duvetyn to deemphasize certain parts of the background and emphasize others.

Simulating passing traffic

For numerous reasons, it is often preferable to simulate traffic than film in actual traffic conditions. I can't even begin to count the number of shots ruined by idiots that feel they have to honk whenever they see a film crew. Simulating passing traffic is a problem generally left to the gaffer to solve.

Here are a few effective methods:

- *Daylight shoots, use a reflector*   Have a person use a reflector to simulate the light streaking through the car. The person will turn the reflector quickly enough to make it appear as if a car passes by the set car. A gold reflector seems to produce the most attractive light reflections.

- *Night shoots, use a flag over a headlight*   Park an idling car with shining headlights so that it faces the filmed action. Using a flag (such as one you constructed in Chapter 38), have a person cover the headlight and occasionally uncover and recover the headlight. This method actually looks surprisingly good in the final footage.

- *Dolly installed with lights*   You can place lights on a dolly and push it past a stationary actor to simulate cars passing. In my experience, the big trouble with this method is the noise. In reality, it is fairly difficult to quietly push the lights around, especially when the types of scenes shot with simulated passing traffic are generally conversation heavy.

- *Drag signs on rollers by the car*   This method is famously used in one of Tim Burton's early films, Pee-Wee's Big Adventure. Watch the scene closely and you'll notice that one time the camera actually captures the little cart with rollers that is being pulled past the camera.

Rigging flying or rocketing items

One method of rigging a teleporting item or a rocket blast-off is to create the scene upside down. This technique is especially effective with small models. For a rocket, turn the camera upside down. You can build a custom camera mount to accomplish this or strap the hi-hat from Chapter 10 to a board for suspension between two ladders. Perhaps the simplest method of securing the small rocket is with fishing line that can be severed off camera. Start rolling and cut the fishing line. The rocket will launch into the air and you'll not need to do any post-production wire removal.

I've included this technique in the gaffer's section since it would have saved me a nightmarish time on a shoot if I'd have know of it back then. The most difficult part of wirework is not the rigging, but lighting around the wires, so they don't catch the light or create visible shadows. Whenever wirework is needed, it seems like the gaffer is always left holding the bag. Therefore, try to consider and suggest alternatives to the wire and save yourself numerous headaches.

Suggestions

Here are a few suggestions for working the electrical department:

- *Purchase gaffer's tape*   While duct tape is a substitute, it isn't a very good one. Gaffer's tape is made to have a very strong adhesive and yet it leaves little residue. If you don't have a film supply store in your town, order gaffer's tape over the Internet. The most popular type of tape is Permacel P665.

- *Sun Guns provide cheap, portable lighting*   Sylvania created a small, hand-held light for use with 8 mm cameras. These lights, popular in the 1960s and 1970s, were purchased by the thousands. They provide 5600 K daylight-balanced light. I can't recommend them highly enough and they are available used at pawnshops and through eBay for the price of a music CD. If your lighting kit is small, be sure to purchase a few of these. They come in handy.

Grip Introduction

IV

Applications

Grips are responsible for all the set equipment not administered by the electricians. Gripping requires the most manual labor of any position on the set. Grip equipment include flags, stands, dollies and dolly tracks, cranes, jib arms, ladders, rigs, sandbags, clamps, and so on. The start of an average day as a grip can include transporting dozens of heavy sandbags from the truck to location.

As a grip, it's best if you're in at least decent physical shape. Due to the heavy physical demands of the job, grips are primarily male. Women can readily perform in the role of grips, but be aware that on a professional film the brute strain can push you to the edge of your limits.

Often on guerilla films, the roles of grips and electrics are combined since the lighting needs are minimized while there is nearly always a great deal of non-lighting equipment to setup and handle (including large reflectors and diffusion for outdoor shoots). No matter what the film, the grips and electrics work together extensively, so you should try to learn the basic skills in each of these departments to promote effective communication.

The easiest way to define the difference between grips and electrics is to say that electricians are responsible for lights and electricity, and grips are responsible for everything else. On a large-budget shoot, the electricians generally don't even handle the flags, diffusion, or other items in front of the lights. On these shoots, the electricians limit themselves to handling the lights themselves and the electricity on the set.

Note that I'm describing the roles in the United States and you may find quite a bit of variety around the world. Each country has its own traditions for the limitations and latitude of the roles of each crew member.

Of all the items presented in this section, the C-stand is likely the most important tool in the grip arsenal. Since it is used so often in so many different situations, the C-stand takes a long time to learn how to quickly and effectively setup and place. Only experience can teach you how to setup a C-stand properly for the hundreds of different applications where it will be used. If you're going to construct any equipment for film production, choosing to make several C-stands is perhaps the most practical.

> **NOTE→** You may have noticed that I located construction of dollies and dolly tracks in the Camera Department section of the book. Although on a professional set the dolly is a responsibility of the grips (specifically the dolly grip), on most guerilla films the camera operator owns the camera and therefore takes responsibility for managing the dolly. For this reason, I didn't locate that equipment in the Grip Department section although a grip will often still be called upon to setup or at least drive the dolly.

Suggestions

Here are a few general suggestions for working as a grip:

- *Stretch before working* Common injuries on a set occur from pulled muscles and strains. Many of these injuries can be avoided by a simple regimen of stretching in the morning. Many shooting days begin early in the morning when people haven't had time to work the stiffness out of their muscles. Doing a few minutes of stretching before the shoot can make a great contribution to your continued health.

- *Don't jump while carrying equipment* One of the first things a key grip taught me was avoid grabbing heavy equipment and then jumping off the back of the grip truck. All the added weight lands squarely on your knees and can cause tremendous extra strain. Many grips have told me that the damaging results crop up later in life and can be horrendous. Take the few extra moments to set down the equipment (this includes heavy cables), jump down, and then pick it up again. Your knees will thank you.

- *Treat people's property with respect* When on location, particularly when that location is a private home, get permission before drilling, stapling, or nailing into a wall or other structure. There is no better way to get kicked out of a location (and I've seen it happen) than to damage something that way specifically flagged to be avoided. Guess who gets fired? Try your best to get permission for any activity that may not be reversible.

- *Learn your knots* Make sure you know all of your knots. Practice, practice, practice. On set it can be dangerous to tie a knot improperly that may give way. Do your best to learn the knots well enough, so you can tie them all quickly without thinking.

Grip's Belt

Belt Equipment

Chapter 29 contains a complete description of an electrician's belt. A grip's belt is very similar with the most noticeable exception being that no electrical equipment is included. However, there are a number of other differences.

Like the electrician's belt, a grip belt should contain:

- Leather work gloves;

- Multi-tool;

- 6 or 8″ crescent wrench;

- Small portable flashlight;

- Tape measure;

- Allen wrenches.

The grip belt contains fewer items than an electrician's belt, so it's also lighter – which is good because a grip has to move around a great deal. Since a grip has heavier items to carry around and frequently climb ladders, some grips use suspender straps. These straps ensure that the belt remains in the same place and doesn't rub and irritate you.

Make sure that you keep rope on you or at least nearby. Rope is one of the most important grip tools and is used for almost every imaginable purpose from raising equipment to the roof to stabilizing a stand to holding up a sheet of duvetyn. Sash cord is the most common type used by grips and is generally supplied by the production.

Grips must carry a larger variety of

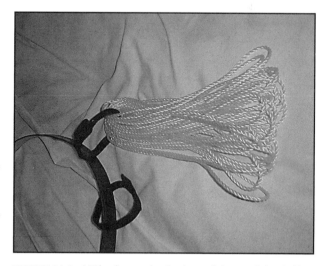

FIGURE 31.1 *A Velcro loop can be placed around the main belt to hold items such as rope.*

miscellaneous items such as rope, clips, etc. For this reason, Velcro loops are very useful. A loop can be easily placed around the main belt (see figure 31-1). When you need to carry anything like a rope, simply unzip and re-zip the Velcro around the rope. These loops are available inexpensively at most hardware stores. You'll find them much more convenient than carabineers.

Grips are also constantly in need of clothespins (C47s in industry-speak). You can make a small cord loop and easily carry a bunch on your belt. In figure 31-2, you'll see such a loop that has C47s and a couple of grip clip #1s on it.

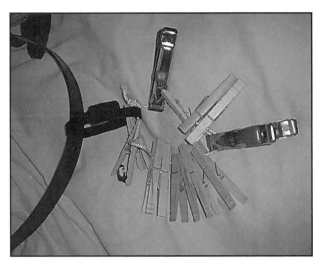

FIGURE 31.2 *A handy loop to hold C-47s and a couple of grip clip.*

Suggestions

Here are a few suggestions to help you:

- *Any strong belt will do* The belt itself doesn't need to be of any specific quality. I myself use the cheapest type of web belt available. It has a convenient snap, so I can take it off and put it on quickly. I used to wear an army surplus pistol belt. It was inexpensive, the quality was excellent and it was very rugged. The only problem was it was too wide for most commercial pockets.

- *Use your forearm as a measure* You'll find that you often need to roughly measure things whether it's the length of a rope or the span of a doorway. Measure the length of your forearm. You can then use your forearm to roughly estimate a length without having any tools. A grip showed me this technique and I've used it hundreds of times since then.

- *Avoid gaffer's tape on painted surfaces* Gaffer's tape (and duct tape) will often lift paint when it is removed. If you need to tape something to a painted surface, try to use paper tape instead because it's far less destructive.

C-stand

Applications

The C-stand (properly named the Century Stand for its hundreds of uses) is the film industry workhorse for holding flags, diffusion, backdrops, set pieces, and sometimes small lights. Figure 32-1 shows a standard C-stand with its tri-leg base, two risers (extensions), and head with extendable arm. When I made the transition from making my own movies to the professional world of filmmaking, it was clear to me that the humble C-stand was the item most critical to low-budget filmmaking and yet also the most unknown outside the professional ranks.

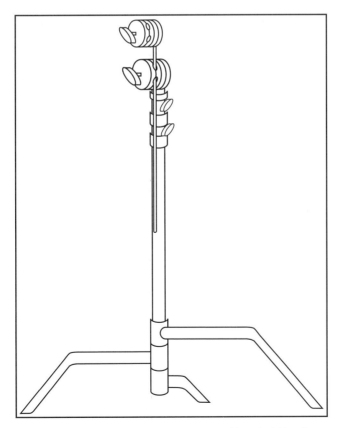

FIGURE 32.1 *The C-stand is the film industry workhorse for holding flags, diffusion, backdrops, set pieces, and sometimes small lights.*

While a C-stand is almost required equipment on sets from high to low budget, it can be prohibitively expensive to buy (a single used C-stand costs about the same as a mid-range DVD player). Since it's usually handy to have about three of them for even a minimal shoot, it's more affordable to make your own. While the C-stand you'll build in this chapter is not as quick to configure as a professional stand, your custom-built stands will have two big advantages: they're cheap and they can be more portable than a professional stand when you don't have a grip truck to haul them around.

PARTS

Qty	Item
4	PVC T-joints
4	$\frac{1}{2}'' \times 12''$ threaded steel pipes
4	$\frac{1}{2}''$ pipe flanges
1	$\frac{1}{2}''$ four-way coupling
4	$2\frac{1}{2}''$ machine screws with nuts
1	Sheet of non-slip material
2	$\frac{1}{2}'' \times 36''$ iron pipes
1	$\frac{1}{2}'' \times 24''$ iron pipes
1	$\frac{1}{2}''$ coupling
4	$\frac{1}{2}''$ pipe clamps
4	$2\frac{1}{2}''$ eyebolts, $\frac{1}{4}''$ 20, 2'' shaft
2	$\frac{1}{2}'' \times 1''$ threaded steel pipe nipples
1	$\frac{1}{2}''$ pipe union
1	$\frac{1}{2}'' \times 8''$ steel pipe
4	Small dumbbell weights

General Instructions

Some of the traditional uses of the C-stand can be seen in the following figures. Figure 32-2 shows a stand being used with a flag to block off light from spilling onto the background. Flags are also commonly used to shield the camera from the sunlight (much like a matte box) and crew members from the wind or sun (known as a courtesy flag). Flags can be used as a "lenser" to block a light source from shining directly into the optics of a camera and creating artifacts such as a lens flare.

Figure 32-3 shows the stand holding a reflector that might provide a fill light for an actor. C-stands are perfect for quickly placing and stably holding reflectors in place. They are also commonly used to hold diffusion material in front of a light.

FIGURE 32.2 *A flag blocks off light from spilling onto the background.*

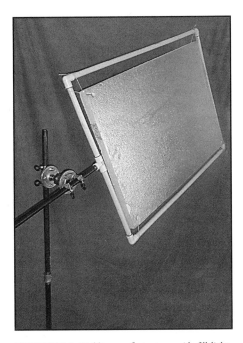

FIGURE 32.3 *Holding a reflector to provide fill light for an actor.*

Figure 32-4 shows a small fill light attached to the stand. The stand allows the height and angle of the light to be quickly altered. Note that you shouldn't use the stand for any heavy or large lights as the stand isn't intended to handle heavy weights.

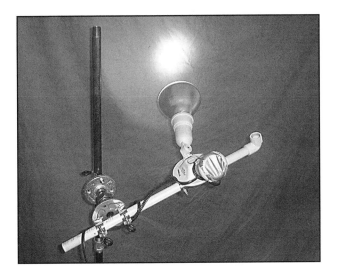

FIGURE 32.4 *A small fill light attached to the stand.*

Another very common use is to utilize two stands to hold up a backdrop. While a colored backdrop is often used for interviews, the C-stand rig most commonly holds a large sheet of duvetyn (black cloth) to block light from coming in a window. The light that must be blocked may be ruining the light balance of an interior shot or you may be filming a day-for-night scene.

Construction

These instructions show you how to construct a very modular stand that is easy to use. Most of the construction for the stand involves screwing various pipes together. The stand can be disassembled in the same way – consequently providing the stand's great portability. Basic breakdown consists of unscrewing the post from the base and disassembling the segments of the post into lengths that will fit into your vehicle.

Assembling the base

To create the C-stand, you'll begin by putting together the base that will hold the rest of the structural pipe. Figure 32-5 shows a top view of the assembled base. The central hub of the base is made of two flanges that sandwich a four-way pipe coupling between them. Four bolts run through the flange holes and secure the two flanges together.

To create the hub, follow these steps:

1. Cut two pieces of non-slip material large enough to cover the top and bottom of the four-way coupling. Non-slip material is available at most dollar stores and hardware warehouses. The material will prevent the coupling from slipping between the two flanges.

2. Place the flanges on either side of the non-slip material with the threaded couplings face out. You should now have a sandwich that consists of a flange, non-slip sheet, four-way coupling, non-slip sheet, and flange.

3. Insert the four $2\frac{1}{2}''$ machine screws through the bottom flange holes and feed them up through the top flange holes. These screws should fit perfectly between the cross members in the coupling such that all four threaded opening face outward unimpeded.

4. Place a nut on each screw and tighten it down. Your completed hub should look like the one shown in figure 32-6.

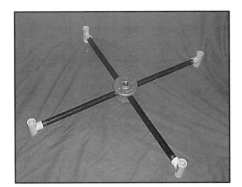

FIGURE 32.5 *A top view of the assembled base.*

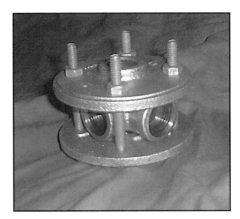

FIGURE 32.6 *The completed hub.*

Once the hub is complete, you'll need to screw the four 12″ iron pipes into the coupling to form the legs. Screw these pipes as tightly as possible. Since the legs and the hub provide the main structural strength of the stand, you might even consider using some type of locking compound to ensure that none of the legs become accidentally unscrewed.

Finally, you need to add the four leg risers. These risers are made using the $\frac{1}{2}''$ PVC T-joints (see figure 32-7) that are screwed onto the ends of each of the four pipes. You might have noticed the screw mount of the bottom flange prevents the stand from sitting levelly on the floor. The risers provide the clearance from the floor to allow the stand to sit evenly.

Cut two 3″ lengths of $\frac{1}{2}$″ PVC pipe. Since the risers are actually T-joints, they will accept this small piece of PVC pipe. Insert these small PVC pipes into the top of one of the risers (see figure 32-8) and another riser on the exact opposite side of the hub.

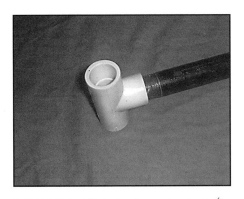

FIGURE 32.7 *Add four leg risers made using the $\frac{1}{2}$″ PVC T-joints.*

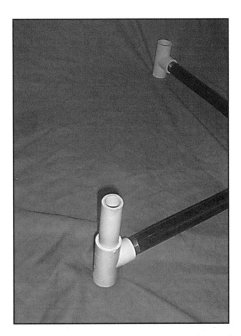

FIGURE 32.8 *Insert small PVC pipes into the top of the risers.*

These small pipes provide the stubs where you'll place weights to hold down the stand. Place some small dumbbell weights on each of the weight stubs (see figure 32-9). The holes of standard dumbbells are the perfect size to accept a $\frac{1}{2}$″ PVC pipe. If you don't have any spare weights sitting around, cheap weight sets can be commonly found at garage sales and listed in the classified ads.

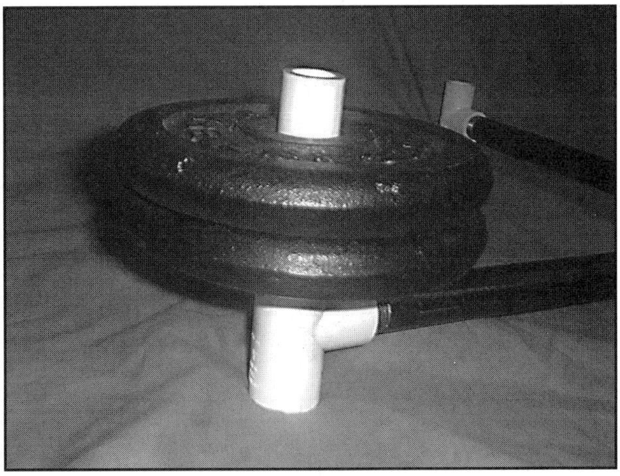

Be sure to place an equal amount of weight on the opposite stub (see figure 32-10). You may want to place stubs and weights on the other two risers if your stand will be handling a heavier load.

The T-joints have one further use. Often you'll find you need to place two stands in very close proximity. For example, one stand might hold a small light and another stand must hold the diffusion material directly in front of the light. As they are now, it would be difficult to place the stands close together without overlapping that can jeopardize the stability of both stands.

FIGURE 32.9 *Place small dumbbell weights on each of the weight stubs.*

FIGURE 32.10 *Be sure to place the equal amount of weight on the opposite stub.*

A solution is to cut four small 3″ lengths of PVC pipe and insert them into the bottoms of each of the T-joints for one of the stands. The pipes will raise the stand high enough so that the legs of one stand can be placed over the legs of another (see figure 32-11).

TIP ▶ *The risers, made of PVC plastic, provide a surface that will minimize the potential of the stand scratching a wooden floor. You might glue a soft wooden base or non-slip surface to the bottom of each riser to further prevent any possibility of floor damage.*

FIGURE 32.11 *These pipes will raise the stand high enough for the legs to be placed over another stand.*

Assembling the post

The post requires either a very small amount of assembly or none at all. Depending on your needs, you'll have to decide how long to make the central post and how many segments you'll need to attain the desired height. Typically, yard-long (1 m) iron pipes are used for the stem. These pipes can be replaced easily with a single 6' (2 m) iron pipe if this length is convenient for you to transport. Likewise, smaller 2' pipes could be used if even more portability is necessary.

Most likely, you'll want to create a post about 8 ft high. This size allows you to handle almost any lighting situation including the placement of a diffusion panel overhead to filter the sunlight striking a 6 ft tall actor. To achieve this height, you'll need two 3' pipe segments, one 2' pipe segment, and two joint connectors. When I assemble this type of stand, I generally put the 2' segment on the bottom, attach a 3' segment, and keep the final segment in reserve in case I need it (see figure 32-12).

Although this setup is the most convenient, there is a reason for wanting a long single-length post. The stand head is attached to the post and then slides up and down until the desired height is reached for the flag, diffusion, etc. When using a single post stand, a single adjustment allows you to move the head from a level close to the ground all the way to the top of the pole.

When the segments are broken up by connecting joints, the head can only be moved up and down the length between each joint. To position it elsewhere, the

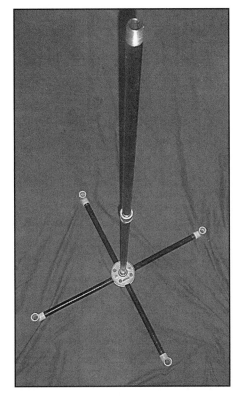

FIGURE 32.12 *Put the 2' segment on the bottom and attach a 3' segment above it.*

joint must be removed and the head re-attached to another segment. In practice, I haven't found this situation to occur very often and when it does, it's usually easy to remedy quickly. However, it's important to consider this predicament and plan ahead for it when performing setup on your stands (e.g., make sure to have at least one head on a low post).

> **TIP ▶** *It is generally a good idea to either spray the threads of the main post segments with a rust inhibitor or to oil them. This type of steel can easily rust if used or stored in damp conditions. By coating them against rust, you will save yourself the unpleasant circumstance of the rust either preventing the rods from being screwed together or from taking them apart.*

Assembling the head and arm

The arm of the stand will actually carry a majority of the load of the stand. Since the arm is assembled from readily available parts, it is not as versatile as a custom-manufactured C-stand arm. Therefore, even if you're comfortable using a professional stand arm, be sure to practice with the new arm before the shoot. That way you can understand the strengths and the limitations of this arm.

1. Take the union and screw one 1" nipple into each side. Secure each nipple with the liquid bond-soldering agent. Using the bonding agent will prevent loosening of the shoulder joints and ensure all the torque placed on the arm will be transferred to the union.

2. Screw the other end of each nipple into a flange (see figure 32-13). Secure the flanges with the liquid bond-soldering agent.

FIGURE 32.13 *Screw the other end of each nipple into a flange.*

3. Attach two conduit hangers on each flange.

4. Replace the screws in each conduit hanger with eyebolts (using the same method shown in Chapter 11). With the eyebolts you can quickly and easily tighten or loosen the brackets to slide them up and down the post.

5. Slide the brackets of the first flange over the central post of the stand (see figure 32-14).

6. Slide the rod that will be used as the arm into the brackets (see figure 32-15).

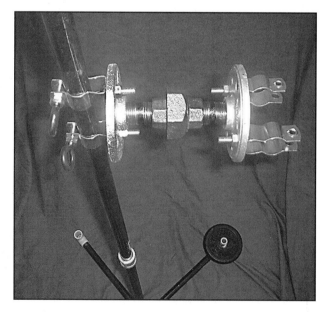

FIGURE 32.14 *Slide the brackets of the first flange over the central post of the stand.*

Now that your C-stand is complete, you will need to construct some flags and diffusion frames (see Chapter 45) to use it properly. When you want to tighten the arm, position the angle where you want it, tighten the ring of the union, and then hold onto the ring as you push the arm slightly downward (see figure 32-16). This will tighten the union to hold the arm precisely in place.

FIGURE 32.15 *Slide the arm rod into the brackets.*

FIGURE 32.16 *Hold the ring as you push the arm slightly downward.*

Be careful not to overload the arm. Not only might the stand tip over, but the force downward will tighten the screw of the union. If a large amount of weight is used, the union may be screwed down so tight that it is difficult to loosen. I did this once and it took a pipe wrench to break the union free.

Suggestions

Here are a few operating suggestions to help you get the best use from the C-stand:

- *Use more base weight than you need* C-stands get bumped into, overloaded, and unbalanced. The rule of thumb is to place more weight (in the form of sandbags or dead weight) on the base than absolutely necessary in order to accommodate unexpected shocks and weights.

- *Make more C-stands* Because of the variety of uses for a C-stand, you'll find that you're almost always one short. Therefore, build as many stands as you can afford to make and transport.

- *Don't use PVC in key places* It's tempting because of the low price, lightweight, and seeming durability of PVC to substitute it for some of the joints and poles, but don't. When PVC breaks, it simply shears off dropping everything attached to it to the ground (including lights, flags, false walls, etc.). You don't want equipment ruined or actors harmed because substandard materials were used in construction.

Sandbags

Applications

Sandbags, or more generally any type of dead weight, can be really important for use and safety. As soon as you use sandbags regularly, you'll find them indispensable on a film set. They are helpful in a multitude of situations:

- **Securing stands** C-stands, light stands, and tripods are all stands that are commonly stabilized or held in place using sandbags. The dead weight holds the stand in place and minimizes vibration and possible toppling if the stand is bumped or struck.

- **Holding down cables** When a cable must run along a walk path, placing a sandbag on each side will hold it close to the floor to prevent it from being easily tripped over. It someone does trip over it, the weight of the sandbag will help reduce the strength of the tug being directly transferred to the item where the cord is attached.

- **Camera mount** For low camera shots, it is often possible to use a few sandbags to provide the proper cushioning and support the camera at the desired shot angle.

- **Stabilizing and blocking weight** Sandbags are often place atop camera dollies and other surfaces to provide stabilizing weight. They are also used to block dolly wheels to prevent the dolly from moving between shots.

- **Standing or kneeling surface** Whether an actor needs a height boost, to stand on a solid surface (despite soft ground), or kneel on a hard floor, sandbags provide a perfect temporary and relatively soft stage.

- **Platform leveling** For anything that needs to be leveled (dolly track, tripods, furniture, etc.), placing one or more sandbags under the surface can help support the item and provide a level surface.

Often on an extremely low-budget film, sandbags are minimal or missing altogether. While sandbags are readily available from a studio supply house, even the transport weigh can be prohibitive to a guerilla production looking to travel light and get in and get out. For these reasons, a number of sandbag types and alternatives have been presented. You can use the solution most appropriate to a given situation. Be sure to choose at least one or two of these solutions, however, because the flexibility of your production will be greatly diminished without some form of dead weight load.

General Instructions

Professional movie sandbags are generally heavy canvas bags that have two pockets to hold the sand and a center handle for transport. In figure 33-1, you can see two sandbags, one on each leg of a low-roller stand. These sandbags are extremely flexible because they can be easily carried and placed straddling the leg of a stand or tripod.

If you don't have access to these movie sandbags, here are some alternative dead weights that may be useful:

- **Dumbbell weights** The plastic/concrete ones are the best for film production since they have the least chance of scratching surfaces such as wood floors. If you use traditional steel weights – which have the advantages of being smaller and more durable – try to obtain canvas bags just bigger than the weights to provide a soft cover.

- **Water jugs** Jugs used for drinking water are one of the most useful dead weight items for the guerilla filmmaker. They are generally built sturdily (for rough handling in grocery stores). The huge advantage to this type of weight is you can transport them empty to most locations and fill them once you arrive. Almost all houses and businesses have running water, so the source is rarely a problem. Additionally, the carrying handle of the jug provides the ideal grip through which you can run a rope to secure the weight to a necessary surface.

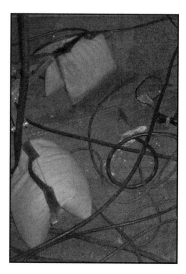

FIGURE 33.1 *Two sandbags – one on each leg of a low-roller stand.*

- **Real sandbags** Sandbags are generally used to secure areas from flooding. For this reason, you'll find the bags at many hardware stores. Better yet, sandbags and sand are often available for free at most fire stations. Think of it as your tax dollars at work to support independent filmmaking.

- **Concrete or bricks** Concrete can be cheap and it's easy to pour into any shape you want. When you pour the concrete, be sure to embed an eyebolt or some other type of anchor, so the dead weight can be tied to the desired item. Alternately, you can use red bricks as weight. For either concrete or bricks, be sure to find some sort of cover as both materials are abrasive and could damage the surface on which they're set.

- **2 liter soda bottles** A soda bottle is an excellent container for poured concrete. The neck and the flair at the top of the neck are perfect for securely fastening a rope which won't slip off. Although these bottles can be used for water or other fluids, they aren't very rugged and tend to spring a leak when abused.

- **Lead weight** The density of lead makes it an ideal dead weight, however, lead is a toxic substance. Once it enters the body it never leaves. Therefore, if you're using any type of lead weight, be sure it is covered with some type of plastic or non-porous material. Lead weights are often used with camera crane and jib arms, and these weights are never handled without first donning a pair of gloves.

No matter what substance you decide to use for your dead weights, transportation may pose a problem. If you need a great deal of weight for a particular application, try to transport it to the location before the shoot begins. Since most dead weight is made of materials that have little intrinsic value, you can often leave the weight out with little fear that it will be stolen.

Suggestions

Here are a few suggestions to help you get the best use of sandbags:

- **Treat sandbags with care** Whether you're using professional or hand-made sandbags, they are not indestructible. While you don't need to treat them with kid gloves, you can destroy them with outright abuse. The most common way to wreck a sandbag is to throw it from a height of over 6 ft (2 m). The sandbag is a tool and like most tools, the better you treat them, the longer they last.

- ***Don't get sandbags wet*** A wet sandbag will not only weigh a great deal more, but often turns either chunky or into a rock once dry. Try to keep them away from water.

- ***Take care when lifting dead weight*** I've seen many grips hurt themselves trying to be macho and carry more sandbags than they should. Be careful when lifting this weight, so you don't hurt yourself. Better yet, use some type of wheeled cart (wheelbarrow, grocery cart, dolly, etc.) to transport the sandbags around the set.

- ***Be careful when putting weight at a high location*** I've seen sandbags placed on the tops of ladders and negligently left there. I've seen bags accidentally knocked from the top of a wall and almost injuring a pedestrian walking below. Recognize that weight in an elevated position can pose serious danger if it falls from that height. Handle these situations with care.

- ***Watch for leaking sandbags*** If a sandbag begins leaking even a little, set it aside. Leaking sand can scratch wooden floors, get it equipment, ruin dolly wheels, and generally play havoc. Set any leaking sandbags aside and mark them clearly for later repair.

Flags, Reflectors, and Diffusion

Applications

Flags, reflectors, and diffusion screens are used to control light. While barn doors, spot/flood adjustments, and dimmers may alter a light source in a basic way, flags and diffusion screens allow you to determine exactly the place shadows will fall (see figure 34-1) and the type and strength of light. In this chapter you'll learn how to construct a general frame to which you can attach any type of flag or diffusion material.

This frame is made to be used in conjunction with the C-stand that was demonstrated in Chapter 32. This frame is also useful in many other situations, particularly where it can be mounted with tape or rope. You may also hold the flag in position by hand, also known as "Hollywooding" it.

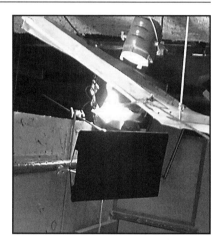

FIGURE 34.1 *Flags and diffusion screens let you determine exactly where the shadows will fall.*

PARTS	Qty	Item
	4	90° PVC bends
	1	Threaded PVC T-joint
	1	Can of PVC cement
	2	$\frac{1}{2}'' \times 8'$ PVC pipe
	1	$\frac{1}{2}'' \times 12''$ threaded iron pipe

General Instructions

A flag may seem like the simplest device possible, but achieving a particular effect takes a little practice. The role of a flag is simple: blocking light. How this is achieved takes some experience. You should also learn some terminology that's used as a method of shorthand on the set for people to communicate the desired role of a specific flag.

The DP may call for a *topper* which means that a flag should be placed to cut off the top of the light. A bottomer cuts off the bottom of the light and a sider is used for one side or the other. Setting a lenser means placing a flag such that it prevents light from entering the optics of a lens and serves the same purpose as a matte box (see Chapter 9).

It is generally a good idea to hold up the flag by hand to determine where the shadow will be cast. Once you have a good idea of the proper location, then you can bring in the stand and mount the flag. This prevents knocking around an unwieldy stand while trying to find the proper angle and location.

To create a soft edge on the shadow caused by the flag, place the flag near the light source. For a hard shadow, place it away from the light source. Most often, when a hard shadow is desired, the flag is placed just out of frame.

If the shadow has a really soft edge, it can sometimes be difficult to know where the shadow caused by the flag ends (as opposed to other natural shadows). You can stand in front of the flag and wave your hand to determine the bounds of the shadow. When your hand disappears, you know it's being hidden by the flag.

> **WARNING→** When you put a flag on a stand, it will act like a large sail. If used outside, that means that any gust of wind will push against it, sometimes strongly. Therefore, make sure that the flag is well anchored, so wind doesn't tip over the stand.

Materials for the frame

The possible materials that you can use in the frame are limited only by your imagination. For a complete list of diffusion and reflector materials, see Chapter 28. Whatever material you use, remember that you'll be placing it in front of hot lights. If there's any possibility that it might catch fire, don't use it.

The flag is really simply a black solid which has the function of blocking and absorbing light. Here is a list of suggestions for commonly available materials that can be used for flags:

- *Black foamcore* I highly recommend using either black foamcore or the black side of a foamcore sheet. Foamcore is light, yet it doesn't catch fire easily. It can be cut to size and is available in large 4′ × 8′ sheets (available from most expendable suppliers).

- *Black cloth* The cloth must be very thick to make sure that the light doesn't filter through the material. A good test is to hold it up to the sun and look through it. That will tell you how opaque the material may be. Also be certain that the cloth you buy is flame-retardant.

- *Painted cloth* Just about any surface painted with matte black paint can become an effective flag. Canvas drop clothes are available cheaply and can be painting with inexpensive craft acrylic paint to provide an excellent flag. You might choose the black paint that's available for painting an outdoor grill as it is very flame-retardant and usually fairly cheap.

> **WARNING→** Note that professional materials are treated and tested to minimize their flammability. If you use other flag materials around hot light, be very careful that there is no fire hazard. Be sure to read the fire retardation qualities of the material you choose and do not use them outside the bounds specified. Make sure you put any material a good distance from the light it is absorbing.

When the materials aren't mounted in the frame, there are several effective ways you can transport them. Cloth and more durable material can be rolled up and kept in a cardboard tube. For materials that must remain flat, you can purchase an inexpensive artwork portfolio traveling case.

Construction

To construct a frame to hold your flag, diffusion, and reflector materials, follow these steps:

1. Cut the PVC pipe of the following lengths: two of length 38″ (97 cm), two of length 12.5″ (32 cm), and one of length 26″ (66 cm).

2. Create one side of the frame by taking the two 21″ pieces and joining them with the PVC T-joint. The threaded end of the T-joint should be left open (see figure 34-2). Use the PVC cement to glue the pieces into place. Note that the cement sets in less than 30 s, so you have to have everything ready for quick placement immediately after application.

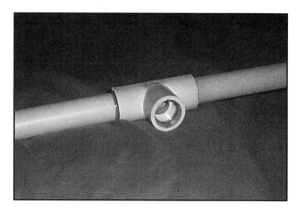

FIGURE 34.2 *Create one side of the frame by taking the two 21″ pieces and joining them with the PVC T-joint.*

3. Put the rectangle together with the 36″ pieces forming the top and bottom sides, the 24″ forming the right side, and the T-joined pieces forming the left side. Your frame should look like the one shown in figure 34-3. Use the PVC cement to glue them into place.

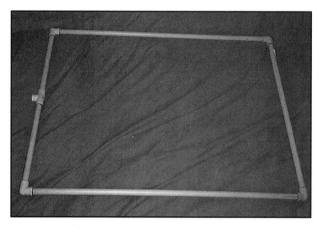

FIGURE 34.3 *Put the rectangle together with the other pieces.*

Now that the frame is complete, there are several ways that material can be attached to it.

The simplest method is to tape the material directly to the frame. You can use duct tape to secure it, but this silver material can cause unwanted reflections. A much better idea is to use black gaffer's tape as the adhesive is very strong and the surface is a non-reflective matte black.

Cord ties (see figure 34-4) are a very effective means of securing soft material. The cord ties are used with the shoelace knot variation demonstrated in Chapter 37. The biggest problem with this method is the time it takes to change the material on the frame. Often you have to switch out level of diffusion or the reflector type at a moments notice. Untying one material and re-tying another can take some time.

You may choose to use elastic string (see figure 34-5). The elastic is convenient because it can be very quickly slipped on or off the frame for nearly instantaneous changing of the frame materials. You will have to occasionally replace it, however, as the elastic tends to lose its strength over time.

You can also place strips of Velcro around the edges of the frame. The other side of the Velcro strip is then adhered to the flag or diffusion material. There are different strengths of Velcro available, so try to use the strongest Velcro you can find.

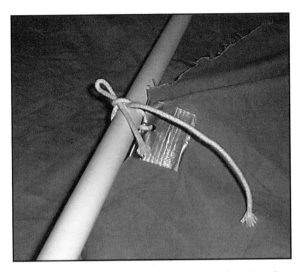

FIGURE 34.4 *Cord ties are a very effective means of securing soft material.*

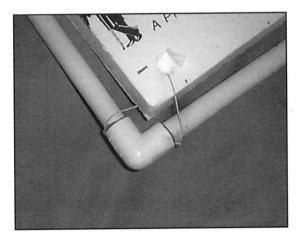

FIGURE 34.5 *Elastic string is convenient because it can be very quickly slipped on or off the frame.*

NOTE→ Velcro is extremely convenient and one of the most versatile methods of affixing various materials. However, I discovered the problem with it on a very windy exterior shoot one day. Each time a large gust of wind would blow, the Velcro would come a little undone. While the material didn't come off the frame, that Velcro tearing sound was enough to ruin the soundtrack on several takes. Perhaps if I'd used a stronger type of Velcro this wouldn't have been a problem. Just be aware that this is a potential drawback of using Velcro.

If the material can be secured to a stiff board such as foamcore, you can actually glue button snaps directly to the frame. Place the other side of the button on the flag or reflector board and you can quickly and easily snap your material into place.

Suggestions

Here are a few suggestions to help you get the best use from a flag:

- *Make several frames* Since the frame is so cheap, light, and easy to construct, you might consider making four or five to keep them on hand. That way you could leave a different material mounted on each frame for quick utilization.

- *Place a union on the end of each flag* When you're using the flag with the C-stand shown in Chapter 32, releasing it from the head can take time. You'll have to loosen the brackets and then slide out the holding arm. This process can take some time, especially if you're leaving the stand where it is and simply swapping out the flag for another material type. You might instead place a small nipple on the flag, attach a union to that, and finally add the extension arm. If all of your frames have a union attached, you can simply unscrew the union and switch frames in seconds.

- *Bring extra soft material* For material that is soft, you'll find that they may be damaged in transportation. A silk with a tear down the middle can be frustrating because it will be rendered useless. For material that damages easily, be sure to bring extra fabric, so you can repair any tears and still obtain the needed shots.

Reflector/Shiny Board

Applications

For exterior shoots, one of the most useful pieces of equipment in the grip truck is the reflector or shiny board (see figure 35-1). A reflector is essentially a large soft mirror that can be used to reflect the sun into a scene. The reflector can be panned and tilted and once properly positioned, locked into place. Shiny boards provide a fantastic way to light a scene without using a full lighting package.

As opposed to attaching a large piece of reflector fabric to an 8′ × 8′ frame, a shiny board is smaller (generally 3′ × 3′) and made to be specifically targeted on an area, and re-targeted. Generally one person is assigned to the reflector so that when the sun moves, adjustments can be made to keep the highlight in the same place.

A shiny board is mounted on a head, so it can be quickly panned left or right. The reflector board itself is attached to a swivel head, so it can be tilted for correct light placement. Most exterior shots benefit from the use of a reflector to add a little brightness to the scene, a rim light to an actor, or highlight detail in the background.

	Qty	Item
PARTS	6	$\frac{1}{2}''$ 90° PVC elbow bends
	2	$\frac{1}{2}''$ 90° PVC elbows w/1 threaded end
	2	$\frac{1}{2}''$ T-joints
	4	1″ to $\frac{1}{2}''$ adapters
	1	1″ coupling
	2	$\frac{1}{2}''$ thread adapters
	1	$\frac{1}{2}''$ plastic union
	1	$\frac{1}{2}''$ steel union
	1	$\frac{1}{2}'' \times 3''$ threaded steel pipe
	1	$\frac{1}{2}'' \times 12''$ threaded steel pipe
	1	$\frac{1}{2}'' \times 36''$ threaded steel pipe
	1	$\frac{1}{2}''$ four-way steel joint
	3	$\frac{1}{2}'' \times 10'$ PVC pipe
	1	C-stand base (see Chapter 43)

General Instructions

A shiny board should have two sides: a hard side and a soft side. The soft side can be provided with aluminum foil. For the hard side, you're going to have to purchase a sheet of Mylar (available at most party stores). You may want to scuff the Mylar surface a bit to make sure the reflected light isn't too

FIGURE 35.1 *For exterior shoots, one of the most useful pieces of equipment is the reflector or shiny board.*

harsh. For the board itself, an insulation panel is nearly perfect. One of the advantages of using insulation panels is that they're sturdy enough to withstand the wind without bending, yet they're still fairly light.

The reflector is typically mounted on a sturdy junior stand. Since the board is used outside and has such a broad flat surface, wind can easily catch it and knock it over. The shiny board you'll create in this chapter will be mounted on the C-stand you created in Chapter 32. Since the C-stand isn't very heavy, make sure you excessively weight down the base to make certain that the stand isn't blown over. Additionally, bring along some spare rope you can use to secure the frame to nearby buildings or fences.

Construction

You can see a complete diagram for the shiny board in figure 35-2. The union at the bottom allows the frame to pan and adjust the reflected light to the left or the right. The assembly on the left side of the frame is essentially a socket that allows the panel to be tilted or even freely spun end over end. The assembly uses a nail like a cotter pin to secure the tilt at a particular angle.

On the right side, a plastic union has been modified to allow the panel to freely rotate. While the right side union can be replaced with an assembly like the one used on the left side, the assembly is more expensive and complicated to make than simply purchasing a union.

For stability, be sure to use PVC cement on all the (non-rotating) pieces to make sure the structure is solid. As always, don't glue on piece that makes the assembly of another piece impossible. For example, don't glue the reflector mount together before you place the reflector panel between the union and the left assembly or you won't be able to insert the frame.

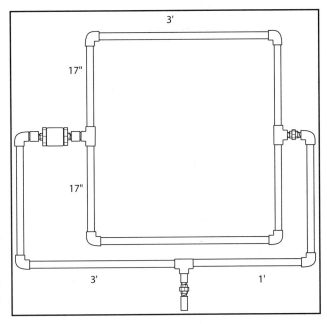

FIGURE 35.2 *A complete diagram for the shiny board.*

Creating the base

Start by creating the base of the reflector. It's the same construction as the one used for the C-stand. Turn to Chapter 32 for instructions and construct the base, so it appears as the one shown in figure 35-3.

Once you have the base assembled, be sure to purchase enough lengths of pipe to raise it high. You will also probably need more height than the C-stand as a shiny board is often extended to 8–10 ft (about 3 m) in height. Since a shiny board needs to be in the light to direct it, this often means catching light over small trees, fences, and other obstacles.

> **TIP** ▶ *If you'll be working with the reflector a great deal (re-positioning, moving, re-directing, etc.), be sure to bring along a stepladder. You may need to put it higher than is convenient to reach.*

Creating the reflector panel

The reflector panel can be made of any type of thick Styrofoam board. I've found that insulation board is about an inch thick (2.5 cm) making it the perfect thickness for this application.

To create the reflector panel, follow these steps:

1. Cut a piece of insulation foam into a square 3′ × 3′ (1 m × 1 m). Most of the standard size boards at the hardware store are 2′ × 4′, so you might have to go to a home warehouse supply to buy the large sizes to trim down. Otherwise, patch two smaller boards together to obtain the correct size.

2. Cut lengths of $\frac{1}{2}''$ PVC pipe to the following measures: two lengths of 36″ (1 m) and four lengths of 17″ (43 cm).

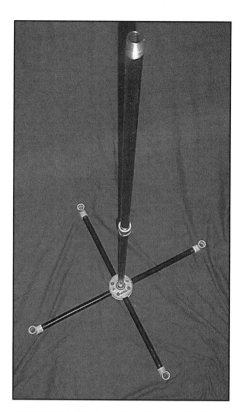

FIGURE 35.3 *The base of the reflector is identical to the one used for the C-stand.*

3. Create the frame with four 90° elbows and two T-joints as shown in figure 35-4.

4. Place the foam square into the frame and make sure it fits snugly. If not, trim the PVC pipes until the frame is the right size.

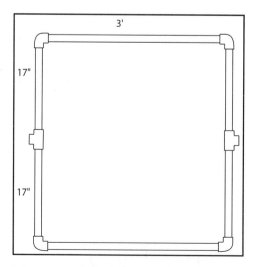

FIGURE 35.4 *Create the frame with four 90° elbows and two T-joints.*

5. Attach the aluminum foil to one side and the Mylar to the other. Although I've found it easiest to simply staple the reflecting sheets onto the insulation board, attachment with glue might be more durable.

6. Drive screws through the frame into the insulation board (see figure 35-5). I used 3″ (7.5 cm) drywall screws to act like pins to hold the insulation board in place. I only needed two screws per side of the frame to steadily anchor the board, so it didn't move. Use as many as you feel are necessary. Be sure to drill holes through the PVC pipe before you drive the screws through to make sure they go straight into the insulation board.

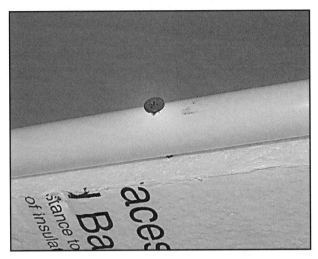

FIGURE 35.5 *Drive screws through the frame into the insulation board.*

Once the panel is complete, you'll begin construction on the reflector mount. The mount will allow the reflector panel to tilt.

Creating the reflector mount

The mount is the most complicated part of the reflector. The mount must allow the reflector to be spun freely since either the soft or hard side might be chosen for a particular shot (and may be called for at any time). However, once the soft or hard side has been chosen and a reflector angle selected, the reflector must be locked into that angle and stay solidly in place despite wind or other factors.

We'll start by creating the left assembly. The left assembly is shown in figure 35-6. From left to right, the assembly consists of: a short length of $\frac{1}{2}''$ PVC (attached to the panel's T-joint), a $\frac{1}{2}''$ threaded adapter, a 1″ to $\frac{1}{2}''$ adapter, a 1″ coupling, a 1″ to $\frac{1}{2}''$ adapter, a $\frac{1}{2}''$ threaded adapter, a short length of $\frac{1}{2}''$ PVC, and a 90° elbow. You may not be able to see the first short length of PVC pipe since in the figure it's joining the threaded adapter to the T-joint of the panel frame.

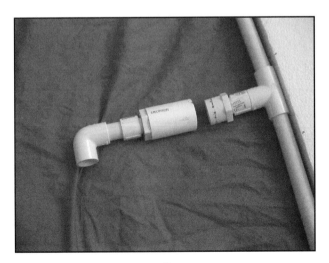

FIGURE 35.6 *Create the left assembly.*

Before you begin assembly, some modifications need to be made to the 1″ coupling and one of the 1″ to $\frac{1}{2}''$ adapters. To make things easier, first take one of the 1″ to $\frac{1}{2}''$ adapters and use PVC cement to glue it into one side of the coupling. The glued adapter will remain stationary with the frame while the other adapter spins to allow the panel to spin.

Take the coupling and sand out the open end. Sanding off a small layer will create enough room for the second adapter to spin freely within it. Don't sand so much that the adapter is loose in the coupling end. Don't worry if the adapter seems a little tight since you'll be putting some oil into it later to reduce the friction.

Insert the second adapter into the coupling and drill a small hole through the coupling into the adapter (see figure 35-7). In this hole you'll insert a nail to use as a cotter pin to hold the panel at a selected angle.

Withdraw the second adapter and you should see the hole generated by drilling through the coupling. Measure the distance from the end of the adapter to this hole. All the holes you drill in the adapter should be at the same distance from the end. You should now drill holes around the barrel of the adapter (see figure 35-8). For my reflector, I drilled 12 holes allowing me to position the panel in 30° increments (360°/12 holes = 30° between holes). Drill more or less holes depending on your needs.

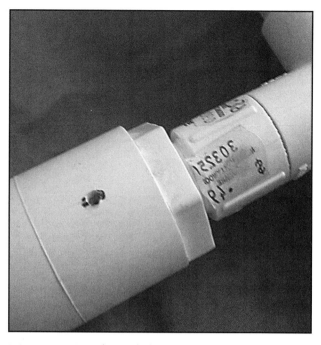

FIGURE 35.7 *Insert the second adapter into the coupling and drill a small hole through the coupling into the adapter.*

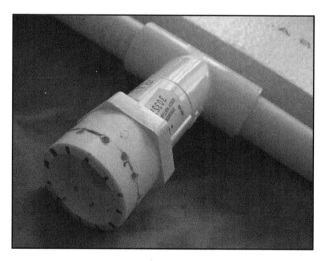

FIGURE 35.8 *Drill all the holes around the barrel of the adapter.*

TIP ▶ *I've found that the easiest way to obtain evenly spaced holes is to wrap a small sheet of paper around the pipe. On the paper, place a mark on the paper where the wrapping overlap occurs. Unroll the paper and you should have a mark that indicates the complete circumference of the pipe. Use a ruler to measure this length and divide the value the number of holes you need. Make marks on the paper at the appropriate intervals (the end of the paper will indicate the first marker). Wrap the paper around the pipe again and mark on the pipe where the holes should go.*

Once all the holes are drilled, place the adapter back into the coupling and try to insert the nail at each of the increments. If the nail won't enter, you may have to widen either the hole on the coupling or some of the holes in the adapter. Make sure you don't widen the holes too much so that you don't have a snug fit or your panel may move when the wind hits it.

Rub a small amount of oil for lubrication on the inside of the coupling. Put the assembly together as shown in figure 35-9. It's a good idea to use PVC cement to glue together all the parts except for the coupling and the second adapter (which should spin freely). If you're not sure you understand how the mount will go together, wait to glue until you can see how you'll complete the construction.

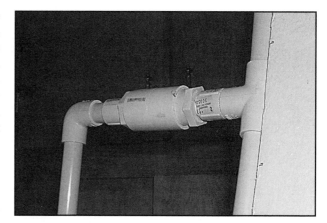

FIGURE 35.9 *Put the assembly together.*

To create the other side of the panel mount, you'll need to make a slight modification to the plastic union piece. In figure 35-10, you can see that the union, when disassembled, is actually three different pieces. The piece on the left has no threads and spins freely in the union. The threaded piece on the right is screwed into the housing (the center object) and can be tightened down until the unthreaded piece can't move. You're going to use PVC cement to bond the threaded piece to the housing such that the unthreaded piece can still spin freely.

FIGURE 35.10 *The three different pieces of a disassembled union.*

Before you get out the glue, try tightening down the threaded piece. Do you feel how the unthreaded piece can't move? Now back off the threaded piece enough, so the unthread piece can freely move (about a quarter turn with the union I've used). Do you feel how the unthreaded piece can spin freely? That's how you're going to create a freely revolving socket.

First, disassemble the union and take out the unthreaded piece. Apply some oil to the rim to ensure the piece will rotate smoothly. Place the unthreaded piece back into the housing. Remember PVC cement dries very quickly, so you'll have to work fast on this next part.

Put PVC cement on the threads of the threaded part. Screw it all the way into the housing and then back it out the number of turns to keep the unthreaded part free (probably a quarter turn). Now grasp the housing and spin the unthreaded part to make sure the PVC cement didn't get on that part (and bind it to the housing). The cement should set in under a minute and you now have a freely rotating socket!

When the union is mounted on the other side of the panel, it will appear as shown in figure 35-11.

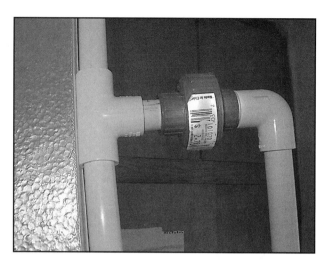

FIGURE 35.11 *The union mounted on the other side of the panel.*

Next you'll put together the main head bracket that uses iron pipes to hold up the panel. Since it uses fixed length iron pipes, you will want to wait to complete the panel mounting because you will need to cut the final PVC pipes to make it fit the bracket.

Mounting the panel

The assembly of the main head bracket consists mostly of screwing together various parts.

1. Screw the steel union onto the top of the pipe on the base of the stand.

2. Screw the 3″ steel pipe nipple into the top of the union.

3. Mount the four-way steel joint onto the top of the nipple. You can use a T-joint instead, although I chose the four-way to have an extra position for placing a securing rope.

4. Screw the 12″ pipe into one end and the 36″ pipe in the other end of the four-way joint (see figure 35-12).

5. Add a threaded 90° elbow at the ends of the pipes. Note that I used these PVC elbows because they were available with one end threaded and the other plain to allow easy insertion of the panel mount. You can use a metal elbow instead, but you'll also have to add thread adapters to the ends of the PVC pipes on the mount.

6. Measure the length between the two elbows on the bracket.

7. Complete assembly of the mount (see figure 35-13) and make it match the length of the mounting bracket by cutting the PVC lengths on the left and right ends just before the 90° elbows.

8. Cut two PVC lengths that provided enough room between the panel 90° elbows and the top of the bracket (see figure 35-13).

9. Insert the lengths into the elbows and put the entire panel mount onto the bracket (see figure 35-14).

FIGURE 35.12 *Screw the 12" pipe into one end and the 36" pipe in the other end of the four-way joint.*

FIGURE 35.13 *Complete assembly of the mount.*

Your reflector is now complete. It is a good idea to use some string to attach the nail/cotter pin to the frame, so it won't get lost. For transporting the reflector, it can be easily broken down into three pieces. Unscrew the bracket at the metal union and the whole head will come free as one piece. Unscrew the rod for the second piece. The base is the third piece.

FIGURE 35.14 *Cut two PVC lengths that provided enough room between the panel 90° elbows and the top of the bracket.*

Suggestions

Here are a few operating suggestions for the reflector:

- **Light the background** Reflectors aren't often used to light the main actors (except as a fill light). Most often, the actors are placed in the direct light, perhaps with a sheet of diffusion on a frame between them and the sun. The shiny board can then be used to add a rimlight, provide a background pattern in conjunction, or highlight features of the background that sit in shadow.

- **Position the reflector with a hand** Especially with the soft side, it's often difficult to accurately position the center of the reflection. Have someone stand in the scene with their fist where the light should be focused. Then you have an easy target to concentrate the light on.

Knots, Hitches, and Bends Overview

Applications

In making a film, your life will be greatly simplified if you know a number of basic knots. A few fundamental knots can be useful for everything from transportation to steadying equipment. I can't count the number of times I've seen camera operators secure expensive camera equipment with knots and lashings that I wouldn't trust to anchor a bag full of garbage. You'll find that the most varied problems can be solved with a handful of well-understood knots.

Keep in mind that learning knots is not easy for most people, so don't get frustrated if you tie a knot perfectly one day and can't remember how the next. The twists and turns of the knot, the different types of rope, and the orientation of the rope all conspire to make a familiar knot seem completely alien.

I'm not a natural knot maker, so it took me a while to master these knots. One technique that helped me was to imagine the rope as a highway on an aerial map. I then thought of a car moving down the highway across underpasses and overpasses. That helped me remember how the pieces of rope were overlapped or how one underlies another. If this technique doesn't help you, try to find something familiar to use as a model. Learning a knot in terms that already make sense to you can dramatically decrease the time needed for mastery.

Knot learning takes, more than anything else, a good deal of practice. Keep a length of practice rope around. Two feet of clothesline will do nicely. Practicing your knots can be a great activity when you're on the phone. Only the first few ties should require your attention and then your hands will learn how to do it almost automatically.

> **WARNING→** Knots you learn for rope should not be used for metal cable. Knots depend on the friction caused by the rope straining against itself. Cable is slick and smooth, so the very foundation of a knot is defeated.

Types of ropes

There are three primary types of rope you will find in stores:

- **Polyrope** Made from many different types of polymers, a polyrope will generally be cheaper than ropes of other materials. Polyrope, since it's made of plastic, won't rot if it gets wet. Some polyrope is very slick which means that knots (which need rope friction) won't hold as well as when done with natural rope types.

- **Nylon rope** Nylon rope is generally soft, pliable, and shiny. Being of artificial material, it also doesn't rot in water. Nylon rope is generally the most attractive type of rope and as such was used for many of the pictures in this book.

- **Natural rope** Made from organic fiber such as cotton or hemp, natural rope is usually the most preferred type of rope to use. The rope is soft and pliable and because it's an organic fiber, it knots tighter and has less of a chance of slipping than the synthetic rope types. However, natural rope is generally weaker than artificial rope and will rot if it is stored after it's been wet.

As you can see, each type of rope has its own strengths and weaknesses. I would recommend that you use some type of thick cotton rope when first learning to tie knots. The width of the rope makes it very easy to handle and will help you see the twists and turns clearly.

Once you've learned a knot, however, be sure to try it with as many different types of rope as you can find. Often a knot which seems simple to create with thick rope can be much more difficult with thin twine. On a film location, you'll never know what type of rope you'll need to tie.

Strength of rope

When you buy rope, it will generally be marked with the amount of weight the rope can handle. It then seems a simple matter to determine the weight you need to pull or lift (say 100 pounds) and get a rope with the proper amount of capacity.

But wait – a knot in a rope actually decreases the amount of weight a rope can handle. Knots typically decrease the strength of rope between 40 and 60%. That means that if you tie a holding knot in 100-pound rope to a dead weight of 100 pounds, it will probably give way under the load. Therefore, be sure to plan in the necessary weight factors when determining the rope you need.

On one film I worked, the owner of a dancehall was going to loan us a large disco ball for set decoration. All I needed to do was get the ball down from the ceiling. It was held by a length of chain on a hook and the ball itself weighed 75 pounds. The owner had put it up by having two people stand on the top of a tall (and very unstable) ladder and wrestle it into place. Since I had no desire to give up my life to retrieve a disco ball, I figured I could get it down by lowering it with some rope.

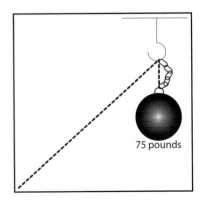

FIGURE 36.1 *The ceiling hook acts as a type of fulcrum.*

Most of the rope at the local home warehouse had a carrying strength of around 100 pounds. I knew that by the time I made a knot in the rope, the situation could become dangerous. By purchasing rope that had a carrying strength of 250 pounds, I knew that the rope would have no problem carrying the load with room to spare.

In figure 36-1 you can see the way I used the ceiling hook as a type of fulcrum. The disco ball lowered easily and after we were finished filming it, we put it back into place quickly and safely.

Cutting and sealing the rope end

Sealing the end of the rope prevents fraying. If the rope is going to be used for any length of time (such as rope used for tying coiled cable), the little extra time spent sealing it will pay off dramatically in time saved replacing frayed rope.

With natural rope, you can create a small binding on the rope end with twine or string. Check out a book on knots from the library for the wide variety of end bindings. Alternately, you can easily use a spot of normal white glue.

A method commonly practiced on film sets is to wrap the point on the rope to be cut with a wide strip of tape. The cut is then made in the middle of the tape leaving both ends with a tape binding.

For polyrope or a rope made of nylon (or any type of plastic), you can use a cigarette lighter or match to seal the end. The fibers at the end will melt together and provide a good binding seal. Make sure you perform the melting outside or in a well-ventilated area as the fumes are generally slightly toxic and very unpleasant.

Knot terminology

When tying knots, there is some terminology that you need to know to clearly understand the written instructions. These terms include:

- *Hitch* The name of a knot used to tie a rope to a post.

- *Bend* Used for tying two ropes together.

- *Bight* A bend or turn in the rope.

- *Standing part* The long part of the rope that isn't doing anything.

- *Working end* The free end of the rope that you're using to make the knot.

If you can understand and duplicate the knots from the demonstration pictures, you may still want to learn these terms. They are standard in the world of knot tying and will help you learn other knots. Just last week I went on the Internet and found instructions on how to make and use a cowboy lasso. The instructions used the above terms to describe the process.

Types of knots

There are six important knots to a filmmaker:

- *Shoelace knot (reef knot)* For day-to-day work, this knot is used most often for everything from binding a package to securing cables. Since you presumably know how to tie your shoelaces, you already know the basics of this knot.

- *Figure-8 knot* The figure-8 knot is a stopper knot for the end of a rope. By tying a figure-8, you can prevent a rope from slipping through a grommet or other hole where the rope has been fed.

- *Bowline knot* This knot creates a loop that won't collapse even under stress. In the scouts, you're taught that if you only learn one knot, it should be this one.

- *Clove hitch* A simple and quick hitch that allows you to secure a rope to a standing load such as a post or pole.

- *Trucker's hitch* The trucker's hitch is essential for securing cargo. It allows you to tie the load and then pull all the slack from the rope thereby binding it tightly.

Each one of these knots is described in the following chapters. Keep in mind that there isn't a really objective reference source for knots like the Oxford English Dictionary is for the English language. You might know these knots under different names or you might know different knots under these names!

For example, a grip first showed me how to do the clove hitch for attaching frame lines to a pole quickly. I looked in all the knot books I could find and while the finished knot is the same, his technique for tying it differed from the many other ways shown. As long as you can tie a knot, how you do it or what you call it isn't very important.

Double Half-hitch

The double half-hitch is the workhorse of many knots. It can be tied quickly and easily and won't bind, so it's easy to untie. A half-hitch is a simple loop around a pole (see figure 36-2). After a turn is made around the pole, the working end is brought under and behind the standing end and then fed through the loop close to the pole.

FIGURE 36.2 *A half-hitch is a simple loop around a pole.*

By itself, a half-hitch doesn't have much holding strength. However, add another half-hitch (see figure 36-3) and any stress on the rope will tighten the knot and make the binding more secure. A double half-hitch is commonly used as an anchoring knot, such as the initial anchor point when creating a trucker's hitch (see Chapter 52).

FIGURE 36.3 *A double half-hitch is commonly used as an anchoring knot.*

Reef or Shoelace Knot

Applications

I'm sure you already know how to tie a shoelace knot. In film production, this knot is handy for several reasons. Since everyone knows how to tie it, even untrained volunteers can use it for everything from binding diffusion material on a 6′ × 6′ frame to fastening a cable tie.

A shoelace knot is actually a reef knot with double draw loops. The name of the reef knot comes from sailing where it was used to tie a rolled-up or "reefed" sail to the cross spar. A reef knot is also known as a square knot or Hercules knot (see figure 37-1). You can see that in a properly tied knot, on each

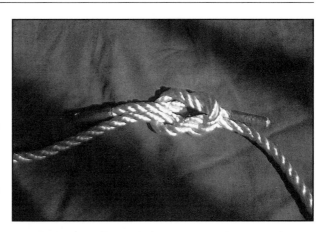

FIGURE 37.1 *A reef knot is also known as a square knot or Hercules knot.*

FIGURE 37.2 *The granny knot is unreliable and can slip and jam.*

side of the knot the two lengths of the rope pass through the same side of the bight (they're side by side).

When tied in the opposite manner with the lengths coming out on opposite sides of the bight, the knot formed is a granny knot (see figure 37-2). The granny knot is unreliable and can slip and jam.

To loosen a reef knot, hold both lengths on one side of the knot in one hand and the opposite two lengths in the other hand. Push them towards each other to make the knot loosen. The reef knot should only be used to tie ropes together if both ropes are the same size. If different sized ropes are used or if one end is stiffer than the other, use a sheet bend. You can easily find directions for making this bend on the Internet.

> **NOTE→** Do not use the reef knot in critical situations such as when people or heavy weights are involved. Since this knot can jam or be easily undone, it's not safe enough for critical applications.

Shoelace Variation

A variation of the reef knot commonly used on movie sets is shown in figure 37-3. Instead of making two draw loops as in a shoelace, a single draw loop is used so that only a single end must be pulled for the knot to release. This variation is commonly used to tie a silk, a solid, or diffusion material to a frame (see Chapter 34), or to knot the ties on coiled cables.

To create this knot, tie the first part just like you would a shoelace and then make a single loop (see figure 37-4).

Push the draw loop around and under the opposite working end as shown in figure 37-5.

Hold the loop and pull the opposite working end until it tightens down on the loop. To release the knot, simply pull the end of the draw loop.

FIGURE 37.3 *This variation is commonly used to tie silk, solid, or diffusion material to a frame.*

FIGURE 37.4 *Tie the first part just like you would a shoelace and then make a single loop.*

FIGURE 37.5 *Push the draw loop around and under the opposite working end.*

Thief Knot

There is a related knot very similar to the reef knot that's known as the thief knot. It has the same basic properties as a reef knot, but it's tied differently so that the working ends complete in opposite corners of the knot rather than both on the top (see figure 37-6).

Legend says that sailors would tie their valuables with a thief knot. If a thief would untie it, he would likely re-tie the knot as a standard reef knot making the tampering obvious to the sailor. If you keep valuables on a set, you might practice the same technique.

FIGURE 37.6 *The thief knot, tied differently than the reef knot, has the working ends complete in opposite corners of the knot.*

Figure-8 Knot

Applications

A figure-8 knot (see figure 38-1), also known as a Flemish or Savoy knot, is a stopper knot. The knot looks like its name and is used to temporarily bulk-up the end of a rope. It can stop a rope from fraying, provide a hand-hold knot, or be used in conjunction with another knot or hitch (see Chapter 39).

Very commonly on a film set, the figure-8 knot is used as a stopper when a length of rope has been fed through a grommet (such as those found in tarps or tents). The figure-8 knot is used in preference to the overhand knot (the most basic stopper knot) since the figure-8 knot is easier to undo after a load has been placed on it.

The knot is tied using either the twist method or the traditional method. The twist method is quicker and easier to remember. The regular method is most often used in a complicated rope setup or when the figure-8 knot is being integrated into the tying of another knot.

FIGURE 38.1 *A figure-8 knot is a stopper knot.*

Twist Method

Take the working end of the rope and fold it over as shown in figure 38-2, so it forms a bight.

Grasp the working and standing ends with one hand and the peak of the bight with the other. Twist the bight away from you until it turns 360° (see figure 38-3). Because your wrist can only easily turn 180°, you will need to do two twists to complete the 360° revolution.

Figure-8 Knot **233**

FIGURE 38.2 *Take the working end of the rope and fold it over so that it forms a bight.*

FIGURE 38.3 *Twist the bight away from you until it turns 360°.*

After you've completed the two turns, push the working end of the rope down around the loop and pull it up through the hole (see figure 38-4). Pull the working end and the standing end in opposite directions and you'll have a figure-8 stopper knot.

This knot is useful at the end of a rope (or even a shoelace) if it begins to fray. Simply pull the knot tight and snip off the excess.

Traditional Method

To tie the knot using the traditional method, take the working end and wrap it around the standing end (see figure 38-5).

Pass it down behind the loop. Bring the working end up through the loop (see figure 38-6). Pull on both ends to make the knot tight.

FIGURE 38.4 *Push the working end of the rope down around the loop and pull it up through the hole.*

FIGURE 38.5 *Take the working end and wrap it around the standing end.*

FIGURE 38.6 *Bring the working end up through the loop.*

Figure-8 Knot **235**

The advantage of the traditional method over the twist method comes if you want to loop the knot to make it stronger. A double figure-8 can be tied with a loop and is commonly used by climbers to secure a rope to a carabineer (see figure 38-7). This version of the knot should be used if the knot will sustain a heavy load.

To make the double figure-8, make sure that there is a good amount of extra rope at the working end. Complete a figure-8 knot, but don't pull it tight. Twist the working end around the pole or carabineer and then feed it back into the loop. Essentially, the working end should retrace its path through the knot. Once it has completed its journey, pull the knot tight and you have a strong double figure-8.

FIGURE 38.7 *A double figure-8 knot can be tied with a loop and is used by climbers to secure a rope to a carabineer.*

You can also tie a double figure-8 by using the traditional method of tying, but form a loop of the working end and run this through the pattern. This method can be used to quickly tie a double figure-8 in a standing line.

Bowline Knot

Applications

If you were in the scouts, you may already know how to tie a bowline (see figure 39-1). Many wilderness survival books say that it's the one knot you should know that can save your life. The bowline (generally pronounced "boelinn") is useful for less dangerous work in film as well.

The bowline creates a loop that doesn't tighten or collapse when stress is placed on it. A non-collapsing loop can be good for a thousand and one uses. The loop is useful for any job where a rope needs to be slipped over a pole or hook. Since it doesn't tighten, there is no binding that needs to be loosened when it needs to be removed.

On a film set, this knot is often used for loading or suspension. For example, the bowline provides a non-collapsing loop that will easily be slipped around a light for hoisting it onto the roof of a building. Other applications include securing frame lines to a post, creating an ad hoc handle for carrying packages, or making a climbing footstep.

FIGURE 39.1 *Many wilderness survival books say that knowing the bowline can save your life.*

> **TIP ▶** *While the bowline is a strong knot, under extreme conditions it can fail. For added security, tie a stopper knot (such as figure-8 knot) at the working end of a completed bowline to guarantee that the knot won't slip. Even better, use two half hitches to bind the final working end to the standing end.*

Traditional Method

Tie the bowline with the standard method. You may have heard the following story to help you remember how the bowline is tied:

> **The rabbit comes out of the hole, runs around the tree, and goes back down the hole again.**

Keep this saying in mind as you learn to tie the knot. It can help you remember how the knot is tied even after long absences from tying it.

To begin, you will need to create the rabbit hole. Form a loop (see figure 39-2) in the working end of the rope. The direction of rope overlap in the loop is important, so this time make sure that the standing end is below the working end as shown in the figure.

Bring the working end up through the loop (the rabbit comes out of the hole). Twist the working end behind the standing end as shown in figure 39-3 (the rabbit runs around the tree).

Finally, the rabbit needs to go back down the hole. Push the working end back through the loop (see figure 39-4). You can tighten up the knot by grasping the two parts of the rope (the working end and the loop in one hand, the standing end in the other) and pulling in opposite directions.

Try making this knot from various perspectives. Tie it around a pole. Tie it around your waist. Tie it using thick rope or narrow sash cord. These variations will help you learn how to tie the knot in a variety of conditions.

FIGURE 39.2 *Form a loop (see figure 50-2) in the working end of the rope.*

FIGURE 39.3 *Twist the working end behind the standing end.*

FIGURE 39.4 *Push the working end back through the loop.*

One-handed or Sailor's Method

The one-handed method of tying the bowline is a handy trick. To learn this method, it's a good idea to begin by tying it around your waist. As you get better at it, the knot can be tied anywhere. If you'll be using your right hand to tie the knot, run the rope around your back, so the standing end is on your left and the working end is held in your right hand. For lefties, do exactly the opposite.

Grasp to working end in your hand near the end of the rope. Move your hand under the standing end as shown in figure 39-5.

The next move is difficult to diagram well, so you'll have to practice until you understand it. Twist your wrist under the standing end and then move your wrist up and out. This will form a loop around your wrist as shown in figure 39-6.

You now have the familiar rabbit

FIGURE 39.5 *Grasp the working end in your hand near the end of the rope and move your hand under the standing end.*

hole loop as described in the last section. Use your fingers to weave the working end up around the "tree" and back down through the loop (see figure 39-7). Once complete, grab both the tip of the working end and the part before the bight and pull them downward together until the knot tightens.

FIGURE 39.6 *Twist your wrist under the standing end and then move your wrist up and out.*

FIGURE 39.7 *Use your fingers to weave the working end up around the "tree" and back down through the loop.*

Double Bowline

If the line needs to carry a large amount of weight, be sure to tie a double bowline (see figure 39-8). It's almost 80% stronger than a single bowline and takes only a few more moments to tie.

A double bowline is tied by creating a double starting loop as shown in figure 39-9. Then the bowline is tied in the traditional manner only the line goes through both loops before it goes around the standing line (see figure 39-10). Then it returns through both loops and the knot is tightened.

FIGURE 39.8 *If the line needs to carry a large amount of weight, be sure to tie a double bowline.*

FIGURE 39.9 *A double bowline is tied by creating a double starting loop.*

FIGURE 39.10 *The line goes through both loops before it goes around the standing line.*

CHAPTER 40

Clove Hitch

Applications

A clove hitch, also known as a builder's knot, is a standard knot used in sailing. It's employed for many common tasks on a film set such as attaching a rope to a pole or a stake.

Most often, I've used this hitch for tensioning guidelines when a large reflector or diffusion cloth is mounted on a 12′ × 12′ frame. The guidelines, usually attached to a fence or stake, hold down the frame in case a strong wind blows on the framed material. When the breeze catches it, a large cloth reflector acts essentially like a large sail.

The clove hitch is also frequently used as a cable tension relief. Tension reliefs are very common when using large HMI lights (12 K and above) where the feeder cable is extremely heavy.

The cable tension relief rope ties the cable to the bail or yoke (the metal bracket that holds the light). The weight of the cable is then held by the tension relief rope instead of pulling on the connector that attaches the cable to the light. The hitch is tied around the feeder cable and the rope ends are tied in a box knot around the light's bail.

The clove hitch is fast and easy to tie and rarely jams. It's also quick to loosen later, even after a strain has been put on it. Be aware that the pull to the standing end of the rope should be steady at a 90° angle. If the line is pulled around backwards, it can loosen the knot.

As with all knots, be sure to repeat this one until you can do it without much thinking. With practice, the clove hitch can be tied with one hand.

Around a Pole

Most often, you'll use a clove hitch around a pole. Before beginning the knot, determine the direction of the pull on the line. In this example, the pull will be in the downward direction from the bar. Therefore, lay the working end of the rope over the pole and bring tip around and over the standing end (see figure 40-1). Put the working end over the pole and bring it around again (see figure 40-2). Feed the working end under the loop you just made as shown in figure 40-3. Pull on the working end to tighten the knot and you're done.

As long as the pull to the standing end of the rope remains in the predetermined direction, the hitch will hold steady. Try pulling the standing end in the opposite direction. See how it threatens the integrity of the hitch? Untie the hitch you made and try tying the hitch where the pull will be coming from the opposite direction.

FIGURE 40.1 *Lay the working end of the rope over the pole and bring tip around and over the standing end.*

FIGURE 40.2 *Put the working end over the pole and bring it around again.*

FIGURE 40.3 *Feed the working end under the loop you just made.*

To remove the hitch, simply loosen the binding and pull the rope free. If it's stuck, pull the working end at various angles until the binding loosens.

If you need to make the hitch more secure, use the working end to tie two half hitches around the standing end. That will prevent the hitch from releasing.

Around a Stake

There are often times when you need to tie down a line to a stake but there remains a lot of extra rope at the working end. With too much spare rope, pulling the working end through several loops can be time-consuming and tedious for both tying and untying.

The following version of the clove hitch can solve this problem if the rope is being attached to an open-ended shaft such as the end of a pole or a stake.

Create two loops, so they look like mouse ears (see figure 40-4). You might think of the first loop forming a "9" and the second loop forming a "P." These two loops don't need to be created at the end of the rope, they can be made anywhere along the rope length. From the figure, you can see that the first loop after the turn goes over the junction. In contrast, the second loop goes under the junction.

Slip the first loop (the one from the left side in the figure) over the end of the pole as shown in figure 40-5. Take the top of the loop as shown in figure 40-6 between your fingers.

Place the second loop over the end of the pole without turning the loop or changing its direction (see figure 40-7).

FIGURE 40.4 *Create two loops so that they look like mouse ears.*

FIGURE 40.5 *Slip the first loop over the end of the pole.*

FIGURE 40.6 *Take the top of the loop between your fingers.*

Pull the rope ends tight in opposite directions and you have a clove hitch (see figure 40-8). To remove it, loose the hitch and pull it off the end of the pole. There is no knot, so the rope will pull right out.

This version of a clove hitch is also handy to secure a rope to a carabineer (see Chapter 31 for more information). Simply make the two loops and click them into the latch of the carabineer as if you were sliding the loops over the end of a pole.

FIGURE 40.7 *Place the second loop over the end of the pole.*

FIGURE 40.8 *Pull the rope ends tight in opposite directions to complete the clove hitch.*

Trucker's Hitch

Applications

The trucker's hitch (see figure 41-1) is a valuable knot for tying down a load in a truck, car, or van. Once you've learned the trucker's hitch, you'll wonder how you ever got along without it. It lets you tie down a load and pull out the slack from the holding loop, creating a very secure fastening. The trucker's hitch is particularly useful in a grip or prop truck where the horizontal wood slats that run the length of the inside body can be used as anchoring posts and the desired load can be bound secured in place.

There are a number of different ways to create a trucker's hitch. The type I'll describe won't release unintentionally if the weight is released from the standing end – a shortcoming of some trucker's hitch implementations.

FIGURE 41.1 *The trucker's hitch is a valuable knot for cinching down and securing a load.*

General Instructions

You first need to tie down one end of the rope to a secure foundation such as a binding post, eye-hook, rail, or wooden slat that will hold it steady. This will be your primary anchor knot. I typically use a double half-hitch on the primary anchor since it's quick and reliable.

Once the anchor knot is in place, pull the rope around the load to be bound. Try to make sure that the rope isn't sticking on something where it will slip off during the journey. If the rope were to slip too far, the entire binding may go slack and the fastening won't provide the solid anchoring that was originally intended.

On the far end of the rope, you'll be making a variation of the figure-8 stopper knot as the foundation of the trucker's hitch. Stretch the rope to the point where you want the hitch. Placing the hitch half the distance between the primary anchor and the destination anchor is a good rule of thumb (see figure 41-2).

Make a looped figure-8 knot (see Chapter 38). Do this by making a double-twist for the 360° turn and then making a loop in the working end. Slip this loop through the double-twist loop (see figure 41-3). Pull the figure-8 loop tight.

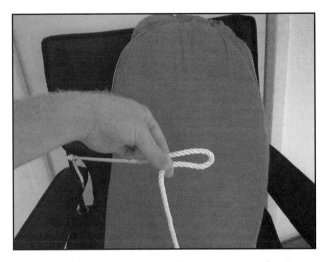

FIGURE 41.2 *Place the hitch about half the distance between the primary anchor and the destination anchor.*

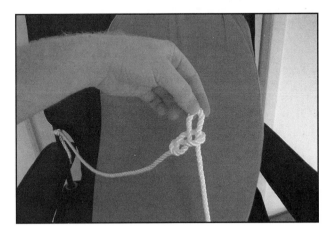

FIGURE 41.3 *Slip the new loop through the double-twist loop.*

Stretch the working end to the destination anchor point. Slip it around the destination anchor and pull it back toward the hitch. Don't pull too hard or the figure-8 loop will be undone. Slip the working end through the figure-8 loop (see figure 41-4) and pull the working end back toward the destination anchor. The slack will be taken up and the binding will be pulled tight. Keep pulling on the working end until you have the tension you want on the load you're securing.

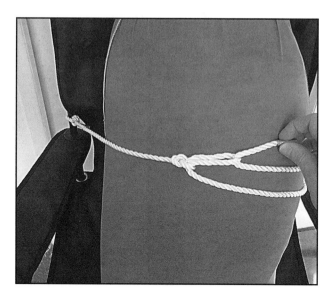

FIGURE 41.4 *Slip the working end through the figure-8 loop and pull toward the destination anchor to tighten.*

Finally, use a double-half hitch to tie off the working end to the standing end of the rope before the bight. Since the trucker's hitch gives you a lot of leverage, make sure you don't pull it so tight that the load you're binding is damaged.

Cable Ties and Coiling

Applications

One of the first things you learn when working in film is the value of cable ties. A cable tie is a short length of rope attached near one or both ends of a cable. Rather than tying a cable with itself or separate piece of rope, the ties are used to secure the cable as shown in figure 42-1.

Two ties (one at each end) are only necessary for very long cables (greater than 50 ft) or very thick ones. When completing a shoot or "wrapping," the ties allow a cable to be quickly coiled, bound, and stored. I find that cable ties to be extremely useful both at home and on set.

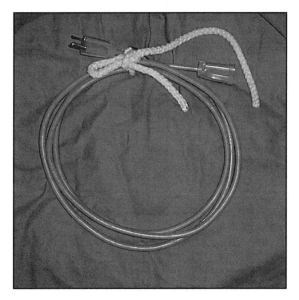

FIGURE 42.1 *Ties can secure a cable more conveniently than tying a cable with itself or separate piece of rope.*

General Instructions

I would recommend that you include ties on all the cables that you'll be using on a shoot. Most common extension cords (stingers) are coiled, tied, and then stacked inside milk crates for easy transport and storage. However you haul your cables, try to make sure that the cable ties are in place before you go to location. It will make cleanup and packing much easier.

Choosing tie material

Some thought should be given to the type of rope that you'll use for the ties. If a poor rope is chosen, cable ties can be more frustrating than helpful. Try to avoid using slick or thin rope. I've found that cotton- or cloth-based rope is best since it doesn't slide (like most polyrope), so your ties will hold better.

However, natural fiber rope does require the ends to be bound to avoid fraying, where you can simply melt the ends of polyrope. I've found that clothesline polyrope is light, thick enough for easy tying, and holds fairly well. An advantage of polyrope is that it doesn't rot if it gets wet – which cable ties often do.

Although any color of rope may be used, try to use rope that's white in color. There is nothing more frustrating than wrapping cables in a poorly lit location after a long shooting day and not being able to see the cable ties clearly. There has been many a time that I've cursed a rental house which provided cables with black rope ties.

Adding the cable tie

To add a cable tie, cut a length of rope about 12″ in length. Twelve inches is plenty for most cord 50 ft and under. For cord greater than 50 ft, it's a good idea to cut two ties, one for each end. If the cable is longer or thicker than a traditional extension cord, increase the size of the tie as necessary.

Use a clove hitch (see Chapter 40) to make the tie around the cable as shown in figure 42-2. Be sure that the two ends of the tie are the same length. This makes the tie easy to knot regardless of which end is chosen as the working end.

Once you've tied the clove hitch, coil the cable and tie the two ends together around the coil. You can use either the shoelace knot (see Chapter 37) or a variation of it. Is the length of tie rope long enough to making knotting easy? If not, discard this tie and cut a longer length.

Now put on a pair of work gloves. Try to tie the knot again. Is the rope thick enough for easy handling? Most rope coiling is done with gloves since the cable may have been used outdoors in dirt, mud, or other grime. You should make your ties such that they can be knotted while wearing work gloves.

Once you're satisfied with the cable tie, use a piece of duct tape or similar to secure it to the cable (see figure 42-3). This will hold the tie in place and prevent it from sliding down the cable or coming loose.

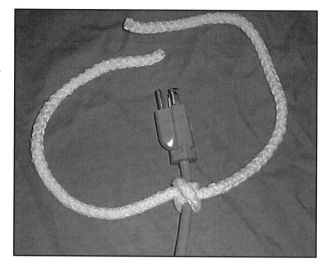

FIGURE 42.2 *Use a clove hitch to make the tie around the cable.*

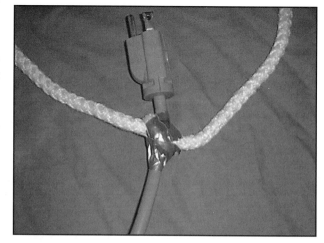

FIGURE 42.3 *Use a piece of duct tape or similar to secure the tie to the cable.*

Coiling

Coiling a cable can take a little practice, but the results are well worth the time spent. Once you begin to coil your cables properly, the skill will quickly become second nature. Proper coiling makes the process much easier and conditions the cables to lie flat for easy storage.

First, make sure you *always coil in a clockwise direction*. You can see a cable being coiled properly in figure 42-4. If the cable seems to be fighting you, flip it over and try again. Don't shrug and coil it counter-clockwise because you'll be breaking a habit for yourself and possibly breaking the conditioning of the cable.

Next, make sure that you *coil a cable the same way each time*. The cable will become "trained" so that with each add-itional coiling it's easier to create the same spiral. Once properly trained, a cable will

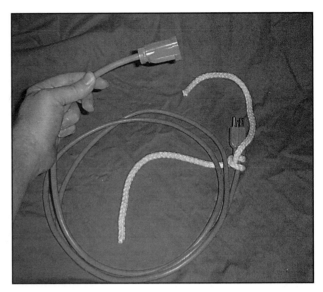

FIGURE 42.4 *Always coil in a clockwise direction.*

coil easily without fighting and without becoming the frustrating mess of an improperly coiled cable.

Coiling should *never be done around your elbow*. People often use the length between the hand and the elbow to force unmanageable rope or cable into a coil. This can break the cable conditioning and also helps to damage and breakdown the wires or fibers.

Except when coiling extension cords (which coil from the plug) always start coiling from the device (light, fan, etc.). By coiling from the item, any twists in the cable generated by the coiling can spin out at the end. For extension cords (stingers) or open power cords (such as generator cables), you coil from the pins or plug. This applies whether the power cord is a simple extension cord or heavy 4/0 generator cable.

Proper coiling is so useful that I find that even my vacuum cleaner cord at home, once a rat's nest of curls, is now trained to coil perfectly.

Using the ties for differentiation

Once you have a tie on each cable, the tie itself can be used as an effective non-written identification system when the cable is in use. For example, if four cables lead into a single power strip or gang box, different knots in the ties of each cable can tell you which cable belongs to a specific light or item. A particular strength of this system is that it can be read even in the dark.

In figure 42-5, you can see a series of knot patterns for cable ties that can be used. These knots are used on

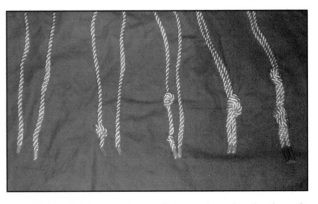

FIGURE 42.5 *Knot patterns in the cable ties can be used to identify specific cables by touch or in the dark.*

professional sets to identify particular lines from a generator. The following is a list of the knots shown in the picture in order from left to right:

1. ***No ties*** the blue leg of the generator power.

2. ***Single knot in one rope*** the red leg of the generator power.

3. ***Two knots in one rope*** the black leg of the generator power.

4. ***Single knot tying ropes together*** the neutral line of the generator.

5. ***Double knot tying ropes together*** the ground line of the generator.

While these standards are useful to memorize, don't let that stop you from using a knot system customized to your own needs. However, be sure to notify your co-workers if a non-standard system is being used to prevent confusion or accidents.

Light ties

Whatever type of lighting you'll be using, it's helpful to have a tie that secures the coiled cable directly to the light. As you can see in figure 42-6, this is a fairly simple proposition. A short length of rope or cord tied between the bail (the metal bracket that holds the light) and the positioning knob does an excellent job of fastening the cable.

You can tie this securing line any way you want. I find that a double half-hitch is good for the bail. To create a loop that will easily slip on and off the positioning knob, tie a small bowline of the appropriate size.

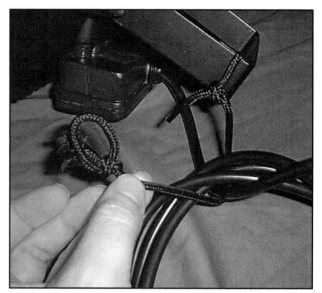

FIGURE 42.6 *A tie can secure a coiled cable directly to the light.*

Apple Boxes

Applications

After C-stands, apple boxes are probably used more often and in more different ways than any other item on a film set. These simple wooden boxes (see figure 43-1) are sturdy enough to be used as a platform for standing and sitting, a mount for a camera, a stand for elevating items, and so on. A set of apple boxes can take up a fair amount of space on the grip truck, but they prove their usefulness again and again.

As you can see in figure 43-1, there are four different standard sizes of apple box: full apple ($8'' \times 12'' \times 20''$), half apple ($4'' \times 12'' \times 20''$), quarter apple ($2'' \times 12'' \times 20''$), and pancake ($1'' \times 12'' \times 20''$). The full apple is twice the size of the half apple, the half apple is twice the size of the quarter, and so on. On a typical movie shoot, a grip truck will at a minimum include a complement of four of each type (four fulls, four halves, four quarters, and four pancakes). The boxes are kept on the taco cart (grip cart) for easy transportation.

FIGURE 43.1 *Apple boxes are sturdy enough to be used as a platform for standing and sitting.*

	Qty	Item
PARTS	1	$4' \times 8'$ sheet of $\frac{3}{4}''$ plywood
	200	$2''$ #6 fine drywall screws
	50	$1\frac{1}{4}''$ #6 fine drywall screws
	1	Clear waterproof wood finish

General Instructions

How many boxes you should construct will depend on how much room you'll have for their transportation. You may have to bring fewer than you'd like because you can't fit them in your vehicle. Full apples tend to be used the most often on a set, so you're better off skimping on the smaller ones if your space is limited.

> **TIP ▶** *Before you decide the number and sizes of boxes to construct, be sure to figure out where you'll keep them when not filming. Apple crates, while extremely useful, are a pain to store. Take the size measurements of the crates and multiply the dimensions by the number you think you'll need. Make sure you have enough space that they can be stored conveniently.*

Construction

The following instructions describe how to create one of each size of apple box from a single $4' \times 8'$ sheet of $\frac{3}{4}''$ plywood. While the professional boxes use $\frac{1}{2}''$ or thinner plywood, I've used thicker material here for safety. Although these boxes are a little heavier, they're almost unbreakable even in extreme circumstances. If the boxes are too heavy for you, I would suggest substituting plywood no thinner than $\frac{1}{2}''$.

The top and bottom panels of all the apple crates are the same measurements regardless of size. Since these panels are the largest pieces of each apple box, it simplifies planning. The largest pieces should be allocated first to maximize remainders.

> **NOTE→** You'll need a couple of special tools to make apple box construction fast and easy. "Hole" drills bits (like the one shown in figure 43-9) can make large holes quickly. Bits of 1" and $1\frac{1}{2}''$ diameters are used to make holes for the box hand-holds. Also, a keyhole saw (see figure 43-10) will conveniently remove the wood between two holes. Although you can use a traditional drill bit (drilling multiple holes to make one big hole) and a standard saw, the hole bits and keyhole saw make life much easier.

Templates and cutting

To begin your construction, create a diagram to determine how you're going to partition the plywood sheet into the individual apple box panels. Although it may be tempting to cut off pieces as you need them, planning out the cuts in advance will save a great deal of material in the long run. You should try to leave the largest uncut rectangle of remaining material, so you have flexibility in cutting other pieces.

In table 43-1 you'll see the list of pieces that will be needed to create four apple boxes (one of each size). Note that these measurements are based on the plywood being $\frac{3}{4}''$ thick. For example, the full apple

Qty	Size	#	Description
8	12" × 20"	1	Top and bottom panels
1	12" × 18.5"	2	Full apple support board
2	8" × 12"	3	Full apple front and back
2	4" × 12"	4	Half apple front and back
2	2" × 12"	5	Quarter apple front and back
2	9.5" × 20"	6	Full apple side panels
2	5.5" × 20"	7	Half apple side panels
2	3.5" × 20"	8	Quarter apple side panels
2	1.5" × 20"	9	Pancake side panels

TABLE 43-1 *Pieces needed for apple box set.*

support board (part #2) is $1\frac{1}{2}''$ shorter than the top and bottom panels (20″ long) since the support board will be sandwiched between the front and back panels ($\frac{3}{4}'' + \frac{3}{4}'' = 1\frac{1}{2}''$). However, lumber is never actually the labeled size ($\frac{3}{4}''$ wood is not actually $\frac{3}{4}''$), so you will have to do small trims to make the pieces fit together precisely.

Also, don't forget that each cut will eliminate a certain amount of material. Depending on the type of saw used, this loss is usually $\frac{1}{16}''$ to $\frac{1}{8}''$. With the number of cuts required here, the total amount lost may not be insignificant, so be aware of it.

In figure 43-2, you'll see the basic layout to cut the plywood sheet into the necessary pieces for one box of each size. I've noted the measurements of each panel where appropriate. The lower right corner of each piece shows the part # in parentheses that correlates with the earlier table. The gray areas indicate left over unused pieces of the original $4' \times 8'$ sheet.

Copy the lines of the template onto the plywood sheet. I used a ruler and a straight edge to make sure the measurements were accurate. The more precisely the lines are drawn, the better the chance that all the pieces will fit together perfectly.

Cut the board into the outlined pieces. I used a battery-powered circular saw that worked very well after

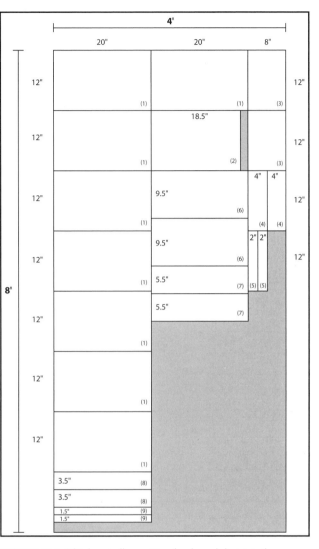

FIGURE 43.2 *This layout allows cutting the plywood sheet into the necessary pieces for one box of each size.*

I suspended the sheet between two sawhorses. Be very careful whenever you use any power tools. I would suggest you find a buddy or family volunteer to help you hold down the board or catch the cut pieces.

Once all the pieces are cut, I would suggest that you coat each piece with wood sealer. Even if you sand down the edges later and need to re-coat certain areas, the primary sealing is best done before assembly. Although sealing can be done after the boxes are complete, that will mean that only the outer sides of the wood are protected. If water or other contaminants get inside the box, they can rot it from the inside out.

Full apple

The pieces of each box are attached together with drywall screws. Assembly is easiest if you have a clamp to hold the pieces in place until the screws are fastened securely in place. If you can afford a set of four 90° clamps (see figure 43-3), I would suggest you buy them. These clamps will dramatically speed apple box construction. They'll hold the edges together while you drive the screws into the wood.

Start your construction by putting the top panel board over the side-boards. Put four screws evenly spaced through the top board (see figure 43-4) into the side panel. The two outside screws should be the longer 2″ length screws while the two inside screws should be the shorter $1\frac{1}{4}″$ length screws. The shorter length provides extra space so when you cut the hand-holds into the side panels, you don't strike the body of a screw. Following the same process and put four screws in the other side.

Flip the assembled sides over and use eight more screws to attach the bottom panel. Once complete, you should have a sturdy box like the one shown in figure 43-5.

FIGURE 43.3 *A set of four 90° clamps makes putting together the boxes a snap.*

The full apple includes an internal board for structural support, so it's the most complicated of all the boxes. Draw a centerline on the sideboard. You can find the centerline by measuring the width of the board, dividing that length in half, marking a few points at that measurement (about 4″ from the side), and drawing a line through the points (see figure 43-6). You'll use this line as a guide to drive the screws and align the support board.

Draw a similar line on the opposite panel. Insert the support board and eyeball its placement until the center of the board sits in position for both lines. Drive four screws into each side of the structural board (see figure 43-7) along the template lines. The box should be extremely sturdy at this point. Before you put on the sideboards, you'll want to cut the hand-holds into the box.

FIGURE 43.4 *Put four evenly spaced screws through the top board into the side panel.*

You'll need to draw lines to guide the placement of the holds. Each hold will measure 6″ long. Make two lines, one on either side of the centerline you drew for the support board. Each line should be at a midpoint between the centerline and the edge of the board (about 2″ from the side).

Once you've drawn these two lines, place a mark $\frac{3}{4}″$ from each end of both lines (see figure 43-8) for a total of four marks. These marks will be the point at which you place the hole drill bit. Since the hole will be $1\frac{1}{2}″$ in diameter, placing the marks at $\frac{3}{4}″$ (half the bit diameter) will make the hold holes exactly the right width.

Use the $1\frac{1}{2}''$ hole bit to drill a hole at each marker. When complete, you should have four holes like the ones shown in figure 43-9. To expand the holes into holds for convenient carrying, you'll need to remove the wood between each pair of holes.

Use a small saw (such as a keyhole saw) to take out the wood that remains between each pair of holes (see figure 43-10). Make one cut between the tops of two holes and another cut between the bottoms of the holes. Perform these two cuts on the other pair of holes and you should have two holds on the end of the box.

Flip the box over and repeat the procedure, so you have two more hand-holds. After the handles are complete, attach the two side boards (see figure 43-11) and you'll have a complete full apple!

FIGURE 43.5 *Use eight more screws to attach the bottom panel.*

Half apple

Construction of the half apple is nearly the same as the full apple (see figure 43-12). The only differences are that no support board is required for the half apple and only a single hand-hold is needed per end.

The hand-holds are excellent for conveniently carrying the apple boxes around the set. You can hold two boxes in each hand as shown in figure 43-13. If needed, you can carry four full apples at once.

Quarter apple

The quarter apple has the same construction as the half apple except the hand-holds are slightly different (see figure 43-14). Since the box is narrow, a proper hand-hold is not really possible. Instead, use the 1″ diameter bit to drill three holes so that you can hold the quarter apple with your fingers.

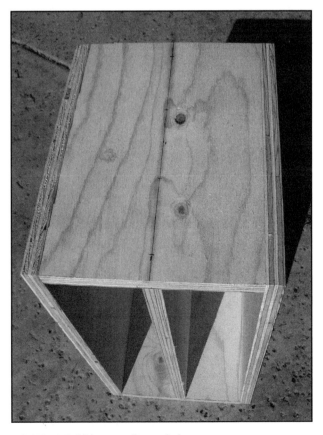

FIGURE 43.6 *Make a centerline on the box.*

FIGURE 43.7 *Drive four screws into each side of the structural board along the template lines.*

FIGURE 43.8 *Place a mark $\frac{3}{4}''$ from each end of both lines for a total of four marks.*

FIGURE 43.9 *Use the $1\frac{1}{2}''$ hole bit to drill a hole at each marker.*

FIGURE 43.10 *Cut out the wood that remains between each pair of holes.*

FIGURE 43.11 *After the handles are complete, attach the two side boards.*

FIGURE 43.12 *Assembling a half apple is nearly the same as the full apple.*

FIGURE 43.13 *The handholds let you hold two boxes in each hand.*

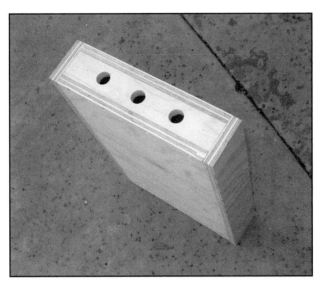

FIGURE 43.14 *The quarter apple has different handholds than the half apple.*

FIGURE 43.15 *A pancake is simply two boards attached together by two sideboards.*

Pancake

Finally, the pancake (see figure 43-15) is simply two boards attached together by two sideboards. You can create the pancake by screwing the top and bottom panels directly together and ignoring the sideboards. However, including the sideboards makes the pancake the same width as the other apple boxes, making it convenient for stacking.

Suggestions

Here are a few suggestions to help you get the best use from the apple boxes:

- *Sand the edges and corners* Slightly rounding the edges of the boxes can minimize the sharp edges and reduce the possibility of getting slivers. Make sure you seal any edges after you've sanded them.

- *Ratchet straps* Apple crates and ratchet straps go hand in hand. With a ratchet strap, you can attach almost anything (including a camera mount) to an apple box. You can also ratchet strap an apple box to something else (such as a ladder). Make sure you have at least two ratchet straps to go along with your set of apple boxes.

- *Beaverboard from a pancake* Beaverboards are used for holding a monitor on top of a C-stand or mounting a light close to the ground. A beaverboard is simply a wall plate attached (with four wood screws) to a pancake. The wall plate has a standard "baby" stub that can be inserted into a light receptacle or into the top of a C-stand. Once a beaverboard is mounted on a C-stand, a ratchet strap is used to secure the video assist monitor to the board for a portable "video village."

- *Raise cable connections* Under wet conditions, place apple boxes under any cable connection to keep them off the wet ground. Likewise, if you're using any gang boxes or power strips in these conditions, use the boxes to elevate them out of the way.

- *Bring some type of box to the shoot* Even if you have no time to create apple boxes, find something else, perhaps milk crates, to bring to your shoot. Having some type of box can be critical to accomplish many of your filming objectives.

Sound Introduction

V

Applications

Good sound production relies on quality equipment much more than technique. A good boom mic can't be replaced by home-made equipment. No matter how good the sound department, low-grade recording equipment will not reproduce the grade of sound that is expected from a professional film. Despite the fact that the poor sound seems to be the number one technical reason for audience apathy and disapproval, many low-budget productions skimp on the sound department. Most audiences will forgive poor picture quality, poor lighting, cheap sets, and so on if the story is good. However, provide a soundtrack where it's difficult to hear or understand the actors and you'll have people rejecting your movie.

Therefore, the number one rule for any production sound is to invest in a decent boom mic and sound recording device. For video and DV filmmakers, most video recorders and cameras provide an external mic jack that lets you record the audio right onto the tape at CD-quality levels. Since an essentially free high-quality audio recording device is readily available, there's little excuse for poor sound on a video shoot.

> **NOTE→** Most professional sound people I know are preparing for a coming revolution in digital recorders. Although most productions use DAT or (more rarely) Nagra analog records, many predict that digital recording to CD-R or DVD-R will quickly overtake the market. Therefore, think carefully before purchasing a high-end DAT system. Although you can never avoid technical obsolescence, you don't want to buy high-end devices right before a coming innovation.

Here are a few general guidelines for the sound department:

- *Have plenty of extra batteries on hand for wireless and boom mics* All good mics require power of some sort, generally in the form of AA or 9 V batteries. Have plenty of spare batteries on hand to prevent hold ups to the production when you must send a PA to get fresh supplies.

- *With external audio recording, buy high-quality tape* Generally, high-quality tape costs only 10–20% more than cheap tape. Some DAT tape has special anti-static coatings to ensure that particles that can create dropouts don't stick to the tape. Quality tape is cheap – re-recording sound is not.

- *Wireless mics should be your second choice* I have never worked in the sound department when we haven't experienced some problem with wireless mics. The problem may be interference, dead batteries, malfunctioning connectors, or even an actor leaving the set with his expensive mic still attached to his coat. To many inexperienced filmmakers, wireless mics seem like a convenient and effortless method of capturing good sound. The reality is much different. Use wireless mics only when you need to use them.

- *Use tape to secure your cable* Cables are very easy to trip over, so a little gaffer's tape can hold the cable securely to the floor and prevent accidents and damage to sound equipment. You can also use sandbags to hold cable to the floor, particularly when the cable runs over carpet or other difficult to tape surface.

- *Bring the necessary adapters* There are a large number of types of audio plugs ($\frac{1}{4}''$, $\frac{1}{8}''$, balanced, unbalanced, etc.) and you had better be prepared with the proper adapters to allow you to plug them into one another. If you are recording directly into the camera, make sure you have the necessary adapters to allow sound sources to feed into the AUX jack.

Suggestions

Here are a few general suggestions for working sound:

- *Even when it seems silly, take sound* A person looking through a pile of papers or caressing the face of a lover may seem like shots where sound is unnecessary. However, the shuffling of papers or an accidental bumping of the cocktail glass can be a terrible pain to reconstruct in post. It takes only a second to record the take and may save you hours and hours of work.

- *Take care of your cables* Cables that are poorly treated or badly stored won't last nearly as long and will fail you at the most inopportune moment. Always coil your cables in the same direction.

- *Don't forget to take room tone* Room tone is the ambient noise of a room (or outdoor setting). By recording 30 seconds to a minute of room tone, you make it possible for the editor to splice this sound over difficult areas of the soundtrack. Background coughing, a dropped tool, or an airplane flying above can all be quickly replaced in post-production with the room tone. Additionally, you'll need room tone as the background noise if you need the actors to ADR any of their lines.

- *Workout with a broom* If you're facing your first time as boom operator, the muscles in your shoulders and arms probably aren't ready for holding up the boom for long periods of time. Practice by holding a broomstick over your head. Over a couple of weeks, steadily increase the length of time that you hold it in place. The longest sustained time I've ever had to hold a boom was for a 7-min take. Most takes average between 1 and 3 min. Try to practice as if you were shooting a film by holding overhead for 1 min, then 30 seconds rest, then hold for 2 min, then rest, and so on.

- *Shoot children MOS* When shooting kids, it is sometimes best to shoot the second take MOS. That way the director can direct the child explicitly and sound can be taken from another shot or created later using ADR.

Boom Pole

Applications

The aspect of a film that audiences are least likely to forgive is poor sound. It seems that the hallmark of a poorly done guerilla film is a muddy soundtrack with a great deal of background noise. Having a good boom microphone mounted on good boom pole, when used properly, can make a fundamental difference in sound quality.

Note that there is no suggestion in this book of an effective replacement for a decent boom microphone because there really isn't one. Rent or invest in a good microphone and it will pay for itself many times over in saved frustration and difficulty. Although a good boom mic can cost about the same as a mid-range computer monitor, it's worth every penny in increased production quality. Any boom mic can be easily mounted on the boom pole you'll learn to make in this chapter.

	Qty	Item
PARTS	1	6′ length of $\frac{3}{4}''$ PVC pipe
	1	4′ length of $\frac{3}{4}''$ PVC pipe
	1	Roll of duct tape
	1	90° bend joint for $\frac{3}{4}''$ PVC pipe
	1	Boom microphone

General Instructions

When I started making short films, I thought that any sound problems could simply be re-dubbed in post-production. Not only does re-dub sound terrible when compared against properly captured sound, but also it's a difficult, time-consuming, and tedious process. It can extend the time spent in post-production by 20%. Additionally, getting your actors to come back and redo their lines is a challenge in itself.

Although skimping on the microphone itself is problematic, the boom pole is another thing entirely. Microphones tend to be very light, so they can be easily mounted on a variety of extensions. The professional graphite boom poles will telescope to various lengths and are made to be very light. They are, however, very expensive and you can do almost as well with a PVC boom pole that can be constructed for less than the price of this book.

Construction

The most popular material to use for a boom pole is $\frac{3}{4}''$ PVC pipe (see figure 44-1). The pipe should be cut to about a 6 ft length as this length is long enough to reach most locations, yet short enough so the PVC pipe doesn't bend tremendously.

After you have the pipe cut to the proper length, you'll need to fix the mic mounting bracket to the end. Your boom mic should have included the bracket. You're going to attach this bracket to the PVC pipe for easy use. Duct-tape the microphone holder to the end of the pole (see figure 44-2). If you're using a rental, use gaffer's tape instead or you'll be spending some time cleaning the adhesive gunk off the mounting bracket before you return it.

Spiral the mic cord around the top of the bracket and down the length of the pole. Be sure to leave a little slack near the mic so that the bracket can be tilted without running out of cord. Also, place two or three small pieces of tape on the cord spiral down the length of the pole. This will hold the cord to the pole to prevent any unraveling. The boom pole is now ready for use.

Boom bend pole

If you have an inexperienced boom operator, it's likely their arms will grow tired during the length of a long shooting day. You want to avoid that because it means they'll stop paying attention to the scene, won't follow the dialogue properly, and generally allow the sound quality to fall short of what you want. In figure 44-3, you can see a boom bend pole made of two pieces of PVC for easy handling.

The same 6 ft length of PVC is used for the vertical part of the bend pole. A 90° joint connects it (see figure 44-4) with a horizontal pole of 4 ft. I've found the 4 ft length to be about the maximum length before excessive sagging occurs.

For many shots, a boom operator can simply hold the vertical length against their shoulder, so it requires little energy. Although the 90° boom mount is easier to hold, it is much less flexible than a standard boom pole. It casts a larger boom shadow and is easier to bump causing noise in the soundtrack. Be sure to only use it when situation demands.

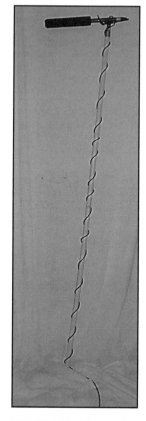

FIGURE 44.1 *A boom pole made with $\frac{3}{4}''$ PVC pipe.*

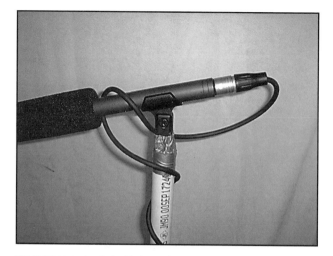

FIGURE 44.2 *Attach the bracket to the PVC pipe by using duct tape on the microphone holder.*

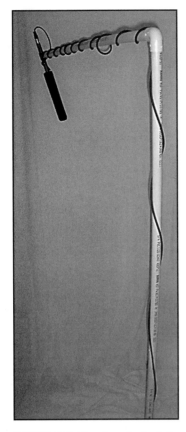

FIGURE 44.3 *Use a boom bend pole for easier handling.*

FIGURE 44.4 *A 90° elbow joint connects the poles together.*

Suggestions

Here are a few operating suggestions to help you:

- ***When recording a conversation, twist the pole*** When you're recording two people having a conversation, use the standard boom pole. Then, instead of moving the microphone back and forth between them, simply locate the mic at the middle point and twist it to point at the person speaking.

- ***Watch the boom shadow*** One of the most common ways to ruin a shot is to have the boom cast a shadow onto the background. Since the shadow is subtle, it's easily missed until the dailies are watched where it becomes annoyingly obvious. Try to be sure to watch for the shadow to make sure it doesn't end up in the shot.

- ***Place the boom mic below the frame and point up*** One of the most common mistakes made by beginning boom operators is to think that the boom always needs to be positioned above the frame. Many conversations, however, can be caught excellently if the microphone is under the actors pointed up. This position is particularly useful when filming exterior walking conversations. The sun can cast a bad boom shadow and catching the sound from below ensures that the shadow won't fall across the actors.

- ***Don't rest the mic against something while filming*** Although you may be tired and it sounds like there is no sound created by leaning the mic against an object, any shift or bump will result in a noticeable thud on the soundtrack. It's best just not to do it.

Boom Mount

Applications

When you attach the microphone directly to the boom pole, any jars or bumps to the pole itself will be picked up by the microphone. To avoid this problem, professionals use a boom mount such as the one shown in figure 45-1. The boom mount suspends the microphone in an elastic cradle, so any jars are absorbed by the mount itself without being transferred to the microphone.

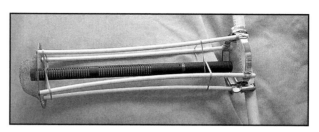

FIGURE 45.1 *A boom mount suspends a microphone in an elastic cradle, so any jars are absorbed by the mount itself.*

Additionally a boom mount allows for a fake fur windscreen to be placed over it. When wind blows against a microphone, it can be heard very plainly. The windscreen absorbs and deflects the wind, yet only muffles the incoming sound slightly. The windscreen is an essential accessory when shooting exterior scenes on even a slightly windy day.

PARTS	Qty	Item
	4	Plastic hangers
	4	Self-tapping wood screws
	8	Rubber bands
	1	4″ screw-adjustable metals band
	2	3″ screw-adjustable metals bands
	1	4″ diameter strainer
	1	Sheet of fake fur
	1	6″ length of $\frac{3}{4}$″ PVC pipe

General Instructions

A professional boom mount can be extremely expensive, despite the simplicity of its construction. You can make one of your own with almost the same functionality for a fraction of the cost. The windscreen does block some of the sound, so it shouldn't be used except on exterior shoots. The boom mount, however, provides excellent protection from bump sounds, so it can be used at any time.

Construction

To begin construction, you'll need to create the four rods that form the body of the mount. You can cut wooden dowels for the support rods. However, I've found lengths of lightweight plastic are strong enough yet far lighter than wooden supports. Plastic rods can be easily obtained by cutting apart simple plastic hangers (see figure 45-2). You can use a saw to cut the four identical rods or use a PVC cutter to make them. The length will depend on the length of your boom mic. For my mount, I cut the rods to $14\frac{1}{2}''$.

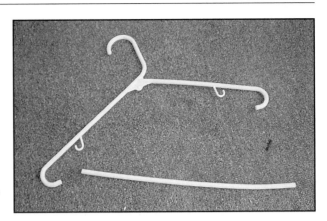

FIGURE 45.2 *Plastic rods are obtained by cutting apart simple plastic hangers.*

For the end cap of the boom mount, a kitchen strainer is used. Use an inexpensive kitchen strainer with the 4″ diameter as it forms a perfect half sphere to cap the end of the mount. I found a mesh drain strainer (see figure 45-3) that worked very effectively. The grid mesh blocks very little sound, but provides a useful structural mount for the windshield.

Use the self-tapping screws to attach the four rods to the strainer (see figure 45-4). Put the four screws at approximately four corner positions of the strainer. Tighten the screws, so the strainer won't move in relation to the rods.

You'll need to add rubber bands for the suspension of the microphone before you continue construction. Slip two rubber bands so that they encircle the top two rods. Add two more rubber bands to encircle the bottom two rods. Finally add one rubber band to each rod (four bands in total).

Use a saw or a knife to cut a $1\frac{1}{2}''$ slit into the end of each of the rods. These slits will allow the rods to slip over the edge of the adjustable metal band. You can hold the band up to the ends of the rods to get

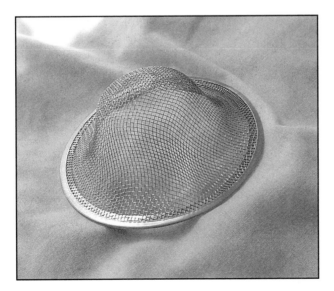

FIGURE 45.3 *An inexpensive kitchen strainer makes a perfect half sphere to cap the end of the mount.*

FIGURE 45.4 *Use the self-tapping screws to attach the four rods to the strainer.*

a general idea of the angle that each cut should be made. Once the cuts have been made, slip the metal band into the slits.

Now you're going to use a wrapping technique on each of the individual rubber bands that you put on each rod. Start by pulling a rubber band to the edge where the rod inserts into the slit (see figure 45-5).

Twist the rubber band around back and down around the band (see figure 45-6). Pull the band back up and around (see figure 45-7). Keep twisting around until the rubber band is taut. When the band is tight, slip the rubber band on the top of the post (see figure 45-8).

Cut a length of PVC pipe that can connect to the boom pole from the last chapter. This pole will be attached to the metal band. Because the microphone is suspended in the boom mount, it cannot be removed easily and quickly like it could from the standard mic clip. For this reason, I find it most convenient to attach the mount to a small 6″ section of PVC.

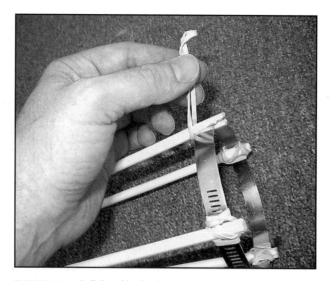

FIGURE 45.5 *Pull the rubber band to the edge where the rod inserts into the slit.*

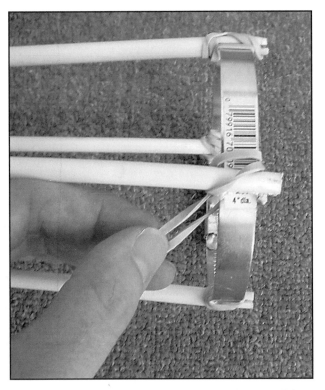

FIGURE 45.6 *Twist the rubber band around back and down around the metal band.*

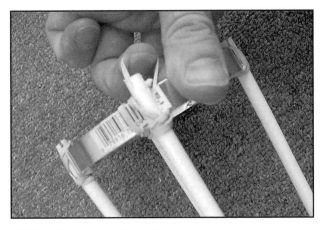

FIGURE 45.7 *Pull the rubber band up and around.*

The 6″ section is then connected to the end of the boom with a simple joining segment. That way, even if you're going to leave some equipment on the set overnight, you can easily and conveniently take your expensive microphone with you without having to either remount it or wrangle the entire boom pole off the set.

Hold the PVC pipe up to the metal band and make two cuts into the pole that matches the diameter of the band (see figure 45-9).

Use the 3″ adjustable metal bands to secure the PVC pipe into place (see figure 45-10). You can accomplish putting the bands around both the PVC pipe and the band by first turning the screw

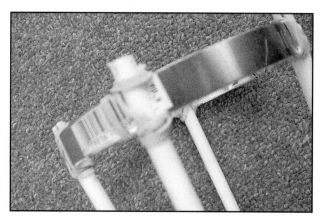

FIGURE 45.8 *Keep twisting around until the rubber band is taut and then slip it on the top of the post.*

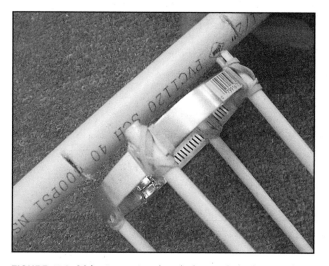

FIGURE 45.9 *Make two cuts into the pole that match the diameter of the band.*

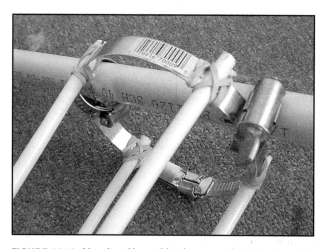

FIGURE 45.10 *Use adjustable metal bands to secure the PVC pipe solidly into place.*

counter-clockwise until the band has come free of the adjustment mechanism. You can then wrap the band around the pipe and band until the band slips back into the mechanism. Tighten down both bands until the pipe is secure.

Now is the time to mount your boom microphone. Pull the rubber band on the bottom rods over the front of the mic, and then pull the top rubber band over the top of the mic (see figure 45-11). This will suspend the mic between the bands.

Do the same suspension procedure for the back of the mic (see figure 45-12). The boom mount itself is complete. When you attach the mic cable, be sure to leave some slack between the back of the mic and the point where the cable begins wrapping around the boom pole. Otherwise the cable can tug the microphone creating jarring noise and defeating the purpose of the boom mount.

FIGURE 45.11 *Pull the bottom rubber band over the front of the mic and then pull the top rubber band over the mic.*

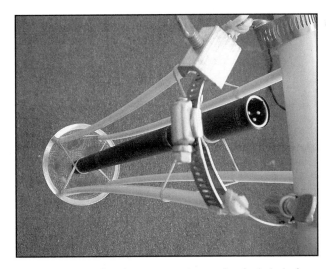

FIGURE 45.12 *Perform the same suspension procedure for the back of the mic.*

To create the windshield, cut an area of fake fur (see figure 45-13) that is big enough to create a cylinder that will cover the boom mount. Remember that it should be long enough to cover the mount itself and have enough material for flaps on the front and back.

If you have sewing skills, you can sew the proper cover. I found it easier to staple the cover together. I did sew some buttons onto the shield for the front and back flaps. On professional windshields they commonly use zippers and occasionally Velcro. I always try to avoid Velcro near my sound equipment since even a little of the tearing sound (caused by the wind, a bump, etc.) will destroy your soundtrack.

FIGURE 45.13 *Cut an area of fake fur big enough to create a cylinder that will cover the boom mount.*

Suggestions

Here are a few suggestions to help you get the best use from the boom mount:

- *Get a mount transport box* I bought a transparent plastic container at a dollar store and used it as a boom mount transport box. While not fragile, it is easy for the mount to be twisted and damaged by other heavy equipment. You should get or make some type of transportation container.

- *Remove your mic when not in use* Although you would probably store your microphone separately anyway, it is important to save the elasticity of the rubber bands. Eventually you'll have to replace the bands anyway, but removing the mic and letting them remain slack for storage will maximize the lifespan of each band.

- *Make a windshield from a stuffed animal* If you can't find fake fur for an inexpensive price, you can always skin a stuffed animal. One soundman I know found a large bear at a thrift shop and made three or four windshields from the toy.

Art Introduction

VI

Applications

The art department is one of the most difficult departments to work on a film. Unlike the camera, electrical, grip, and even wardrobe departments that solve many of the same problems over and over, there is very little repetition in the art department. Today you might need to create a ray gun, tomorrow decorate a college dorm room, the next day re-construct a villain's mountain hideout, and round out the week with the construction of a realistic prison cell, all within a minimal budget.

But the art department has its own rewards. Unlike camera operators, grips, and electrics whose work simply facilitates the shoot, all of your work will actually be seen on screen and used by the actors. No one can describe the thrill of seeing a set, painstakingly constructed from scratch, appear like an inhabited living space on the big screen. Or the sense of satisfaction when an actress shapes a major part of her character's personality around a prop you've delicately crafted.

In the following chapters, I've tried to include solutions I've seen and used to solve some of the more difficult art department problems. More than any other area of film production, you must use your taste and ingenuity to find ways to make the artificial seem real. I hope you'll be able to adapt these projects and suggestions to generate screen magic in your own films.

Suggestions

Here are a few general suggestions for working in the art department:

- *Always carry a notepad* Whether you need to jot down a continuity note or draw a diagram to explain something to the director, a small notepad and pen are invaluable. I always carry one of the 60-sheet 3″ × 5″ (7.6 cm × 12.7 cm) memo books. Before production begins, I write all the key crew phone numbers on the front page for easy reference. One shoot I tried to replace my notepad with a PDA, but it didn't work half as well. In addition to other problems, I couldn't make a list and tear off a sheet to hand to an assistant.

- *Take free construction classes* Most home warehouse stores provide free classes that teach you how to do everything from painting faux finishes to staining wood. You will need this type of information, maybe for your current film or maybe for two films down the road. This information is free and well worth the time to learn.

- ***Visit the websites of paint manufacturers*** During preproduction, the Internet can be a valuable tool for set decoration visualization. Some websites, particularly the one for Behr paint (www.behr.com), have spectacular color and interior decorating suggestions. The painting color schemes on the websites demonstrate matching color patterns for walls, curtains, sheets, etc. and can help you select a set color motif.

- ***Try not to worry*** Art people seem to have the most regrets during a shoot. Wish you had more time to prepare the set decorations. Wish you had a larger budget. Wish you'd had the right prop at the right time. Wish you could have found that tool when you needed it most. Wish the shot had included the mural that took 3 weeks to paint. The fact is that because the art department is not repetitious, you won't have time to perfect everything and many aspects of the filming is out of your hands. Sometimes it seems like the most thankless job on the production. Know that all art people go through the same thing. Just do your best. We're all in this together.

On-set Box

Applications

For the art department, a well-stocked "on-set box" is critical when going on location. Depending on the size of the shoot, sometimes more than one is needed. An on-set box contains all the supplies and materials for modifying, patching, taping, gluing, or maintaining the sets or props. It should contain all the items you may need at a moment's notice. The better organized your on-set box is kept, the more useful it will be to you.

In this chapter, I've described the most common items I keep in my on-set box. This list is by no means exhaustive and will change depending on the type of film (drama, comedy, sci-fi, etc.) you are making. You'll find that no matter what type of film you're working on, this general set of tools will be indispensable whether you're working as an art director or prop master or somewhere in between.

On-set Boxes

On-set boxes are commonly large transparent plastic boxes, so the items inside can be quickly seen. Most standard is the plastic box with the jigsaw covers (see figure 46-1). These types of boxes are available in a variety of sizes and depths, and are constructed to allow them to be conveniently stacked.

FIGURE 46.1 *On-set boxes are commonly large transparent plastic boxes with jigsaw covers.*

You can find these boxes cheaply at most office supply stores. There are two common sizes:

- **36″ tall** The 36″ tall box is the most common size and it can store a large number of items.

- **18″ tall** Although it can contain fewer items than the 36″, there are a number of reasons why these boxes are preferable for most film jobs. The shorter size allows the box to fit in most standard car trunks (which the 36″ won't) and that makes the box more convenient if you don't have a dedicated prop truck. Also, a large amount of time is wasted on-set digging for items at the bottom of the on-set box. This time is drastically reduced since you can see most items in this shallow box instantly. When the crew is waiting for the art department to find a missing item, this can be a godsend.

Once you have your box, it's a good idea to label it art department, so other members of the crew won't casually place their own items inside. Also, if you have the time, make a list of the items contained in a box and tape it to the lid. The list will allow you to inventory to find missing items or replenish expendable items that you've used.

> **TIP** ▶ *Several art directors I've worked with have inexplicably used black canvas bags for their on-set boxes. These canvas bags seem to promote disorganization. If you're using any type of opaque on-set box, be sure to closely examine the contents each time before you go on a shoot. This will help you to minimize the length of time spent searching through the contents to locate a particular item.*

Within your on-set box, it's a good idea to store items within smaller boxes. I keep one for tools, one for drawing implements (see figure 46-2), and another for expendables. These small boxes allow me to send someone to "bring the small toolbox" rather than have them search endlessly for a tool we may know by a different name.

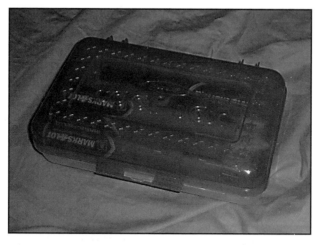

FIGURE 46.2 *Store loose items in your on-set box within smaller boxes.*

Standard Items

The list of standard items includes all the tools and supplies that will find a permanent home in the box. You should always try to return the item to the box once you've finished using it. This habit will prevent you from losing things on the set and having to replace them.

Purchasing all these items at once can get expensive, so build your on-set box over time. You may find that some of the items you'll never use so they wouldn't be worth obtaining anyway. Think in terms of items you use around the house for repair and maintenance. These items provide a good start for the tasks you'll need to complete on a set.

> **TIP** ▶ *For tools, it is always a good idea to spend the extra money to buy quality tools. However, many tools I've purchased even though I didn't know if I'd ever need them. In those cases, I buy the cheapest version I can find (often from the dollar discount stores), so I'll have it just in case. If I find myself using that tool, I replace it with a quality counterpart.*

The items are listed roughly by order of importance with the most critical items listed first and tools primarily optional near the end. The standard items in the on-set box include:

- **Battery-powered drill** This is the most critical tool in the art arsenal. You can use it to quickly screw in wood screws, mix paint, drill holes, and a thousand other uses. If you will be working on a number of films, make sure you invest in a good one. The money saved with a low-cost drill is not worth the slow battery charge time and marginal performance. Also, buy at least two spare batteries and keep them charged. You never know when you'll end up on a location that doesn't have any available power.

- **Tape measure** The old saying of "measure twice, cut once" to save time and material is very applicable on set. A small 10–15 ft tape measure is useful for measuring space for furniture placement, estimating paint surfaces, determining the width of the elevator (to make sure whatever you're elevating can actually fit), etc.

- **Set of screwdrivers or multi-bit driver** Many art people seem to think a screw gun is enough, often to the dismay of their crew. Screw guns are terrible at reaching into tight spaces or dislodging those stubborn jammed or partially stripped screws. Additionally, there is commonly only one screw gun which means people are waiting in line to use it. Although it has become increasingly popular to use the multi-bit drivers, I still recommend a small set of flat/blade drivers and two (small and large) Philips head drivers. Despite being magnetic, I have irretrievably lost many bits reaching into tight spaces.

- **Hand-held vacuum** Great for when cleaning up is necessary for multiple takes of spilled non-liquid items.

- **Trash bags** Useful for everything from storing trash to segregating props to simulating latex. Be sure to put a masking tape label describing the contents of the bag or you will soon have a prop truck filled with anonymous plastic bags that you'll have to look through to find what you want.

- **Hot glue gun** A glue gun (see figure 46-3) is one of the most indispensable items in your kit. Make sure you have one of these for quick and stable bonding of nearly any two types of materials.

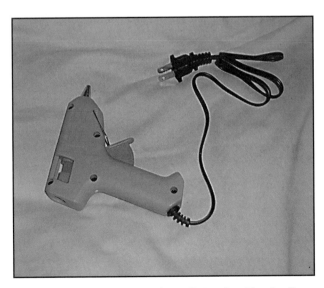

FIGURE 46.3 *A glue gun is an indispensable item for quick and stable bonding of nearly any two types of materials.*

- ***Paint brushes*** Just one or two will be great for quick paint touch-ups or spreading liquid glues.

- ***Staple gun*** When hanging temporary curtains or sheers, you can staple into wood window frame or door trim. Try to avoid using the staple gun in drywall as the staples will leave holes when they are removed.

- ***Plastic paint drop cloth*** Plastic drop cloth is useful for painting, preventing scratches to wood floors, or covering furniture while using spray guns or saws. When folded, a large plastic cloth is small and cheap and handy to have around.

- ***Coping saw w/steel cutting blade*** In addition to the usual art sawing needs, a small coping saw with the proper blade can be used to cut off the head of a stripped screw or inaccessible nail. Stripping screws occurs all the time with the combination of inexperienced help and power tools.

- ***Steel wool and sandpaper*** Keep various strengths of both these items for everything from aging to prop refinement.

- ***Magic markers in various colors*** You never know when you'll have to quickly create a sign or modify an existing one. Almost more importantly, you may have to eliminate trademarked product names in order to show the item in a scene. This practice, known as "greeking," is used to mask trademarked items from beer bottles to soap. At a minimum, keep a black and a red marker, each with a big tip.

- ***Shoe polish*** Quicker and cheaper to use that a large black marker.

- ***Tape ring*** You'll find that the number of different kinds of tape you use will multiply quickly. Paper tape, cloth tape, double-stick tape, colored tape, and electrical tape to name a few. Rather than having all these rolls float freely in your on-set box, it is a good idea to make a ring out of thick rope and attach them together (see figure 46-4). You might alternately use a clipped strap, so you can easily open the clip to take off or replace one of the rolls.

- ***Gloves*** Whether you have to clean a very dirty house, pull shrubs away from a wall for a better shot, move potted thorny roses onto a porch, or a million other tasks, having a decent set of gloves is extremely worthwhile. A good pair of gardening gloves is usually better than leather gloves for art department work. Leather gloves can get very warm, especially if you're working outside. Gardening gloves are better suited to most art tasks.

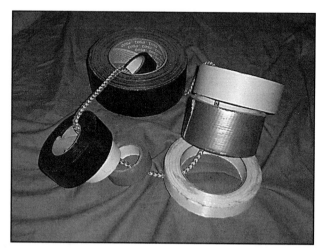

FIGURE 46.4 *A ring out of thick rope can hold all your tape rolls together.*

- ***Window scraper*** You might even consider getting the dual-width scraper to save time (see figure 46-5). These are cheap, so it's good to keep two or three. That way if the job is large and time is small, you can recruit some PAs to lend a hand. Also, these are useful for taking off alarm stickers from the exterior windows of a house that will be used as a location.

- ***Jeweler's screwdrivers*** Whether replacing batteries, prying up little covers, repairing damage to a miniature, or undoing a tiny screw, keep a jeweler's screwdriver set in your art box.

- **Drawing compass** Useful for making signs or stencils and marking painting areas. It is usually a good idea to include a large and a small one in your box.

- **Hole punch and clip ring** For continuity snapshots, it is useful to punch a hole in each picture and put it on a clip ring (see figure 46-6). The ring can then be easily carried or clipped onto a belt loop.

- **Laser pointer** While not strictly necessary, a laser pointer is an excellent device when you're communicating with the director or another member of the crew. You can quickly and specifically point to places in a room or particular items on the location.

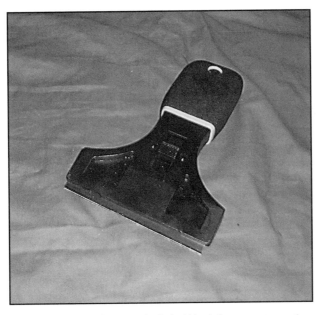

FIGURE 46.5 *Consider getting the dual-width window scraper to save time.*

FIGURE 46.6 *Use a hole punch and clip ring to hold together continuity snapshots.*

- *Labeled color chart* A color wheel available at any fine-art store is perfect for quickly examining complementary or tertiary color schemes, especially when quick matching with wardrobe is necessary. Also useful to communicate a particular color to the director to avoid misunderstanding.

- *Fireplace lighter* If you need to light cigarette after cigarette for the use of the actors or a large number of candles, it is usually easier to use a fireplace lighter. Cheap disposable lighters have problems in the wind and heat up with repeated use while a fireplace lighter can be used effortlessly.

- *Knee pads or a knee cushion* Working in the art department, you spend a lot of time on your knees – fixing and painting sets! These items come in especially handy when you're working on a sound stage with a concrete floor. Resting comfortably on your kneepads is a lot easier that trying to squat all the time. I find a knee cushion (see figure 46-7) to be most convenient.

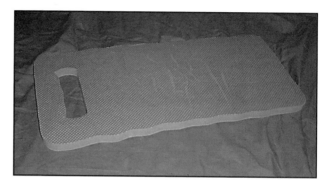

FIGURE 46.7 *A knee cushion is convenient and saves your knees.*

- *Hand-held sewing machine* Can be perfect for sewing fake curtains, adjusting cloth items such as sofa covers, and quickly making backdrops. Make sure you have spare batteries!

- *Paint mixer* This cheap little tool, usually available for about the cost of a can of soda, can make your painting life much easier. Just put it in the bit of a drill and it can mix paint quickly and easily.

- *Label machine* A machine that can make instant labels can be useful for labeling props or art equipment. These machines are cheap and convenient to use.

- *Sanding block* It seems like art department workers are continually sanding. Whether you're roughing up a surface for painting or taking edges off newly fabricated props, it'll save your fingers to use a sanding block (see figure 46-8).

FIGURE 46.8 *A sanding block is excellent for roughing up a surface for painting or taking edges off newly fabricated props.*

- *Various types of cigarette lighters* A lighter is a very common prop that can look good on film. It is often forgotten until the day of the shoot. By keeping several lighters in the art box, you can quickly supply the right lighter to match the desired character.

Expendable Items

Expendable items are items that you'll use up during the process of filming. You probably won't have to refresh your expendables at the end of every shoot, but is a good idea to keep an eye on how much has been used. Also, if the art department has a budget, be sure to include the expendables in the budget so the expense won't come out of your pocket.

Keep a list of expendables with each box, so you can easily and quickly check it before you start filming and refill any items that are short. Often, directly after a shoot is over, the on-set boxes are stored away and forgotten. Weeks or months can pass before your next shoot. By quickly checking the list against the contents when a new shoot is starting, you can replace any missing items.

Keep the following expendables in your box:

- *Paper towels* Useful for everything from masking during painting to cleanup to paper mache prop fabrication material.

- *Temporary hair coloring spray* The most popular brand among art directors, Streak-n-tips, is used for everything from aging materials to covering light bulbs to covering chrome to avoid reflections.

- *Black spray paint* For untold number of uses, especially for "greeking" (rendering trademark names illegible) on large labels or signs.

- *Blue painting tape* If you are doing any painting, blue masking tape is invaluable. In contrast to standard masking tape, painting tape is specially made to avoid leaving residue or peeling up existing paint when it's removed. This can be critical if you are using someone's home as a location and painting where existing trim or other objects that need masking has paint that's in poor condition.

- *Double-stick tape* Time and again, props will need to be secured to desktops, walls, and serving trays. You can use the foam-backed double-stick tape as it holds fairly well. For applications where the tape needs to be transparent, don't use normal double-sided tape because it doesn't hold very well. Get clear hairpiece tape (such as Topstick) for a solid, transparent hold.

- *Mounting spray* There are a wide variety of aerosol sprays of mounting fluid. Spray Mount (by 3M) is the most popular since it is very solid, yet it can still be removed at the end of the shoot. Super 77 (by 3M) is useful for permanent spraying and Remount (by 3M) is for very temporary applications as it provides the same adhesive that's found on the back of those little sticky notes.

- *Fuller's Earth or Schmere!* This fake dirt is useful for dirtying everything from walls to lampshades. It is made to come off easily, so the item can be restored to its original cleanliness.

- *Wood screws* Bring a number of different sizes of wood screws (see figure 46-9) for everything from mounting pictures to hanging drapes.

- *Hand wipes* Hand wipes are available in small packages that are convenient to keep in your art box. With all of the painting, spraying, and cleaning you'll need to do on set, hand wipes are fantastic.

FIGURE 46.9 *A number of different sizes of wood screws.*

- *Polaroid film* Polaroid cameras are the most popular method of taking continuity snapshots. If the film is put in the on-set box, make sure the box isn't left in the sun as this can ruin your film.

- *Fake money* Good fake money is increasingly hard to find. Keep your eyes open and you can sometimes find good fake money in stores or older businesses. You never know when you'll need a realistic looking wad of cash.

- *Bottle of water* Not for drinking, but to wash your hands, clean paint brushes, dilute paint, clean hairspray from surfaces, and for numerous other uses.

- *Fishing line* For hanging props or securing fixtures. Unless a light shines directly on the line, it's transparent to the camera.

Suggestions

Here are a few suggestions for your on-set box:

- *Keep your on-set box in a safe location* Don't bring your box onto the set until you have a safe location to put it. If left out, you'll find people taking things out of your box or even putting trash in! Find an out-of-the-way place that is easy to get at it.

- *Bow to the wishes of your superiors* I can't tell you the number of shoots that I've worked where the head of the art department was a disorganized, haphazard decision-maker which led to untold numbers of mistakes and distress on the part of the subordinates. Sometimes it seems that "artiste department" would be a more appropriate label. However, a lesson I still haven't completely learned (to my continued distress) is being careful when offering suggestions of a "better" way of doing things. Do what you can, but in the end – right or wrong – do it their way.

- *Keep the closest eye on your power tools* Power tools disappear from sets with alarming frequency. Since they're fairly expensive, easy to grab, and useful to almost everyone, they are very commonly stolen. Write your name with a permanent marker prominently on each tool as this seems to help deter thieves. Make sure that when you loan out your tools, it isn't to "the grips" but to one particular person who will be responsible for getting the tool back to you.

- *Preparation is very important* You will almost never, ever have extra time while on a shoot. Therefore, any organization you can do in preproduction is an investment that will pay off a 1000-fold during production. Although you will undoubtedly be given very little time for preparation before a shoot, make sure you take the time out of that sparse allocation to prep your on-set boxes.

Set Design and Construction

Applications

Set design and construction is an art in itself. This chapter contains a brief overview of structures and techniques that are used on professional sets that you may not have been exposed to yet. The primary obstacle to set construction is finding a place where a set can be created. However, guerilla filmmakers often overcome this problem by locating an unused warehouse or barn that can be rented for little or no cost.

> **TIP ▶** *If you find an unused location where you can film, be sure to consider where you'll obtain electricity for your equipment. A generator is often a necessity since power will be shut down at the location. This may offset the savings you obtained by using the empty structure.*

Constructing a Flat

The basic structure on most sets, a flat, is essentially a thin, light wall. Three flats can be joined together, painted, and decorated to represent a room in a house, an office, or an apartment. Flats are made to be light in weight, so they can be moved and stored easily. They are bolted together, so a flat can be easily added or quickly removed in case a special camera angle is required.

Flats allow you to create a set that is often better than a location. Locations, by definition, have set geography making it difficult to obtain some desirable shots. Additionally, low ceilings can make overhead lighting impossible. A flat doesn't suffer these problems since the geography of a room can be altered with a moment's notice and, unless desired, a room created from flats has no ceiling allowing easy placement of lights.

In figure 47-1, you can see the basic design of a flat. This figure shows the frame of the flat. The front of the frame is generally covered with a thin and inexpensive wood such as luon. Luon is great because it is almost as light as balsa wood, yet it is much stronger and less brittle. It is also

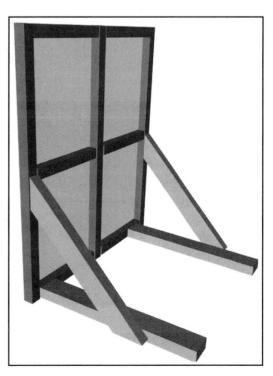

FIGURE 47.1 *The basic frame design of a flat.*

possible to break through the luon (or in one project I worked on, stab through with a butcher's knife) for a particular scene.

The structural frame members are generally 2 × 2 boards cut to proper length and nailed together. The angled boards that provide the supporting members are often 2 × 4 boards attached to the frame. Their weight and support holds up the wall. The back support legs are secured to the floor with sandbags. On a wooden stage, the legs are screwed directly to the floor with drywall screws.

Luon can handle the weight of mounted lighting fixtures, although it would not be strong enough to mount a bookshelf on. To mount something as heavy as a bookshelf, run a supporting beam along the back and attach it to the frame. The shelf would be attached through the luon to this weight-bearing member.

If you have an outside area with a surface such as a flat concrete slab, you can construct a three-wall set as they did in the early black and white film era. Back then, indoor lights were expensive and difficult to use. By suspending diffusion material (such as white bed sheets) from the top of the flats, you can use the sunlight to provide a majority of the interior light. This type of setup has the drawback of putting your filming schedule at the mercy of the weather. However, it may provide an effective solution if you can't afford a full lighting package.

Making an Arch

Traditionally, arches for set decoration have been difficult to create since they often have to fit the width of a specified doorway expanse and the height of a desired frame. A production designer showed me a simple method for making an arch that can be customized to all of your requirements.

You'll need a length of cloth that will cover the distance of the arch you desire. Additionally, you'll need some white glue and a bucket. Dilute the white glue with water in a ratio of 1:1 (one part water for every one part glue). Dip the cloth in the glue.

> **TIP ▶** *You can also use the standard papier-mâché mixture of flour and water if the glue is too expensive.*

While the cloth saturates with the glue and water mixture, suspend it between two flat surfaces (identical tables are good) as shown in figure 47-2. When the cloth dries, it will harden in the shape of the desired arch. You can now mold foam over the arch to provide any structural support needed.

FIGURE 47.2 *Suspend the saturated cloth between two flat surfaces such as identical tables.*

Breakthrough Wall

Many movies that I've worked on have needed a breakthrough wall. That means a wall that some object (human fist, motorcycle, baseball bat, and so on) bursts through and enters the room. Breakthrough walls are simple to construct and provide a cheap and impressive visual effect.

To construct a breakthrough wall, follow these steps:

1. ***Create a wall frame*** I generally use 2 × 4 boards to provide enough structural support to survive the impact.

2. ***Using finishing nails to attach drywall to the frame*** Drywall is cheaply available in sheet from most hardware and construction shops. It is also soft enough for an actor to drive his fist through if necessary.

3. ***Use covering tape or spackle to cover the nail heads*** The first breakthrough wall I made, I didn't cover with anything and it took me seemingly 100 coats of paint to cover them. If you aren't familiar with drywall finishing, ask the guy at the hardware store. You can use the same techniques that are used to place drywall in a home.

4. ***Score the back of the drywall*** Drywall is made up of three basic layers sandwiched together: cardboard, gypsum, and cardboard. You should score through the first layer of cardboard and through as much gypsum as you can without coming through the front piece of cardboard that will be facing the camera. Score in the pattern that you need the break. If an actor is punching through the wall, a basic X will do. If an object is coming through, you might want to create a cloud shape perhaps with an uncut portion so the piece breaks but the remaining flap will hold the piece in place. Any accidental cuts through the camera facing cardboard should be repaired with covering tape or spackle.

5. Paint the wall facing the camera.

6. ***Attach background material to the back of the wall*** When the punch or object comes through the wall, the camera will see behind it. I've found that instead of trying to dress the background set, it is far easier to attach a dark sheet or cut trash bags over the back area. That way the camera just sees a black background behind the object that bursts through the wall. This look is generally convincing even in daylight.

7. ***On the day of the shoot, add flour and drywall chunks*** People know about the white dust that is created when drywall is broken. Unfortunately, just breaking through doesn't create enough dust for the camera to capture effectively. Therefore, it is a good idea to dump flour on the backside of the wall. When the object breaks through the wall, the flour will plume through the rupture and create an excellent visual cloud with the help of the extra debris.

If you are using a film camera, it is often a good idea to overcrank the camera when photographing the breakthrough event. By overcranking (and essentially creating slow motion footage), you'll capture all the detail that in real time can seem instantaneous. It is far easier to speed up this slow-motion footage in post-production to show the detail you desire, than slow down normal speed film which may not have captured the detail you desire.

Suggestions

Here are a few suggestions for set design:

- ***Multiply your set dimensions by 1.5*** Generally, you should make your sets 150% or more of the size of a real location. For example, a 10′ × 10′ room should be made 15′ × 15′. While the extra size won't be noticed by the audience, it will be heaven for the film crew that often has to operate in the small, confined space.

- ***Make sure you have clearance for posters and paintings*** Using paintings and posters to cover wall space is probably the most common method of decoration by set designers. However, you need legal clearances to use the images that will appear in a film. If you were to place a Michael Jordan poster prominently in the center of a wall, your film can be in legal jeopardy unless the proper clearances are obtained. It is usually a good idea to find a local artist and use the legal release in Chapter 6 to get clearance to use the art in your film.

- ***Determine whether the floor will be seen*** Before beginning construction on a set, talk to the DP (cinematographer) and see if he has shots that will see the floor. Floors are one of the most problematic aspects of set dressing. If the floor will be seen, you may have to plan for carpet, linoleum, tile, or other materials. I haven't seen an effective method of floor covering that is simple and cheap, so generally guerilla films avoid shooting the floor.

Prop Fabrication

Applications

Prop fabrication is one of the most exciting and interesting jobs in the art department. When you work on a low-budget film, you'll be called upon to make an unbelievable number of props. Prop houses are a great place to rent the objects you need, but you may not have one near you or your budget may not allow it. Further, many props are still difficult or very expensive to obtain such as an assault rifle, an Academy Award (until you win one), or a uranium transport container. Some props simply do not exist outside of the imagination of the screenwriter/filmmaker.

Because of the limited time and budget, bad-looking props are usually a hallmark of low-budget films. In this chapter you'll learn some basic techniques to make a variety of realistic props with readily available materials. Before you begin to fabricate a prop, always consider how the real thing might be obtained or whether an available substitute prop might be used. There's nothing more realistic than the real thing.

> **WARNING→** None of the materials described in this chapter are appropriate for constructing items that will be used for food (such as plates, utensils, etc.). Some of the materials are actually toxic when ingested and should never be used in this capacity. I would recommend against fabricating items that will touch food that the actors might consume.

Prop Examples

The type of prop you'll need to construct will be largely determined by what is called for in the script. Often, however, you will need to make a simulation of an existing item. For example, if the villain with a metal ashtray knocks the lead actor unconscious, you'll need to construct a fake ashtray to make certain there is no possible injury to the actor.

Some common items that I've had to construct (or help construct) include:

- Prop telephones;

- Old time microphones;

- Replica handguns;

- Badges;

- Swords;

- Surgical instruments;

- Mock consumer items (toothpaste tubes, hairspray, etc.);

- Prison shivs;

- Fake knives and switchblades;

- Ash trays.

Lighting can do a great deal to make the fake look real, so after you've created a prop, take some still pictures of the item. Use bright lighting, low lighting, and so on to see variations. You can examine these pictures to aid you in determining what lighting is most effective with the item. Over time, you can learn to customize the props to fit the type of lighting that will be used in the movie. For example, dark moody films almost require shiny reflective objects, otherwise the item will appear like a black blob in the footage.

Fake binders

If you need to create stacks of three ring binders (maybe for a lawyer's office), filling them with paper may require hauling hundreds of pounds to the set. If only binding of the folder will be seen, you can blow up a zip lock bag with air and then tape or glue it to the inside of the folder. Folders with this filling can then be stacked, maybe with some random paper sticking out here and there to simulate a huge stack of filled folders using only a fraction of the weight.

Using Polymer Clay

Polymer clay has been a godsend to prop makers. Previous to polymer clay, materials available were difficult to work with, very expensive, toxic, or required elaborate curing processes. Polymer clay is non-toxic, malleable, and bakes hard in a standard cooking oven. Once hardened, the object can be painted, sanded, dyed, coated, or used to create a mold from which many duplicates can be made. It's available in colors that include primary and earth tone, fluorescent, translucent, glow in the dark, and countless others. You can use it to create everything from a futuristic phone to a ray gun to a Maltese falcon.

The two most popular brands of polymer clay are FIMO and Sculpey. There are several different types of polymer clay in each product line that vary in malleability and hardness. The softer clay is easier to shape, but blemishes such as a fingernail scratch or fingerprints can easily mar these soft materials. I would recommend you buy a block of each and find which one is best for your application.

There are only two minor disadvantages to polymer clay: the cost and oven size. While not expensive, polymer clay is also not cheap. If you're buying small quantities, watch for sales or coupons at your local arts and crafts stores. For large quantities, it's best to shop online and buy the 1-pound blocks of standard colors such as white and black. Since this material can be very heavy, be sure to check the shipping weight charges before ordering.

The size of the prop that can be constructed from polymer clay is limited to the size of your oven. Since the oven cures the clay, the piece must fit entirely and safely inside before it can be baked. Luckily for larger props, the hardened clay can be used with any number of glues and epoxies. Therefore separate pieces can be created and cured, then glued together to create the final piece.

Modeling

Modeling polymer can be done with almost anything from your hand to a set of professional modeling tools. Even if you buy a set of tools, makeshift tools can be used to great effect to create custom distinctive pieces.

Here are a few common household items I've found useful for sculpting props:

- *Plastic utensils* Plastic spoons and knives are some of the simplest but most effective tools you can use for modeling. Additionally, you can make a good gouger if you break off all the tines of the fork but the middle one.

- *Manicure set for tools* I've found these tools to be really great for detail work. You can even use the files for adjustments after the clay has been fired.

- *Turkey skewers* These are cheap, sturdy, and readily available. You can use the pointed end as a gouger and the round end for smoothing and texturing.

- *Crochet needles* Needles are excellent for gouging and producing line detail on the clay surface.

- *Outer tube of a Bic pen* Remove the inside pen head and ink tube, and the outer tube is perfect for many surface indentations. Be careful to make sure that any color clay stuck inside the tube is removed before using the tool on a different color of clay.

- *Custom-made tools* With an electric sander and some wood, you can easily make your own clay modeling tools.

- *Metal or brass stencils* These are excellent for making text impressions in the clay.

- *Rubber stamps* You can use a rubber stamp to create embossed text in a clay object.

Structures and frames

The expense of polymer clay means that any technique that minimizes its use can really help your budget. One of the best methods of minimizing the amount of required clay is to use aluminum foil as an inner core material. Aluminum foil can be easily shaped into the basic rough outline of the desired prop. Once the core has been shaped, polymer clay is built up on the surface for the final appearance. Aluminum foil works very well since it is light, cheap, readily available, and will heat in the oven during the curing process and helps the inner side of the clay shell to harden.

> **TIP** ▶ *You may consider including extra metal within the frame or structure to add weight to the item. If you're creating an artificial gun, you will force on the actor the need to pretend it has the weight of the real thing if the gun is featherweight. By adding the necessary weight, you can help add to the realism of the performance.*

For framing, you can create armatures with standard small gauge wire. This wire can be readily bent into the desired shapes to support the polymer clay. It can even be used as a basic frame around which aluminum foil may be wrapped. The clay can then be affixed on top of the foil.

> **TIP** ▶ *A wire frame presents an ideal method of ensuring proper proportions for the designed item. As any proficient artist knows, maintaining the proper proportions is critical to making an item, shape, or sculpture appear properly. It is much easier to measure and set these proportions using the line-like wire than the amorphous clay or aluminum shape.*

A frame should be used for larger pieces because polymer clay gets soft before it gets hard. An extended arm on a figure, for example, may droop as it is being cured if there is no frame to keep it structurally in place. The wire will ensure your object emerges from the oven in the same shape as when you placed it inside.

Finishing

Finishing is perhaps the most critical step for a prop maker. You have to be sure that the item will appear real on film. There are many different surfaces that might need to be simulated where you'll have to use your own ingenuity to find the surface you think will pass for real. Finishing is the one area that I always consult a more experienced prop master for suggestions.

Here are a few tips to help you achieve some of the surfaces you might need:

- Use a hand-held shoe polisher to buff a surface to shine.

- Scouring pads can be great for distressing or aging the surface.

- *Use ink-jet T-shirt transfer paper with polymer clay to create a permanent, waterproof image* After you preheat the oven, put the object with the transfer paper in for 5–7 min. Then remove the paper backing and put the item back in oven to complete baking.

- *Use Rub & Buff silver on clay to simulate pewter* Available at almost any craft store, Rub & Buff can add a number of metallic surface looks to your props. I've found that silver is excellent for providing a pewter look to plastic.

- *Use brake fluid to remove paint* Surprisingly, brake fluid is a great paint remover for many types of non-enamel paint. Try it if you need a non-abrasive method of removing paint.

- *To apply gold leaf, use a blush make-up brush* Rub the brush against your cheek for static electricity buildup. Peel that single layer off the stack and apply to surface. Smooth with brush. Recognize that fingerprints can cause tarnishing, so try to avoid touching the leaf.

Creating Molds

There are so many compounds for moldmaking that only from experience you can determine which compound is best for the job. To get started, check your local hobby store. Hobby stores generally have molding materials and casting compounds for making scenery for model train sets. These compounds are excellent for introductory experience. For volume, however, you'll find that they are extremely expensive.

Search the Internet for excellent deals on mold compounds. Synair Corp, Smooth-On, and Ace Resin all have websites where you can order cheaply available starter kits. The starter kits will have mold material and casting resin, so you can inexpensively experiment.

Before you start working with molds, be sure to buy cheap measuring spoons and cups. I usually get them at a local dollar store. You won't be able to use them for food items and often have to replace them after a few uses, so be sure to buy them cheap. You'll need many for measuring and mixing the mold materials.

Mold use

On one low-budget film I was working, I was suddenly and unexpectedly promoted to prop master. The person that vacated the position left few notes and even less completed work. According to the shooting schedule, in 48 hours we needed a sculpture for a pivotal scene. The script wasn't very specific in details, especially information relating to props.

In the critical scene, the lead detective stumbles upon a copy of a neo-modern sculpture and recognizes that the original sculpture might be a fake. The script gave no indication how the detective knows that the sculpture he stumbles upon is a copy. I discussed the problem with the production designer and we decided that the original and the copy of the sculptures would be in two different materials. The different materials would visually show the viewer that there must be a mold of some sort from which the different copies might be cast.

A mold was necessary because I needed two or more copies of the same sculpture in different materials. With a wire frame, aluminum foil, and polymer clay, I constructed a neo-modern head. Since time was extremely limited I needed a quick piece that would be visually recognizable and at the same time could be cast in a single-piece mold (see figure 48-1). A two-piece mold would mean that the sculpture could be more complicated, but it would make the timeline impossible.

Creating the mold

After I completed the original piece, I painted it with rubber latex (manufactured by Amaco) that I purchased over the Internet. This mold was risky to accomplish within the time frame, since I knew it would take 3–4 coats and each coat would take about 3 hours to dry under the lights. Nonetheless, the mold was created with about 16 oz. for latex and dried on time (see figure 48-2). I was now ready to cast.

Visually, I thought that clear acrylic would be perfect to let the audience know that there was a copy. I also thought it would give the DP (the cinematographer) something interesting to

FIGURE 48.1 *This piece could be cast in a single-piece mold.*

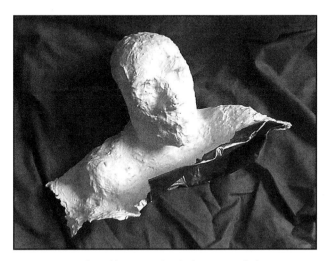

FIGURE 48.2 *The mold was created with about 16 oz. for latex.*

light. After I cleared the idea with both the DP and the production designer, I set to work. I use the acrylic that comes as two separate liquids: the resin and the catalyst. Once combined, they create a chemical reaction that solidifies to a solid clear plastic.

I started by filling the mold with water and then dumping the water into a large measuring bowl. That measure indicated how much acrylic I was going to need (a lot!). I completely dried the mold with a hair dryer to make sure that no wetness remained to interfere with the acrylic compound.

Normally, to prevent distortion of the latex mold, you'll want to cast a plaster backing around it. This prevents the weight of the material you pour into the mold from bending it out of shape. I knew that I didn't really have time to create this backing, so I taped the base of the mold to metal rods and suspended it upside-down in a box. I then filled the box with fine sand (from a friend's fish tank, actually) so that the outside of the latex mold would be supported.

Finally, I mixed and poured the acrylic. First I poured a small amount of acrylic into the mold and swirled it around making sure the entire inside surface was coated. Now comes the tedious part. Your enemy in creating a flawless final piece will be air bubbles. The first few times you make a cast you will probably end up with one or two air bubbles in exactly the right place to ruin your piece. The more pieces you make, the more experience you will have knowing where air might be trapped and how the proper jiggle here or there can dislodge all but the most stubborn air bubbles.

For the next hour, I babysat the mold and tapped it every 15 min or so. I wanted to do my best to prevent the bubbles that would ruin the cast and ruin my schedule. The chemical reaction of the acrylic heats up the cast and it grows very warm. When it became cool, my cast was finished. I carefully peeled-off the mold and the finished piece looked almost like I wanted it (see figure 48-3).

FIGURE 48.3 *The finished clear acrylic piece.*

TIP ▶ *Be sure to wait until the acrylic is cool, otherwise you're likely to peal-off the outer layer of the cast. It will stick to the inside of the mold.*

I then used the same mold to make another copy, this time in cast stone. Cast stone can be poured like cement – only it is available to provide a variety of surfaces including marble and granite. Both the acrylic and the stone statues I was going to sand down and polish, but the director decided he liked the rough surfaces. Critical props were completed only 4 hours before they were used on-camera – now that's guerilla filmmaking!

Suggestions

Here are a few suggestions to help you fabricate the best props:

- ***Spend extra time on props used in exterior scenes*** Low lighting is often used to hide the lack of detail on the prop. For exterior daylight shoots, using low light is generally not an option. Therefore, spend extra effort on exterior props since the bright sunlight will often make a mediocre prop look laughable.

- ***Use floor polish to remove scratches from acrylic*** You can use an acrylic floor polish to fill in cracks and scratches in acrylic material. Let the polish dry on the object at least overnight before handling.

- *For rugged use, dye plastics and polymer clays* If a prop is used heavily, the paint may chip off or wear away. You can use vinyl dyes available at auto parts stores (some is made by the Plasti-Cote manufacturer) that will actually dye the plastic. Using dye is especially effective if the prop has to be aged with sandpaper since the dye will look worn away rather than sanded off.

- *Use sandable auto primer on plastic or metal for a smooth, hard finish* After applying the primer, use 320 wet/dry sand paper to sand down rough edges or drips. Do the fine sanding with 400–600 sand paper.

Smoke Box

Applications

On a movie set, smoke is both a blessing and a curse – although far more often it's a curse. I have never, ever worked on a film set with a smoke machine where it hasn't malfunctioned, spurted smoke at inopportune times, made soundtrack-destroying noises, caused an allergic reaction for one of the cast, or simply failed to perform when activated. Further, smoke is difficult to control and keep at a constant level. However, I think we've all seen it create life in a dead scene or provide a special type of atmosphere that can't be duplicated any other way.

I just want you to realize what you're getting into by deciding to use smoke. You'll face large delays and, if smoke is used extensively, I can almost guaranty your shooting schedule will slip. Now that you have a general idea of what you're getting into, think twice before using smoke.

Smoke machines are available for rent from many film rental houses. These machines are often poorly maintained and malfunction regularly. Generally these machines generate smoke that has the light smell of burnt wood chips. Although most people are unaffected by the smoke, some people do have a slight skin reaction to large amount of smoke.

If you have plans to do a lot of smoke work, I would recommend checking party stores shortly after Halloween. I purchased a better smoke machine than is used on most sets for 70% off. If you don't have access to a commercial smoke machine, there are many ways to generate your own smoke.

WARNING→ The smoke machines in this chapter use fire and therefore should not be attempted by minors without adult supervision. Adults should practice great care when using anything flammable, so the fire has no chance to spread and cause a danger to people or property. If you can't be reasonably certain that no danger will be involved in your attempting these projects, please don't.

PARTS	Qty	Item
	1	L-bracket $1\frac{1}{2}''$ wide with $3''$ strut lengths
	1	$4''$ mounting ring
	1	Empty cat food container
	1	Can of Sterno cooking fuel
	1	12 oz. packet of ground corn

General Instructions

Smoke is generally used to best effect if it is backlit. Although difficult to demonstrate in still black and white pictures, in figure 49-1 you can see a horse figure that is lit from the front. Some smoke is visible, but in reality the horse is nearly surrounded by smoke.

With the same smoke level, you can see the smoke much more clearly in figure 49-2 when the smoke is backlit. You can see the puffs of smoke to the right of the horse as well as trails in front near the horse's hooves. Whenever you use smoke, lighting is even more critical than normal situations.

Because I wanted to show the smoke distinctly, I used a spotlight on the horse figure. In general use, flat light such as that generated by fluorescent bulbs tends to work the best. It's difficult to explain, but if you make some test footage using traditional tungsten lights and then try fluorescents you'll see that the fluorescent results are generally far more appealing.

FIGURE 49.1 *Front-lit horse figure shows little smoke.*

TIP ▶ *If you're considering using smoke effects with a DV camera, I would suggest you don't. When I started making short films I envisioned creating an atmospheric look akin to Blade Runner for a DV film-noir mystery. After lot of wasted time and energy, I believe it's nearly impossible to use atmospheric smoke effects on DV for more than the most minimal shots. DV simply lacks the exposure range in all but the most perfect circumstances to capture the smoke effectively. Instead, you're left with a bunch of low-contrast footage that looks like the scene wasn't lit properly.*

FIGURE 49.2 *Backlit smoke appears much more clearly on the negative.*

Smoke machine

You can create a very simple smoke machine (see figure 49-3) that will generate large quantities of smoke. I would recommend only using this smoke machine with models and miniatures since it takes some time to master and works best when you can control the pace of shooting. To give you an idea of the amount of smoke that will be generated, I used three of these to fill a small bedroom completely with smoke.

Construction of this machine is simple. Fill the cat food-can with ground corn (see figure 49-4) to about $\frac{1}{2}''$ level. You can grind up corn or corn-cobs yourself. You can also find ground corn at pet food store both as feed and as natural cat litter. The grind doesn't have to be fine, you just want to avoid any kernels of corn actually popping.

Take the mounting ring (see figure 49-5) and open it until it fits around the cat food-can. Make sure you leave extra space in the ring since it will need to be fitted over the steel of the L-bracket.

Slide the mounting ring over the top of the bracket and use a screwdriver to tighten it enough to hold it in place. You should place the can near the top of the bracket (see figure 49-6), but allow for some adjustment.

Before you start the smoke machine, get a big pair of pliers or a pair of duck-bill pliers. After 20 min of burning, the entire machine including the L-bracket and the cat food-can will heat up. If you need to move the machine, you don't want to touch it with your bare hands. With a good pair of pliers you can easily grip the main arm of the bracket and move it as needed.

To start the smoke machine, light the Sterno fuel and place it under the cat food-can (see figure 49-7). Sterno fuel is available at nearly any grocery store and of course at most camping outlets. The can should be suspended about 1″ above

FIGURE 49.3 *A simple smoke machine will generate large quantities of smoke.*

FIGURE 49.4 *Fill the cat food-can with ground corn to about $\frac{1}{2}''$ level.*

FIGURE 49.5 *Take a mounting ring and open it until it fits around the cat food-can.*

the can of fuel. You want the corn to slowly brown and then turn to charcoal to get the best smoke.

After lighting the fuel, it will take about 20 min to begin generating substantial quantities of smoke. The bracket will get hot, so be sure to place it on a non-flammable surface such as a brick or marble block. Once it reaches full smoke level, it will continue to smoke for about 20–30 min. The room you use it in will smell strongly of burnt corn.

As the corn burns, it will turn to a solid charcoal block. If you're going to need continuous smoke for a particular length of time, prepare several of the machine and light them at specific intervals. That way when one runs out of material, the next can be used.

You can use aluminum flashing to great effect to concentrate and funnel the smoke. Aluminum foil is another material that can focus smoke at a particular location, but you'll have to seal it rather well or much of the smoke will leak through places where the foil is not secured.

FIGURE 49.6 *Place the can near the top of the bracket.*

WARNING→ If the cat food-can becomes hot enough, the corn will ignite in open flame. In most cases, you can simply blow out the flame and add more ground corn and raise the can further from the flame to prevent it from flaming again. However, make sure to have water nearby to put out any potential fire.

FIGURE 49.7 *Light the Sterno fuel and place it under the cat food-can.*

Smoke box

There are many situations where a smoke machine just won't fill the needs called for. Small amounts of smoke such as from a smoking cigarette or smoldering ashes can't be simulated effectively with the volume of smoke produced by a smoke machine. These situations can be handled by creating a simple smoke box. The smoke box can then be hidden out of frame and left to smolder.

WARNING→ The incense coal in the smoke box will be burning, so you need to take very great care that no fire hazard is created. While inside the smoke box, there should be little danger, but don't set the box on any flammable material. Also be careful that the box is isolated, particularly when exposing the burning coal.

Incense coal is available cheaply through most religious supply stores. This coal is fairly inexpensive as one coal costs about the same as a single hard candy. If you can't find a local vendor, there are many sources of the coals on the Internet.

You will need two cake tins: one will be the top and the other the bottom of your smoke box. You will also need a non-flammable surface such as a brick to place the smoke box upon.

Use an ice pick to punch some holes in the top tin. The smoke will escape from these holes, so make them about the same size you'll need to simulate the desired source. If you are going to have the smoke come out as a distant location, punch a single hole in the top, feed the hose into the hole, and seal the hose to prevent leaking.

Place the coal in the bottom cake tin. Fill the bottom of the tin with vegetable oil until about half of the height of the coal is covered. Use an extended lighter to light the coal. The coal will act as a wick, and absorb and burn vegetable oil as it needs it. Put the top tin over the bottom. Use the binder clips from the office supply store to hold the tins together.

Suggestions

Here are a few suggestions for working with smoke:

- *Turn off your smoke alarms*! To my dismay I learned that even a commercial smoke machine with set off smoke alarms. In a commercial building, this can mean an automatic call to the fire department or even sprinkler activation that can ruin expensive lighting and camera equipment not to mention hair and costumes. Make sure this is your first step when using a smoke machine or you'll most likely regret it.

- *Keep a fire extinguisher near* Even if your commercial smoke machine presents little fire potential, turning off the smoke alarms can put a densely populated set in jeopardy. Have fire extinguishers where they are easily accessible for safety reasons.

- *Use smoke in a place of controlled ventilation* A place with excellent air circulation (such as outdoors) will mean that you can never achieve the critical mass of smoke you desire. Poor circulation means you can't clear out smoke between takes. A place where you can close off ventilation and activate it at will is perfect.

Fake Body

Applications

There are many scripts that call for a situation where an artificial body is needed. Perhaps the lead actor is beating up the body on the floor. Maybe a corpse must remain absolutely still for the length of the shooting day. Sometimes a dummy must be thrown from the roof of a building.

Sadly, most of the time on guerilla shoots, clothes are simply stuffed with newspaper to provide a clearly false and unnatural replica of a body. Even with a good framing practice, these rudimentary fake bodies generally look awful. They don't have the illusion of the weight and structure of a real corpse, so they appear on camera just as they do in real life – cheesy.

The way to solve this problem is to create a carcass that has the same general characteristics of a real body. That is, the fake body should have a rudimentary skeleton and some musculature. In this case, you'll create the skeleton out of PVC pipe (for bone) and foam furniture padding (the muscle).

TIP ▶ *It is often a good idea to visit stores just after Halloween. You can usually get wigs, facial masks, and hands or gloves at blowout prices. Also check thrift stores and the Salvation Army stores for a ready source of a variety of these types of items. With the proper stuffing and a little repainting, these items can make your fake body even more realistic.*

	Qty	Item
PARTS	1	18' (6 m) of $\frac{1}{2}''$ PVC pipe
	1	$\frac{1}{2}''$ PVC four-way coupling
	1	$\frac{1}{2}''$ PVC T-joint
	1	Roll of duct or gaffer's tape

General Instructions

To begin construction of the body, start with the skeleton. For this skeleton, you'll use $\frac{1}{2}''$ PVC pipe for the bones. The $\frac{1}{2}''$ stock is light and the simplest to put together. If your body will be taking a great deal of abuse, you may want to use $\frac{3}{4}''$ or greater PVC. However, if you want a particular effect such as a fight scene where an actor breaks the arm of the body, the $\frac{1}{2}''$ pipe is just about the correct hardness for a nice break and will provide a satisfying snap!

Construction

The following instructions are used to create a body that is roughly 6 ft (2 m) tall. If you need a smaller body, scale the dimensions appropriately. Use PVC cement to secure the pipes into the couplings and joints, so the body doesn't come apart during handling.

The skeleton is a number of PVC pipes connected by flexible tubing. The more comprehensive you can make the skeleton, the more realistic it will move (such as when it's falling). Make the skeleton primitive if the fake body is meant to simply lie on the living room carpet. However, you should always include a skeleton, no matter how primitive, in order to provide the authentic layout of the limbs and body.

To create the skeleton, follow these steps:

1. Cut PVC pipe of the following lengths: two pipes of each of these lengths: 9″ (23 cm), 13″ (33 cm), 11″ (28 cm), 5″ (13 cm), 14″ (36 cm), 21″ (53 cm), and 10″ (26 cm). Cut single pieces of each of these lengths: 7″ (18 cm), 3″ (8 cm), and 21″ (53 cm). The skeleton will be laid out as shown in figure 50-1.

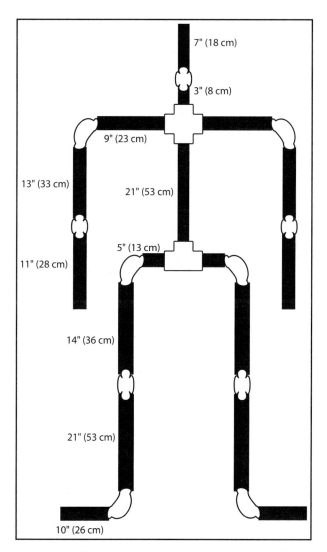

FIGURE 50.1 *The skeleton can be created with PVC pipe cut to the designation lengths.*

2. Insert the two 9″ (23 cm) lengths into opposite sides of the four-way coupling.

3. Insert the 3″ (8 cm) length and the 21″ (53 cm) length into the two remaining sockets of the four-way coupling.

4. Take the free end of the 21″ (53 cm) pipe and insert it into the top of the T-joint.

5. Insert the 5″ (13 cm) pipes into the remaining sockets of the T-joint.

The rest of the assembly will depend on your needs. You can place flexible joints at any point where it will help the story. Figure 50-1 shows places where these joints may be used effectively. To create a joint, take a piece of tape and fold it over on itself a few times (see figure 50-2). The folded tape should be flexible, but not too weak.

Take this tape and using another piece of tape, bind it to one of the PVC bones (see figure 50-3). You are going to be binding it to the other bone in the same way. With that structure, the joints will only fold in one direction, just like real arm and leg joints.

Tape the folded tape to the other bone (see figure 50-4). The joint should now be complete. You can add as many joints as you want to your skeleton. However, the more flexible pieces used in the skeleton, the more unmanageable the body.

In figure 50-5, you can see an example of a completed skeleton. Notice that I only needed joints at the elbows so that the rest of the skeleton is solid.

For the head you can use a stuffed Halloween mask, a custom head, or even a large doll head. Mannequin heads or Styrofoam heads are usually avoided because of noise-related problems. If the Styrofoam scrapes on the floor or one of your actors is assaulting the head off camera, the distinctive noise can ruin your soundtrack.

The muscle is supplied by lengths of furniture padding. I use lengths of rope to bind the stuffing to the skeleton although you can use soft tape if you prefer. Furniture padding is good

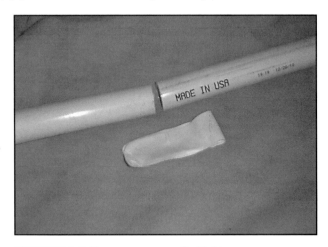

FIGURE 50.2 *Fold tape over to create a flexible joint.*

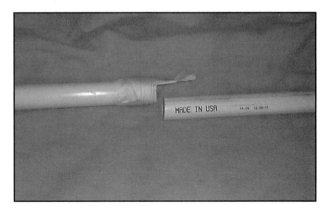

FIGURE 50.3 *Take the tape length and use another piece of tape to bind it to one of the PVC bones.*

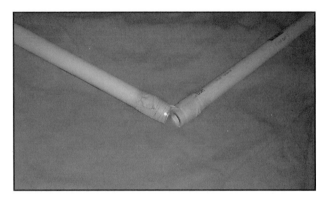

FIGURE 50.4 *Tape the folded tape to the other bone.*

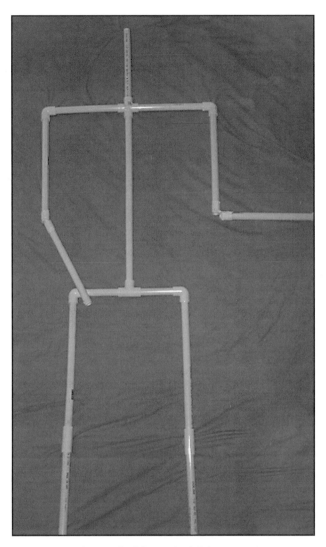

FIGURE 50.5 *An example of the completed skeleton.*

because it's robust, has some give, and yet is silent when prodded or bumped. You can use old clothing as muscles instead of padding, but I find the furniture stuffing to be much easier to attach to the skeleton.

Once you've completed the muscles, put the necessary clothes on the body. Remember that the clothes should cover all areas, so there isn't any exposed skin. If there will be parts exposed, you can use tan-colored stockings for an approximate skin tone. Be aware, however, that this only looks even passable when filmed from a distance.

Suggestions

Here are a few suggestions for your fake body:

• ***Coordinate with wardrobe*** Read the script and coordinate with the wardrobe people what clothes that the actor will be wearing when the substitute dummy is to be used. You don't want the actor wearing a tank top and shorts in the scene since creating a believable dummy with these clothes will be nearly impossible.

- ***Bring extra furniture padding to the set*** Sometimes a fake body looks fine in preproduction, but looks flat in the camera frame. Have some extra padding on hand in case the body needs to be plumped up a bit.

- ***Leave the body in the prop truck until the shot is ready*** Crew members seem to have an almost obsessive need to play with a dummy left unattended on a set. Most of the time this play involves placing the dummy in obscene poses, having it pick its nose, etc. You don't want your prop broken because someone feels the need to amuse themselves with it.

Securing Loads

Applications

The art department has the opportunity to rent and handle some of the most beautiful and intriguing items used on a film. The department must transport everything from unique props to striking set decorations to fake walls. Regardless of whether you're packing a prop truck, sharing space on the grip truck, or using a minivan, there's a great deal of responsibility in effectively hauling and securing loads. It can be a critical skill to master and one that should be taken seriously. Besides keeping the items safe, the better you are at moving, the less chance that someone (most likely you) will be hurt.

The demands of movie transportation are much different from the general practice of moving. In traditional moving, packing and unpacking are activities only performed once per job. For the art department, moving is an ongoing process with items acquired at various stages and each set requiring different items. Careful planning can minimize the breakage, the amount of needless searching, and frequent need for complete re-packing of the transportation vehicle.

General Instructions

As with improving any skill, you'll get better at set packing the more practice you have at it. Below are several guidelines I've learned during the numerous shoots I've worked. Because an art department worker is always handling different types of items, only experience can prepare you for the variety of challenges you'll face. The goal of effective packing is more than just achieving a level of efficiency – it's also about minimizing the amount of L&D (lost and damaged items). If you're renting from prop houses, L&D can ruin your budget since charge-back costs can be enormous. If you're using borrowed items, you want to minimize the amount of ill will caused by breakage.

Proper procedures, whether using a furniture dolly or securing a load effectively with the trucker's hitch, can help you complete a shoot with a minimum of heartache. If there are more experienced workers on your crew, be sure to listen to them as they're probably full of hard-won experience.

Using a packing list

You should use a packing list to ensure everything you need for a particular set will be placed in the transportation vehicle. I can't tell you the number of forgotten, lost, or misplaced props and decorations that result from not using a packing list. The art department shoots I've worked that went smoothly always used a packing list. On any shoot, there are simply too many items to keep track of accurately without one.

The packing list serves three major purposes: loading checklist, unloading checklist, and communication device.

- *Loading and re-loading* Not only does the list allow you to check off items that are loaded for the shoot, it also allows you to make sure everything is re-loaded once the set is struck. This can help you prevent leaving behind important items that may be expensive to replace.

- *Unloading* During unloading, the packing list can help you be sure that all the items that are needed for the shoot are on set.

- *Communication* The list provides a central communication device that allows the entire department to know exactly what's onboard the truck. This means that when you ask for someone to get an item, you'll know you're not sending them on a fool's errand.

Whenever you consider not using a packing list, think about the time and frustration caused by a missing prop or the time it will take to go and re-acquire a decoration. Like many things, the time you invest up front will be greatly repaid later.

> **TIP ▶** *I have encountered many art directors who steadfastly refuse to make a packing list and then observe as mishap after mishap occurs during the shoot. If you're working for someone that's resistant to a packing list, I would suggest that you try to make a list of the items for which you're responsible. I've found a personal list has provided me with at least a little peace of mind despite the inevitable calamity that occurs by not having an overall one.*

Packing and labeling items

In the rush of a shoot, many people don't think through the packing job ahead of them. Before you're ready to shoot, you'll probably have numerous props and set decorations for many different locations contained in the same truck. You'll save a great deal of time if you plan your packing order in advance and label the items appropriately.

Whether you're using a prop truck or a personal vehicle, pack all the props of a particular location together. This practice usually takes extra time at the beginning because you'll have to unload everything before repacking it. However, that time will be saved when you get to the location. Set aside a separate area (usually the last area packed for quick access) for items that you'll use on multiple sets. This area will include space for your on-set box, tools, and other materials.

After you've separated the items by location so that they can be easily retrieved, it's a good idea to use colored tape to denote which item belongs to which set. I use colored electrical tape, because it's cheap, available in packs of six different colored rolls, and the adhesive tends to be weaker than many tapes. This means that it generally doesn't leave a sticky residue (provided it is removed within a few weeks of application).

If you have more than a couple of people in the art department, you'll find that this color coding is wonderful for set decoration. Everyone can be instructed to bring the blue labeled items to the set. That eliminates everyone asking the art director "Does this go to the set?" with each of the thousand items stored in the truck.

Using a furniture dolly

A furniture dolly is simply a small carpeted board with wheels (see figure 51-1). You will find these indispensable when moving furniture, file cabinets, book shelves, and other cumbersome items. Furniture dollies are available for rent from most truck rental companies or you can purchase one from a local hardware warehouse. I would advise against buying one unless you're doing a great deal of moving since they're a pain to store and seldom needed when production isn't underway.

While you can move equipment onto a dolly by lifting it and setting it down on top, there is a better way. I always muscled equipment onto furniture dollies until a set decorator showed me how the dolly can be used for leverage. If you have an item with a solid flat bottom, tip the load onto one of its edges.

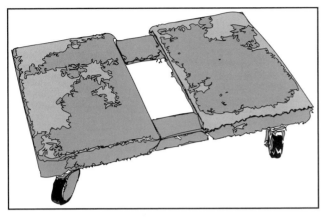

FIGURE 51.1 *A furniture dolly is a small carpeted board with wheels.*

Scoot the dolly under the load and tip the dolly up until the top of the dolly rests against the bottom of the load (see figure 51-2).

Now tip the item and the dolly back together to the horizontal (see figure 51-3). You might have to put your foot in front of the dolly wheel to act as a stopper, so the dolly isn't pushed out from under by the weight of the object. This technique works great because the dolly itself acts as a lever to pry the heavy object off the ground.

Ratchet straps

Ratchet straps are some of the most useful items you can have for securing a load. They can be used quickly and surely, and the ratchet mechanism allows the strap to be tightened down into place. If you're using a prop or a grip truck, there are wooden slats that run down the length of the body. There is an accepted proper way of affixing a ratchet cord to these slats.

First of all, it's not recommended to put the hook of the strap directly on the slat. It can too easily come loose, especially from jostling while the truck is driving. The hook should go down and around the slat and hook back onto the strap itself (see figure 51-4). Also, the opening of the hook should

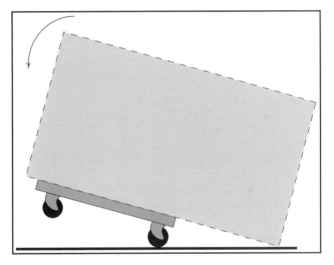

FIGURE 51.2 *Scoot the dolly under the load and tip the dolly until the top of the dolly rests against the bottom of the load.*

face down, so a jolt to the bottom of the truck doesn't allow the strap to jump out of the hook.

Securing rope

Although ratchet straps are the preferred method of securing heavy loads, you will almost certainly need lengths of rope to tie down other objects. If the load is too big to fit a strap around or you're simply out of ratchet straps, rope can be invaluable. If you have a single long length of rope, you can simply coil the rope and hang

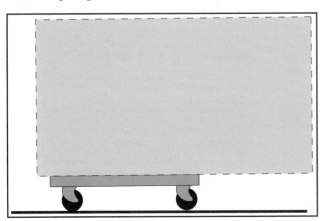

FIGURE 51.3 *Tip the item and the dolly together back to the horizontal.*

it in some convenient place. However, more often you have several lengths of shorter rope that are available for tying items. It's convenient to keep these ropes secured on the slats when they're not in use.

First, coil the rope so each loop of the length is about five times the width of the slat. Once you have the coil, feed it up behind the slat as shown in figure 51-5.

Pull the top of the coil down and feed it through the bottom edge of the coil (see figure 51-6). Pull the coil tight and it will remain secure on the slat. Make a series of secured coils for all the rope you have. When the rope is needed, it can be quickly and easily retrieved from the slat.

Proper use of the trucker's hitch

Chapter 41 demonstrates how to tie a trucker's hitch to secure a load. Proper use of the hitch can mean the difference between a secure item and the one that may come loose and allow damage to the stored items. Therefore, here are a few suggestions to help you ensure that it is being used properly:

FIGURE 51.4 *The hook should go down and around the slat and hook back onto the strap itself.*

*   ***Pull the load tight*** Although you don't want to break anything, pull the hitch as tight as you can. If anything isn't packed firmly, a little movement when you pull can tell you that. This practice is important because something may look well seated, but it can shift during transport.

*   ***Make a loop around a piece of a large item*** Use one of the front items you are tying down as a sort of bookend for the rest of the objects. Make a loop around an open part of an item (such as the arm of an armchair) in the length of rope before the loop for the trucker's hitch.

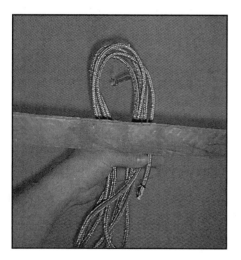

FIGURE 51.5 *Coil the rope and feed it up behind the slat.*

FIGURE 51.6 *Pull the top of the coil down and feed it through the bottom loop of the coil.*

- ***Don't run the line around an object that can move or slide*** Try to avoid putting light items or items with wheels on the front line next to the securing rope. They may move during transport and create havoc. Try to put these items in the middle of the objects you're securing.

Suggestions

Here are a few suggestions to help you when you're transporting items:

- ***Always bring a tape measure*** Whenever you're moving or placing something, it's a good idea to measure before you expend the energy. If a couch won't fit through a doorway, it's a good idea to know this before dragging the couch up two flights of stairs.

- ***Watch out for bungee cords*** These cords may be pulled tightly around an item and releasing them may cause them to snap violently. You don't want to loose an eye because you weren't paying attention when handling a simple elastic band.

- ***Call out before activating a truck lift*** For grips, standard practice requires you to call out "going up" or "going down" before activating the lift gate on the back of a truck. Often art department people don't follow this simple etiquette and endanger or injure others because of it. This simple warning tells everyone around the back of the truck to be aware that things are moving. Please, please, please make the effort to perform this simple task.

Make-up Introduction

VII

Applications

Make-up and wardrobe go hand-in-hand on most guerilla productions. While they are seldom handled by the same person, still they are closely coordinated and generally located in the same location or trailer. While wardrobe on most small productions is very rudimentary, many people don't realize that make-up is an art as complicated as cinematography. There are hundreds of techniques and numerous materials that must be mastered to perform the craft of make-up. Facial make-up is an art not unlike oil painting. A make-up artist applies color and highlights one layer at a time. Every face is different, so the make-up work is specialized to the unique surface of each actor's face.

There are three primary categories of movie make-up:

- *Beauty make-up* Also known as "flat" make-up, beauty make-up generally seeks to make the actors appear normal or as if they aren't wearing any make-up. The art of beauty make-up requires subtly enhancing the face or body of the performer to make them appear normal to the viewer, yet more attractive than they would ordinarily look in real life.

- *Character make-up* This type of make-up involves transforming an actor into a character that is different from the actor's normal appearance. The performer is made to look sick, fat, old, young, thin, stupid, lecherous, period, and so on. Wigs, false teeth, rubber or latex appliances, and bald caps are all familiar items used to alter the looks of an actor. In my experience, character make-up is the least used type of make-up outside of big-budget films.

- *Effects make-up* When most people think of movie make-up, they immediately think of effects make-up. Gore, alien faces, monster guises, wounds, and scars are all popular aspects of effects make-up. Effects are particularly difficult because of the continuity and matching required for shots made over several days or weeks.

Whatever area of make-up you'd like to learn, practice on yourself and use a still camera to capture the results. Some effects can look wonderful in real life but the camera sees them poorly. Likewise, some make-up (such as hard lines to accentuate stomach muscles) will look terrible in the light of day, but will appear spectacularly in a photograph. If you live near a film school, see if you can find an aspiring cinematographer who is willing to collaborate with you. You can experiment together to find the optimum visual image.

When applying make-up, be sure to take your time. While you shouldn't work slowly, recognize that trying to rush make-up application will either produce poor results or require additional time to correct mistakes made during the hurry. Practice on any friend or family member that will let you since the variety of complexion and skin types is staggering, so broad experience will decrease the amount of time required on the set.

> **NOTE→** The fields of stage make-up and movie make-up are tremendously dissimilar. Stage make-up requires boldness and pronounced make-up effects to allow the audience in the back rows to see and understand the characters. Stage make-up is also generally made to withstand the rigors of long hours of performance and sustained physical activity. Movie make-up is generally much more subtle and comfortable for the actors. Don't assume that techniques from one venue can successfully be applied to the other.

If you're considering a career in movie make-up, there are many schools that provide excellent instruction. Effects make-up artists in particular require a portfolio of images of previous make-up jobs. The make-up school can supply the instruction and practical applications for assembling your portfolio.

Suggestions

Here are a few general suggestions for working make-up:

- *Develop a good chair-side manner* Most actors and actresses enjoy the make-up chair because they can relax, gossip, talk about the news, or get to know the make-up artist. I've heard before that a good make-up person is a father confessor, gossip columnist, and comedian rolled into one. Careers in this field are made by getting a rising star to take you along with them. Therefore a pleasant disposition is required for this position.

- *Use the right tools for the job* Make-up has its own set of professional application tools including brushes, pencils, cotton balls, cotton swabs, sponges, and so on. Learning the proper use of each tool is critical to achieving the application results that you desire. Since these items are inexpensive, experiment with each of them to find where they can be used to best effect.

- *Create a basic make-up kit* Even if you don't intend to do a lot of make-up, you should begin to create a basic kit that contains all the primary make-up tools, materials, and adhesives. In addition to the basic make-up items, the kit should contain a number of make-up removal liquids such as petroleum jelly, cold cream, tissues, and so on.

- *Consider compositing screen colors* You might be doing make-up or wardrobe for actors that will be performing in front of a blue or green screen. If this is the case, avoid using shades of make-up or fabric that are near the color of the screen that will be used for compositing. This suggestion may seem simple at first, but many make-up artists fail to check the script for continuity. This oversight can result in inappropriate colors being used in a normal scene without recognizing that the scene that follows is a blue screen shot. Check with the director or the DP to determine the shots that will use the blue screen and plan around them.

- *Avoid making wardrobe items* Most hand-made wardrobe items will look as fake on screen as they do in the real world. Avoid making any pieces if possible. It is far better to add slight modifications to existing items than to have a piece that will quickly attract the attention and dismissal of the final viewer. While most clothes available at thrift shops will appear very used (and therefore unsuitable), estate sales often have inexpensive used (but not threadbare) clothes from times gone by. Watch your local paper for them.

Character Look

Applications

Establishing a character is the responsibility of the actor. Providing the costuming and accessories that help the actor find and convey the character is the responsibility of wardrobe. To assist you in thinking about wardrobe there are a large number of things to consider aside from the basic necessities of period and socio-economic level.

This chapter will provide a number of suggestions and possibilities for wardrobe that can help add that distinctive flair that can give a character his/her "look." Wardrobe should never be an afterthought since the proper costuming can help an actor become the role that is being played.

General Instructions

Wardrobe is a difficult department to work in because it requires coordinating with many people with strong opinions. Wardrobe personnel have to please the actors and the director at the same time coordinating with the DP and production designer. At the same time, the costumes and accessories can complement and augment the heart of the film in ways lighting and performance cannot.

On guerilla films, wardrobe personnel are often thrown into the deep end with little professional training. To help you, here are a few tips for general selection of wardrobe:

- *Better oversize clothing than under* As a general rule, wardrobe on adults looks better oversize than under. However, extremely ill-fitting clothing may be perfect to emphasize a character's awkwardness or poverty. Charlie Chaplin's suit on the Tramp character is an excellent example.

- T-shirts with custom text is one of the easiest, fastest, and cheapest ways to say something about a character. With all of the iron transfer paper for ink-jet printers these days, you can easily create shirts on short notice.

- *Top/skirt pairs are better than full-length dresses* Tops and skirts can be easily unpaired, mixed and matched, re-used for several different characters, etc. A full-length dress tends to be recognizable and is therefore much less flexible for use on a guerilla shoot.

- *Have the actors bring their own shoes* It is nearly always better to either have the actors use their own shoes or have the film allocate a budget to buy them. The actors will have to stand in them all day, so aside from the sanitary problems of used shoes, it's best to have shoes that fit well.

- *When altering clothing, use large stitches* Large stitches are much easier and quicker to undo than tight stitches.

- *Get a hand-held sewing machine* Portable hand-held sewing machines are cheap and light, so be sure to include one in your kit. They can be used to make quick adjustments and repairs.

- *Fake tattoos* While tattoos are a make-up item, it is important to plan wardrobe around tattoos that are key to the character. While the tank top is the most common way to show off body art, I've seen strategic ripping worked into the story and used very effectively.

- *Uniform patches* A very under-used costume item, patches can be custom made with generic but realistic names. They might be sewn on a jacket, a baseball cap, or even glued to a backpack.

Shirt Comportment

Beyond selecting a shirt type for a character, there are a many things you can do to give the shirt its own personality. Are the sleeves rolled up? Is the tail of the shirt hanging out? Tucked in? Are buttons missing? Is the pocket torn? Is there junk in the shirt pocket?

Real people wear their shirts for long period of time and treat them differently and abuse them. Much like the art department is called upon regularly to age set decorations, wardrobe looks at aging clothes. What about a stain? Better yet, how about an area where spilled bleach has turned the colored fabric white? Coffee stains provide a close likeness for grease stains, particularly for clothing worn by workers at a greasy spoon.

How about adding an overshirt? What about using clothing as an accessory? Maybe an overshirt tied around the character's waist. Perhaps tied over the shoulders for that classic 1980s' yuppie look? Use your imagination.

Spend some time considering how alterations to a shirt can affect the overall look. Is there a way you can distress several pieces of clothing so they "match" in their sense of wear? Finding good clothes is wonderful, but modifying them to perfection will give the film substantial added polish.

> **TIP ▶** *To simulate sweat stains on the armpits of a shirt, use a laundry detergent such as Era or Tide. These detergents will darken the fabric appropriately and they don't dry or evaporate. They also generally have a pleasant smell.*

Accessories

Accessories can involve almost anything that the character wears that is not a prop. Jewelry, glasses, hats, gloves, fans, umbrellas, parasols, handbags, earrings, and so on can all be used to provide a character with a unique identity. Actors often like to have accessories as it provides them a way to add another dimension to the performance (such as tugging on an earring when nervous or precisely straightening a handkerchief in a suit pocket).

Here are a few suggestions for selecting and handling accessories:

- *Consider the scene before the accessories* The scene, and actions of each performer within it, takes precedence over any wardrobe considerations. Therefore, carefully consider whether a particular costume or accessory can actually be used in a scene before selecting it. In an extreme example, a woman in jeopardy can't easily climb a mountain to escape if she's carrying a parasol.

- *Collect hats* Good hats are difficult to come by in this age where baseball caps and snowcaps are the only two types in wide use. Thrift stores seemed to have a smaller and smaller collection of hats. Try the Internet instead where some wonderful items can be obtained through online auction sites such as eBay. If you meet someone with a great worn hat, you might offer to trade a new hat for the authentically aged one.

- *Buy watches from street vendors* A cheap watch bought in a store almost never looks like an expensive watch. Luckily most cities have street vendors that sell knock-offs of expensive name brand watches for a small fraction of actual cost. In most circumstances, costume watches don't even have to work, so it won't matter if the one you bought from a street vendor stops ticking in month.

- *Add detail with belts* One fashion conscious friend of mine says that you only need to look at a person's belt and shoes to see how much attention they pay to style. While a belt may be little seen on screen, it can provide an excellent opportunity to add that little extra polish to the overall look of the character.

- *Stuff in pockets* On a tight-fitting pair of pants, filling the pockets with junk can make a character look slovenly or overworked. Try to avoid anything that jingles. While realistic, these items never sound very good on the soundtrack.

Glasses

Glasses can be wardrobe's best or worst friend because they say so much about a person. However, some actors hate glasses because they cover the eyes and rob the actor of some range of expressiveness. Make sure to have a variety of different types since you never know which the actor will find comfortable or appropriate.

Are glasses a prop or are they wardrobe? It seems to vary from shoot to shoot. Make sure you determine whose responsibility these types of items belong to before the shoot begins. Otherwise, you could lose an important item the first day of shooting – never a good omen.

Be aware that some glasses, particularly some type of sunglasses, can have very reflective lenses. They must be avoided since they might show the camera and crew when doing close-ups. Be careful to check whether a pair of glasses has this problem before purchasing them.

Some common types of glasses include:

- *Monocle* Common mostly in period dramas and comedies, the monocle is a single lens for one eye. It's wedged between the eyebrow and the upper part of the cheek. If you need one, be sure to get it early so the actor that will use it will have time to practice with the lens.

- *Bifocals* Glasses with a visible line between the upper and lower parts of each lens. If the actor doesn't wear bifocals, check the prop rental shops as they usually have these glasses with fake lenses.

- *Granny glasses* Granny glasses can be used to advance a character's fear or acceptance of old age. Historically George Washington used them to great dramatic effect. A similar theatrical impact can be seen in Star Trek II when William Shatner produces a pair in the middle of a conflict.

- *Steel rimmed* Usually worn by a bookish sort of character.

- *Pince-nez* Once only used in period dramas, the Matrix movies have altered the connotation of pince-nez glasses.

Sunglasses can be found at dollar stores that will fool the camera to appear like expensive designer glasses. However, while cheap glasses may look fine on camera, they are usually not the most comfortable to wear for a long shooting day.

General Warnings

On the guerilla shoots I've worked, the wardrobe department usually has little time, littler money, and tremendous demands for authenticity. In the whirlwind of preparation, it can be easy to forget the simple rules of making certain that the clothes will actually show up properly on camera.

Here is a general checklist to keep in mind when putting together the costuming for the shoot:

- ***Bright red and yellow shirts can reflect colored light onto other actors*** This can be particularly problematic in close-ups of actors embracing. If you're afraid that this might be a problem but believe a particular item is perfect for the actor, discuss the situation with the DP. If the DP is concerned, he may suggest some test shoots to determine if this is a problem.

- ***Avoid dense stripes on shirts, jackets, ties*** I'm sure you have seen even professional movies and television shows where the patterns cause distracting and irritating moiré patterns on the screen. Dense stripes and small checkerboard patterns provide the worst examples of these types of problems and should be avoided like the plague.

- ***Avoid bright white clothes*** These types of clothes generally blowout on the footage and look like a large undifferentiated blob of white. If you have to go for white, try for an off white or eggshell coloring to minimize the problem.

- ***Avoid very dark clothes on dark people*** Dark clothing can be interesting on a character especially since it sucks up the light and can tell you something about the character's state of mind or general demeanor. This can mean that special lighting such as rim lighting or silhouette is required. This special lighting becomes problematic if the skin tone of the actor is dark because there is less contrast range to work with to differentiate the skin from the clothes. Try to avoid this combination unless you develop a particular strategy to overcome it (e.g. a light blue shirt with a dark blazer).

- ***Check with the DP for lighting concerns*** When color filters, colored light, or special processes (such as skip-bleach) are being used on a film, it is important to consider the impact on wardrobe. For example, if a room is lit with all blue light, a red dress won't reflect that color light and will appear on film as a black mass. Be sure to talk with the DP about any special optic or lighting effects that will be used.

Blue/green Screen Considerations

Day by day, advanced special effects are becoming inexpensive enough to be used by even the lowest budget film. Therefore, you might need to wardrobe actors for work against a green or blue screen that will be later composited with computer effects or a different background. Here are a few wardrobe suggestions when costuming for a blue or green screen:

- ***Check what color screen will be used*** When a blue screen is used, the costumes and accessories cannot be blue. When green screened, no green. Therefore, you need to know the type of screen to be used and choose the wardrobe accordingly.

- ***Avoid feathers, fur, and frills*** Fine hair causes enough problems for compositors without worrying about the boundary problems created by a wardrobe item with fine, semi-transparent edges such as feathers, fur, or similar materials. Try to avoid choosing costume pieces with these types of fringes.

- ***Avoid transparent or reflective accessories*** Objects as simple as the crystal face of a watch can cause great problems during post-production. Try to avoid anything that is partially transparent or reflective.

Suggestions

Here are a few suggestions to help you with wardrobe:

- ***Always keep a lint brush near*** Everything from pollen to cat hair can get stuck to clothing during a shoot. Be sure to have a lint brush to save the day!

- ***Hit the library*** Even the smallest library seems to have a large number of books on fashion and clothes making. These books are especially useful for movies set in the recent past (1980s, 1990s, etc.), as it is often difficult to remember the distinctive clothing of a period outside of a few extreme examples.

- ***Try to stock throwaway clothes*** There are many times when a change is made to a scene that requires clothing to be destroyed. For example, the director decides to have a supporting character, initially assigned to the far side of the room, to stand next to the lead as he is shot covering the supporting player with blood. With a throwaway shirt on hand, the important wardrobe for this character can be saved.

- ***Keep a box of safety pins of all sizes*** Safety pins are the workhorse of the wardrobe department. Make sure you have plenty in a variety of sizes. Also, paint a few safety pins with matte black spray paint. There are occasions where you can't effectively hide the pin and having matte black pins will prevent the camera from catching a glint of light reflected from them.

Make-up Techniques

Applications

The most common type of make-up for film differs from everyday make-up since it's generally supposed to make the actor or actress look "normal" or as if they aren't wearing make-up. In the film industry, this is known as *flat make-up*. A majority of all make-up applied is flat make-up. Effects make-up, which is fascinating to many people, occupies only a small part of the needs of the movie-making community.

There is a magazine dedicated to movie make-up artists called Makeup Artist Magazine (http://www.makeupmag.com/). It focuses on professional movie make-up people, interviews, and techniques. Make-up professionals discuss various techniques and display procedures in color photos. If you are considering doing any substantial amount of movie make-up, it would be an excellent idea to consider obtaining a subscription.

If you want to do make-up research on the web, check out the Makeup411 (www.makeup411.com) site. Makeup411 is an excellent site that details the actual make-up used by professionals for a particular look. For example, one article details the make-up used on each of the individual actresses on the show *Sex in the City*. The descriptions include the products and techniques used for the skin, foundation, concealer, powder, blush, eye shadow, eyebrows, eyeliner, lashes, lips, and body for each actress.

For any type of movie make-up, one of the key problems is consistency. Scenes that occur within moments of each other in the final film may be shot weeks or months apart. Therefore, continuity pictures are critical. In effects make-up, continuity is even more critical than in flat make-up. Try to avoid improving on effects make-up as time progresses. Your skills will improve and you'll want to make the effect look more realistic. However, this can cause a mismatch with scenes shot earlier of the same effect, so resist the temptation.

The brands I've seen used most often on set are Ben Nye (http://www.wyb.com) and Mehron Cosmetics (http://www.mehron.com). Both vendors have flat make-up as well as special effects make-up and appliances (such as bald caps, extra hair, etc.). Many make-up people I asked about their preferences agreed that the product lines from each of these companies are excellent.

Flat Make-up

Flat make-up is used to make the actor appear "normal" on screen. Much make-up is used to provide the appearance of improved facial structure.

The following general tips will give you some sense of the techniques of the field:

- *For long wear, use oil-based make-up* Oil-based make-up is hotter to wear than water-based, but it lasts much longer. It can be particularly important when doing an exterior shoot in varying weather conditions.

- Whenever you're doing make-up, be sure to have hair clips handy. These can be critical for keeping hair out of the actor's face while applying the make-up. Loose hair can quickly mess up an excellent make-up job that has yet to dry.

- *Use soap to minimize large eyebrows* Rub a thin piece of wet soap through large or bushy eyebrows and press them flat.

- *Airbrush make-up application* Many make-up artists use an airbrush to apply the make-up, especially when large areas need to be covered evenly such as when a tattoo needs to be covered or a nude scene is being filmed.

Make-up layer order – male

Make-up on males can be critical to making the face appear healthy. There is the famous story about the 1960 first-ever televised presidential debate between Jack Kennedy and Richard Nixon. Kennedy, an image savvy candidate, wore make-up to make him look healthy and robust. Nixon refused the make-up and appeared sweaty and flushed. To this day political scientists argue whether Nixon's appearance on this debate tipped the scales to lose him the election.

For men, make-up is generally applied in the following order:

1. *Skin cleanser* Make-up will apply best and easiest if the skin is clean. Therefore, use some type of skin cleanser to remove the oil and dirt from the face.

2. *Foundation* Available in either water-based cakes and cream sticks. Apply broadly at first and then use a sponge, slightly dampened to blend the foundation for even leveling. Use a light wash of cake make-up.

3. *Powder* Helps to even the skin surface and will prevent skin shine. Also absorbs mild perspiration, although multiple applications may be required in hot circumstances.

4. *Eyebrows* Eyebrows can be groomed with a clean eyebrow brush.

5. *Lip color* Sometimes natural color lipstick is used on men, primarily to blend the line between the lips and the beginning of the base make-up.

You may need some or all of these steps to help the male actor look his best. Most commonly, the foundation is required at a minimum to even out skin tone. Few people have perfect skin, but a basic foundation will go a long way to improving the look of average skin on the film image.

Make-up layer order – female

If you don't have a make-up artist, it is generally still better to designate someone to handle the make-up chores – most likely a woman. Having actresses apply their own make-up is usually a bad idea, since continuity will generally suffer.

For women, make-up is generally applied in the following order:

1. *Skin cleanser* The cleanser will remove all make-up, dead cells, oil, and dirt, so the make-up will have a fresh surface.

2. *Foundation* Foundation will make the surface of the skin even. Make sure that the base of the foundation matches the underlying color of the skin. Apply the foundation with a cosmetic sponge. Pay special attention to blend the foundation under the jawline, into the hairline, and on the earlobes.

3. *Shading and highlights* You can use make-up for shading and highlights to improve bone structure. You can add dark brown color around the brow bones, across the tip of the nose, and under the cheekbones. Add skin color tones along the center of the nose, on the cheekbones, under eye bags, and to cover any blemishes visible through the foundation.

4. *Eyeshadow* Since eyes are the focal point of the face, eyeshadow can be some of the most important make-up applied. Eyeshadow provides color to the entire eyelid. Add eyeshadow at the outer corners of the eyes to extend the shadow and create the appearance of rounder eyes.

Use minimal shadow on the lids near the temples or the eyes will appear sunken. Dry powder or cake type of eye shadow holds up best under film lights.

5. *Top eyelines* Use eyeliner on the base of the eyelids to enhance the shape and size of the eyes.

6. *Bottom eyelines* Optionally add eyeliner to the bottom of the eye for a more dramatic appearance.

7. *Mascara or false lashes* Added to eyelashes. Mascara looks far more natural than false eyelashes, although the "fake" look may be useful for the character or scene. Color mascara should be avoided as it may pick up oddly on camera and appear as a photography artifact.

8. Eyebrows.

9. *Blush or dry rouge* Blush should be put on almost last and it should match the rest of the make-up. As a general guideline, the blush color should resemble the color of the actress' cheeks after exercise. Use blush to emphasize the bone structure of the face. Don't blend the blush.

10. *Lipstick* Consider outlining the lips with lip pencil before applying lipstick.

> **TIP** ▶ *Keep in mind that make-up will need to be taken off once a shooting day is complete. Be sure to bring the necessary skin-cleaning products so that the applied make-up can be easily removed.*

Effects Make-up

Effects make-up can be anything from special contact lenses to Marlon Brando's famous wadded cotton balls in the cheeks to change the facial structure. False teeth are perhaps one of the easiest ways to alter the look of a character. Narrow mustaches can be drawn using eyeliner or eyebrow pencil. Although effects make-up is beyond the scope of this book (there are many volumes dedicated to the subject), I've included some basic information here that might come in handy.

> **TIP** ▶ *Many of the basic items in a make-up kit such as spirit gum, mustaches, etc. are available from general stores during the Halloween season. Wait until after Halloween and shop to get the make-up items at a tremendous discount.*

Wigs

For a guerilla film, I would advise against using any type of wig. I had a character with a wig in one of my films and it was a complete disaster. Continuity problems, fake-looking footage, and complaints from the actress were only a few of the problems that resulted. Unless the character is supposed to have a bad-looking wig or toupee, try to avoid using them.

If you must use a wig, here are a few general tips:

• Cover the natural hair of your actor with a stocking cap or top.

• Use gel or mousse to mat down the hair. This will prevent stray strands from becoming visible over the course of the shooting day.

• When putting on a wig, it should be pulled on from front to back.

Take continuity pictures often. For some reason while a performer seems content to leave alone even a heavily sprayed hair style, they can't seem to stop themselves from fiddling with a wig. I suspect that this results from a feeling that the wig is moving, falling forward, or falling off despite being securely fixed in place.

Continuity pictures can help you repair accidental changes to the wig wrought by the performer. They can also help you match the wig's position from scene to scene.

> **TIP** ▶ *To apply a mustache, first clean the skin where the mustache will be placed. Add a layer of spirit gum to the lip and let it dry. Then add another layer of gum to the skin and put the mustache on it.*

Scars

Scars are difficult to maintain for continuity, so use them judiciously. Keep in mind that there are alternatives to some scars that are much easier to maintain. A shaved slit in an eyebrow can indicate an old fight or cut. A patch on the beard or mustache where hair no longer grows can provide a similar effect.

Try using a piece of tissue paper for scars and scabs. Tear off a small piece so it has jagged edges. Paint spirit gum on the skin and then press the tissue onto it. Don't use too much gum so that the tissue becomes saturated. Brush colored eyeliner in red or darker color onto the tissue. Most cuts and scars are thin at the ends, but wide at the center, so try to make your scar in this shape.

Suggestions

Here are a few suggestions to help in the make-up department:

- *Create a fashion file* There are numerous different looks that are needed in a typical movie. For example, an actress may have to look glamorous, dumpy, goth, tacky, and so on. To achieve these looks, it is usually most helpful to work from a reference photo. For this reason, you should begin a file of magazine and newspaper clippings of photographs of the spectrum of human appearances. A picture of a street person, for example, may provide the perfect model for dirt smudges, under eye bags, and a ravaged complexion. You can use these photos for reference to reconstruct the desired look with make-up.

- *Categorize basic facial types* People's faces can generally be divided into basic shapes such as square, round, or oval. If you think in these terms, it makes make-up easier to approach in terms of choosing the appropriate techniques to achieve a desired look. For example, you would rarely want to make a long oval face appear longer unless an emaciated look was needed. Thinking of a face in these terms provides a method of shorthand that will allow you to choose the proper approach quickly.

- *Pay special attention to men* Guerilla filmmakers often assume a male actor can work without make-up – that is a bad idea. Since an inexperienced actress probably understands make-up basics from her real life while an inexperienced actor probably has no such understanding, males pose special problems. Make sure you apply make-up and do general tests prior to principal photography or your male actors may appear like clowns in the shot footage.

- *Toothache medication for an anesthetic* If you need to perform simple but possibly painful operations such as plucking from eyebrows, nose, or ears, spread toothache medication on the area. It will deaden the area, so the pain isn't felt. This can be especially useful if you need to do plucking after other make-up has already been applied since plucking often causes sneezing and eye tearing.

Post-production
Introduction

Applications

For better or worse, when post-production begins work, most of the primary footage is already in the can. Post-production staff is expected to be particularly clever in figuring out how to pull all the elements together for the final release print. Post-production covers a broad range of potential jobs, but unlike production, most of the jobs occur while sitting at a desk.

The post-production department generally has the following responsibilities:

*   *Telecine* Pronounced "Tell-a-sinny," this process transfers the images of film to videotape. Commonly, film is transferred to BetaSP or DigiBeta for editing through the digital proxy.

*   *Editing* Editing takes all the source footage and makes a coherent story (or incoherent story if that is the intention) from it. When footage doesn't fit, post-production often has to find a way to solve the problem to minimize re-shoots. For guerilla filmmakers, editing generally means either the editing package Final Cut Pro or Adobe Premiere. These programs are incredibly powerful and duplicate a large number of the features available in high-end packages such as Avid.

*   *Dailies* The post-production staff is generally required to handle processing and screening of the daily footage for the director, DP, and other crew members.

*   *Effects* Effects can represent a wide range of visual aspects of image treatment including computer graphic imagery (CGI), compositing, color timing, film processing, and so on. Modern summer movies tend to spend a large share of their budgets in adding post-effects.

*   *Title and credits* The titles and credits sometimes comprise almost a short film themselves – telling the viewer about the film they're about to see.

*   *Foley and sound effects* Most common sounds (doors slamming, cars starting, etc.) are available in sound libraries and are designated as sound effects. If the sound is custom-generated, it is considered foley work.

*   *ADR* Audio digital recording is the process of having actors overdub the lines they performed during principal photography. If the sound is poorly recorded, a great amount of money will be spent in studio ADR sessions.

- **Sound sync** Sound is rarely recorded on the visual media (film, for example). Instead, an external audio recording source (such as a DAT or Nagra) is used to record the sound. Once the visual images and audio sources have been transferred into the editing system, they must be synchronized. Often, this process is automatically handled by the editing software, but in cases where the synchronization is faulty, manual sync may be required.

- **Scoring** A soundtrack, or score, provides the background music for a film. Famously, people such as John Williams have substantially increased the dramatic impact of a visual film with a moving score.

The post-production techniques presented in this book are primarily techniques and effects that guerilla filmmakers need to use frequently, yet I haven't seen them well described in other books. Most of these effects focus on my experience on MiniDV-based films and may be accomplished using inexpensive hardware and software. High-end post-production technology changes so fast that this book isn't the proper place for detailing that type of information. The techniques introduced in the following chapters should be applicable to low-budget production for many years to come.

Suggestions

Here are a few general suggestions for working in post-production:

- **Duplicate an existing graphics effect or a commercial** Most artists know that when beginning a new discipline, making copies of the works of past masters is the surest route to achieving mastery in a given technique. Likewise, post-production masters usually begin by attempting to duplicate the effects or edited sequences of existing work. This duplication will help you learn from a master who has many years of experience in perfecting the post-production craft.

- **Check end credits on the final medium** I can't tell you the number of short films I've seen on VHS where the end credits were impossible to read. Credits may appear great on your razor sharp editing console monitor, but completely greeked on a normal television. Avoid forcing your cast and crew into anonymity by making sure the end credits are legible.

- **Go to at least one day of the shoot** When I've worked in post-production, I've been amazed at how often I've heard the cast and crew disparaged by the editors because the perfect footage wasn't supplied. Spending a little time on set would quickly make apparent the number of obstacles that had to be overcome to get any footage at all. Being on a shoot can not only make you appreciate the difficulty of production, but will also allow you to productively converse with the people that can make your life easy or difficult.

Skip-bleach Simulation

Applications

You may have noticed a number of films that share a particular look of desaturated colors and high contrast. A short list of films affecting this look includes: Seven, Minority Report, Fight Club, Saving Private Ryan, Lost Souls, Panic Room, Pitch Black, The Grifters, Shipping News, and Kansas City. All these films use a post-production technique called the skip-bleach process to achieve a visual tone that helps the audience feel the mood of the story.

Skip-bleach desaturates the color palette, crushes the blacks, and increases the contrast of the picture. In figure 54-1, you can see the untreated image that shows a house in a normal peaceful neighborhood. If the film is a murder mystery about dark truths hidden under placid surfaces, this location may be excellent. Adding the skip-bleach look would give the audience the impression that despite the surface, something is odd.

Once the frame has been put through the simulated skip-bleach process, the house looks far more sinister (see figure 54-2). The scene itself hasn't changed, but the changes set a completely different tone. Although a black and white picture will fail to demonstrate the full screen impact of this effect, you can get a general idea of the level of difference.

FIGURE 54.1 *An untreated image shows a house in a normal peaceful neighborhood.*

FIGURE 54.2 *In the treated image, the house looks far more sinister.*

NOTE→ While detail is lost in the dark shadows and the bright highlights, the middle tone area (particularly through the front window of the car) hasn't lost its features. This effect is one of the strengths of the skip-bleach process over simply increasing the contrast of the exposure. By keeping the middle-tone detail, soft surfaces (particularly the faces of the actors) don't become stark landscapes of black and white.

The skip-bleach look is actually known by a wide variety of names including ENR, skip-bleach, bleach bypass, CCE, NEC, silver tint, leave-out-the-bleach, silver retention, and other names. The exact look of the final image and how that is achieved varies depending on which process is used. The legendary cinematographer Vittorio Storaro pioneered the ENR process which adds a black and white developer after what would normally be the bleach step.

While skip-bleach is difficult and expensive to accomplish with film, if you're using MiniDV, duplicating the effect is a snap. While the effect is easiest to accomplish when using a post-production program such as Adobe After Effects, the look is achievable with almost any standard editing program. This chapter will provide instructions for simulating the skip-bleach process using Adobe After Effects.

PARTS	Qty	Item
	1	Copy of Adobe After Effects

General Instructions

Perhaps it's best to start by providing a basic description of how the film-based skip-bleach process is performed. In the skip-bleach process, a stage of developing the film is skipped. After film has been exposed, it goes through a number of chemical baths that make the image on the negative visible. One of the final steps in traditional film processing is a bleach bath that removes the remaining unnecessary silver crystals now that the dye image is already in place.

Developing film goes through the following stages: prebath, color developer bath, stop bath, first fix bath, bleach bath, soundtrack application, wash, second fix bath, wash, and stabilizer bath. The skip-bleach process essentially skips the bleach bath step, so the silver crystals remain on the film. Since the remaining silver is essentially a black and white image of the frame, a color and a black and white image are merged together. The retention of the silver makes the exposed areas darker (since the silver is still attached) and also subtracts some of the exposed color that leads to a desaturated image.

The process does not have to be all-or-nothing skip-bleach step, but instead may be a partial bleach bath. The film can be removed from the bath when half of the process is complete or 30% or other level of partial bleaching.

> **NOTE→** DV footage is very suited to simulating this process, because it had less to lose than film. If you've ever entirely desaturated a DV image, you may have noticed that the black and white image looked almost better than the color original. This is because while the DV format has excellent resolution, much of the data lost in DV compression is color information.
>
> While film records a huge amount of color data, DV does not. Therefore, when you desaturate the image through this process, you clear away some of the distraction caused to the viewer who subconsciously notices the poor DV color reproduction.

The final result is a picture that has muted colors, blacks that are more black, darkened shadows, blown-out highlights, more grain, and higher contrast. This creates a specific mood with images that are gritty and more surreal, all of which helps the viewer to understand that we're not in Kansas anymore.

> **TIP ▶** *For best effect, skip-bleach shouldn't be simply a post-production addition. If you know that you'll be applying the process, principal photography should adjust the lighting scheme to maximize the impact of the look. Generally this means that footage is slightly underexposed and flat lighting (such as that available from fluorescents) is used.*

Reproducing the skip-bleach effect on DV footage isn't difficult since Adobe After Effects provides filters to radically alter source footage. Therefore, the process can easily be simulated and applied to any digital footage that can be loaded into the program. The simulation is a three-part process of desaturating the color, crushing the blacks, and increasing the contrast.

> **NOTE→** If you don't have Adobe After Effects, you can still follow the instructions using Adobe Photoshop. Photoshop has the same filters available (although the user interface is slightly different), so you can make the same modifications to a still photograph to see the effect. Look up Adjustment Layers in the Photoshop manual for instructions on adding these filters to achieve the skip-bleach look.

Construction

You can use almost any version of Adobe After Effects to complete these steps. Many editing programs (such as Premiere and Final Cut Pro) can also be used to achieve the desire look although they generally don't have the flexibility or elegance of After Effects for this type of work.

The effects are stacked so the output of one is fed into another. Therefore, to duplicate the results shown here, you will need to add the filters in the order given. Changing the order will produce different results.

Crushing blacks and blowing out highlights

Crushing blacks involves taking colors that are very near to black and making them actual black. That means that dark grays that would show only a little bit of detail and generally muddy the image are converted to be simple black. Likewise, blowing out highlights involves taking colors that are bright white and making them white. Blowing out the whites gives the look of overexposure in the lighter areas of the image.

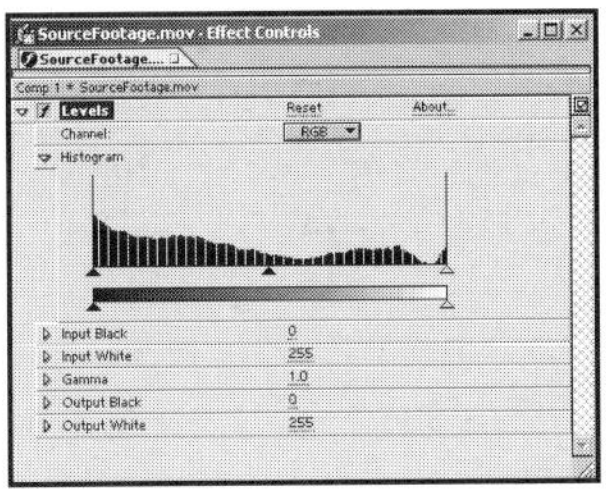

To modify the color palette at the two ends of the spectrum is simple using the Levels filter. The Levels filter uses a bar chart to show the histogram of the color levels for the image (see figure 54-3). The three triangle arrows at the bottom of the image are the controls that interest us. Right now, one is set on the far left, one in the exact center, and one on the far right. These arrows represent the position of absolute black, the middle tone, and absolute white, respectively. The Levels filter allows the arrow positions to be changed and thereby changing the levels in the final image.

FIGURE 54.3 *The Levels filter uses a bar chart to show the histogram of the color levels for the image.*

Follow these steps:

1. Load the footage you want to modify.

2. Apply the Levels filter. It's generally available under the Effect > Adjust menu, although this will depend on the After Effects version you're using.

3. Drag the left arrow (see figure 54-4) until the blacks have darkened to the level you desire. Don't worry at this point if the entire image became

FIGURE 54.4 *By moving the arrow, the color information to the left of the arrow was converted to black.*

darker than you wanted it. The next step of the process will lighten the picture. As you adjusted the left arrow, what you were doing was converting all the color information shown on the histogram to the left of the adjustment arrow to black.

4. Drag the right arrow to the left until the highlights are blown out to the level desired.

5. Change the center arrow if the overall picture brightness needs adjustment. When you're changing the left or right arrows, the center arrow stays centered between them. That means that typically very little manual adjustment is needed for an attractive image.

Increasing contrast

To increase the contrast, you'll need to add a brightness/contrast filter. This filter is generally found on the Effect > Adjust menu. Increase the contrast level until you find an appropriate level (see figure 54-5). Don't overdue the contrast or you'll lose a lot of your picture detail.

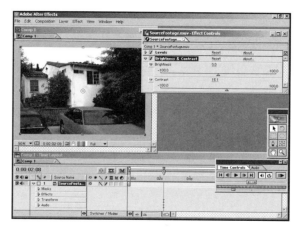

FIGURE 54.5 *The brightness/contrast filter lets you increase the contrast level.*

Desaturating color

Finally, add a Hue/Saturation filter from the Effect > Adjust menu. Decrease the Master Saturation setting until you reach the level you want (see figure 54-6). This setting is generally the most subjective since it can make your picture black and white or just take away a little of the color.

I've found that it usually works best for me to totally desaturate the picture (setting of −100) and add the color until I think it looks right. To check what changes you've made, click on the italic "f" to turn off the filter to see the image with full saturation. You'll often be surprised how garish and oversaturated the normal image looks when compared with the level you've chosen.

The only remaining step is to render out your final footage. Computer screens are pretty much never accurate to how a television will look, so output the render to television (through your camcorder) to make the final adjustments.

I would make one final recommendation. Get a video or DVD of a film that you liked that used the skip-bleach effect. If possible, find a shot or location that's similar to the one you've been treating. Freeze-frame that footage and compare it side-by-side with your treated footage. Have you achieved the look you intended? Is there too much contrast? Too little color? Performing this comparison will help you get a somewhat objective sense of how your final footage appears.

FIGURE 54.6 *Add a hue/saturation filter and decrease the Master Saturation setting.*

Suggestions

Here are a few suggestions to help you with this effect:

- *Use with discretion* For a while, the skip-bleach look became trendy and was seen in every other commercial and music video, whether it was appropriate or not. Like other tools of cinematography, a little goes a long way. Try to use this technique where it will add to the story, rather than simply using it because it looks neat.

- *Use your imagination* Although this chapter provides a clear way to simulate the skip-bleach effect, you can use this information as a beginning instead of an end. Now that you see how to alter the color palette, I would encourage you to experiment and see if you can find an interesting visual effect you might use. Try to save several samples of new things you find for examination later (usually a couple of days). Sometimes with a fresh pair of eyes the experiments you thought were failures are actually beautiful and the effects you judged as clever are in fact tedious.

- *Realize that you may need to adjust scene-by-scene* Light levels and the general look of each scene you photograph will probably be different. Professional films will go through a final step known as color timing where light levels for each scene are adjusted individually, so the final print colors and levels match. So although the skip-bleach process is applied the same way for all the footage, the final levels are adjusted in color timing. For best effect, you'll need to perform this timing while adding the After Effects filters.

DV Softener

Applications

Guerilla filmmakers are always trying to squeeze the highest quality images out of the lowest budget equipment. One common goal is to use a prosumer-grade DV camcorder to obtain film-grade images. There are a number of guides on the Internet with suggestions for obtaining these results. One problem that I haven't seen addressed is the level of sharpness in a DV image.

Film is essentially an analog image, so the exposure is even across the entire exposed frame. Digital pictures capture images using small blocks of color called pixels. For this reason, a DV picture is overly sharp and can even feature jagged edges or stair step effects on solid lines. With a simple filter application in Adobe After Effects, it's possible to soften the original image in post-production.

PARTS	Qty	Item
	1	Copy of Adobe After Effects

General Instructions

There are often times when a softer image is desired. During principal photography, special softening filters can be used. In post-production, however, using a blur filter will usually make the image seem out of focus. To obtain a general image softening without this effect, you can double the size of the image, blur the pixilated version, and then reduce it back to normal size. At first this may seem like it wouldn't have much effect, but give it a try. In most normal contrast footage, it has a subtle but significant effect on the final output.

> **NOTE→** I haven't included before and after figures of the softening process. I didn't think any noticeable difference would be visible once the frame was converted to black and white and then reduced to fit on the printed page. However, I would recommend that you perform a comparison test. Output a clip of the source footage and then output the same clip as treated footage. It is good to do a couple of output tests with various levels of blur applied to find the optimal setting for your footage.

Construction

You'll need to start by executing After Effects. Generally, you should avoid using an editing program such as Final Cut Pro to create this effect, since it requires a composition to be rendered before it can be placed inside another composition. Performing this process would be tedious and requires double the amount of storage needed for the final render.

To create a DV softener process, follow these steps:

1. Open After Effects and create a project with the source footage.

2. Create a composition double the normal size. In the case of DV footage, a size of 1440 × 960 is double the normal dimension.

3. Import source footage into the composition.

4. Scale the source footage until it's double the size and fills the entire composition frame. Generally, using the Snap To Grid option makes scaling and placement easier. You'll notice that the image is very pixilated at this large size (see figure 55-1).

5. Select the image and add a Gaussian blur filter. You'll most likely find this filter under the Effect > Blur & Sharpen menu.

6. Set the Blurriness value to around 1.0 (see figure 55-2). You will notice that the pixelation disappears almost entirely. Don't set the blur value too high or the image will appear out of focus.

FIGURE 55.1 *Scale the source footage to double size and the image will become very pixilated.*

FIGURE 55.2 *Set the Blurriness value to around 1.0.*

7. Close the composition.

8. Create a new composition. This composition should be the standard DV size (720 × 480).

9. Import the first composition.

10. Scale the imported composition to 50% or normal size.

11. Render footage from composition.

The rendering process will probably take some time given that the Gaussian blur is one of the more processor-intensive filter effects. Always test the process on a small clip of the source footage to make sure that you're getting the results you want. By examining the test, you can make any necessary adjustments before spending the time to process the entire source footage.

Suggestions

Here are a few suggestions to help you use the softener:

- *Speed rendering time with other blurs* Although the Gaussian blur seems to provide the best picture, it's also the slowest. That can mean that rendering a large amount of footage can take a prohibitively long time. You can try a Fast Blur effect and see if it provides the quality level you need.

- *Use 3:2 pulldown and frame blending* A standard motion picture is 24 frames per second, while standard DV is 30 fps (or 29.97). To obtain a more film-like appearance, you can convert your footage to 24 fps. Then convert it back to DV using 3:2 pulldown and frame blending. This technique is especially useful with action footage where the extra DV frames create an overly sharp almost freeze-frame clip. Film has substantially more blurring which more closely approximates human perception.

Scoring

Applications

Adding a musical soundtrack to your film can be one of the most frustrating parts of making a movie. You can't add contemporary music because paying the license fees to obtain copyrighted music will cost you an arm and a leg. Stock music is typically expensive or cheesy or both. Even if you can find good stock music, it's difficult to find music that will properly match the emotional parts of the narrative.

Hiring a musician to create a custom score is one of the best options if you're lucky enough to know a good, reliable musician that will work cheap and has the proper recording equipment. You may want to make changes to the film after you've screened it and received valid suggestions for improvement. At that point you'll find that it's much easier to tighten up the visual aspects of the film in editing than re-adjusting the musical score to the change. Usually this process means going back to the musician which can be a frustrating and expensive process.

There are methods of obtaining a modifiable score if you have a reasonably powerful computer. These methods work best if you want either an electronic, techno or classical score. Realize in advance that your soundtrack won't sound like a John Williams orchestra piece. However, you should be able to create a workable soundtrack that can be customized to the film and will cost you almost nothing.

Classical Scores and Old Melodies

To start, one great way to obtain free classical music is to scan and use the works of any of the great composers. Classical scores or old sheet music (see figure 56-1) can be read into a computer and used without any license fees. All the work of the greatest composers (Bach, Beethoven, Mozart, etc.) is older than 75 years and out of copyright – hence in the public domain.

Begin by looking for these scores at your school or local library. Most libraries either stock or can make requests to other libraries for musical scores and books of music. Make sure that you obtain the original score and not a modern (copyrighted) arrangement of that music.

FIGURE 56.1 *Classical scores or old sheet music can be read into a computer and used without any license fees.*

> **WARNING→** A great deal of the sheet music in books will have been arranged by a modern author. That means that someone took the original classical piece (such as Beethoven's Symphony #9) and rewrote, adapted, or simplified it. The new arrangement may have a modern copyright and hence can't be used without paying the author a copyright fee. While the likelihood is very low that someone could identify a specific arrangement by hearing it on your soundtrack, the safest route is to use the original scores or arrangements that were created by the original author.

If you don't need a complete score or you have some musical ability, you can look for melodies to old folk songs that you can build upon. Folk songs are a great source of music because they're nearly all in the public domain. These classic melodies are also meant to express various emotions such as happiness, loss, melancholy, etc. which makes them particularly suited to adaptation for movie soundtracks. They also tend to be memorable otherwise they wouldn't have survived this long.

You can find books of folk songs including both the music and the lyrics. It is usually a good idea to use a melody less identifiable than "Old Susannah," but by the time you put it through a variety of instruments and effects, it may sound familiar, but not readily recognizable.

Scanning Scores

Once you have a melody or complete sheet music, you might wonder what to do with it. If you have a musician to work with, you can provide this music and indicate you want the score constructed from those pieces. You'll be much closer to your intentions than if you'd asked the musician to start from scratch. Most likely it will also be much simpler for the musician to work from these building blocks than to have to create musical themes without any direction.

If you don't have a helpful musician, you'll have to turn to the aid of the computer. The notes from the sheet music can be entered into the computer by hand. For a simple melody, there is a variety of free software that will help you accomplish this task (check the Internet). Some of these programs even turn your computer keyboard into a simple piano that will allow you to play the music directly.

However, for a complete score, this is a tedious process and can require a great deal of knowledge of the music program you'll be using. Instead, there are a number of programs that, when used in conjunction with a scanner, can convert sheet music into a playable music file. These programs have an accuracy of 90–95%, so you'll probably have to do some proofreading and correction after the scan.

Some of the more popular programs include:

- *SharpEye Music Reader (www.visiv.co.uk)* SharpEye seems to work very well and provides a 30-day trial version that can be downloaded for free.

- *Scorscan* Optical music recognition that stores the music in Score compatible files.

- *Photoscore Lite* Free plug-in for the scoring software Sibelius. A professional version is available.

- *MP Scan* Plug-in for the Music Publisher program. Music Publisher doesn't include any MIDI features, so the scanned score cannot be exported.

- *SmartScore Lite* Free plug-in with scoring software Finale. A professional version is available.

Once the music is in the computer, it can be easily transposed to a different key, sped up or slowed down, cut into sections, assigned various instruments, and finally output to MIDI. MIDI is one of the most powerful technologies that you can use for creating and modifying your music.

MIDI

MIDI synthesis is excellent for some types of music and poor for others. New age and synth pop are two styles that were born on synthesizers and are therefore very appropriate. The most difficult types of instruments for MIDI to replicate are stringed instruments (guitar, violin, standing bass, etc.). That creates a problem for orchestral style soundtracks. While a flute section might sound pitch perfect, the cello and the violin sections will most likely have that distinctive synthesizer sound.

The broad number of meanings of the term MIDI can be confusing to someone that isn't steeped in computer music. On the simplest level, MIDI is a standard that defines how musical devices can exchange information such as notes and intervals. From there it becomes increasingly complicated. There are MIDI ports (see figure 56-2) that can be used to connect a MIDI device (such as a keyboard) to other MIDI devices or a computer. MIDI ports can be hooked together to create a daisy chain of various MIDI devices.

On a computer, the information that is exchanged over a MIDI port can be stored in a file called a MIDI file. On Windows-based computers, these files have a .MID extension. All the notes and their intervals are stored in the file, as well as the instrument number for the notes played. An accepted numbering standard of instruments is contained in the classification of GM or General MIDI instruments. However, it's up to the particular synthesizer to play the instrument, so how an Oboe might sound is completely up to the machine that's playing it.

FIGURE 56.2 *MIDI ports can be used to connect a MIDI device (such as a keyboard) to other MIDI devices or a computer.*

Whether you have a Macintosh or Windows-based machine, your operating system has a form of software synthesizer built into the machine. This synthesizer can play all the different instrument types, although the quality tends to be very low and inappropriate for all but the most rudimentary musical performance. Therefore, even if you have a wonderful score scanned into the computer, you may not be able to output it at a level you would find acceptable.

To obtain excellent sound, there are generally two options: use either a quality external hardware synthesizer or a professional software synthesizer. A hardware synthesizer will require you to have a MIDI interface and a set of cables through which the score is sent to the machine. A professional software synthesizer works just like the software synthesizer included with your operating system, but the difference in output is like night and day.

> **TIP** ▶ *On a Windows-based platform, go onto the Microsoft website and search for the Microsoft DirectMusic Producer program. It's a free download. Although not particularly user-friendly, it is very robust and was designed to add soundtracks to game programs. You'll find that game soundtracks are very similar to movie soundtracks and that many of the features included in the program are ideal for scoring.*

Hardware synthesizers

If you have a friend, neighbor, or relative that has a quality hardware synthesizer, you may be able to get that person to output your musical composition. Since these machines generally require a certain level of know-how to run properly, it would save you a great deal of time and frustration to have an experienced user setup and output the audio tracks.

Note that although the most common hardware synthesizers are built into a keyboard, there are many professional ones that are created as a simple box or rack-mount container. These boxes contain MIDI In and Out ports as well as some form of analog and/or digital output. These machines can be attached to a MIDI output keyboard or computer that can control them and send the musical information they need to play a song.

If you don't have a friend who has a decent synthesizer, you can rent MIDI equipment from a music store. Although the rates may seem a little pricey at first, realize that if you have the score properly prepared, you should be able to simply rent the equipment, make the output, and return the equipment in a very short time. Once you know what you're doing, you might even see if they have special rates if you return the equipment the same day.

To hook up the keyboard to the computer, you will need a MIDI interface. Most sound cards have a built-in interface and you only have to buy the adapter cable (see figure 56-3) to use them. The same cable can vary in price dramatically from store to store, so be sure to shop around to get a good deal. The web is a good place to find a deal on these cables. You might try www.musiciansfriend.com as they usually have very reasonable prices on music equipment.

If your computer doesn't have a MIDI interface or you're running on a portable, you can buy an adapter to provide a MIDI port through either your USB or Firewire ports. A USB MIDI adapter such as the one shown in figure 56-4 can be very handy and are available for prices that won't empty your bank account.

In addition to the interface or adapter, you may need at least one MIDI cable. Some adapter interfaces require a separate cable (they have female jacks), while others such as the one pictured in figure 56-4 have the cables built into the adapter. A separate MIDI cable is a good item to have even if your adapter doesn't need it because the cable will allow you to extend the length, so the keyboard or synthesizer doesn't have to be so close to the computer.

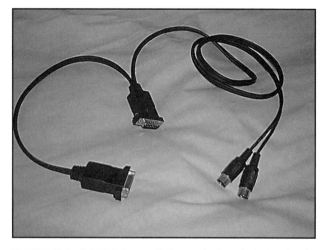

FIGURE 56.3 *A MIDI adapter cable lets you hook up the keyboard to the computer.*

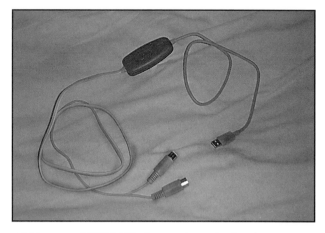

FIGURE 56.4 *A USB MIDI adapter can be very handy and inexpensive.*

Remember also that the quality level of the sound is proportional to the quality of the equipment and the amount of time spent in mastering it. Many filmmakers would be happy to have the quality level found on the CDs of the singer Enya who produces most of her music on a synthesizer. However, even with equipment identical to her's, it takes knowledge, time, and experience to produce that depth of sound.

Professional software synthesizer

Software synthesizers have made huge leaps forward in recent years and in many cases rival or surpass their hardware brothers. Pick up a magazine such as Computer Music to find out the latest state of the art. Unlike the hardware synthesizer market which remains somewhat static, there is a newest, latest, and greatest software synth out every other month it seems.

Despite the power of a software synth, there are two primary drawbacks for the novice user: complexity and computer power. Unlike a hardware synth that, once the MIDI cables are plugged in, is somewhat straightforward, most software synths are not programs in and of themselves. Rather they are plug-ins for other musical programs such as CuBase or Cakewalk. Therefore, you have to know how to configure and navigate an oftentimes unfriendly user interface to use them properly.

Additionally, each voice or track that the software synth must play requires additional computer power. Where hardware synths are constructed to play a specific number of voices (and only that number), a computer can begin to slow down or skip if it doesn't have the necessary processing power.

As with the hardware synthesizer, it would be best to find someone that is already experienced in the use of these synthesizers to output your soundtrack. If that person's setup is already in place, it will take them only minutes for something that will take you countless hours.

Mod Programs

As an alternative to a MIDI program or MIDI synthesizer, you might try using a sampling program. While a synthesizer will "synthesize" each note by using a computer algorithm specific to each instrument, a sampling program uses a small piece of recorded audio of the actual instrument (or a voice or a sound or whatever). The sampling program knows how to speed up or slow down the recorded audio (say a recorded note C) to change the pitch to match a particular note (to play a D# note).

A sampling program has an advantage of sounding much more realistic because it is playing a sound that is from the actual instrument. It also generally requires far less computer power to play the same number of voices.

NOTE→ Sampler programs have the same difficulty with string instruments that synthesizers do. The problem with duplicating stringed instruments is primarily related to two factors that make these instruments so warm and compelling: note attack and harmony.

A good deal of the sound of each note on a guitar is generated by how a string is plucked, struck, dampened, or twanged. Although the note remains the same, the sound generated by the string can be significantly different. The randomness and variety found in everything from guitars to violins is difficult to replicate in the computer.

Further, stringed instruments allow multiple notes to be struck at once. These notes resonate together in the body of the instrument and mix, blend, and merge to create the final harmonic sound that you hear. The strings of an electric guitar, although it doesn't have the body of a cello or a traditional guitar to reverberate, still mix the sounds of the notes together. Simulating this type of resonance mixing is extremely complicated, difficult, and processor-intensive.

Although it isn't impossible to achieve a realistic string sound, don't expect to achieve it for less than the cost of hiring stringed musicians to actually play your score.

One of the best things about sampling programs is that there are a number of robust programs that are available for free! Check the Internet for numerous websites devoted to sample-based programs that create files known as Mods. Unfortunately, Macintosh-based sampling programs are very limited. You'll have to search to find what is available. Two of the most popular Windows-based sampling programs are ModPlug (www.modplug.com) and Buzz (www.buzzxp.com).

ModPlug looks something like a spreadsheet with the different voices taking up different columns. If you don't have deep-rooted reverence for the traditional clefs, bars, and measures of sheet music, you'll find that this interface is fairly user-friendly and quick to navigate. ModPlug can play a wide variety of sample files (Mod files) including .IT and .XM formats. It can also import the notes from a MIDI file to use as the basis for a creation of an Mod.

The disadvantage of Mod files is that they require you to supply all the instruments. While there are numerous free instrument samples available online, you'll have to take the time to download them and insert them into the program. On the bright side, you can also create your own instruments whether they're based on your favorite instrument (kazoo perhaps?) or a random sound or vocal sample.

There are a large number of sample music files available to allow you to hear the type of music you can create with these programs. Try downloading a Mod Player and search for the song "Ancient Stories.xm" by Victor Vergara. It will give you an idea of the amazingly cinematic level of audio possible through these Mod programs.

If you want a simple rhythm soundtrack, download Hammerhead Rhythm Station which is actually freeware. It comes with a basic number of instruments and allows you to put in your own samples. The user interface is the essence of simplicity and you'll be creating great sounding rhythm tracks in about 10 min.

For professional sampling software, Sonic Foundry's Vegas (www.sonicfoundry.com) is a popular program used by many production companies. It generates extremely high-quality output quickly and easily. Vegas is used in Hollywood for everything from trailers to commercial soundtracks.

Computer-generated Music

Finally, if you don't have a musician that you trust and you can't find an existing musical score that fits your needs, you can use your computer to create a score for you. The levels of sophistication for computer-generated music programs vary dramatically.

For classical music, you can find a variety of public domain or freeware programs that will generate a MIDI file of a score. AutoScore Deluxe is one such program. By simply entering a few values for such factors as the length of score and tempo, you can have these programs generate a complete score. You can find these programs on the Internet by searching for computer music composition. It's often useful to look at college music program websites as these institutions are the primary researchers into this field.

There are several more sophisticated commercial applications such as Jammer and Band-in-a-Box (www.pgmusic.com). These programs supply a wide variety of styles (jazz, rock, new age, etc.) and can play the various parts on a broad range of instruments (electric guitar, saxophone, xylophone, etc.). Once you input the basic chords for your composition, the program will generate the entire score, including such embellishments as guitar solos and random changes in the prepared pattern.

Using computer-generated music seems like a magic solution, but it has two problems: sound quality and feeling. All the programs invariably output to a MIDI device or MIDI file, so they have all the problems inherent to computer music. That means that even if an acoustic guitar is chosen, it still sounds like a synthesized acoustic guitar, so don't think that a program will take the place of a flamenco guitarist.

The other problem is one of feeling. In my opinion at least, the computer-generated music I've tested sounds somewhat sterile. Even with the randomized factors, the notes strike at precise intervals and all the subtle emphasis of a performer is lost. The biggest problem with this lack of feeling is that a generated soundtrack fails to generate the type of emotional involvement a filmmaker wants from an audience.

Suggestions

Here are a few operating suggestions for scoring your movie:

*   *Use a temp-track at your own peril* Professional filmmakers usually create a temp-track of existing music while they're editing to achieve the emotional feeling of the movie before the final sound-track is ready. Since you probably don't have a full orchestra at your beck-and-call, the final sound-track of your film is almost guaranteed to *not* live up to your temp-track. That means that you'll always feel like something is missing or that your film is tainted by an amateur soundtrack. It's best not to go there. I recommend either forgetting the temp-track or using a primitive MIDI sound-track. That way your final music will certainly be better than what you've heard before.

*   *Choose a style that tells the emotional story of your movie* This suggestion is particularly appropriate to dark comedies. Many independent dark comedies are scored with a dark, brooding musical style. This style tells the audience that it's not a comedy, but a serious and disturbing drama. While a bright and silly soundtrack wouldn't be appropriate, something a little odd or quirky can be used to great effect to tell the audience that what they're seeing on the screen shouldn't be taken at the surface level. Give some thought as to what style of music you can use to tell the audience about the core theme of the film.

*   *Don't wait until the film is in the can to think about the soundtrack* It's an oft-told tale that James Cameron listens to particular set of CDs while writing a script to provide him with the emotional feeling of the characters and events. Just considering the style of music while you're in pre-production can provide some core insight into everything from set decoration to shooting style.

Shortcut Keys

Applications

If you're editing a lot of footage in Final Cut Pro or Adobe Premiere, you'll need to learn the keyboard shortcuts to use it most efficiently. Professional editors have special keyboards with all the important editing commands written directly on the keys. Film editors sometimes almost look like typists the way they tap the keyboard to activate sequences of commands.

If you want to maximize the time you spend in editing, you'll need to learn as many of these commands as you can. To help you overcome the substantial learning curve, it can be incredibly useful to have these shortcuts affixed directly to the appropriate keys. This chapter provides templates for the most common shortcuts in Final Cut Pro and Adobe Premiere. You can copy or print a template onto an adhesive-backed sheet of paper. Once the sheet is printed, individual labels can be cut out with a scissors and attached to the proper keys. While these labels won't last forever, they should be useful long enough for you to learn all the individual commands.

	Qty	Item
PARTS	2	Sheets of adhesive copier or printer paper

General Instructions

There are literally dozens of shortcut keys for any application. Editing programs are different from other programs since many of the important shortcuts don't require key modifiers such as the Option, Ctrl, Shift, Command, or Alt keys. The labels included in these templates only show the single-key activation commands since including the modifier-based functions will make things cluttered and difficult to read. For a complete list of modifier keys, check the manual of your editing program.

The following templates are made for general key sizes. However, since there's no actual standard among full-sized keyboards (let alone for portable keyboards), you may need to enlarge or reduce the template size to match your keys. Laptop keys are often 89% of their full-sized cousins.

If you have a scanner, you can easily scan the template into the computer and reduce or enlarge it to exactly the size you need. Otherwise, you'll need to use trial and error with a copier that has reduction and enlargement capabilities.

Construction

The labels have been designed to fully cover each key, so they include the letter or symbol of the key in the upper-left corner. The shortcut is shown in the lower-right corner of the key. I've found these font sizes to be about the smallest size that is easily readable. Because of the size limitations, I've abbreviated some of the words in the shortcut description.

Final Cut Pro shortcuts

Figure 57-1 contains the template for the Final Cut Pro keyboard. Keys without shortcut commands have been included for completeness, but the bottom-right corner has been left blank. The function key commands have been included at the top of the figure.

Premiere shortcuts

Figure 57-2 contains the template for the Adobe Premiere keyboard. Keys without shortcut commands have been included for completeness, but the bottom-right corner has been left blank.

Suggestions

Here are a few operating suggestions to help you:

- *Buy a cheap keyboard* Keyboards have become staggeringly inexpensive at computer stores, so you might consider buying one strictly for use when editing. After placing the labels on the keys, you can attach it to the computer only when you need to edit. That will maximize the lifetime of the labels and leave your main keyboard pristine.

- *Use the labels as a learning device* When a label wears out, don't replace it. Remove the remnants of the sticker from the key and then use it normally. This will help you learn the most common keys by heart. It will also assist you when you edit on a keyboard without the labeled shortcuts.

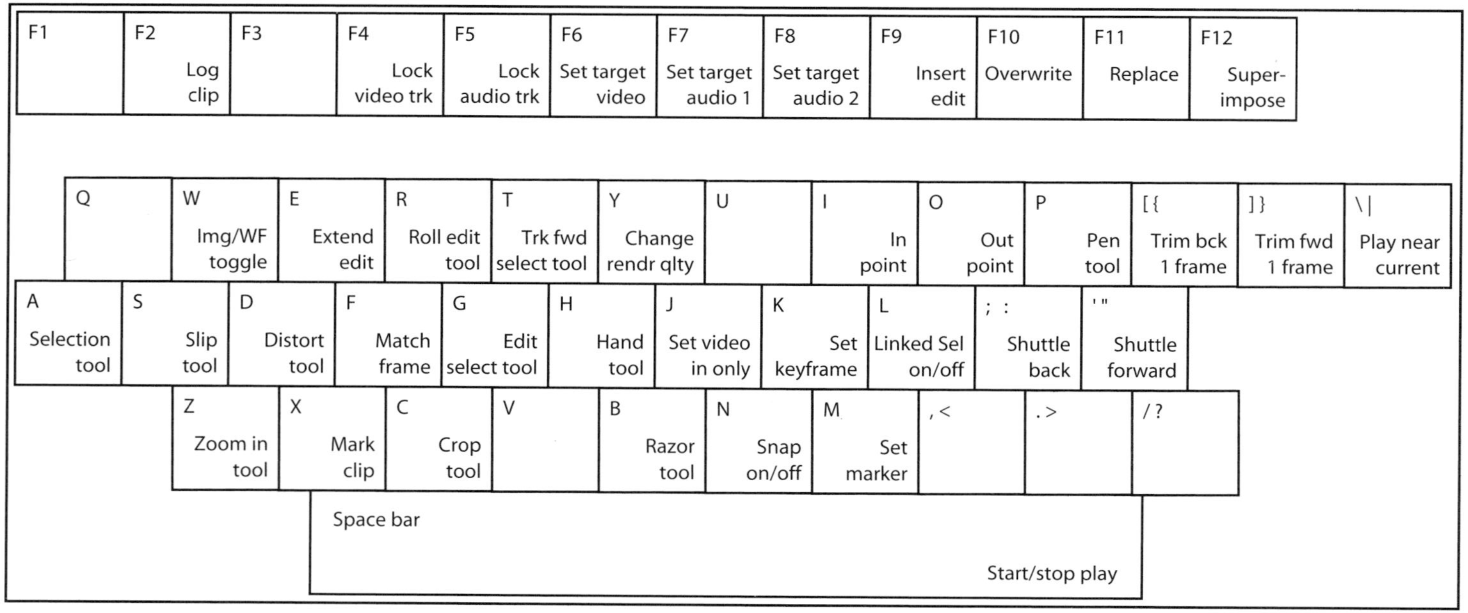

Q W E R T Y U I O P keyboard template (Final Cut Pro)

F1	F2	F3	F4	F5	F6	F7	F8	F9	F10	F11	F12
	Log clip		Lock video trk	Lock audio trk	Set target video	Set target audio 1	Set target audio 2	Insert edit	Overwrite	Replace	Super-impose

Q	W	E	R	T	Y	U	I	O	P	[{	]}	\\\|
	Img/WF toggle	Extend edit	Roll edit tool	Trk fwd select tool	Change rendr qlty		In point	Out point	Pen tool	Trim bck 1 frame	Trim fwd 1 frame	Play near current

A	S	D	F	G	H	J	K	L	;:	'"
Selection tool	Slip tool	Distort tool	Match frame	Edit select tool	Hand tool	Set video in only	Set video in keyframe	Linked Sel on/off	Shuttle back	Shuttle forward

Z	X	C	V	B	N	M	,<	.>	/?
Zoom in tool	Mark clip		Crop tool	Razor tool	Snap on/off	Set marker			

Space bar — Start/stop play

FIGURE 57.1 *A template for the shortcut commands of a Final Cut Pro keyboard.*

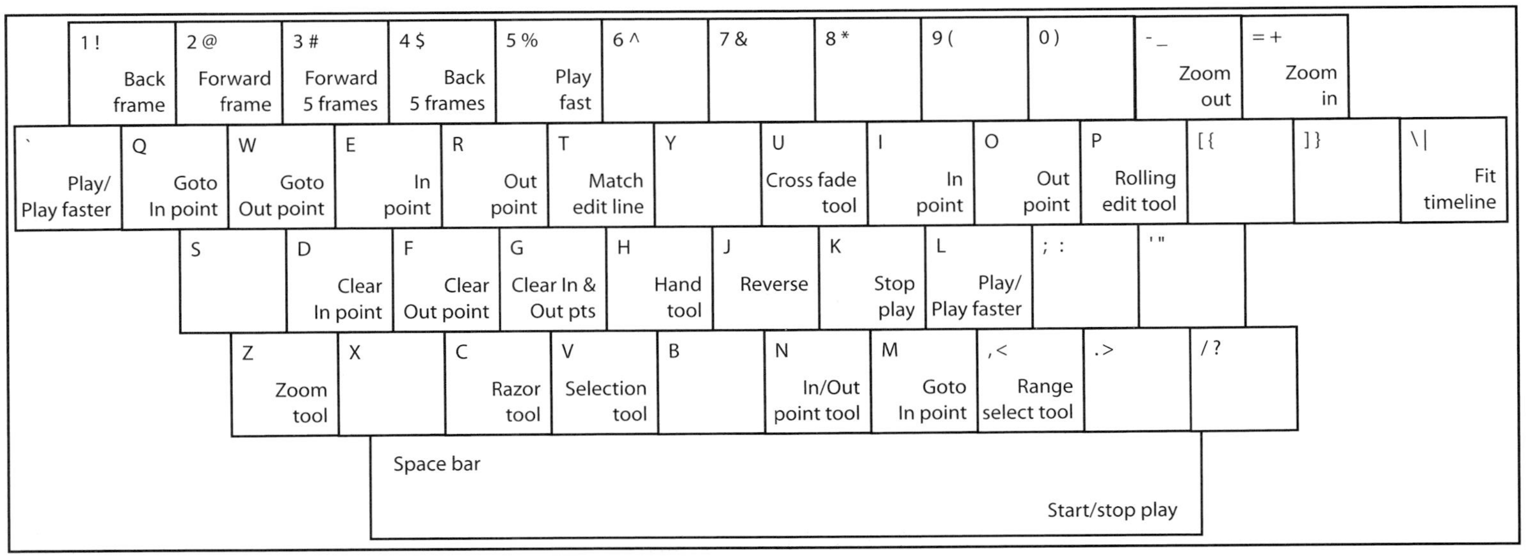

FIGURE 57.2 *A template for the shortcut commands of an Adobe Premiere keyboard.*

Glossary Introduction

Applications

When a person sets foot on a professional set for the first time, it can seem like none of the crew is speaking English. The amount of industry-specific vocabulary used by a film crew can be absolutely staggering. One of the primary skills a person gains working on the first few films is becoming familiar with the commonly used expressions.

In this glossary, I've tried to include most of the common terms you'll hear on a set. I felt it important to include this list since a first visit to a professional set can be disconcerting just because of all of the new terminology, even if you have enough experience to know what's actually going on. Many of these terms I haven't seen documented anywhere else as I had searched for such a glossary to ease the bewildering time I was having when I first started working in production.

No glossary for the film industry can ever be complete since much of the vocabulary is slang (which changes all the time) or based on film technology (which seems to change even faster). Since slang has different meanings in time and location, some of the meanings may vary depending on the distance from Hollywood, California, in the early 2000s. Further, many times the crew will call something by its brand name ("Bring me the Chimera!") and brands fall in and out of popularity.

To keep up with the technical terms and products, I try to read professional filmmaking magazines, and I'm not talking about entertainment weekly. Not only is a lot of the current equipment advertised, but often the articles will quote statements made by filmmakers that tend to be rife with industry jargon. For camera and lighting, I would recommend that you subscribe to the International Cinematographer's Guild magazine (ICG) as it provides useful articles on how specific lighting and film techniques are achieved on A-list films. Also check out their website at www.cameraguild.com for interviews that contain a lot of film-speak.

Glossary

12 by, 10 by, 8 by, 20 by Specifies the size of diffusion material to fit a frame such as 12′ × 12′, 10′ × 10′, 8′ × 8′, or 20′ × 20′.

16:9 A popular screen ratio (ratio 1.78), 16 × 9 is the most popular ratio for HD TV.

180° line An imaginary line that intersects the actors. Once shooting begins, crossing this line makes editing a problem because actors won't look like they're looking at each other.

3:2 pulldown Process of conversion from 24 to 30 fps. Typically used to convert 16 or 35 mm film to television or MiniDV.

35 mm Standard motion picture film type. Generally a 35 mm negative is cropped so that the displayed frame has a ratio of 1.85.

5:1 Surround sound audio standard that is most commonly used on DVD.

500T See Kodak Vision film.

5279 See Kodak Vision film.

7279 See Kodak Vision film.

ADR Automatic dialogue replacement, also known as dubbing, is the process of recording dialogue in a studio separately from the dialogue shot during principal photography. Most often used to replace dialogue made unusable by noise or problems on the original recording track.

AFI The American Film Institute is a popular string of schools, the most famous of which is located in Los Angeles.

Anamorphic Special set of shoot and projecting lenses that create an extra wide picture (2.35 ratio). The shooting lenses compress the horizontal width of the image while the height remains the same. The projecting lens expands the image on the negative to display the extra wide frame.

Antihalation backing Dye used on the back of most films to absorb extra light that passes through the emulsion. Prevents light from reflecting back into the camera.

Aperture The iris of the lens through which the light passes to expose the film. Aperture settings are denoted in t/stop and f/stop settings. The greater the stop number (i.e. f/22), the smaller the aperture and the less light that passes through it. The smaller the number (i.e. f/2.4), the wider open the lens and the more light that strikes the film.

Apple An apple box is a sturdy wooden box that is used for everything from keeping cables off the ground to giving an actor a heightened place to stand. Apple boxes come in a variety of sizes with the standard ones being: full apple, half apple, quarter apple, and pancake.

Art Dog Generally used as an affectionate term for someone in the art department.

ASA See ISO.

Aspect ratio The ratio of width to height for a shooting or display format. For example, television has an aspect ratio of 1.33 that means for every 1.33 unit of width, there is 1 unit of height. This produces a nearly square picture. Movies with a 1.85 ratio are more of a long rectangle.

B See CTB.

Baby A type of 1 K light fixture that uses a Fresnel lens.

Baby stud An adapter that provides a $\frac{5}{8}''$ stud to which a light can be mounted.

Ballast A ballast is the power supply for an HMI light. The ballast is a separate box that is attached to the HMI light through a feeder cable. There are two primary types of ballast: electronic and magnetic.

Barn doors Metal doors attached to the face of a light that allow control of the light throw pattern.

Baseball bat A long and narrow flag.

Beaver board A wall plate attached to a pancake apple box. Most commonly the beaver board is turned upside down and the baby stud is inserted into the top of a C-stand. A monitor is then ratchet strapping to the flat surface for a video village monitor display.

Blackwrap Black metal sheets similar in feel to very thick aluminum foil. Blackwrap can be placed on surfaces that will be hot (such as light housings) and will prevent light leaks.

Bleach bypass A technique during development of the film negative that creates a blacker, desaturated final image. Variations of this technique are known under a variety of names including silver retention, skip-bleach, CCE, NEC, and ENR.

Blonde A type of tungsten light rated at 2000 W.

Bottomer A flag that is positioned to cut off the bottom cast of a light.

Breakaway glass A type of fake glass that is made to shatter without injury to a person or property. Most often breakaway glass is made out of some type of sugar, hence the moniker candy glass.

Bullet See C47.

C47 A standard clothespin. Typically used by electricians to attach a gel to the front of a light. Also called a C47, CP47, or a bullet.

Candy glass See Breakaway glass.

CCE See Bleach bypass.

CGI Computer graphic imagery defines any type of computer-enhanced scene, but is most commonly used to describe 3D graphics footage.

Cheat Arranging objects in a frame, so it enhances the composition of the shot, despite the fact that may not be in real life. For example, a table may be shown to be in the center of the room in an early wide shot. For a fight scene, however, more room is needed between the table and the wall. For these closer shots, the table is "cheated" over a couple of feet to provide this extra room.

Chicken coop Overhead soft light for top lighting that usually includes six 100 W globes (bulbs).

Chimera An attachment to the front of a light that makes the light soft and warm. Essentially a more flexible and more expensive version of a soft box.

Chroma Blue Chroma Blue is the specific bright color of blue that is used in blue screen or compositing applications. Chroma Green is the green used for green screen applications. Both colors are available as tape, paint, and cloth.

Color timing Process of setting and locking in the colors as they will appear on the final film print.

Compositing The act of combining two or more pieces of footage into a single run of footage. Most commonly used to combine actors and objects shot against a blue or green screen with other background footage or CGI images.

Courtesy flag Flag placed to block the wind or the sun, generally provided for the camera crew.

CP47 See C47.

Crab Specifies the crab-like movement setting on a camera dolly.

Cribbing Short lengths of 2 × 4 that are kept on the taco cart and used with wedges to level various things such as dolly track.

CTB Color temperature blue is a particular type of gel that is used to modify the color of light toward the blue range.

CTO Color temperature orange is a particular type of gel that is used to modify the color of light toward the orange range.

Cut-in See Cutting.

Cutting Process of editing a scene so that the various runs of footage fit together properly to tell a visual story.

Dance floor Piece of smooth wood, generally plywood, used to allow a dolly with wheels to steadily move over the surface.

DAT Digital audio tape is the most common method of recording audio for a film. DAT is generally synchronized to the time setting on the camera to allow for automated synchronization of the audio track recorded on the DAT with the final footage.

Dolly A wheeled vehicle that holds the camera to allow for moving shots. There are numerous types of dollies from simple platforms (doorway dollies) to advanced motorized dollies with camera mount arms and hydraulic lifts.

Doorway dolly Simple type of dolly that is essentially just a platform with wheels. A tripod or other camera mount can be placed on top of the doorway dolly for shooting.

Dulling spray Spray used to dull reflective surfaces to avoid highlight flares or reflection of the camera crew into the lens.

Dutch angle Tilting the camera so that the horizon is not a level horizontal line, but instead a sloped diagonal. Generally used to give the viewer a sense of unease.

ENR See Bleach bypass.

Eyeline The direction an actor is looking in relation to the camera. Usually record in the script supervisor's notes to make certain eye contact is maintained during reversal shots in a dialogue sequence.

Eyemo Small camera that provides a special POV such as that of a small animal or machine.

Fischer Used to refer to the J.L. Fischer brand of dolly.

Flat make-up Make-up that is used to make the actor or actress appear normal in the footage.

Float it See Hollywood it.

Floppy A type of 4′ × 4′ flag that has an extra flap of 4′ × 4′ black material attached to it by Velcro. When the flap is extended, a flag 4′ × 8′ is created.

Fresnel A type of lens that magnifies the light beam. A Fresnel light allows the bulb to be moved back and forth in relation to the lens so that the light throw will vary between flood (near the lens) and spot (distant from the lens).

Full apple See Apple.

Furni blanket Furniture blanket or pad that is used to cover items for moving, to prevent damage, or to dampen noise (such as placement over the camera). Also used as a makeshift pad if an actor needs to fall to the ground.

Gangbox Plugs into a single female power outlet and provides multiple female outlets. Used like a traditional power strip except generally built more ruggedly and designed to handle larger power loads.

Gary Coleman stand The smallest size of C-stand.

Gel A piece of translucent plastic that is generally placed over a light source to change the color of the light. Most commonly CTB and CTO gels are used, but a magenta gel may be used to correct florescent lights and other colors are available for atmosphere.

Genny Short for generator.

Globe Most common way on a set to refer to a light bulb.

Golden hour Hour near dusk where the light is perfect for shooting soft beautiful footage.

Greek Make illegible. The art department generally has to greek labels of products such as beer to avoid any legal difficulties of that product being used in the movie. The object of greeking is to make the covering transparent, so the viewer doesn't notice that the label has been modified or removed.

Grip clip Steel spring clip that comes in three basic sizes: 1, 2, and 3.

Half apple See Apple.

Half-B See CTB.

Half-O See CTO.

HHB Brand name of popular DAT tape for on-set sound recording.

Hi-hat Camera mount that is a piece of plywood with a mount for a camera head on top. Used when the camera needs to be placed in an odd location such as ratchet strapping it to the top of a ladder.

HMI Type of light that provides very bright daylight temperature source for relatively low power. See also Ballast.

Hollywood it To have someone hold something in place rather than securing it on a C-stand or light stand. Generally, you "Hollywood" a reflector when the actors are moving or when setting up a stand is more trouble than quickly assigning someone to hold it in place.

Insert Small amount of footage such as a hand placing a wallet into a pocket that provides either additional information to the scene or exists as a cut-away from the main action. Often inserts are filmed using stand-ins since the actors' faces are not seen.

ISO Exposure value for a particular type of film stock. The higher the ISO number, the faster (the less light required) the film. For example, 500 ISO films can obtain a correct exposure with less light (and therefore more quickly) than slower 250 ISO films. Fast films tend to be grainier than slow films.

Kodak Vision film The Kodak Vision film line is the staple of the motion picture industry in the United States. Vision 500T is the most popular type of film for indoor shooting.

Leave-out-the-bleach See Bleach bypass.

Lens flare An optical artifact when a light source shines directly into the lens of a camera. Reflections occur on the individual pieces of glass in the lens to create small circles. Lens flares are generally avoided unless the DP seeks to use them for artistic reasons. See also Lenser.

Lenser A flag that operates with much the same purpose as a matte box to shield the optics of the camera from a light source. See also Lens flare.

Mafer Type of clamp that looks like two right angles. Mafer clamps are excellent for holding poles such as speedrail.

Martini shot The last shot of the day.

Maxibrute A light fixture that holds a grid array of bulbs in a 3 × 3 configuration for a total of nine par lights. Each par globe can be turned on and off separately. Often maxibrutes are used to simulate sunlight shining in a window.

Meat axe Rectangular type of flag.

Midget A type of tungsten light rated at 200 W.

MOS Specifies a scene will be shot without sound. Generally held to have originated from German filmmakers who said "mit out sound".

Mylar Reflective material most often seen in party balloons. Available at party stores or on the Internet, Mylar is generally available on rolls. Used on film set as a reflector.

Nagra Type of analog sound-recording equipment that was generally the standard method of recording pre-DAT.

ND Neutral density is a type of gel or filter that decreases the light level while not affecting the color temperature. ND filters are commonly used on exterior shoots on bright days. ND gels are typically attached to windows to bring down the light levels of sunshine coming through them.

NEC See Bleach bypass.

Nine-light See Maxibrute.

O See CTO.

Opal Plastic diffusion material that softens the light. Often mounted on a 4′ × 4′ frame.

PA Production assistant. The PA is the lowest position on a set and usually acts as a gofer for everything from food to supplies.

Pancake See Apple.

PAR The term PAR refers to a specific type of light bulb (parabolic reflector bulb) where the reflector is sealed into the bulb such as a household flood bulb. Par bulbs cast a beam with a specific point of focus as opposed to a fixture where the bulb and the reflector are separate and their distance relation can be adjusted (such as in a Fresnel light).

Pepper Pepper is a brand name of lighting products. Usually refers to small accent lights.

Platypus clamp Type of clamp that looks light two hand-sized metal plates attached to the jaws of a vice-grip tool. Generally used to hold reflectors and bead board.

Power balancing The process of balancing power on a generator that has multiple phases. General rule of thumb is to keep all legs within 50 A of each other. Often power balancing is performed by placing a "ghost" light on a particular leg that casts no light into the shot but burns power to keep the power balanced.

Prep day The day before principal photography where the electrical staff organizes the equipment, the truck, and all the gels.

Quarter apple See Apple.

Quarter-B See CTB.

Quarter-O See CTO.

Redhead A type of tungsten light rated at 800 W.

Reversal film Also called positive film (as opposed to negative), reversal film captures the actual image instead of a negative version of the image. Common slide film is an everyday example of reversal film. Reversal film has less-contrast latitude than negative film, but can save steps and expense in the film-developing process.

Room tone The background noise of the room when no one is talking. The soundman must take about 30 seconds of room tone to make sure that in post-production work (such as an ADR session) room tone can be added to make the new sounds match the rest of the audio.

Russian Type of dolly that is like a doorway dolly only bigger and more rugged.

Scrim Used to cut the amount of light from a light without diffusing it. Usually consists of a steel frame with a tight weave metal grid inside.

Sekonic Popular brand of light meter.

Selective focus Using an aperture setting to provide shallow depth-of-field thereby keeping only the selected actor or object in focus while blurring the foreground and background.

Silver retention See Bleach bypass.

Skip-bleach See Bleach bypass.

Soft box Light box fixture that casts a soft warm light. Soft boxes are often hand-made by the DP and are used to provide flattering wraparound light for the actor's faces, eye lights, or light-reflective surfaces.

Soft focus The image captured is diffuse and slightly fuzzy. This technique generally uses a special filter and is often used either for a dream sequence or to soften the lines and wrinkles of an actress or actor.

Sound blanket See Furni blanket.

Specular highlight A reflective area that provides a bright reflection on the footage with little or no detail.

Spot meter Type of light meter that will take a reflected light reading for a very small area, usually a 1° or 3° cone.

Straight make-up See Flat make-up.

Super16 40% more image area than 16 mm, single perf, negative cannot be directly edited, ratio 1:1.66.

Taco cart Special cart for grip that holds gel frames, flags, apple boxes, C-stands, wedges, mounting hardware, and expendables.

Television Broadcast standard television in the United States has a ratio of 1.33.

Timing See Color timing.

Topper A flag that is positioned to cut off the top cast of a light.

Tweenie A type of tungsten light rated at 650 W.

Video village Location of one or more monitors that show the camera image. Often set-up for the director to examine framing or when a small set is being used and a minimum of personnel can be near the shooting.

Vision2 See Kodak Vision film.

Vision500T See Kodak Vision film.

Wall plate Also called a pigeon plate or nail-on plate, a wall plate mounts to a surface with nails or screws and provides a mount for a light fixture, camera, or clamp. Most commonly used are the plates that provide a baby stud. See Beaver board.

Wall spreader Steel mounts that are placed at each end of a piece of timber that is wedged between two walls creating a mounting surface for lights.

Wedge Piece of wood in a wedge shape that is kept on the taco cart. Wedges are most often used with cribbing to level a dolly track.

Western dolly Type of platform dolly that is larger than a doorway dolly and smaller than a Russian dolly.

Wild track Sound footage that is taken without accompanying film footage being shot. Often a wild track is extra dialogue (such as "Look out below!") that occurs off camera and will be added in post-production.

Xenon Type of extremely bright arc discharge light that provides light in the daylight color temperature range. Generally used for shafts of very bright light.

Index